Wings of Home Science

Wings of Home Science

Sangeeta Rani

RANDOM PUBLICATIONS
NEW DELHI (INDIA)

Wings of Home Science

ISBN 978-93-5111-847-3

Published in 2016 in India by

RANDOM PUBLICATIONS

4376-A/4B, Gali Murari Lal, Ansari Road
New Delhi-110 002
Phone : +9111-43580356, 011-23289044, 011-43142548
e-mail: sales@randompublications.com,
info@randompublications.com, randomexports@gmail.com

Reprinted 2023

Type Setting by : Friends Media, Delhi-110089
Digitally Printed at: Replika Press Pvt. Ltd.

Preface

One of the first to champion the economics of running a home was Catherine Beecher, sister to Harriet Beecher Stowe. Catherine and Harriet both were leaders in mid-19th century North America in talking about domestic science. They came from a very religious family that valued education especially for women.

The Morrill Act of 1862 propelled domestic science further ahead as land grant colleges sought to educate farm wives in running their households as their husbands were being educated in agricultural methods and processes. Iowa, Kansas, Nebraska, Illinois, Minnesota and Michigan were early leaders offering programs for women. There were women graduates of these institutions several years before the Lake Placid Conferences which gave birth to the home economics movement.

Home Science is the profession and field of study that deals with the economics and management of the home and community. It is also known as home economics or home science. The field deals with the relationship between individuals, families, and communities, and the environment in which they live. As a subject of study, home science is taught in secondary schools, colleges and universities, vocational schools, and in adult education centers; students include women and men. It prepares students for homemaking or professional careers, or to assist in preparing to fulfill real-life responsibilities at home. As an academic profession, it includes educators in the field and human services professionals. The field represents many disciplines including consumer science, nutrition, food preparation, parenting, early childhood education, family economics, human development, interior design, textiles, apparel design, as well as other related subjects. Family and Consumer Sciences education focuses on individuals and families living in society throughout their lifespan, thus dealing not only with families but also with their interrelationships with the communities. Other topics such as sexual education, and fire prevention may also be covered.

– ***Author***

Contents

Preface .... *v-vi*

1. Food and nutrition **1**

introduction 1
Expected Consequences of Disasters on The Food Chain 1
Possible Adverse Effects of Large-Scale Food Distribution 3
Setting Priorities 3
Immediate Relief 3
Estimating Food Requirements 4
Procurement 5
Surveillance 5
Understanding the Nutrition 6
Carbohydrates 8
Fat 10
Protein 11
Minerals 12
Vitamins 13
Water 14
Antioxidants 15
Phytochemicals 15
Intestinal bacterial flora 17
Nutrition: What, When and How to Eat? 17
Food and Nutrition Guidelines for Healthy Adults 30
Nutrition and health 31
Vision 34
Strategic goals 34
Diet for Women 36
Health Diets for Patients 45
Low Carb Diets—How They Work? 47
Weight Loss After Pregnancy 50
Eating Tips During Holidays 52
Tips for Easy Weight Loss 53
Healthy Eating Guidelines 54
Food Items 55

Keys to a Healthy Diet 67
Role of Food and Nutrition for Health Maintenance 69
Daily Food Intake 76
Classification of Foods 84
Flesh Foods 88

2 . Protein 97

An Overview 97
Protein methods 98
Structure of Protein 99
Protein Food 109
Protein Function 111
Source of Protein 112
Importance of Protein 112
Food guide pyramid 114
How much protein need each day? 119
How to choose healthy protein 119
Protein and Disease 120
Protein and Weight Control 121
Why nuts are healthy for the heart 122
Quality of Proteins 123
Protein Requirement 123
Protein purification 124

3 . Carbohydrate 128

The role of carbohydrates in nutrition 133
The role of carbohydrates in maintenance of health 148
Dietary carbohydrate and disease 151
The role of the Glycemic index in food choice 156
Factors influencing the blood glucose responses of foods 158
Goals and guidelines for carbohydrate food choices 160

4. Fats 164

An Overview 164
Types of Fats 167
Why do we need fats? 168
sources of fat 169
How can you reduce fat in your diet? 170
Function of Fats in Our Life 171
Food Sources of Fat 173
Daily Usage of Fats 174
Nutritional Safety 174
Side Effects 174
Recommendations 174
Fats and Heart Disease 175

5. Vitamins 178

Water-Soluble Vitamins 178
Vitamin B2 179

Vitamin and Mineral Fortificants ... 180
Vitamin A ... 185
Overview of vitamin A metabolism ... 185
Vitamin B12 in human metabolic processes ... 191

6. Meal Planning for an Individual ... 196

Menu ... 199
Level of Services ... 204
Interior design ... 208
Atmosphere ... 210

7. Food Preservation ... 235

Food Preservation by Heat ... 235
Canning ... 235
Pasteurization ... 236
Freeze-drying Food Preservation ... 252
Raw Materials ... 252
The Manufacturing Process ... 253
Freeze-Drying ... 257
Properties of freeze-dried products ... 259
Applications of freeze-drying ... 259
Freeze-drying Equipment ... 261
techniques used by food industry ... 262
Canning Food Preservation ... 264
development of canning ... 265
How Canning Preserves Foods ... 267
Ensuring Safe Canned Foods ... 267
Double seams ... 270
Canning Foods ... 272
Home Canning Food Preservation ... 275
Zucchini Relish Canning Process ... 281
Homemade Applesauce ... 282
How to can Tomatoes ... 283
Peach Marmalade Canning Process ... 287
Salting Food Preservation ... 287
Salting ... 288
Salt-Preserving ... 288
Salt and Food Technology ... 290

Bibliography ... 296

***Index* ... 298**

1

Food and nutrition

INTRODUCTION

The nutritional status of a population depends on the availability of food, its consumption, and its biological utilization. A natural disaster may affect the nutritional status of the population by affecting one or more components of the food chain depending on the type, duration, and extent of the disaster, as well as the food and nutritional conditions existing in the area before the catastrophe. Slow-onset disasters such as drought are more likely to affect long-term nutritional status than sudden-onset disasters such as earthquakes and hurricanes. Not all sudden-onset disasters produce food shortages severe enough to cause harmful changes in the nutritional status of the population. The effect of any type of disaster on the nutritional status of the affected population is never immediate. Large scale food distribution is not always an immediate relief priority, and its long-term implementation may, in fact, produce undesired effects. To plan and implement successful food relief operations, nutrition workers responsible for humanitarian operations must be familiar with the possible nutritional outcomes of specific types of natural disasters, as well as the food and nutrition situation in the affected area prior to the disaster. A nutrition officer trained in emergency management must be part of the disaster planning and response teams.

The immediate steps for ensuring that a food relief programme will be effective include:

- Assessing the food supplies available after the disaster;
- Gauging the nutritional needs of the affected population;
- Calculating daily food rations and needs for large population groups; and
- Monitoring the nutritional status of the affected population.

EXPECTED CONSEQUENCES OF DISASTERS ON THE FOOD CHAIN

Hurricanes, floods, land- or mud-slides, volcanic eruptions, and sea surges directly affect food availability. Standing crops may be completely destroyed, and seed stores and family food stocks may be lost, especially if there is no warning period. Volcanic eruptions can cause widespread crop destruction: food crops may be burned, defoliated, and buried under ashfall; reduced photosynthesis resulting from ash clouds limits subsequent production.

Earthquakes, on the other hand, generally have little direct impact on the long-term total availability of food. Standing crops are unaffected, and food stocks can often be salvaged from family, wholesale, and retail stores. However, temporary food problems may result as a consequence of the breakdown of the transportation and marketing systems.

If an earthquake strikes during a labour-intensive period such as harvest, the loss of labour from death or its diversion from agriculture may cause short-term scarcities.

The most likely consequence of any kind of sudden-impact disaster will be the disruption of transportation and communications systems and upheavals in routine social and economic activities. Even when food stocks exist, they may be inaccessible due to disruptions in the distribution system or the loss of income with which to buy food.

Destruction of cash crops also will have an effect on the economy of families. When destruction of a greater magnitude occurs, leading to the death of livestock and the loss of crops and stored foodstuffs, the short-term dilemma can leave a more severe, long-term crisis in its wake. Moreover, evacuation and resettlement of communities during the post-disaster period are often necessary, creating foci in which total food supplies will have to be provided for the duration of the encampment. Hospitals and other institutions may require emergency food supplies as well. Livestock may have to be sacrificed if they cannot be fed, and they are likely to die when vast tracts of land are flooded for long periods.

While the meat can be used immediately for distribution among the affected population, or salted for later distribution, in the long run it results in food and economic shortfalls. The effect of disasters on the biological utilization of food, that is, intestinal absorption and subsequent utilization of nutrients, is indirect, and dependent on factors such as the impact of the disaster on the environment, particularly on water supply and sanitation. This is an issue of concern, particularly in regard to gastrointestinal infections since they affect the absorption of nutrients.

Other infectious diseases increase the demand for nutrients. These effects are more likely to occur among the young and vulnerable groups. If there is an increase in undernutrition rates among young children soon after a disaster, it will most likely be the effect of gastrointestinal illness rather than actual food shortages. This is something to keep in mind in the implementation of surveillance mechanisms. Outbreaks of infectious diseases are uncommon after natural disasters, especially in the Americas.

POSSIBLE ADVERSE EFFECTS OF LARGE-SCALE FOOD DISTRIBUTION

The decision to distribute large amounts of food, although made at the political level, should be based on the most accurate information available. If unnecessarily large quantities of food are brought into an area, this may hinder recovery. Food distribution requires transport and personnel that may be better employed in other ways, and small farmers may face hardship due to depressed market prices.

Perhaps the most serious side effect is that maintaining a population by free food distribution, if not accompanied by essentials such as seeds and tools needed to restart the local economy, may create dependence on relief.

SETTING PRIORITIES

The priorities in alleviating food problems are to:

- Supply food immediately where there appears to be an urgent need, namely to isolated populations, institutions, and relief workers;
- Make an initial estimate of likely food needs in the area, so that steps can be taken towards procurement, transport, storage, and distribution;
- Locate or procure stocks of food and assess their fitness for local consumption; and
- Monitor information on food needs so that procurement, distribution, and other programmes can be modified as the situation changes.

IMMEDIATE RELIEF

During the first, usually chaotic, days after a disaster strikes, the exact extent of the damage is unknown, communications are difficult, and the number of people affected seems to double by the hour. Food distribution must start as soon as possible to keep people fed, rather than prevent clinical malnutrition. Given the large variety and small stocks of commodities sent in as aid by governments, agencies, private organizations, and individuals, however, food distribution is initially a day-to-day exercise.

Planning nutritionally sensible food rations during this period is impossible. What matters during this "chaotic stage" is to provide a minimum of 6.7 to 8.4 Megajoules (1,600 to 2,000 kcal) per day, per person. As an immediate relief step, available food should be distributed in sufficient quantity to any group that is at high risk or appears to be wanting, to ensure survival for one week (3 or 4 kg per person). Food may be included automatically, for example, in supplies sent to communities isolated by earthquake or displaced by flooding.

Where fuel shortages are likely, it may be better to distribute cooked food such as boiled rice or bread rather than dry food. No detailed calculations need be made of the precise vitamin, mineral, or protein content of the food distributed in the initial phase, but supplies should be acceptable and palatable. The most important thing to be provided is sufficient energy. If no other items can be obtained, distribution of a cereal alone will be sufficient to meet basic nutritional requirements. When a population can find some of its own food, it may be possible to supply only part of the ration, or one food item that complements the basic or staple food lacking in their available supplies.

ESTIMATING FOOD REQUIREMENTS

As soon as possible after a disaster, a rapid assessment of the food and nutrition situation should be made to get a rough estimate of likely bulk food items needed. This is based on the population affected, its composition, distribution (for example, isolated villages, refugee camps), and locally available foods. This will enable managers to take the necessary steps to locate and procure stocks, storage, and transport. Hoarding is not uncommon and leads to over-response. In the absence of detailed information, an estimate of food requirements must be based to some extent on judgement in the light of the initial assessment, but it should take into account the following factors:

- The probable effect of the disaster on food availability (e.g., a tsunami may have destroyed all household supplies);
- The approximate size of the population affected;
- Normal food supply and variations within the area (e.g., the approximate percentages of the population who are subsistence farmers and those who depend wholly on purchased food);
- The impact of seasonal factors. In subsistence areas just before the harvest, for instance, household and traders' stocks may be depleted and the population may be more dependent on the market.

The nutrition officer should prepare estimates of foods on the basis of a family unit (usually considered to consist of five people) for one week and one month. Logistically, food distribution on a family basis for one month may be considered the most practical approach. The nutrition officer also should prepare estimates of commodities required by large population groups, for instance, on the basis of 1,000 people for one month.

Two simple and useful rules of thumb are:

- 16 metric tonnes of food sustain 1,000 people for one month,
- To store one metric tonne of food, about two cubic metres of space are needed.

Proper storage is extremely important to avoid food losses due to rain, pests, or looting.

When calculating the composition of daily rations, the following points should be kept in mind:

- The ration should be kept as simple as possible;
- To facilitate storage and distribution, nonperishable food commodities that are not bulky should be chosen;

- Substitution of items within food groups should be allowed for.

The food ration should be based on three food groups: a staple, preferably a cereal; a concentrated energy source such as a fat; and a concentrated source of protein, such as salted or dried fish or meat. In practice, the diets will be dictated by the availability of ingredients. A standardized ration may be impractical as availability will change daily and according to areas. Whenever possible, vulnerable groups should receive a food supplement in addition to the basic diet. Among these groups we include children under 5 years old, who are growing very fast and may suffer permanent damage if malnourished, and pregnant and lactating women, who require more nutrients. Breastmilk is the best food for infants under six months of age, and Health Disaster Coordinators should not allow the emergency situation to become an excuse for flooding the country with infant formula.

PROCUREMENT

If the calculated amount of food required exceeds immediate local availability, and if it is anticipated that food will have to be distributed for several months, steps must be taken to obtain food from elsewhere in the country or abroad. A rough estimate of local food transport requirements should also be made for this contingency. Food for the initial emergency distribution phase should be obtained from national government or wholesaler stocks, or from bilateral or international development agencies (e.g., World Food Programme, NGOs). If large quantities of food are required from abroad, procurement and shipping may require several months.

Approaches to suitable agencies should hence be made at the earliest possible date. It is critical that Health Disaster Coordinators advise potential donors of the eating habits and preferences of their populations. Food not eaten is of no nutritional benefit. The need for special infant foods ("baby foods") immediately after disasters is often exaggerated.

Improving maternal nutrition and assisting mothers economically is more cost-effective and safer than airlifting strained baby foods. Since vitamin requirements are of little concern during the acute emergency phase after sudden-impact natural disasters, multivitamin tablets should not be requested as a separate relief item. The population's specific vitamin and mineral needs will have to be assessed for the long-term.

SURVEILLANCE

If long-term food supply problems seem likely, as in areas with subsistence agriculture and poor communications, the nutritional status of the community should be monitored. This can be accomplished by making regular physical meas-urements of a suitable sample of the population. Since young children are the most sensitive to nutritional changes, the surveillance system should be based on them, remembering that the most serious malnutrition results from an acute exacerbation of chronic under nutrition. In emergency situations, weight-for-height will provide the best indicator of acute changes in nutritional status. If height and weight cannot be measured, arm circumference, which is simple and easy to measure, may be used to gauge changes in communities. As the results of the first needs assessments become available, more accurate information will make it possible to adjust preliminary estimates of the proportion of the population most in need of long-term food distribution.

Surveys of need should make sure to cover not only food availability, but also identify areas where problems of labour, tools, marketing, and other variables affecting distribution have arisen. As soon as an area is able to return to normal consumption patterns, distribution should be phased out.

UNDERSTANDING THE NUTRITION

Nutrition (also called nourishment or aliment) is the provision, to cells and organisms, of the materials necessary (in the form of food) to support life. Many common health problems can be prevented or alleviated with a healthy diet. The diet of an organism is what it eats, which is largely determined by the perceived palatability of foods. Dietitians are health professionals who specialize in human nutrition, meal planning, economics, and preparation.

They are trained to provide safe, evidence-based dietary advice and management to individuals (in health and disease), as well as to institutions. A poor diet can have an injurious impact on health, causing deficiency diseases such as scurvy, beriberi, and kwashiorkor; health-threatening conditions like obesity and metabolic syndrome; and such common chronic systemic diseases as cardiovascular disease, diabetes, and osteoporosis.

Nutrition science investigates the metabolic and physiological responses of the body to diet. With advances in the fields of molecular biology, biochemistry, and genetics, the study of nutrition is increasingly concerned with metabolism and metabolic pathways: the sequences of biochemical steps through which substances in living things change from one form to another. Nitrogen is needed by animals to build proteins. Carnivore and herbivore diets vary in their source of nitrogen, which is a limiting nutrient for both. Herbivores consume plants to get nitrogen and carnivores consume other animals to obtain nitrogen. Nitrogen is a common element in the atmosphere but exists in a state that is not usable by most living organisms, certain fungi and bacteria are able to convert atmospheric nitrogen into a form plants can adsorb and utilize.

The human body contains chemical compounds, such as water, carbohydrates (sugar, starch, and fibre), amino acids (in proteins), fatty acids (in lipids), and nucleic acids (DNA and RNA). These compounds in turn consist of elements such as carbon, hydrogen, oxygen, nitrogen, phosphorus, calcium, iron, zinc, magnesium, manganese, and so on. All of these chemical compounds and elements occur in various forms and combinations (e.g., hormones, vitamins, phospholipids, hydroxyapatite), both in the human body and in the plant and animal organisms that humans eat.

The human body consists of elements and compounds ingested, digested, absorbed, and circulated through the bloodstream to feed the cells of the body. Except in the unborn foetus, which receive processed nutrients from the mother, the digestive system is the first system involved in breaking down food prior to further digestion.

Digestive juices, excreted into the lumen of the gastrointestinal tract, break chemical bonds in ingested molecules, and modulate their conformations and energy states. Though some molecules are absorbed into the bloodstream unchanged, digestive processes release them from the matrix of foods. Unabsorbed matter, along with some waste products of metabolism, is eliminated from the body in the feces. Studies of nutritional status must take into account the state of the body before and after experiments, as well as the chemical composition of the whole diet and of all material excreted and eliminated from the body (in urine and foeces).

Comparing the food to the waste can help determine the specific compounds and elements absorbed and metabolized in the body. The effects of nutrients may only be discernible over an extended period, during which all food and waste must be analysed. The number of variables involved in such experiments is high, making nutritional studies time-consuming and expensive, which explains why the science of human nutrition is still slowly evolving. In general, eating a wide variety of fresh, whole (unprocessed), foods has proven favourable for one's health compared to monotonous diets based on processed foods. In particular, the consumption of whole-plant foods slows digestion and allows better absorption, and a more favourable balance of essential nutrients per Calorie, resulting in better management of cell growth, maintenance, and mitosis (cell division), as well as better regulation of appetite and blood sugar. Regularly scheduled meals (every few hours) have also proven more wholesome than infrequent or haphazard ones, although a recent study has also linked more frequent meals with a higher risk of colon cancer in men.

There are six major classes of nutrients: carbohydrates, fats, minerals, protein, vitamins, and water. These nutrient classes can be categorized as either macronutrients (needed in relatively large amounts) or micronutrients (needed in smaller quantities). The macronutrients include carbohydrates, fats, protein, and water. The micronutrients are minerals and vitamins. The macronutrients (excluding water) provide structural material (amino acids from which proteins are built, and lipids from which cell membranes and some signaling molecules are built), energy.

Some of the structural material can be used to generate energy internally, and in either case it is measured in Joules or kilocalories (often called "Calories" and written with a capital C to distinguish them from little 'c' calories).

Carbohydrates and proteins provide 17 kJ approximately (4 kcal) of energy per gram, while fats provide 37 kJ (9 kcal) per gm., though the net energy from either depends on such factors as absorption and digestive effort, which vary substantially from instance to instance.

Vitamins, minerals, fibre, and water do not provide energy, but are required for other reasons. A third class of dietary material, fibre (*i.e.*, non-digestible material such as cellulose), is also required, for both mechanical and biochemical reasons, although the exact reasons remain unclear.

Molecules of carbohydrates and fats consist of carbon, hydrogen, and oxygen atoms. Carbohydrates range from simple monosaccharides (glucose, fructose, galactose) to complex polysaccharides (starch). Fats are triglycerides, made of assorted fatty acid monomers bound to glycerol backbone. Some fatty acids, but not all, are essential in the diet: they cannot be synthesized in the body. Protein molecules contain nitrogen atoms in addition to carbon, oxygen, and hydrogen. The fundamental components of protein are nitrogen-containing amino acids, some of which are essential in the sense that humans cannot make them internally. Some of the amino acids are convertible (with the expenditure of energy) to glucose and can be used for energy production just as ordinary glucose in a process known as gluconeogenesis.

By breaking down existing protein, some glucose can be produced internally; the remaining amino acids are discarded, primarily as urea in urine. This occurs normally only during prolonged starvation. Other micronutrients include antioxidants and phytochemicals, which are said to influence (or protect) some body systems. Their necessity is not as well established as in the case of, for instance, vitamins.

Most foods contain a mix of some or all of the nutrient classes, together with other substances, such as toxins of various sorts. Some nutrients can be stored internally (e.g., the fat soluble vitamins), while others are required more or less continuously. Poor health can be caused by a lack of required nutrients or, in extreme cases, too much of a required nutrient. For example, both salt and water (both absolutely required) will cause illness or even death in excessive amounts.

CARBOHYDRATES

Carbohydrates include sugars, starches and fibre. They constitute a large part of foods such as rice, noodles, bread, and other grain-based products. Carbohydrates may be classified chemically as monosaccharides, disaccharides, or polysaccharides depending on the number of monomer (saccharide or sugar) units they contain.

Monosaccharides, disaccharides, and polysaccharides contain one, two, and three or more sugar units, respectively. Polysaccharides are often referred to as complex carbohydrates because they consist of long, sometimes branched chains of single sugar units. Mono- and disaccharides are called simple carbohydrates. Dietary advice frequently but erroneously suggests that complex carbohydrates are superior to simple because they take longer to digest and absorb. Simple carbohydrates, on the other hand, are said to cause a spike in blood glucose levels rapidly after ingestion. These traditional claims are false. In fact, many digestible polysaccharides are processed as rapidly and simple sugars in the human body. On the other hand, some simple carbohydrates (fructose, for example) are processed in a different way and do not spike blood sugar. Thus the distinction between "complex" and "simple" does not predict the nutritional value or impact of carbohydrates. A better way of determining what effect particular foods may have on blood sugar and ultimately on health in general is the glycemic index. Carbohydrates are not essential nutrients (with the likely exception of fibre), but are typically an important part of the human diet. While it would not be accurate to categorize all carbohydrates as "bad" nutritionally, some carbohydrate sources may well have deleterious effects on health, especially when consumed in large quantities. Highly processed carbohydrates (sugars and starches) as well as fructose consumed in large quantities have been implicated in negative.

FIBRE

Dietary fibre is a carbohydrate (or a polysaccharide) that is incompletely absorbed in humans and in some animals. Like all carbohydrates, when it is metabolized it can produce four Calories (kilocalories) of energy per gm. However, in most circumstances it accounts for less than that because of its limited absorption and digestibility. Dietary fibre consists mainly of cellulose, a large carbohydrate polymer that is indigestible because humans do not have the required enzymes to disassemble it.

There are two subcategories: soluble and insoluble fibre. Whole grains, fruits (especially plums, prunes, and figs), and vegetables are good sources of dietary fibre. There are many health benefits of a high-fibre diet. Dietary fibre helps reduce the chance of gastrointestinal problems such as constipation and diarrhoea by increasing the weight and size of stool and softening it. Insoluble fibre, found in whole-wheat flour, nuts and vegetables, especially stimulates peristalsis—the rhythmic muscular contractions of the intestines which move digesta along the digestive tract. Soluble fibre, found in oats, peas, beans, and many fruits, dissolves in water in the intestinal tract to produce a gel which slows the movement of food through the intestines. This may help lower blood glucose levels because it can slow the absorption of sugar. Additionally, fibre, perhaps especially that from whole grains, is thought to possibly help lessen insulin spikes, and therefore reduce the risk of type 2 diabetes. The link between increased fibre consumption and a decreased risk of colorectal cancer is still uncertain.

FAT

A molecule of dietary fat typically consists of several fatty acids (containing long chains of carbon and hydrogen atoms), bonded to a glycerol. They are typically found as triglycerides (three fatty acids attached to one glycerol backbone). Fats may be classified as saturated or unsaturated depending on the detailed structure of the fatty acids involved.

Saturated fats have all of the carbon atoms in their fatty acid chains bonded to hydrogen atoms, whereas unsaturated fats have some of these carbon atoms double-bonded, so their molecules have relatively fewer hydrogen atoms than a saturated fatty acid of the same length. Unsaturated fats may be further classified as monounsaturated (one double-bond) or polyunsaturated (many double-bonds).

Furthermore, depending on the location of the double-bond in the fatty acid chain, unsaturated fatty acids are classified as omega-3 or omega-6 fatty acids. Trans fats are a type of unsaturated fat with trans-isomer bonds; these are rare in nature and in foods from natural sources; they are typically created in an industrial process called (partial) hydrogenation. There are nine kilocalories in each gm. of fat. Saturated fats (typically from animal sources) have been a staple in many world cultures for millennia. Unsaturated fats (e. g., vegetable oil) are considered healthier while trans fats are to be avoided.

Saturated and some trans fats are typically solid at room temperature (such as butter or lard), while unsaturated fats are typically liquids (such as olive oil or flaxseed oil). Trans fats are very rare in nature, and have been shown to be highly detrimental to human health, but have properties useful in the food processing industry, such as rancidity resistance.

ESSENTIAL FATTY ACIDS

Most fatty acids are non-essential, meaning the body can produce them as needed, generally from other fatty acids and always by expending energy to do so. However, in humans, at least two fatty acids are essential and must be included in the diet. An appropriate balance of essential fatty acids—omega-3 and omega-6 fatty acids—seems also important for health, although definitive experimental demonstration has been elusive.

Both of these "omega" long-chain polyunsaturated fatty acids are substrates for a class of eicosanoids known as prostaglandins, which have roles throughout the human body. They are hormones, in some respects.

The omega-3 eicosapentaenoic acid (EPA), which can be made in the human body from the omega-3 essential fatty acid alpha-linolenic acid (LNA), or taken in through marine food sources, serves as a building block for series 3 prostaglandins (e.g., weakly inflammatory PGE3). The omega-6 dihomo-gamma-linolenic acid (DGLA) serves as a building block for series 1 prostaglandins (*e.g.*, anti-inflammatory PGE1), whereas arachidonic acid (AA) serves as a building block for series 2 prostaglandins (e.g., pro-inflammatory PGE 2). Both DGLA and AA can be made from the omega-6 linoleic acid (LA) in the human body, or can be taken in directly through food.

An appropriately balanced intake of omega-3 and omega-6 partly determines the relative production of different prostaglandins, which is one reason why a balance between omega-3 and omega-6 is believed important for cardiovascular health.

In industrialized societies, people typically consume large amounts of processed vegetable oils, which have reduced amounts of the essential fatty acids along with too much of omega-6 fatty acids relative to omega-3 fatty acids. The conversion rate of omega-6 DGLA to AA largely determines the production of the prostaglandins PGE1 and PGE2.

Omega-3 EPA prevents AA from being released from membranes, thereby skewing prostaglandin balance away from pro-inflammatory PGE2 (made from AA) towards anti-inflammatory PGE1 (made from DGLA). Moreover, the conversion (desaturation) of DGLA to AA is controlled by the enzyme delta-5-desaturase, which in turn is controlled by hormones such as insulin (up-regulation) and glucagon (down-regulation).

The amount and type of carbohydrates consumed, along with some types of amino acid, can influence processes involving insulin, glucagon, and other hormones; therefore the ratio of omega-3 versus omega-6 has wide effects on general health, and specific effects on immune function and inflammation, and mitosis (*i.e.*, cell division).

PROTEIN

Proteins are the basis of many animal body structures (e.g., muscles, skin, and hair). They also form the enzymes that control chemical reactions throughout the body. Each molecule is composed of amino acids, which are characterized by inclusion of nitrogen and sometimes sulphur (these components are responsible for the distinctive smell of burning protein, such as the keratin in hair).

The body requires amino acids to produce new proteins (protein retention) and to replace damaged proteins (maintenance). As there is no protein or amino acid storage provision, amino acids must be present in the diet. Excess amino acids are discarded, typically in the urine. For all animals, some amino acids are essential (an animal cannot produce them internally) and some are non-essential (the animal can produce them from other nitrogen-containing compounds). Twenty-one proteinogenic amino acids are found in the human body, along with non-proteinogenic amino acids (e.g., gamma-aminobutyric acid).

Ten of the proteinogenic amino acids are essential and, therefore, must be included in the diet. A diet that contains adequate amounts of amino acids (especially those that are essential) is particularly important in some situations:

during early development and maturation, pregnancy, lactation, or injury (a burn, for instance). A complete protein source contains all the essential amino acids; an incomplete protein source lacks one or more of the essential amino acids.

It is possible to combine two incomplete protein sources (e.g., rice and beans) to make a complete protein source, and characteristic combinations are the basis of distinct cultural cooking traditions. Sources of dietary protein include meats, tofu and other soy-products, eggs, legumes, and dairy products such as milk and cheese. Excess amino acids from protein can be converted into glucose and used for fuel through a process called gluconeogenesis. The amino acids remaining after such conversion are discarded.

MINERALS

Dietary minerals are the chemical elements required by living organisms, other than the four elements carbon, hydrogen, nitrogen, and oxygen that are present in nearly all organic molecules. The term "mineral" is archaic, since the intent is to describe simply the less common elements in the diet. Some are heavier than the four just mentioned, including several metals, which often occur as ions in the body.

Some dietitians recommend that these be supplied from foods in which they occur naturally, or at least as complex compounds, or sometimes even from natural inorganic sources (such as calcium carbonate from ground oyster shells). Some minerals are absorbed much more readily in the ionic forms found in such sources. On the other hand, minerals are often artificially added to the diet as supplements; the most famous is likely iodine in iodized salt which prevents goiter.

MACROMINERALS

Many elements are essential in relative quantity; they are usually called "bulk minerals". Some are structural, but many play a role as electrolytes. Elements with recommended dietary allowance (RDA) greater than 200 mg/day are, in alphabetical order (with informal or folk-medicine perspectives in parentheses):

- Calcium, a common electrolyte, but also needed structurally (for muscle and digestive system health, bone strength, some forms neutralize acidity, may help clear toxins, provides signaling ions for nerve and membrane functions).
- Chlorine as chloride ions; very common electrolyte;
- Magnesium, required for processing ATP and related reactions (builds bone, causes strong peristalsis, increases flexibility, increases alkalinity).
- Phosphorus, required component of bones; essential for energy processing.

- Potassium, a very common electrolyte (heart and nerve health).
- Sodium, a very common electrolyte; not generally found in dietary supplements, despite being needed in large quantities, because the ion is very common in food: typically as sodium chloride, or common salt. Excessive sodium consumption can deplete calcium and magnesium, leading to high blood pressure and osteoporosis (Note: Some sources suggest high blood pressure is due to high water retention per osmosis).
- Sulfur, for three essential amino acids and therefore many proteins (skin, hair, nails, liver, and pancreas). Sulfur is not consumed alone, but in the form of sulfur-containing amino acids.

TRACE MINERALS

Many elements are required in trace amounts, usually because they play a catalytic role in enzymes.

Some trace mineral elements (RDA < 200 mg/day) are, in alphabetical order:

- Cobalt required for biosynthesis of vitamin B_{12} family of coenzymes. Animals cannot biosynthesize B_{12}, and must obtain this cobalt-containing vitamin in the diet.
- Copper required component of many redox enzymes, including cytochrome c oxidase.
- Chromium required for sugar metabolism.
- Iodine required not only for the biosynthesis of thyroxine, but probably, for other important organs as breast, stomach, salivary glands, thymus, etc.; for this reason iodine is needed in larger quantities than others in this list, and sometimes classified with the macrominerals.
- Iron required for many enzymes, and for haemoglobin and some other proteins.
- Manganese (processing of oxygen).
- Molybdenum required for xanthine oxidase and related oxidases.
- Nickel present in urease.
- Selenium required for peroxidase (antioxidant proteins).
- *Vanadium (Speculative*: there is no established RDA for vanadium. No specific biochemical function has been identified for it in humans, although vanadium is required for some lower organisms.)
- Zinc required for several enzymes such as carboxypeptidase, liver alcohol dehydrogenase, and carbonic anhydrase.

VITAMINS

Some vitamins are recognized as essential nutrients, necessary in the diet for good health. (Vitamin D is the exception: it can be synthesized in the skin, in the presence of UVB radiation.) Certain vitamin-like compounds that are recommended in the diet, such as carnitine, are thought useful for survival and health, but these are not "essential" dietary nutrients because the human body has some capacity to produce them from other compounds.

Moreover, thousands of different phytochemicals have recently been discovered in food (particularly in fresh vegetables), which may have desirable properties including antioxidant activity, however, experimental demonstration has been suggestive but inconclusive.

Other essential nutrients that are not classified as vitamins include essential amino acids, choline, essential fatty acids, and the minerals discussed in the preceding part.

Vitamin deficiencies may result in disease conditions, including goitre, scurvy, osteoporosis, impaired immune system, disorders of cell metabolism, certain forms of cancer, symptoms of premature aging, and poor psychological health (including eating disorders), among many others. Excess levels of some vitamins are also dangerous to health (notably vitamin A), and for at least one vitamin, B6, toxicity begins at levels not far the required amount. Deficient or excess levels of minerals can also have serious health consequences.

WATER

It is not fully clear how much water intake is needed by healthy people, although some assert that 6–8 glasses of water daily is the minimum to maintain proper hydration. The notion that a person should consume eight glasses of water per day cannot be traced to a credible scientific source. The effect of, greater or lesser, water intake on weight loss and on constipation is also still unclear. The original water intake recommendation in 1945 by the Food and Nutrition Board of the National Research Council read: "An ordinary standard for diverse persons is 1 milliliter for each calorie of food.

Most of this quantity is contained in prepared foods." The latest dietary reference intake report by the United States National Research Council recommended, generally, (including food sources): 2.7 litres of water total for women and 3.7 litres for men.

Specifically, pregnant and breastfeeding women need additional fluids to stay hydrated. According to the Institute of Medicine—who recommend that, on average, women consume 2.2 litres and men 3.0 litres—this is recommended to be 2.4 litres (approx. 9 cups) for pregnant women and 3 litres (approx. 12.5 cups) for breastfeeding women because an especially large amount of fluid is lost during nursing.

For those who have healthy kidneys, it is somewhat difficult to drink too much water, but (especially in warm humid weather and while exercising) it is dangerous to drink too little. People can drink far more water than necessary while exercising, however, putting them at risk of water intoxication, which can be fatal. In particular, large amounts of de-ionized water are dangerous. Normally, about 20 per cent of water intake comes in food, while the rest comes from drinking water and assorted beverages (caffeinated included). Water is excreted from the body in multiple forms; including urine and faeces, sweating, and by water vapour in the exhaled breath.

ANTIOXIDANTS

As cellular metabolism/energy production requires oxygen, potentially damaging (e.g., mutation causing) compounds known as free radicals can form. Most of these are oxidizers (*i.e.*, acceptors of electrons) and some react very strongly. For the continued normal cellular maintenance, growth, and division, these free radicals must be sufficiently neutralized by antioxidant compounds.

Some are produced by the human body with adequate precursors (glutathione, Vitamin C), and those the body cannot produce may only be obtained in the diet via direct sources (Vitamin C in humans, Vitamin A, Vitamin K) or produced by the body from other compounds (Beta-carotene converted to Vitamin A by the body, Vitamin D synthesized from cholesterol by sunlight).

Phytochemicals and their subgroup, polyphenols, make up the majority of antioxidants; about 4,000 are known. Different antioxidants are now known to function in a cooperative network. For example, Vitamin C can reactivate free radical-containing glutathione or Vitamin E by accepting the free radical itself. Some antioxidants are more effective than others at neutralizing different free radicals.

Some cannot neutralize certain free radicals. Some cannot be present in certain areas of free radical development (Vitamin A is fat-soluble and protects fat areas, Vitamin C is water soluble and protects those areas). When interacting with a free radical, some antioxidants produce a different free radical compound that is less dangerous or more dangerous than the previous compound.

Having a variety of antioxidants allows any byproducts to be safely dealt with by more efficient antioxidants in neutralizing a free radical's butterfly effect. Although initial studies suggested that antioxidant supplements might promote health, later large clinical trials did not detect any benefit and suggested instead that excess supplementation may be harmful.

PHYTOCHEMICALS

A growing area of interest is the effect upon human health of trace chemicals, collectively called phytochemicals. These nutrients are typically found in edible plants, especially colourful fruits and vegetables, but also other organisms including seafood, algae, and fungi. The effects of phytochemicals increasingly survive rigorous testing by prominent health organizations. One of the principal classes of phytochemicals are polyphenol antioxidants, chemicals that are known to provide certain health benefits to the cardiovascular system and immune system.

These chemicals are known to down-regulate the formation of reactive oxygen species, key chemicals in cardiovascular disease. Perhaps the most rigorously tested phytochemical is zeaxanthin, a yellow-pigmented carotenoid present in many yellow and orange fruits and vegetables. Repeated studies have shown a strong correlation between ingestion of zeaxanthin and the prevention and treatment of age-related macular degeneration (AMD).

Less rigorous studies have proposed a correlation between zeaxanthin intake and cataracts. A second carotenoid, lutein, has also been shown to lower the risk of contracting AMD. Both compounds have been observed to collect in the retina when ingested orally, and they serve to protect the rods and cones against the destructive effects of light. Another carotenoid, beta-cryptoxanthin, appears to protect against chronic joint inflammatory diseases, such as arthritis.

While the association between serum blood levels of beta-cryptoxanthin and substantially decreased joint disease has been established, neither a convincing mechanism for such protection nor a cause-and-effect have been rigorously studied. Similarly, a red phytochemical, lycopene, has substantial credible evidence of negative association with development of prostate cancer.

The following table presents phytochemical groups and common sources, arranged by family:

Family	Sources	Possible Benefits
Flavonoids	Berries, herbs, vegetables, wine, grapes, tea	General antioxidant, oxidation of LDLs, prevention of arteriosclerosis and heart disease
Isoflavones (phytoestrogens)	Soy, red clover, kudzu root	General antioxidant, prevention of arteriosclerosis and heart disease, easing symptoms of menopause, cancer prevention
Isothiocyanates	Cruciferous vegetables	cancer prevention
monoterpenes	Citrus peels, essential oils, herbs, spices, green plants, atmosphere	Cancer prevention, treating gallstones
Organosulfur compounds	Chives, garlic, onions	Cancer prevention, lowered LDLs, assistance to the immune system
Saponins	Beans, cereals, herbs	Hypercholesterolemia, Hyperglycemia, Antioxidant, cancer prevention, Anti-inflammatory
Capsaicinoids	All capiscum (chile) peppers	Topical pain relief, cancer prevention, cancer cell apoptosis

Some of the correlations between the ingestion of certain phytochemicals and the prevention of disease are, in some cases, enormous in magnitude. Yet, even when the evidence is obtained, translating it to practical dietary advice can be difficult and counter-intuitive. Lutein, for example, occurs in many yellow and orange fruits and vegetables and protects the eyes against various diseases. However, it does not protect the eye nearly as well as zeaxanthin, and the presence of lutein in the retina will prevent zeaxanthin uptake. Additionally, evidence has shown that the lutein present in egg yolk is more readily absorbed than the lutein from vegetable sources, possibly because of fat solubility. At the most basic level, the question "should you eat eggs?" is complex to the point of dismay, including misperceptions about the health effects of cholesterol in egg yolk, and its saturated fat content.

As another example, lycopene is prevalent in tomatoes (and actually is the chemical that gives tomatoes their red colour). It is more highly concentrated, however, in processed tomato products such as commercial pasta sauce, or tomato soup, than in fresh "healthy" tomatoes. Yet, such sauces tend to have high amounts of salt, sugar, other substances a person may wish or even need to avoid.

INTESTINAL BACTERIAL FLORA

It is now also known that animal intestines contain a large population of gut flora. In humans, these include species such as Bacteroides, *L. acidophilus*, and *E. coli*, among many others. They are essential to digestion, and are also affected by the food we eat. Bacteria in the gut perform many important functions for humans, including breaking down and aiding in the absorption of otherwise indigestible food; stimulating cell growth; repressing the growth of harmful bacteria, training the immune system to respond only to pathogens; producing vitamin B_{12}, and defending against some infectious diseases.

NUTRITION: WHAT, WHEN AND HOW TO EAT?

WHAT TO EAT?

It is very important to eat the right kind of food, but it is even more important to be balanced and use common sense. Those who are moderate in their habits and cheerful can eat almost anything with good results. Of course, people who live almost entirely on such denatured foods as polished rice, finely bolted wheat flour products, sterilized milk and meat spoiled in the cooking, refined sugar and potatoes deprived of most of their salts through being soaked and cooked will suffer.

There are many different diet systems, and some of them are very good. If their advocates say that their way is the only way, they are wrong. Many try to force their ideas upon others. They find their happiness in making others miserable. They are afflicted with the proselyting zeal that makes fools of people. This is the wrong way to solve the food problem. Let each individual choose his own way and allow those who differ to continue in the old way.

Many have changed their dietary habits to their own great benefit. After this they become so enthused and anxious for others to do likewise that they wear themselves and others out exhorting them to share in the new discovery. This does no good, but it often does harm, for it leads the zealot to think too much of and about himself, and it annoys others. Many are like my friend who lunched daily on zwieback and raw carrots. "I think everybody ought to eat some raw carrots every day; don't you?" she said. We cannot mold everybody to our liking, and we should not try. If we conquer ourselves, we have about all we can do. If we succeed in this great work, as suggested, evolve enough tolerance to be willing to allow others to shape their own ends. To volunteer undesired information does no good, for it creates opposition in the mind of the hearers. If the information is sought, the chances are that it may in time do good. It is well enough to indicate how and where better knowledge may be obtained. We should at all times attempt to conserve our energy and use it only when and where it is helpful. Such conduct leads to peace of mind, effectiveness, happiness and health.

The tendency to become too enthusiastic about a dietary regime that has brought personal benefit is to be avoided, for it brings unnecessary odium upon the important subject of food reform. People do not like to change old habits, even if the change would be for the better, and when an enthusiast tries to force the change his actions are resented. He makes no real converts, but as pay for his efforts he gains the reputation of being a crank.

Those who wish to be helpful in an educational way should be patient. The race has been in the making for ages. Its good habits, as well as its bad ones, have been acquired gradually. If we ever get rid of our bad habits it will be through gradual evolution, not through a hasty revolution. We need a change in dietary habits, but those who become food cranks, insisting that others be as they, retard this movement. Only a few will change physical and mental habits suddenly.

If those who know are content to show the benefits more in results than in words, their influence for good will be great. What shall we eat? How are we to know the truth among so many conflicting ideas? We can know the truth because it leads to health. Error leads to suffering, degeneration and premature death. As the homely saying goes, "The proof of the pudding is in the eating." Let us look into some of the diet theories before the public and give them thoughtful consideration. The late Dr. J.H. Salisbury advocated the use of water to drink and meat to eat, and nothing else. The water was to be taken warm and in copious quantities, but not at or near meal time. The meat, preferably beef, was to be scraped or minced, made into cakes and cooked in a very warm skillet until the cakes turned grey within. These meat cakes were to be eaten three times a day, seasoned with salt and a little pepper.

The doctor had a very successful practice, which is attested by many who were benefited when ordinary medical skill failed. His diet was not well balanced. In meats there is a lack of the cell salts and force food. Especially are the cell salts lacking when the flesh is drained of its blood. The animals of prey drink the blood and crunch many of the bones of their victims, thus getting nearly all the salts. But in spite of his giving such an unbalanced diet, the doctor had a satisfactory practice and good success. Why? Because his patients had to quit using narcotics and stimulants and they were compelled to consume such simple food that they ceased overeating. It is a well known fact that a mono-diet forces moderation, for there is no desire to overeat, as there is when living on a very varied diet.

Another fact that the Salisbury plan brings to mind is that starch and sugar are not necessary for the feeding of adults, although they are convenient and cheap foods and ordinarily consumed in large quantities. The fat in the meat takes the place of the starch and sugar. Atomically, starch, sugar and fat are almost identical, and they can be substituted one for the other. Nature makes broad provisions.

Dr. Salisbury's career also serves to remind us that a mixed diet is not necessary for the physical welfare of those who eat to live. Vegetarians dwell upon the toxicity of meat. But Dr. Salisbury fed his patients on nothing but meat and water, and the percentage of recoveries in chronic diseases was considered remarkable. Meat is very easy to digest and when prepared in the simple manner prescribed by the doctor and eaten by itself it will agree with nearly everybody. But when eaten with soup, bread, potatoes, vegetables, cooked and raw, fish, pudding, fruit, coffee, crackers and cheese, there will be overeating followed by indigestion and its consequent train of ills. However, it is not fair to blame the meat entirely, for the whole mixture goes into decomposition and poisons the body.

The cures resulting from Dr. Salisbury's plan also help to disprove the much heralded theory of Dr. Haig, that uric acid from meat eating is the cause of rheumatism. Overeating of meat is often a contributory cause. We are told that the rheumatics who followed Dr. Salisbury's plan got well. They regained physical tone. They lost their gout and rheumatism. They parted company with their pimples and blotches. All of which would indicate that the blood became clean.

The chief part derived from Dr. Salisbury's plan and experience is the helpfulness of simple living and moderation. An exclusive diet of meat is not well balanced. Energy produced from flesh food is too expensive. The good results came from substituting habits of simplicity and moderation for the habit of overeating of too great variety of food. The same results may be obtained by putting a patient on bread and milk.

Dr. Salisbury's patients had unsatisfied longings, doubtless for various tissue salts. The addition of fresh raw fruits or vegetables would improve his diet, for apples, peaches, pears, lettuce, celery and cabbage are rich in the salts in which meats are deficient.

Dr. Emmet Densmore recommended omitting the starches entirely, that is, to avoid such foods as cereals, tubers and legumes. He believed that it is best to live on fruits and nuts. He recommended the sweet fruits—figs, dates, raisins, prunes—instead of the starchy foods. The doctor did much good, as everyone does who gets his patients to simplify. He also had good results before discovering that starch is a harmful food, when he fed his patients bread and milk. Starch must be converted into sugar before it can be used by the body.

The sugar is what is known as dextrose, not the refined sugar of commerce. The sweet fruits contain this sugar in the form of fruit sugar, which needs but little preparation to be absorbed by the blood. Dr. Densmore reasons thus: Only birds are furnished with mills; hence the grains are fit food for them only. Other starches should be avoided because they are difficult to digest, the doctor wrote.

Raw starches are difficult to digest, but when they are properly cooked they are digested in a reasonable time without overburdening the system, provided they are well masticated and the amount eaten is not too great and the combining is correct. Rice, which contains much starch, digests in a short time. We can do very nicely without starch. We can also thrive on it if we do not abuse it. The two chief starch-bearing staples, rice and wheat, contain considerable protein and salts in their natural state.

In fact, the natural wheat will sustain life for a long time. Man has improved on nature by polishing the rice and making finely bolted, bleached wheat flour, deprived of nearly all the salts in the wheat berry. The result is that both of them have become very poor foods.

The more we eat of these refined products the worse off we are, unless we partake freely of other foods rich in mineral salts. Not long ago a lady died in England who was a prominent advocate of a "brainy diet". Her brainy diet consisted largely of excessive quantities of meat, pork being a favourite. She died comparatively young, her friends say from overwork. Such a diet doubtless had a large part in wearing her out. To overeat of meat is dangerous. A gentleman is now advocating a diet of nothing but cocoanuts. This is a fad, for they are not a balanced food. He has published a book on the subject. Perhaps his advocacy is influenced by his interest in the sale of cocoanuts.

The vegetarians condemn the use of meat. Some of them are called fruitarians. It is very difficult to decide who are the most representative of them. Some advocate the use of nothing but fruit and nuts. Others add cereals to this. Others use vegetables in addition. Some even allow the use of dairy products and eggs, that is, all foods except flesh. They say that meat is an unnatural food for man and condemn its use on moral grounds. It is difficult to decide what is natural, for we find that man is very adaptable, being able to live on fruits in the tropics and almost exclusively on flesh food, largely fat, in the arctic regions.

In nature the strong live on the weak and the intelligent on the dull. There is no sentiment in nature. In her domain might, physical or mental, makes right. Sentiments of right and justice are not highly developed except among human beings, and even there they are so weakly implanted that it takes but little provocation for civilized man to bare his teeth in a wolfish snarl. With some vegetarianism is largely a matter of aesthetics, ethics and morality.

Morality is based on expediency, so it really is a question whether meat is an advantageous food or not. Another vegetarian argument is that man's anatomy proves that he was not intended by nature to eat meat. Good arguments have been used on both sides, but they are not very convincing nor are they conclusive. It is hard to draw any lines fairly. Another objection to meat is that it is unclean and full of poisons, that these poisons produce various diseases, such as cancer.

We are also informed that refined sugar causes cancer, and the belief in tomatoes as a causative factor is not dead. Cancer is without doubt caused principally by dietary indiscretions but it is impossible to single out any one food. No matter what foods we eat, we are compelled to be careful or they will be unclean. Those who wish clean meat can obtain it. The amount of poison or waste in a proper portion of meat is so small that we need give it no thought.

Those who eat in moderation can take meat once a day during cold weather and enjoy splendid health. During warm weather it should be eaten more seldom. On the other hand, meat is not necessary. We need a certain amount of protein, which we can obtain from nuts, eggs, milk, cheese, peanuts, peas, beans, lentils, cereals and from other food in smaller amounts. The amount of protein needed is small—about one-fifth of what the physiologists used to recommend. Those who think meat eating is wrong should not partake of it. They can get along very well without it.

The organism can stand it if the life is active in the fresh air, but it will not do for people who are housed. Much meat eating causes physical degeneration. The body loses tone. Experiments have shown that vegetarians have more resistance and endurance than the meat eaters, but the meat eaters get so much stimulation from their food that they can speed up in spurts. The excretions of meat eaters are more poisonous than those of vegetarians.

Eggs produced by hens fed largely on meat scraps do not keep as well as those laid by hens feeding more on grains. In short, meat eating leads to instability or degeneration, if carried to excess. Young children should have none of it and it would be a very easy matter for the rising generation to develop without using meat, and we believe this would be better than our present plan of eating.

However, let us give flesh food the credit due it. When meat eaters are debilitated no other food seems to act as kindly as meat, given with fruits or vegetables. When properly prepared and taken in moderation meat digests easily and is quite completely assimilated. Many make the mistake of living too exclusively on starch and taking it in excess. The result is fermentation and an acid state of the alimentary tract. Dr. Daniel S. Sager says that, "About all that we have to fear in eating is excessive use of proteids."

Experience and observation do not bear out this statement, for it is as easy to find people injured by starch as by protein. One form of poisoning is as bad as the other. The doctor also warns against nearly all the succulent vegetables, saying that on account of the indigestible fibre, most of them are unfit for human consumption. Dr. E.H. Dewey condemned the apple as a disease-producer, and inferentially, other fruits. Dr. Charles E. Page objects to the use of milk by adults, on the ground that it is fit food only for the calves for whom nature intended it. Many writers have repeated this opinion. Most of the regular physicians have a very vague idea of dietetics and proper feeding. When asked what to eat they commonly say, "Eat plenty nourishing food of the kinds that agree with you." They do not point out the fundamentals to their patients. Sometimes they advise avoiding combinations of milk and fruits. Sometimes they say that all starches should be avoided and in the next breath prescribe toast, one of the starchiest of foods. At times they proscribe pork and pickles but they are seldom able to give a good diet prescription. What people need is a fair knowledge of what to do and the don'ts will take care of themselves. All foods have been condemned as unfit for human consumption by people who should know.

However, those who look at these matters with open eyes and open minds will come to the cease that man is a very adaptable animal; that if necessary he can get along without almost all foods, being able to subsist on a very small variety; that he can live for a long period on animal food entirely; that he can live all his life without tasting flesh; that he can live on a mixed diet; that he can adopt a great many plans of eating and live in health and comfort on nearly all of them, provided he does not deprive himself of the natural salts and gets some protein; and finally and most important, that moderation is the chief factor in keeping well, for the best foods produce disease in time if taken in excess.

Those who object to flesh, dairy products, cereals, tubers, legumes, refined sugars, fruits or vegetables, should do without the class which they find objectionable, for it is easy to substitute from other classes. Eggs, milk or legumes may be taken in place of flesh foods. The salts contained in fruits may be obtained from vegetables. The starch, which is the chief ingredient of cereals, is easily obtained from tubers and legumes; fats and sugars will take its place. Commercial sugar is not a necessity. The force and heat derived from it can be obtained from starches and fats.

Outside of milk in infancy, there is not a single indispensable food. Some people have peculiarities which prevent them from eating certain foods, such as pork, eggs, milk and strawberries, but with these exceptions a healthy person can eat any food he pleases, provided he is moderate. We eat too much flesh, sugar and starch and we suffer for it.

This does not prove that these foods are harmful, but that overeating is. Sometimes the food question becomes a very trying one in the home. One individual has learned the fact that good results are obtained by using good sense and judgement in combining and consuming food, and he tries to force others to do as he does. This is unfortunate, for most people object to such actions, and though the intention is good, it accomplishes nothing, but prejudices others against sensible living.

The best way is to do right yourself and let others sin against themselves and suffer until they are weary. Then, seeing how you got out of your trouble, perhaps they will come to you and accept what you have to offer. The attempt to force people to be good or to be healthy is merely wasted effort.

WHEN TO EAT?

Three meals a day is the common plan. This is a matter of habit. Three meals a day are sufficient and should not be exceeded by man, woman or child. Lunching or "piecing" should never be indulged in. Children who are fed on plain, nutritious foods that contain the necessary food elements do not need lunches. Lunching is also a matter of habit, and we can safely say that it is a bad habit. If three meals a day are taken, two should be light. He who wishes to work efficiently can not eat three hearty meals a day. If it is brain work, the digestive organs will take so much of the blood supply that an insufficient amount of blood will be left to nourish the brain. The worker feels the lack of energy. He is not inclined to do thorough work, that is, to go to the root of matters, and he therefore does indifferent work.

One rule to which there is no exception is that the brain can not do its best when the digestive organs are working hard. If there is a piece of work to be done or a problem to be solved that requires all of one's powers it is best to tackle it with an empty stomach, or after a very light meal. If the work is physical, it is not necessary to draw the line so fine. But it is well to remember that hard physical work prevents digestion.

All experiments prove this. So if the labour is very trying, the eating should be light. Those who eat much because they work hard will soon wear themselves out, for hard work retards digestion, and with weakened digestion the more that is eaten, the less nourishment is extracted from it. Those who labour hard should take a light breakfast and the same kind of a noon meal. After the day's work is done, take a hearty meal. Those who perform hard physical labour, as well as those who work chiefly with their brains, should relax a while after the noon meal. A nap lasting ten to twenty minutes is very beneficial, but not necessary if relaxation is taken.

During sleep the activities of the body slow down. Most people who take a heavy meal and retire immediately thereafter feel uncomfortable when they wake in the morning. The reason is that the food did not digest well. It is always well to remain up at least two hours after eating a hearty meal. Most people would be better off if they took but two meals a day. Those who have sedentary occupations need less fuel than manual labourers, and could get along very well on two meals a day. However, if moderation is practiced, no harm will come from eating three times a day.

In olden times many people lived on one meal a day. Some do so today and get along very well. It is easy to get plenty of nourishment from one meal, and it has the advantage of not taking so much time. Most of us spend too much time preparing for meals and eating. Once when it was rather inconvenient to get more meals, we lived for ten months on one meal a day. We enjoyed our food very much and was well nourished. For twelve years we have lived on two meals a day, one of them often consisting of nothing but some juicy fruit. Many others do likewise, not because they are prejudiced against three meals per day, but they find the two meal plan more convenient and very satisfactory. Meat, potatoes and bread, with other foods, three times a day is a common combination. No ordinary mortal can live in health on such a diet. Such feeding results in discomfort and disease, and unless it is changed, in premature aging and death. The body needs only a certain amount of material. Sufficient can be taken in two meals. If three meals is the custom less food at a meal should be eaten. However, the general rule is that those who eat three meals per day eat fully as large ones as those who take only two.

As a rule, the meal times should be regular. We need a certain amount of nourishment, and it is well to take it regularly. This reduces friction, and is conducive to health, for the body is easily taught to fall into habits of regularity and works best when these are observed. There should be a period of at least four and one-half to five hours between meals. It takes that long for the body to get a meal out of the way. Stomach digestion is but the beginning of the process, and this alone requires from two to five hours.

On the two-meal plan it makes very little difference whether the breakfast or the lunch is omitted. After going without breakfast for a week or two, one does not miss it. Miss the meal that it is the most troublesome to get. Dr. Dewey revived interest in the no-breakfast plan. He considered it very beneficial.

The doctor did not give credit where credit is due, for he insisted on going without breakfast. Omitting lunch or dinner accomplishes the same thing. He got his beneficial results from reducing the number of meals, and consequently the amount of food taken, but it is immaterial which meal is omitted.

Heavy breakfasts are very common in England and in our country. On the European continent they do not eat so much for breakfast, a cup of coffee and one roll being a favourite morning meal there. To eat nothing in the morning is better than to take coffee and rolls. To eat enough to steal one's brain away is a poor way to begin the day. Much better work could be done on some fruit or a glass of milk, or some cereal and butter than on eggs, steak potatoes, hot bread and coffee, which is not an uncommon breakfast.

When we consider the best time to eat, we come back to our old friend, moderation, and find that it is the best solution of the question, for if the meals are moderate we may with benefit take three meals a day, but no more, for there is not time enough during the day to digest more than three meals. However, it is not necessary to eat three times a day.

HOW TO EAT?

It seems that all of us ought to know how to eat, for we have much practice; yet the individuals who know the true principles of nourishing the body are comparatively few. Very few healers are able to give full and explicit directions on this important subject. Some can give partial instructions, but we need a full working knowledge.

In one period of our racial history there were times when it was difficult to obtain food, as it is now among some savage people. Then it was without doubt customary to gorge, as it is among some savages now when they get a plenteous supply of food, especially of flesh food. Even among so-called civilized people, the distribution of food is so uneven that some are in want somewhere, nearly all the time.

In parts of Russia, we are informed, the peasants go into a state of semi-hibernation during part of the winter, living on very small quantities of inferior food. With rapid transportation and the extensive use of power-propelled machinery, famine should be unheard of in civilized countries. In our land there is a sufficient quantity of food and people seldom suffer because they have not enough, but considerable suffering is due to excessive intake and to poor quality of food.

Weight for weight, white bread is not as valuable as whole-wheat bread, though it contains as much starch. Measure for measure, boiled milk is inferior as a food to untreated milk, either fresh or clabbered. Such facts make it necessary for us to know how to eat.

The correct principles of taking nourishment to the best advantage have been fairly well known for a long time, and perhaps they have been fully discussed years ago by some authors, but so far as we know Dr. E.H. Dewey is the first one who grouped them and gave them the prominence they deserve.

He employed many pages in explaining clearly and forcibly these principles, which can be briefly stated as follows:

- First, be guided by the appetite in eating. Eat only when there is hunger.
- Second, during acute illness fast, that is, live on water.
- Third, be moderate in eating.
- Fourth, masticate your food thoroughly.

Dr. J.H. Tilden teaches his patients the same in these words:

- "Never eat when you feel badly.
- "Never eat when you have no desire.
- "Do not overeat.
- "Thoroughly masticate and insalivate all your food."

Because these true dietetic principles are so important let us give them enough consideration to fix them in the mind. They should be a part of every child's education. They should be so thoroughly learned that they become second nature, for if they are observed disease is practically impossible. Accidents may happen, but no serious disease can develop and certainly none of a chronic nature if these rules are observed, provided the individual gives himself half a chance in other ways. When the eating is correct, it is difficult to fall into bad habits mentally. Correct eating is a powerful aid to health. Health tends to produce proper thinking, which in turn leads the individual to proper acting.

EAT ONLY WHEN THERE IS HUNGER

Hunger is of two kinds, normal and abnormal. The real or normal hunger was given us by nature to make us active enough to get food. If it were not for hunger, there would be no special incentive for the young to partake of nourishment and consequently many would die comfortably of starvation, perhaps enough to endanger the life of the race. Normal hunger asks for food, but no special kind of food. It is satisfied with anything that is clean and nourishing. It is strong enough to make a decided demand for food, but if there is no food to be had it will be satisfied for the time being with a glass of water and will cause no great inconvenience. Abnormal hunger is entirely different. It is a very insistent craving and if it is not satisfied it produces bodily discomfort, perhaps headache. The gnawing remains and gives the victim no rest. Very often it must be pampered. It calls for beefsteak, or toast and tea, or sweets, or some other special food. If not satisfied the results may be nervousness, weakness or headache or some other disagreeable symptom.

When missing a meal or two brings discomfort, it is always a sign of a degenerating or degenerated body. A healthy person can go a day without food without any inconvenience. He feels a keen desire for food at meal times, but as soon as he has made up his mind that he is unable to get it or that he is not going to take any the hunger leaves. Normal hunger is a servant. Abnormal hunger is a hard master.

A person in good condition does not get weak from missing a few meals. One in poor physical condition does, although this is more apparent than real. In the abnormal person a part of the food is used as nourishment, but on account of the poor working of the digestive organs, a part decomposes and this acts as an irritant or a stimulant. The greater the irritation the more food is demanded. The temporary stimulation is followed by depression and then the sufferer is wretched. This depression is relieved by more food. Please note that it is relieved, not cured. The relief is only temporary.

All food stimulates, but only slightly. It is when the food decomposes that it becomes stimulating enough to cause trouble. It is well to remember that considerable alcoholic fermentation can take place in an abused alimentary tract. The stimulation obtained from too much food is very much like the stimulation derived from alcohol, tobacco or morphine. At first there is a feeling of well-being, which is followed by a miserable feeling of depression that demands food, alcohol, tobacco or morphine for relief, as the case may be, and no matter which habit is obtaining mastery, to indulge it is courting disaster. When a habit begins to assert itself strongly, break it, for later on it will be very difficult, so difficult that most people lack the will power to overcome it.

If there is abnormal hunger, reduce the food intake. Instead of eating five or six times a day, reduce the meals to two or three. It is quite common for such people to take lunches, which may consist of candies, ice cream, cakes, milk or buttermilk and various other things which most people do not look upon as real food. Take two or three meals a day, and let a large part of them be fresh vegetables and fresh fruits. Eat in moderation and the troublesome abnormal hunger will soon leave. By indulging it you increase it.

Many people get into trouble because they believe that they have to have protein, starch and fat at every meal. This is not necessary, for the blood takes up enough nourishment to last for quite a while. A supply of the various food elements once a day is sufficient, which means that protein needs be taken but once a day, starch once a day and fat once a day. Starch and fat serve the same purpose and one can be replaced by the other.

Cultivate a normal hunger, then fix two or three periods in which to take nourishment, and partake of nothing but water outside of these periods. If there is no desire for food when meal time comes, eat nothing, but drink all the water desired and wait until next meal time.

DURING ACUTE ILLNESS FAST

This is so obviously correct that we should expect every normal individual to be guided by it. Even the lower animals know this and act accordingly. This rule we should go without food when ill, but to do so is contrary to the teachings of medical men. They teach that when people are ill there is much waste, which is true, and that for this reason it is necessary to partake of a generous amount of nourishing food, so they give milk, broth, meat, toast and other foods, together with stimulants. Feeding during illness would be all right if the body could take care of the food, which it cannot. In all severe diseases digestion is almost or quite at a standstill and the food given under the circumstances decomposes in the alimentary tract and furnishes additional poison for the system to excrete.

Food under the circumstances is a detriment and a burden to the body. In fevers, the temperature goes up after feeding. This shows that more poison has entered the blood. In fevers little or none of the digestive fluids is secreted, but the alimentary tract is so warm that the food decomposes quickly. Feeding during acute attacks of disease is one of the most serious and fatal of errors. There is an aversion to food, which is nature's request that none be taken.

When an animal becomes seriously ill, it wants to fast, and does so unless man interferes. Here we could with advantage do as the animals do. Nature made no mistake when she took hunger away in acute diseases, and if we disregard her desires, we invariably suffer for it. We should make it a rule to take no food, either liquid or solid, during acute disease.

Those who have had no opportunity to watch the rapidity with which people recover from serious illness may take the ground that sick people would starve to death if they were to be treated thus, for some of these acute diseases last a long time. Typhoid fever, for instance, occasionally lasts two or three months. It never lasts that long when treated by natural means, and it is very mild, as a rule. The fever will be gone in from seven to fourteen days in the vast majority of cases, and then feeding can be resumed.

Chronic disease is often due to neglected acute disease, at other times to the building of abnormality through errors of life which have not resulted in acute troubles. While acquiring chronic disease, the individual may be fairly comfortable, but he is never up to par. Most chronic diseases can be cured quickly by taking a fast, but usually it is not necessary to take a complete fast. The desire for food is not generally absent and there is usually fair power to digest.

One of the most satisfactory methods, if not the most satisfactory one, of treating chronic disease is to reduce the food intake, and instead of giving so much of the concentrated staples, feed more of the succulent vegetables and the fresh fruits, cooked and raw, using but small quantities of flesh, bread, potatoes and sugar. This gives the body a chance to throw off impurities. There are always many impurities in a deranged body.

BE MODERATE IN YOUR EATING

This is often very difficult, for most people do not know what moderation is. In infancy the too frequent feeding and the overfeeding begin. The common belief that infants must be fed every two hours, or oftener, is acted upon. The result is that the child soon loses its normal hunger, which is replaced by abnormal hunger. When food is long withheld it begins to fret.

The mother again feeds and there is peace for an hour or so. When mothers learn to feed their children three times a day and no more there will be a great decrease in infant ills and a falling off in the infant mortality. The healthiest children we have seen are fed but three times a day. They become used to it and expect no more. Another thing that makes it difficult to be moderate is impoverishing the food through refinement and poor cooking.

These processes take away a great part of the mineral salts which are present in foods in organic form. These salts can not be replaced by table salt, for sodium chloride is but one of many salts that the body needs and an excess of table salt does not make up for a deficiency in the others. Children fed on refined, impoverished foods are not satisfied with a reasonable amount. There is something lacking and this makes itself known in cravings, which demand more food than is needed to nourish. We have noticed many times that children are satisfied with less of whole wheat bread than of white bread, and that the brown unpolished rice satisfies them more quickly and completely than the polished rice. In other words, depriving the foods of their salts is one of the factors that leads to overeating. Simplicity is a great aid to moderation.

It is also necessary to exercise the conservative measure, self-control. Some writers suggest to eat all that is desired and then fast at various intervals to overcome the effects of overeating. In other words, they advise to eat enough to become diseased and then fast to cure the trouble. This is better than to continue the eating when the evil results of an excessive food intake make themselves known, but it does not bring the best results. Such people have their spells of sickness, which are unnecessary.

If they stop eating as soon as the disease makes itself known, it does not last long. By exercising self-control sickness will be warded off. By using will power daily it grows stronger and those who force themselves to be moderate at first, are in time rewarded by having moderation become second nature. People should always stop eating before they are full. Those who eat until they are uncomfortable are gluttons. They should be classed with drunkards and drug addicts.

THOROUGHLY MASTICATE ALL FOOD

Horace Fletcher has written a very enthusiastic book on this subject. Enthusiasm is apt to lead one astray, and even if thorough mastication will not do all that Mr. Fletcher believed, it is very important, and we owe Mr. Fletcher thanks for calling our attention to the subject forcibly. Thorough mastication partially checks overeating. Our foods have to be finely divided and subdivided or they cannot be thoroughly acted upon by the digestive juices. The stomach is well muscled and churns the food about, helping to comminute it, but it can not take the place of the teeth. All foods should be thoroughly masticated. While the mastication is going on the saliva becomes mixed with the food. In the saliva is the ptyalin, which begins to digest the starch. Starch that is well masticated is not so liable to ferment as that which gets scant attention in the mouth. Starches and nuts need the most thorough mastication. If thorough mastication were the rule, meat gluttons would be fewer, for when flesh is well chewed large quantities cause nausea.

Milk digests best when it is rolled around in the mouth long enough to be mixed with saliva. To treat milk as a drink is a mistake, for it is a very nourishing food. All kinds of nuts must be well masticated. If they are not they cannot be well digested, for the digestive organs are unable to break down big pieces of the hard nut meats. The succulent vegetables contain considerable starch. If mastication is slighted they often ferment enough to produce considerable gas. Fruits are generally eaten too rapidly, and therefore often produce bad results. Even green fruits can be eaten with impunity if they are very thoroughly masticated. Those who are fond enough of liquors to take an excess should sip their alcoholic beverages very slowly, tasting every drop before swallowing. This would decrease their consumption of liquor greatly. Even water should not be gulped down. It should be taken rather slowly, especially on hot days. During hot weather many drink too much water. This tendency can usually be overcome by avoiding iced water and by drinking slowly.

These four rules should be a part of your vital knowledge. Remember them and try to put them into practice:

1. "Eat only when hungry.
2. During acute illness fast.
3. Be moderate in your eating.
4. Thoroughly masticate all food."

FOOD AND NUTRITION GUIDELINES FOR HEALTHY ADULTS

This chapter presents recommendations for high-priority measures to promote proper nutrition in the years ahead. The National Council for Nutrition, an independent council appointed by the Ministry of Health and Care Services in 2003, has formulated overall health and diet objectives. These are based on nutrition-related challenges and the vision of a healthy diet for lifelong good health.

The nutrition policy is rooted in health policy and builds on the following three documents: recommendations for nutrition and physical activity 2005, which presents updated scientific information on which intake of nutrients is best. Prescriptions for a healthier, which sets outs strategies for nutrition and public health work in a 10-year perspective; and the Global strategy on diet, physical activity and health adopted by the World Health Organization in May 2004. Social disparities in health are a major challenge for nutrition policy.

Eating habits and levels of physical activity vary greatly throughout the population according to education and income. Segments of the population with low income and little education eat more energy-dense foods and fewer vegetables than high-income, highly-educated segments of the population. Reducing social disparities in health is a primary goal in nutrition work. The efforts to encourage a healthy diet are linked to the goal of preventing health problems and promoting good health. Eliminating or reducing the scope of diet-related health problems is of utmost importance.

At the same time, the role of nutrition in treatment merits more attention. The efforts to promote good health through a healthy diet must have a global perspective. Sustainable food production is an aim in food and nutrition policy. A sustainable diet is both healthy, and takes environmental issues like production, processing and transport into account. Promoting a healthy diet requires efforts in a number of sectors. Food and food culture form an important frame-work for day-to-day life. It is vital to ensure that dietary recommendations are based on reliable, up-to-date information.

The National Council for Nutrition attaches great importance to issuing recommendations to the population and the health authorities that are based on solid scientific documentation. Knowledge about the relation between diet and health is comprehensive and growing, but much remains to be learned and new questions continue to emerge. Public health services and social services at all levels must be provided by competent personnel, whether dealing with the prevention or the treatment of diet-related health problems. Schools and day-care centres are key arenas for promoting a healthy diet for children and adolescents.

There are huge economic interests at stake in the food and beverage industry, and reconciling commercial interests and the interests of nutrition can be challenging. The authorities should promote cooperation with industrial players in order to promote healthy diet through the production, and supply of foods. As voluntary organizations also play an important role in nutrition work, the National Council for Nutrition aspires to promote strong alliances for good health.

The National Council for Nutrition's main concern is nutrition as it relates to diet. The Food Safety Authority is responsible for inspecting food production and sales to ensure that food is safe and healthy and complies with regulations. Determining what is necessary for food to be healthy and safe requires knowledge in a broad range of fields. Both the National Council for Nutrition and the Food Safety Authority's Scientific Committee for Food Safety play important roles in this process. Among other tasks, the Scientific Committee carries out risk assessments on foods and food components.

NUTRITION AND HEALTH

Continuing to reduce cardiovascular disease and the prevention of cancer and health problems associated with overweight and obesity are currently the most important challenges facing nutrition policy. Prescriptions for a healthier, and in the WHO global strategy on diet, physical activity and health. A healthy diet and regular physical activity can reduce the incidence of cardiovascular disease and cancer and prevent increases in overweight, obesity and type 2 diabetes.

The nutritional needs and health problems change throughout the life cycle. The risk of developing chronic diseases can be influenced at all ages. Health-promoting and preventive nutrition work must take a comprehensive approach to the human life cycle and to different needs at the various stages of life.

The foundation for health and disease is laid already in utero. The mother's nutrition during pregnancy has consequences not only for the child's health as a newborn, but also for its health later in life. In other words, the eating habits and nutrition of pregnant women and women of childbearing age have consequences not only for themselves but for the next generation as well. It is important to ensure that women in this stage of life have proper nutrition, and that their intake of folic acid and iron meets recommended levels.

Breastmilk is of great importance to infants' nutrition, immune systems and development. The greatest possible number of infants should be breastfed in accordance with recommendations. Infants and toddlers are in a biologically vulnerable stage of life, and it is essential that baby and toddler food is healthy and safe, and contains the nutrients required to meet their nutritional needs.

Commissioned by the Ministry of Health and Care Services and completed in the spring of 2005, the action plan for infant and toddler nutrition identifies measures designed to achieve these objectives. Eating habits established during childhood and adolescence, have an impact on the risk of disease later in life. Food and drinks are important indicators of social and cultural identity for everyone, and perhaps particularly for adolescents. The physiological need for nutrients is greater during adolescence than during childhood, and high-quality diet is important. Given society's obsession with perfect bodies, many young people feel pressured to lose weight, and eating disorders are a problem. Children and adolescents are an important target group for health-promoting nutrition work. People who have developed diet-related diseases may benefit greatly from dietary measures to improve their condition. Most chronic diseases have their onset during adulthood. The need for certain nutrients increases with age. Many elderly people experience a loss of appetite and some eat too little, becoming undernourished and frailer than need be.

Settling in a new country that has a different culture and language can lead to changes in diet, physical activity and health. Dietary changes, including a higher intake of fats and sugar and a lower intake of vegetables, fruits, lentils and beans, have been documented. Immigrants from non-Western countries differ in many ways, and there are substantial differences in health among the various groups. Some nutritional problems, such as overweight and obesity, type 2 diabetes, and iron and vitamin D deficiency, occur more often in certain immigrant groups.

CARDIOVASCULAR DISEASE

Cardiovascular disease is the most common cause of death and has a great impact on morbidity. For people under the age of 70, deaths from cardiovascular disease have been reduced by more than half in the past 30 years. A large part of this decline is due to improvements in diet. In particular, decreased consumption of solid fats has improved the blood cholesterol level in the population. There is great potential for prevention of these diseases through reduced dietary intake of solid fats and salt and increased intake of fruits and vegetables. A combination of a healthy diet, regular physical activity and no smoking plays an important part in preventing and treating cardiovascular disease.

CANCER

Cancer is the second most common cause of death and the overall incidence is on the rise. Obesity and physical inactivity are important risk factors for cancer. Diet plays an important role in preventing and treating cancer. A healthy diet with a high intake of fibre-rich foods, fruits and vegetables combined with a low salt intake can help prevent the development of a number of types of cancer. Cancer treatment not only exacts toil on the body mentally and physically, it may also alter or disrupt eating habits. As a consequence, proper nutrition is crucial when undergoing treatment.

OVERWEIGHT AND OBESITY

Overweight and obesity have become increasingly prevalent in population in recent decades, as in other Western countries. All segments of the population are experiencing weight gain, regardless of age, gender or education level. Nevertheless, overweight and obesity are most common in the lower socio-economic strata. Weight gain is the result of an imbalance between energy intake and energy expenditure. Overweight readily occurs when a reduced level of physical activity is combined with easy access to energy-dense foods.

There is a need for viable treatment options for those who become seriously overweight or obese. Obesity is a risk factor for developing type 2 diabetes, cardiovascular disease, certain types of cancer and osteoarthritis of the hips and knees. Overweight and obesity represent a growing pro-blem for individuals and society-at-large, meaning prevention is of tremendous importance.

DIABETES MELLITUS

Diabetes mellitus is the most common metabolic disorder in Norway. Diabetes is a result of a combination of genetic disposition and environmental factors. Overweight, obesity and physical inactivity increase people's risk of developing type 2 diabetes. These days, people are developing diabetes at an increasingly younger age. Diabetes is a contributing factor to cardiovascular disease, stroke, kidney failure, blindness, foot ulcers and amputation.

It is estimated that many people may have undiagnosed diabetes. Among immigrants from the Middle East and the Indian sub-continent, particularly among females, there is a substantial over-representation of type 2 diabetes. Dietary changes, increased physical activity, smoking cessation, controlling high blood pressure and weight loss play important roles in the treatment of type 2 diabetes. The single most important nutrition-related risk-factor of bone fractures is underweight. It is important to prevent underweight among the elderly. It is also important to ensure an adequate intake of vitamin D and calcium.

VISION

A healthy diet meets the recommendations for the composition of nutrients, is varied, tasty and in harmony with cultural values. It is the sum of what is consumed, how much and how often, that is decisive in the long run. From a health-promoting and preventive perspective, health is more than the absence of disease. In addition to physical health, it encompasses contentment and well-being.

STRATEGIC GOALS

Work in the nutrition sector should contribute to:

- Reducing the incidence of cardiovascular disease;
- Reducing the incidence of diet-related cancer;
- Halting the increase in overweight and obesity;
- Preventing type 2 diabetes;
- Preventing underweight and malnourishment;
- Strengthening the role of nutrition in treating the sick.

High-priority initiatives include:

- Increased consumption of vegetables, fruits, berries and whole-grain products;
- Decreased intake of solid fats;
- Decreased intake of energy-dense, nutrient- poor foods.

Facilitating healthy choices and increasing the health literacy of the population should be given priority in an attempt to achieve these strategic goals.

INCREASED CONSUMPTION OF FRUITS, VEGETABLES, BERRIES AND WHOLE-GRAIN PRODUCTS

Fruits, berries, vegetables, potatoes and whole-grain products are good sources of fibre, vitamins, minerals and a number of other nutrients. There is substantial documentation to show that a diet rich in fruits, vegetables, and whole-grain products reduces the risk of cardiovascular disease and certain types of cancer. Such a diet is not energy-dense and can reduce the risk of obesity. Consumer surveys, the consump-tion of vegetables increased from 80 gm./day in the 1970s to 110 gm./day in 2002, and there was a corresponding increase in the consumption of fruits and juice from 120 gm./day to 170 gm./day. Altogether, consumption has risen from 200 gm./day to 280 gm./day during this period. The consumption of potatoes has declined by half during the same period. Only about 10 per cent of the population has an intake of vegetables and fruits. There are clear social disparities in the consumption of these foods. The intake of grain products has remained relatively stable, but the consumption of whole-grain flour accounts for less than 20 per cent of total consumption. The goal is to increase the consumption of vegetables and fruits throughout the population to an average total intake of fruits and vegetables of at least 400 gm./day by 2009 to meet WHO recommendations.

Meanwhile, another goal is to increase the consumption of whole-grain products and potatoes at the expense of fat-rich potato products.

REDUCED INTAKE OF SOLID FATS (SATURATED FATS AND TRANS FATS)

Saturated fatty acids, and particularly trans fatty acids, in the diet have a negative effect on blood lipid profiles and increase the risk of coronary heart disease. It is estimated that a reduction in the intake of solid fats can substantially reduce the risk of coronary heart disease. In the 1970s, saturated fats accounted for 17 per cent, while the percentage has fallen to 14 per cent today, according to consumer surveys. The diet's content of trans fatty acids has been reduced from 4 per cent to less than 1 per cent of the diet's total energy content in the past 30 years.

The most important sources of saturated fats and trans fats in the diet are milk, dairy products, meat and meat products. Bread products, biscuits and cakes can also contain trans fats. The intake of solid fats should be limited to 10 per cent of total energy intake. By promoting the consumption of foods that are low in fat and foods that contain unsaturated fats, the intake of solid fats as well as the total fat intake can be reduced. The goal is to further reduce the consumption of solid fats to 12 per cent.

REDUCED INTAKE OF ENERGY-DENSE, NUTRIENT-POOR FOODS

A diet rich in energy-dense, nutrient-poor foods is linked to an increased risk of overweight and obesity, type 2 diabetes and caries. This type of diet can also result in a low intake of vitamins and minerals. A consumer surveys, over the past 30 years, total sugar consumption has risen slightly to 15 per cent of energy intake.

Sugar consumption patterns have changed, and the consumption of soft drinks and sweets has increased in particular. The sugar intake of children and adolescents has climbed sharply and is considerably higher than desired levels. Dietary studies among 13-year-olds reveal that sugar accounted for 13 per cent of their energy intake in 1993 and 18 per cent in 2000.

On average, they drank 4–5 dl of sugared soft drinks and fruit drinks a day, and ate 40–45 g of sweets a day. Sugared fruit drinks, soft drinks, and sweets accounted for 65 per cent of 13-year-olds' total sugar intake. Added sugar comprises sucrose, fructose, starch hydrolysate and other isolated sugars, which are used either in their pure form, as components of other food products or in cooking. Added sugar should not exceed 10 per cent of total energy intake. Another goal is to reduce the consumption of sugared soft drinks from some 85 litres per person per year to 60 litres per person annually, corresponding to the level of con-sumption in 1990. An additional goal is to reduce the consumption of sweets, sugared, nutrient-poor beverages, snack foods and fat-rich potato products.

DIET FOR WOMEN

With the way they are conditioned, women end up doing more or less work equivalent to men. However, the kind of recognition they get is pretty less compared to what men get. Many women feel bad when they even put on one pound of weight. They go on crash diet and try and reduce their weight to make it to normal. But fact is many women don't even realise that they are too skinny to go on diets that make them thinner. Iron deficiency in women is definitely a big cause of worry for many women. We do not teach you special kinds of diets, instead as suggested, be discussing about what foods are advised for women, and what are not.

What Foods to Avoid, gives a detail of what type of foods should be avoided, and why. Actually, avoiding bad foods is half the job done to stay healthy. And when you know what foods you avoid, you should also be worried about what gives you a healthy structure and figure. Most of the body weight is constituted by bone weight.

Hence it is important that take foods that give loads of calcium to your body. *Nutrition for Healthy Bones*, will help you understand how to build up healthy bones, and a healthy life.

PREGNANCY DIET

Though not always, many a woman is always in two minds whenever she is confronted with a new situation. The same is the case when a woman gets pregnant. Unfortunately one cannot say that all pregnant women know how to take care of their health during this important time.

NUTRITION DURING PREGNANCY

A stable diet is a critical component of good health always in an individual's life. All through pregnancy, diet is still more significant. The foods that one consumes are the chief suppliers of the nutrients for one's baby. As the baby develops, one will require more of the majority of nutrients.

Prior to becoming pregnant is the most excellent time to commence eating a beneficial diet. Eating correctly prior to becoming pregnant can assist an individual in ensuring that both she and her baby start off with the nutrients that both require.

Supplement

Folic acid is a kind of vitamin that is crucial to the development of the baby, particularly all through the initial months of pregnancy. Not receiving sufficient folic acid in one's diet prior to one becoming pregnant and initially in pregnancy augments the threat of birth flaws, for example neural tube imperfection. Receiving good health care ahead of one becoming pregnant will assist an individual all through one's pregnancy.

Pregnant women are occasionally worried about gaining surplus weight. However, it should be borne in mind that one's diet is the foremost source of energy for the baby. That signifies one has to consume more while pregnant. When an individual is pregnant, she requires approximately 300 calories additionally everyday day than she generally consumes. The amount of weight a woman puts on during pregnancy is dependent on her weight prior to pregnancy.

A beneficial gain for the majority of women is between 25 and 35 pounds. If a woman is obese, she should put on less, but certain weight gain is usual. If a woman is underweight, she should put on additional weight. The initial move in the direction of healthy eating is to take into account the foods in one's everyday diet.

Additional Nutrients:

- Pregnant women may require additional nutrients and these may consist of iron, folic acid and calcium.
- They can be made available as single pills or as an amalgamated pill.
- Occasionally a prenatal vitamin has all that one requires.
- In order to avert neural tube flaws, a woman ought to receive 0.4 mg. of folic acid every day ahead of and all through pregnancy.
- It should be taken for one month ahead of pregnancy and throughout the initial three months of pregnancy.

Women who have had a child with a spine or skull blemish are more liable to have one more child with this trouble. These women require greater amounts of folic acid-4 mg. every day. Milk and additional dairy products are the most excellent sources of calcium in one's diet.

However, several women have indications, for example bloating, diarrhoea, gas and indigestion subsequent to drinking milk or consuming dairy products. This is referred to as lactose intolerance. If a pregnant woman is lactose intolerant, she should ensure that she is receiving adequate calcium.

DIET FOR HEALTHY WEIGHT GAIN DURING PREGNANCY

Acquiring the correct quantity of weight all through pregnancy by consuming a nourishing, stable diet is an excellent sign that the baby is receiving all the nutrients he or she requires and is developing at a healthy rate. It is not essential to consume for two in pregnancy. It's a reality that pregnant women require additional calories from nutrient-rich foods to aid the growth of her baby, but a pregnant woman commonly should consume just 100 to 300 more calories than she did ahead of becoming pregnant to fulfil the requirements of the developing baby.

It is imperative for a pregnant woman to take the advice of the health care provider on the amount of weight she should put on for the period of pregnancy. A woman of standard weight ahead of pregnancy should put on 25 to 35 pounds for the period of pregnancy. Women who are underweight should put on 28-40 pounds for the period of pregnancy. Obese women may require putting on just 15-25 pounds during pregnancy.

Ideal weight gain:

- Generally, one should put on approximately 2 to 4 pounds all through the initial three months of pregnancy and 1 pound a week for the rest of the pregnancy period.
- If an individual is anticipating twins she should put on 35 to 45 pounds for the period of her pregnancy.
- This would be a typical of 1 ½ pounds for every week following the normal weight increase in the initial three months.

The Additional Weight is Distributed in the Following Manner

For the baby it is 8 pounds, for the placenta 2-3 pounds, for amniotic fluid 2-3 pounds, for breast tissue 2-3 pounds, blood supply 4 pounds, fat reserves for delivery and breastfeeding 5-9 pounds and for uterus increase 2-5 pounds. This makes for a total weight of 25 to 30 pounds.

It is by no means risk-free to shed weight for the period of pregnancy since both the mother and the baby require the appropriate nutrients so as to be healthy. In order to gain the required weight during pregnancy one should consume five to six minor, regular meals everyday. One should stock swift, trouble-free snacks on hand, for example nuts, raisins, cheese and crackers, dried fruit, in addition to ice cream or yogurt. It is imperative to apply peanut butter on toast, crackers, apples, bananas, or celery.

A single tablespoon of creamy peanut butter will make available approximately 100 calories and 7gm. of protein. One should include nonfat powdered milk in foods for example mashed potatoes, scrambled eggs plus hot cereal. It is crucial to include condiments in one's meal, for example, butter or margarine, cream cheese, gravy, sour cream as well as cheese. Certainly, patterns of weight increase all through pregnancy differ. It's usual to put on less if an individual is heavier at the time of pregnancy and it is normal to put on extra weight if an individual is expecting twins or triplets or if an individual is underweight prior to becoming pregnant.

WHAT FOODS TO AVOID

Eating proportionate meals is vital at all times, but it is especially crucial when one is pregnant. There are important nutrients, vitamins and minerals that a growing baby requires. The majority of foods are harmless; nonetheless, there are certain foods that one ought to stay away from during pregnancy. Raw seafood and exceptional or undercooked beef or poultry should be shunned due to the danger of infectivity with coliform bacteria, toxoplasmosis, and salmonella.

Deli meats have been acknowledged to be infected with Listeria, which can trigger miscarriage. Listeria has the capacity to traverse the placenta and may contaminate the baby resulting in contamination or blood poisoning, which can be critical. If a pregnant woman is contemplating to eat deli meats, she should ensure to reheat the meat until it is steaming.

Avoiding fish:

- Fish that has high quantities of mercury ought to be avoided.
- Mercury ingested during pregnancy has been associated with developmental hindrance and brain harm.
- Examples of these kinds of fish comprise: shark, swordfish, king mackerel and tilefish.
- Canned, chunk light tuna usually contain less quantities of mercury in comparison to other tuna, but still should only be consumed in restraint.
- Some kinds of fish employed in sushi should also be shunned because of high concentration of mercury.

Frozen, smoked seafood frequently described as lox, nova style, kippered, or jerky should be shunned since they could be infected with Listeria. Preserved or shelf-safe smoked seafood is considered safe for consumption.

Individuals who are pregnant should shun fish from polluted lakes and rivers that may be subjected to high quantities of polychlorinated biphyenyls. Most of seafood borne sickness is attributable to undercooked shellfish, which comprise oysters, clams, and mussels. Cooking assists in averting several kinds of infection, but it does not thwart the algae-related illness that is linked to red tides. Uncooked shellfish create apprehension for everyone and they should be shunned in general all through pregnancy.

Uncooked eggs or any foods that has uncooked eggs should be shunned due to the possible exposure to salmonella. Several home-produced Caesar dressings, mayonnaise, home-produced ice cream or custards, and Hollandaise sauces may be prepared with uncooked eggs. If the recipe is cooked at certain stage, this will reduce the contact with salmonella. Commercially produced ice cream, dressings and eggnog are prepared with pasteurized eggs and do not augment the threat of salmonella. Restaurants also are supposed to be utilizing pasteurized eggs in whichever recipe that is made with uncooked eggs, for example Hollandaise sauce or dressings.

Imported soft cheese may have bacteria recognized as Listeria, which can trigger miscarriage. Listeria has the capacity to traverse the placenta and can contaminate the baby resulting in infection or blood poisoning that can be life-intimidating. Pregnant women should keep away from soft cheese for example, brie, camembert, Roquefort, feta, gorgonzola and Mexican type cheeses that comprise queso blanco and queso fresco.

IRON DEFICIENCY ANAEMIA IN WOMEN

Iron insufficiency anaemia—a shortage of iron in the blood affects a large number of women globally. Iron is a vital nutrient in pregnancy; hence it's imperative to be certain that pregnant women have an ample ingestion. There are three major causes that an adequate iron ingestion to thwart anaemia is vital. First, iron is indispensable for the development of maternal and foetal hoemoglobin, the oxygen-transporting constituent of blood.

As a woman's blood volume swells by 25 to 40 per cent in pregnancy, and the baby is producing blood cells, as well, the requirement for iron rises putting the mother in danger of anaemia. Second, in the final trimester, the baby extracts from the mother a quantity of the iron reserves that it will require in the initial four to six months of life. Third, the augmented blood volume and iron stores aids the mother's body adjust, to certain extent, to the blood loss that takes place in childbirth.

Maternal iron deficiency anaemia:

- Maternal iron deficiency anaemia is linked to an augmented frequency of anaemia in the baby in the initial year of life, in addition to anaemia and reduced iron reserves in the mother.
- Pregnant women with iron deficiency anaemia, chiefly in the first and second trimesters, have an augmented danger for early delivery and for delivering a low-birth weight baby.

The majority of doctors suggest iron supplements for pregnant mothers. In general, an every day 60 mg. iron supplement is recommended to check anaemia, although the suggested quantity of iron in pregnancy is 30 mg. every day. It is for the reason that iron from supplements is not completely assimilated. Receiving 60 mg. of iron daily will make certain that a pregnant woman in reality assimilated the suggested daily quantity of iron. Iron supplements are appropriately assimilated if taken with foods enriched with vitamin C, for example orange, grapefruit, or tomato juice. Absorption is weakened if one takes them with antacids or foods containing calcium for example milk and cheese. Iron supplements occasionally trigger upset stomach, constipation, or nausea.

If such a condition arises one can obtain most of the iron an individual requires from iron-rich foods, for example organ meats like liver red meat, egg yolks, and legumes such as dried peas and beans. Iron deficiency anaemia in pregnant women and in babies in the aftermath of delivery is without difficulty avoidable by the consumption of a stable, wholesome, iron-rich diet and taking iron supplements as stipulated by one's doctor. Iron deficiency anemia is linked to psychomotor and cognitive defects in children. Iron deficiency anaemia in pregnancy has been connected with augmented danger for low birth weight, preterm delivery, and prenatal death. Recent studies entail that maternal iron deficiency anaemia may be related to postpartum melancholy and inferior performance on mental and psychomotor tests in children.

ANTI AGING NUTRITION

Although ageing is unavoidable, physical decay is not. More than a few of the external manifestations of growing old can be decelerated - and life can even be protracted - by sustaining a wise and meaningful approach to diet. As individuals grow old, their bodies' process nutrients less competently, leading to the requirement for individuals to enhance their nutrient ingestion. For instance, Vitamin D is a nutrient necessary for the deterrence of osteoporosis. The human body produces vitamin D when the skin is subjected to sunlight, but when individuals are in their 70s their bodies manufacture merely 40 per cent of it. An ample quantity of vitamin D for people in their 20s is 200 IU; for individuals who are grown-up, 400 IU to 600 IU is required for performing the identical amount of work.

Requirement related to age:

- The requirement for B vitamins rises with age also.
- Three B vitamins—folic acid, vitamin B6 and vitamin B12—are crucial for maintaining levels of a compound described as homocysteine at a low level in the blood; if permitted to increase, homocysteine plays a part in heart-disease threat and probably memory loss, as indicated by studies in the relevant sphere.
- When individuals age it is imperative for them to augment their B6 amount from 2 mg to 5 mg; augment B12 in due course from 2 mcg to 10 mcg.
- Women ought to receive 400 mcg of folic acid every day; pregnant women ought to ingest 800 mcg everyday in order to thwart neural-tube flaws in the foetus.

Women, specifically, should be conscious that their calcium ingestion should augment as they age to avert osteoporosis. Individuals who eat diets rich in fresh fruits and vegetables have reduced ailment rates, additional energy and less danger for weight gain that can result in health troubles in comparison to those who omit these foods.

With the omission of avocados, olives and coconuts, fresh fruits and vegetables are devoid of fat, cholesterol or sodium. Fresh fruits and vegetables are furthermore rich in fibre. Eight servings of fruits and vegetables consumed everyday offers roughly 27 gm. of fibre, which is well inside the everyday requirement of 25 gm. to 35 gm.. Foods rich in fibre reduce an individual's threat for developing age-linked ailments for example heart disease, cancer, diabetes and hypertension. Foods rich in fibre are moreover reduced in calories, nonetheless satisfying; consequently they assist in filling up individuals without filling him or her.

Fresh fruits and vegetables are rich in nutrients, making available sufficient quantities of calcium, iron, magnesium, vitamin C, beta carotene and folic acid, and they are short in calories. Fruits and vegetables also contain longevity-boosting compounds referred to as antioxidants which comprise vitamins C and E in addition to beta carotene. Antioxidants resist free radicals, oxygen fragments that strike and harm cell membranes, life-supporting proteins and even genetic code of cells that trigger aging and ailments.

Diets high in antioxidants check ailment and untimely aging. Antioxidants, moreover, invigourate the immune system and defend the nervous system and brain from the oxidative harm connected with age-linked memory loss.

DIET DURING MENOPAUSE

Menopause is the expression employed to signify the cease of the period of probable sexual reproduction, as demonstrated by the termination of menstrual periods. This is completely usual and happens between 45 to 55 years. Menopause does not reduce women's physical capability, sexual energy and capacity to enjoy life. Menopause fetches specific freedoms to female life. Such as no longer they have to be anxious about the monthly bleeding and about birth control. Still then in this period a woman suffers a great deal of emotional strain. Ovaries discontinue making oestrogen and this result in oestrogen deficiency. This hormonal disparity may trigger short-term symptoms and long term health threat.

Adhering to a healthy diet:

- Sticking to a healthy diet can be beneficial for vitality in general and this in the process assists in providing a woman with better resistance against any troubles during menopause.
- Hot flushes can be diminished by acquiring vitamin E rich foods similar to wheat germ, nuts, eggs and olive oil.
- Vitamin A, D, calcium, phosphorous and magnesium can assist in checking osteoporosis.
- Fish, drumstick leaves, ragi and dairy products are outstanding suppliers of calcium. During menopause women should shun consuming uncooked bran, which hinders calcium absorption and should reduce the consumption of tea, coffee which advances the excretion of calcium.

Many women gain weight which augments the blood cholesterol level. To regulate body weight and blood cholesterol one should choose low fat dairy foods and reduce the consumption of saturated fats such as butter and cheese. Studies indicate that substances from plants identified as phytoestrogens can assist in diminishing the acuteness of hot flushes and additional indications of menopause. Phytoestrogens, which imitate human oestrogen, are obtained chiefly from soybeans and alfalfa sprouts. Soya bean flour can be combined with wheat flour for making bread. Additional soya foods are soymilk, tofu, as well as soy sauce. Carrot in addition to beet root juice is considered to be extremely helpful in menopausal maladies. Oats, corn, barley, brown rice, whole wheat are as well outstanding sources of phytoestrogens.

Frequent exercise is necessary in this period. This stage is to be considered as a usual period in a women's life. Nonetheless the family members ought to understand that this stage in the life of a woman requires a great deal of thought, attention and sympathy to make the daily life stress free. A nourishing diet can not only diminish the indications of menopause, but also bring about an improved lifestyle and augmented energy levels, enabling one to do the types of activities that will support an improved body and an improved lifestyle in general. Foods rich in calcium and supplements are an excellent suggestion if one intends to lead a vigourous way of life during menopause. Calcium is mainly helpful when used with additional vitamins and minerals such as magnesium and vitamin D, which supports superior skeletal health.

NUTRITION FOR HEALTHY BONES

Healthy bones provide the body with power and firmness to defend the internal organs from damage. Significant as the skeleton is, it accounts for merely around 12 per cent of a human being's entire body weight.

Bones are living tissues and are continuously experiencing remodeling since old bone tissue gets worn-out and fresh bone is produced. A subtle equilibrium has to be kept between these two procedures. If that equilibrium is disrupted, problems can take place, including brittle bones and osteoporosis.

Ensuring healthy bones needs:

- Frequent physical exercise and a nourishing, stable diet are equally vital.
- Evading threat factors similar to smoking and strain also add to healthy bones.
- Every individual can do a bit to shape the health of their bones.
- By indulging in weight-bearing physical work out one can promote bone mineralization.
- By eating correctly one can make certain that the essential nutrients are obtainable for bone metabolism.
- These major nutrients are Calcium and Vitamin D.

Calcium is essential for strong teeth and bones and furthermore, plays a vital part in a variety of bodily systems, for example, the health and performance of nerves and muscle tissue.

Superior sources of calcium comprise dairy foods and leafy green vegetables, even though calcium from milk and milk products is more effortlessly assimilated and present in larger quantities. Individuals at various life phases require dissimilar quantities of calcium. Adolescents, young children in addition to elderly women all have bigger than normal necessities. Calcium is one of the vital nutrients required for healthy growth of bone.

Ample calcium ingestion is crucial for the accom-plishment of peak bone mass in the late teen. This is the maximum stage of bone strength which takes place at cease of growth, and consequently results in tough healthy bones, which will prolong the consequences of ageing on the skeleton. It is vital to have a proportionate diet with sufficient quantities of dairy products, which are the principal sources of foods high in calcium.

Vitamin D is the broad name for a cluster of steroid-like substances with anti-rachitic action. Vitamin D is obtained only from animals and there are simply some foods which have vitamin D like oily fish, fish oils, butter and eggs. Different from other vitamins, individuals can in reality produce vitamin D in their bodies as an outcome of contact to sunlight, on condition that ingestion of ascorbic acid is sufficient.

The two major members of this vitamin cluster are ergocalciferol or vitamin D2 and cholecalciferol or vitamin D3. Vitamin D is necessary for the assimilation of calcium and phosphorus from the small intestine, their re-assimilation in the kidneys, and the mineralization procedure of the bones. It therefore promotes healthy bone development. It, furthermore performs a vital role in the appropriate working of muscles, nerves, blood clotting, cell growth and energy utilization.

BREAST CANCER DIET

When an individual is coping with breast cancer, appropriate nutrition becomes especially vital. Nonetheless, a proportionate diet and breast cancer treatment may not be effective simultaneously. The side effects from breast cancer treatments, together with the emotional stress of being afflicted by the disease can make it tough for patients to eat. By pursuing recommen-dations to deal with the side effects when eating; selecting beneficial foods to eat; and drawing assistance and support from others, breast cancer patients can preserve a well-balanced diet during cure and recuperation. While taking into account the diet in breast cancer treatment, one should initiate a hunt for cancer-combating nutrients. Foods with such nutrients should assist in satisfying the palate of the breast cancer patient. One may start by looking for foods that are rich in selenium.

Selenium effective in fighting cancer:

- Selenium is equally an indispensable natural mineral and a helpful cancer-fighting antioxidant.
- Foods rich in selenium require being an ingredient of a diet for breast cancer treatment.
- Selenium aids to fortify the immune system, and helps in easing the action of the thyroid. It also assists in stimulating specific enzymes.
- One can acquire a required ingestion of selenium by consuming tuna, eggs, wheat grain, chicken, liver, garlic as well as Brazil nuts.

The benefits of selenium make it suitable for addition in the diet for breast cancer cure. Studies indicate a connection between the capacity of selenium to initiate the action of specific enzymes and the mineral's ability to defend against cancer threats. An every day ingestion of no less than 70 microgm. of selenium should be the aim of every woman who is concerned with regard to her diet for breast cancer treatment. If an individual consumes a quantity far higher than 100 microgm. every day, then this surplus quantity of selenium can trigger nausea, awful breath, skin complaints, giddiness, feebleness and cold indications.

Ingestion of above 60 microgm. of selenium every day is unsuitable for pregnant women. An excessive ingestion of selenium seems connected with birth problems. However, certain women can include extra selenium to a diet in breast cancer treatment. One more nutrient that should be an ingredient of every diet in breast cancer treatment is indole-3-carbinol, a chemical that is as well described as 13C. This phytochemical, a crucial component of the chemical composition of broccoli and additional cruciferous vegetables has been revealed to be a natural means of averting specific cancers.

The useful 13C utilizes three dissimilar means for supplying its beneficial effects. Initially, 13C disrupts the cancer cell phase; a broken up cycle checks cell division. Second, 13C checks the development of blood vessels in the tumor; with no blood vessels, the tumor cells can not obtain required nutrients. Third, 13C work in a way that is capable of preparing the phase for the death of the cancer cells. The maximum worth of 13C stems from the anticipated product formed when an individual has consumed a diet high in 13C.

HEALTH DIETS FOR PATIENTS

When taking care of various health issues, one has to be extremely careful about one's diet. Doctors advise medicines mentioning what kind of diet should be taken with it. If this diet isn't followed carefully, medicines do not do the complete job.

DIET FOR CANCER

A strict diet is advised for Cancer because some foods directly affect cancer maturity. Fat, especially saturated fats do more harm than any one can imagine.

Hence diets for Cancer should increase as much as only 55gm. of Fat intake daily.

DIET FOR GOUT

Gout is one type of arthritis and is called metabolic arthritis. It is one of the worst types of arthritis. Gout makes sodium urate crystals deposit on the particular cartilage of joints and tendon tissues. It might even cause stones in kidneys. Rich Carbohydrate diet is advised for people who suffer from Gout. Protein intake should be very limited as well.

DIET DURING ACID REFLUX

When someone feels heartburn, or suddenly realises that he or she gets food back into their mouths, they should suspect Acid Reflux. Gastric juices that contain acids are pushed back from stomach to esophagus, and this condition is called acid reflux. Diet for acid reflux starts off with taking smaller meals, more than three times a day. And the diet is all given in the substance called diet during acid reflux.

DIET DURING DIARRHOEA

Diarrhoea is one of the most irritating health problems. It could be cause by contaminated food or even climate change. And importantly one should not stop diarrhea because it is nature's way of eliminating virus.

DIET FOR CONSTIPATION

Constipation is the exact opposite situation of diarrhoea. While you struggle to control defecating in diarrhoea, Constipation doesn't allow easy defecating. Fibre is the most suggested diet for constipation. And make sure you find the correct sources of Fibre from the substance.

DIET FOR OBESE

United States suffers with an ever increasing population of obese people. Though obesity doesn't kill right away, one needs to be specially aware of what it can do to ones body. Obesity isn't a disease but a condition which definitely leads to disease over a period of time. Fat is the mean reason behind obesity.

So, if you think and find that you are growing in weight regularly, you should first consult your doctor. One can be called obese when is unable to see their toes, when they stand straight. All you need to do is avoid food, and you lose weight. But why should any one take food for weight loss? All foods play an important role in the way we act and think daily. Hence if we do not have foods over a period of time, it is imperative that we are not as good as when we have enough food in our bellies. However, we need to understand that certain foods with too much of fat in them, make us fatter, and certain foods have lesser amounts of fat. Hence, taking food that has lesser amounts of fat helps.

LOW CARB DIETS

Food, in general, contains proteins, carbohydrates, fat, minerals, water and other nutrients. In all these we proteins are digested for various activities performed inside the body. Carbohydrates provide energy required for the body to do various physical activities. Fat helps our body in many ways, and it acts as a substitute for carbs. So when carbs fall short, fat is burnt to provide energy. That's how low carb diets help.

SAFE SWEETENERS AND FAT BURNERS

If you crave for that sweet taste and can't get adjusted to not having sugar in your tea and coffee, then sweeteners help you out. These small tablets contain sucralose or saccharin apart from various other ingredients. Importantly they add lesser amounts of calories to your body. Fat burners are dangerous if not taken under a doctor's advice. They simulate burning of excessive calories in your body, and their effect is felt immediately.

HEALTHY EATING

Healthy eating should be made a daily routine and cannot be taken easy. Healthy eating guildelines provide apart from few easy tips for weight loss, with an substance especially for new moms who want to shed weight.

LOW CARB DIETS—HOW THEY WORK?

Low carb diets are anchored in the principle that a diet extremely low in carbohydrate results in a decrease in the body's insulin production, leading to fat and protein stores being utilized as its major energy source.

OBJECTIVE

- The objective of low carbohydrate diets is to compel the body to utilize fat as its chief energy source.
- When this takes place an individual produces "ketone bodies" to stimulate parts of the body that cannot utilize fat as an energy source—the brain, and red blood cells, specifically.
- When this occurs an individual is said to be in a condition of ketosis—typified by stinking breath and side effects for example sickness and exhaustion.

In essence an individual eliminates practically all carbohydrate from his or her diet and increases the protein and fat ingestion. Hence one reduces the consumption of pasta, bread, rice in addition to alcohol, and consumes unrestricted quantities of meat, cheese in addition to butter.

In the short term, the majority of individuals who follow low carb diets do lose weight and they lose it extremely fast. Nonetheless, most of the weight loss happens from loss of water as well as muscle tissue, not fat which one requires to lose to avoid the surplus weight.

In addition, if an individual is attempting to lose weight on a permanent basis, losing valuable lean muscle tissue is similar to damaging one's own body. Even when an individual is relaxing, muscle tissue is metabolically active, and burns calories. A reduction in the quantity of muscle tissue an individual possesses will result in a reduction in the number of calories an individual requires every day to preserve one's weight, making it a great deal tough to keep one's weight under check when one discontinues pursuing the low carb diet. Persons are fascinated by low carb diets since weight loss is extremely fast, and individuals love to observe immediate results on the weighing machine. However, low carb diet is not a very healthy choice. Crucial vitamins and nutrients are obtained from a balanced diet and low carbohydrate diets are definitely not balanced.

One can simply obtain a lot of vital nutrients from fruit, vegetables and grains and low carb diets merely permit extremely small quantities of fruit and vegetables which is certainly not sufficient to offer an individual his or her suggested every day allowance. The crucial point these low carb diets expresses is that carbohydrates advance insulin production, which in the process leads to weight gain. Hence by decreasing carbohydrate ingestion, individuals will shed weight. The reality is that by consuming a low carb diet, individuals do not offer sufficient carbohydrates to his or her body for every day function. Consequently it will begin burning the stored carbohydrates known as glycogen for energy. When a person's body commences burning glycogen, water is discharged. Consequently the severe early drop of weight at the start is merely water one loses as a consequence of burning glycogen.

SAFE SWEETENERS

Widespread obesity and diabetes promoted the expansion of the artificial sweetener industry. Increasing number of people are endeavoring to shed weight or trying to preserve a healthy weight. Sweeteners can be discovered in nearly all chewing gum, diet pop as well as drinks, light yogurt in addition to various frozen ice cream. If a product is labelled sugar free, it is extremely probable that sweeteners are added to them.

Types of sweeteness are:

- Nutritive Sweeteners make available calories to the diet at approximately four calories for every gm., akin to the usual carbohydrate individuals acquire from food.
- Instances of nutritive sweeteners comprise white and brown table sugars as well as molasses, honey in addition to syrups.

- Besides, sugar alcohols obtained from fruits or commercially prepared are as well nutritive sweeteners.
- The majority of widespread sugar alcohols comprise sorbitol, mannitol, xylitol as well as maltitol.
- Every nutritive sweetener supplies calories to the body and may well have an effect on one's blood glucose.
- Nonnutritive sweeteners are the real artificial sweeteners.
- They do not supply calories and will not affect blood glucose.
- These consist of, saccharin, neotame, aspartame, sucralose, stevia and acesulfame potassium.

The safest thing to do is to keep away from all synthetic and chemical sweetener substitutes. They boast of no food value, deceive the body into believing it is consuming something sweet, and they have by-products of damaging poisonous side effects.

Foods having saccharin no more carry a warning maintaining that the utilization of this product may perhaps be dangerous to one's health accompanied by the assertion that such foods have saccharin which has been revealed to trigger cancer in laboratory animals. This caution was removed following indications that saccharin no longer has been associated with cancer in human beings. Saccharin may possibly be there in drugs in large amounts. Intake of the suggested every day dosage of chewable aspirin or acetaminophen tablets in a child of school going age would make available roughly the similar quantity of saccharin enclosed in one can of a diet soft drink. This quantity, comparative to the body weight of a child younger than 9 or 10 years and consumed for extended duration would be regarded as excessive use, as characterized in a key scientific report.

In this report, heavy utilization of artificial sweeteners was connected with a considerably augmented danger for the growth of bladder cancer. Acesulfame Potassium which was permitted for utilization as a harmless artificial sweetener is an offshoot of acetoacetic acid. Regrettably, a number of probable troubles connected with the application of acesulfame have been brought up. They are centred mainly on animal studies because experiments on humans continue to be limited. Aspartame, a dipeptide of aspartic acid and a methyl ester of phenylalanine, is permitted for utilization in pharmaceutical products and is being employed more and more in chewable tablets and sugar-free formulations.

FAT BURNERS

Ripped Fuel, ProBURN, Thermo-Cuts, Metabolift, OptiBurn and Hydroxycut are promoted as fat-burning supplements that will enable an individual acquire a lean shape in a rapid manner. In reality, these fat burners do have a propensity to augment the pace at which a person uses up calories, but as with every product that promises marvel, it is essential for an individual to exercise caution prior to use and care should be taken while using them. A fat burner that an individual selects will more or less at all times have two basic ingredients, namely, ephedrine and caffeine. Ephedrine is a bronchodilator, which is available as asthma medicine or cold medication to augment the body's capacity to carry oxygen into the bloodstream. Additional oxygen in the bloodstream offers individuals the capability to generate more energy in the cells.

More significantly for fat burning, ephedrine is a stimulant that enhances heart rate and blood pressure, thereby stimulating the body during workouts at the gym. In addition, ephedrine has a propensity to hinder appetite and perform as a diuretic. Synephrine, norephedrine, and pseudoephedrine are all related to ephedrine that offers comparable results. Individuals who drink coffee are aware of caffeine's invigourating ability, and packing caffeine collectively with ephedrine augments the thermogenic or heat-producing effect inside the body.Caffeine in addition shows on labels as kola nut extract, guarana paste, and maté leaves. Studies have revealed that adding aspirin to the ephedrine, caffeine pile additionally boosts the thermogenic effect, thus advancing improved weight loss. Whenever the internal temperature of the body is raised, individuals automatically burn more calories and this characteristically leads to weight loss and fat loss in particular. White willow bark is a source of salicin, the primary component of aspirin, and each of these expressions might as well become evident on labels. Products having the ephedrine, caffeine, aspirin stack or its chemical counterparts are time and again described as ECAs.

Lure of fat burners:

- Fat burners are appealing since they have an effect on the body just about straight away.
- When individuals check out these stimulant-based products, they generally experience something immediately and it is the effect of the stimulant.
- This acts as a major reason for people clinging to such products.

The trouble is fat burners shouldn't be used simply by everyone. Not every individual reacts positively to stimulants and individuals on aspirin or heart medicine or an additional kind of asthma medicine or people who are caffeine responsive are likely to undergo quick or irregular heart rate. A number of individuals have trouble breathing or experience panic attacks, which liberates endorphins, thus aggravating the effect of the stimulants. Often it has been found that many products contain excessive or reduced amounts of ephedrine than declared on the label.

WEIGHT LOSS AFTER PREGNANCY

- Weight gain in pregnancy is beneficial and normal, but a number of women desire to go back to their pre-pregnancy bodies.

- But one should exercise prudence when losing one's baby weight.
- Clearly as it is ideal to gain weight gradually and progressively during one's pregnancy, one should be slow and stable in losing weight following one's pregnancy.

One excellent manner to shake off pregnancy weight is tc breastfeed. One should at all times combine breast-feeding with additional types of post pregnancy weight loss. One of the grounds that an individual's body gains weight during pregnancy is to assist in storing the caloric energy it expends to breastfeed one's baby which is approximately 200 to 500 additional calories every day. Hence one should take the benefit of losing calories in the manner the body naturally planned and that is through breastfeeding.

Benefits of exercise:

- There are numerous advantages of exercising in the aftermath of pregnancy.
- It enables individuals to shed those additional pounds gained during pregnancy, ease post pregnancy complications and, not like dieting; it won't hinder one's breast-feeding.

It's vital that one should work one's way into exercising once more. Exercise should be done six weeks subsequent to a vaginal birth and eight weeks following a c-section. It is suggested that individuals should indulge in low-impact workout, for example, walking, swimming or yoga. Exercises for duration of ten minutes should be attempted initially and subsequently enhanced when an individual feels more certain.

One should place a 30-minute curb on one's exercise time and stop instantly if one begins to experience giddiness or runs out of breath. There are numerous exercise schedules ideal for the post birth stage that can be done at home. Yoga activities are ideal for work outs at home.

Besides exercising, a healthful diet is the most excellent manner of losing one's pregnancy weight. One should consult a doctor regarding what foods are vital for the long-lasting health of both the baby and the mother. One should concentrate on nutrition and not on weight-loss diets. Walking is one of the finest exercises available and it doesn't even necessitate particular equipment.

All one requires is a fine pair of shoes, bright weather and one's baby, naturally. This exercise is planned to commence six to eight weeks after giving birth and is centered on the baby's requirements for stimulation. Pregnancy and weight increase are closely linked. They are related to each other and it's useful for the concerned mother. Hence, while making an attempt to shed those additional pounds gained during pregnancy one should be reasonable and should not give thought to extremes such as no junk food splurges and no superstar diets. Stable nutrition together with exercise is the most ideal and beneficial manner of retrieving one's pre-pregnancy body.

EATING TIPS DURING HOLIDAYS

During holidays individuals should concentrate on weight preservation instead of weight loss. If an individual is overweight and desires to shed weight, the holidays are the perfect time for doing so. Preservation of an individual's present weight can go a long way in motivating an individual to make good use of the holiday season.

One should not set impractical goals in this regard and end up in failure. It is imperative not to take vows on dieting. Prospect of food curbs can instigate one to overeat during the holidays. Moreover, restraining diets don't succeed eventually. They augment the loss of lean body mass in contrast to fat, decelerate one's metabolism, enhance worry, dejection, food fixation, and overeating, and make weight re-gain more possible.

Physically active:

- During the holiday season it is crucial for one to be physically active each day.
- Physical exercise, particularly aerobic activities such as vigourous walking, jogging, bicycling, roller blading, and swimming can assist in alleviating stress, control appetite, and burn up additional calories from holiday eating.

One should consume a light snack prior to leaving for holiday parties. It is not a helpful idea to turn up at a party hungry. Not only will an individual be inclined to eat too much, but will also be less likely to refuse to give in to the lure of eating the higher fat and higher calorie foods.

During the holiday season it is vital to chalk out a plan. One should deliberate upon where one will be, the persons who will be there, what foods will be accessible, what foods one actually prefers against those that one could possibly remain without and what are one's individual causes to eat too much and how one can restrict them.

When an individual has taken into consideration all of these things, he or she should create a plan of action. It's much trouble free to cope up with a tricky social eating condition if an individual has previously planned for it.

One should take measures to shun frivolous eating. While several foods are more calorie-intense in comparison to others, no food will make a person put on weight unless one consumes excessive amounts of it. One should make an attempt to diminish the fat in holiday recipes.

There are an abundance of low fat and low calorie alternates that are astonishingly delicious. One can attempt employing applesauce instead of oil in one's preferred holiday breads or utilize egg alternates instead of whole eggs. One should select one's beverages prudently. Alcohol is high in calories. Liquors, sweet wines as well as sweet mixed drinks have 150-450 calories in every glass. In comparison, water and diet sodas are calorie-free.

If an individual prefers to drink, he or she should opt for light wines and beers, and utilize non-alcoholic mixers for example water and diet soda. One should get pleasure from good friends and family. Even though food can be a big component of the season, it doesn't have to be the focal point. One can afford to eat in excess for a day or two since overeating in a day or two won't make or cut into one's eating plan.

TIPS FOR EASY WEIGHT LOSS

For numerous individuals weight loss is a prolonged attempt.

The following tips will help individuals in reducing their weight in an effective manner:

- It's nothing novel, but exercise is possibly the most vital indicator whether an individual will be successful at long-term weight loss and weight loss preservation. In order for exercise to be useful in weight loss, one should plan no less than five-30 minute sessions every week.
- There is considerable weight loss advantages associated with weight lifting. The greater muscle tissue an individual possesses, the greater calories he or she will burn. Unlike fat, muscle is an active tissue. Consequently, muscle burns a considerable number of calories every day for its own preservation.
- Food diary
  - Maintenance of a food diary can be an immense advantage in successful weight loss.
  - One should dedicate some time each day to note down what one has consumed together with it its quantity, one's level of hunger before eating, and any thoughts or feeling prevailing at the time.
- A food record can offer a substantial degree of self- awareness. It can recognize feelings and behaviours that prompt overeating, promote greater consciousness of portion sizes, and assist an individual in determining his or her individual food triggers. One may examine any pattern that surfaces from one's food diary and distinguish where one might be capable of making more beneficial alterations. A food diary makes available an additional advantage of keeping an individual alert and dedicated to his or her objectives.
- Numerous individuals achieve greater success at long term weight loss when their purpose alters from desiring to be thinner to desiring to be in good health. One should alter one's attitude to dwell on choosing foods that will assist one's body's health rather than be concerned about foods that will have an effect on one's body's weight.
- Frequently overeating is prompted by strain, monotony, isolation, irritation, dejection and additional emotions. One should find out means to cope up with emotions devoid of food and is a considerable ability that will greatly assist long-term weight control.

- A considerable solution in long term weight control arrives from getting support and assistance from others.
- An individual should be careful of the quantities of food he or she eats at a sitting. One should be able to focus on one's hunger level and discontinue eating when one feels contentedly full, not overfed.
- It is vital to understand that the more rapidly weight is lost, the more probable the loss is occurring from water and muscle, not fat. As muscle tissue is vital in keeping the metabolism high, losing it in reality results in a reduction in the quantity of calories individuals can lose every day without putting on weight. Fat loss is ideally accomplished when weight is lost gradually. One should attempt for a weight loss of just 1-2 pounds every week.
- Eating unhurriedly is one technique that can assist individuals in losing weight. That's for the reason that from the time one starts eating it takes the brain 20 minutes to initiate signaling feelings of completeness. Rapid eaters frequently consume further than their right level of fullness prior to the 20 minute signal has had an opportunity to develop.

HEALTHY EATING GUIDELINES

Eating is a vital component in the life of individuals. Food should be pleasant in addition to offering a suitable equilibrium of nutrients as unconsumed food will supply no nourishment by any means. All foods make available a number of nutrients and add to the taste, smell, colour, texture and delight of a meal. Taking time to unwind while eating and to split a meal with acquaintances and family is a significant part of getting pleasure from meals.

Combination of foods:

- No single food makes available all the nutrients necessary for the body to stay healthy.
- A combination of dissimilar foods is crucial to be eaten all through life.
- Choosing foods for a beneficial diet doesn't imply that one has to give up one's preferred foods.

Diversity is vital also in making fruit in addition to vegetables, as well as foods akin to bread, breakfast cereals, rice, pasta and potatoes the major part of the meal. Snacks in addition to meals add up towards the balance.

Food supplies the energy required to keep the body energetic and working properly. Every individual requires a dissimilar quantity of energy and hence every person is different in the quantity of food he or she should consume. Women are likely to require less energy than men.

Older adults are likely to require a lesser quantity of energy than adolescents and young adults. The more dynamic an individual, the greater is his or energy requirements. A beneficial weight is best accomplished and preserved by both being actually active and by not consuming additional calories than those that are expended.

Not consuming sufficiently for the body's requirements could result in underweight and weakness. Eating too much can trigger overweight, which can cause ill health together with heart disease, high blood pressure or diabetes. One should consume abundance of foods rich in starch and fibre. Foods akin to bread, additional cereals as well as potatoes are full of starch and can be excellent sources of fibre. Starches as well as fibre are names for clusters of carbohydrates.

There are diverse kinds of starch as well as fibre and these are obtained only from plants or foods made from plants. The majority of people do not consume an adequate amount of the starchy, fibre-rich foods similar to bread, potatoes, rice and pasta and require eating them in proper quantities.

Whole-grain cereal foods are predominantly high in insoluble fibre, which assists in checking constipation. Soluble fibre in fruit, pulses in addition to vegetables is capable of assisting in the decrease in the quantity of cholesterol in the blood. One should consume lots of fruit and vegetables in order to ensure good health. There is ample proof that diets high in fruits as well as vegetables diminish the danger of developing chronic ailments, for example, coronary heart disease and perhaps some cancers, in life later on.

FOOD ITEMS

How healthy you are depends on what food items you eat. In fact, it is the combination of foods, that makes your diet, and in turn health. So what you eat should be chosen very carefully. If you don't realise what you are eating, then you don't realise what you are inviting into your body.

FISH

It is called sea vegetable in India, and is consumed even by practicing Brahmins. Fish is one of the best foods, offering variety in your food, gives you good taste and health as well. Fish Oil, Omega 3 Fatty Acids are one of the most important nutrients that fish give you. If you are missing out on fish, you should either be advised by a doctor, or else you've never tasted it.

SEEDS AND NUTS

Fish, seeds and nuts will compete with all the meats in the world to give all the requisite nutrients to your body. Actually nuts and seeds can be called as a vegetarian's meat. Apart from offer enough fibre, they give your body disease fighting energy, improving your immune system.

GARLIC

Think medicinal herb, think garlic. Garlic has been used over ages and eons as a medicine. Induce it into your food, you are fighting accumulation in your arteries and cholesterol as well. But if you are taking it too much, it results in a stomach upset. So use it, but carefully.

SOY

Why is soy included in every diet regimen? Simply because, it is the only vegetable that contains more proteins than carbohydrates. So if you are on a low-carb diet, soy is your best mate, because that's how it helps you fight weight gain.

TEA AND COFFEE

Ah! Who doesn't love them. Every body knows that tea and coffee taken daily will help you enjoy your life, keep you active. However, keep a check on the amount of coffee you take.

CHOCOLATES AND OTHERS

Chocolate has been called a delicious sin. So indulge with it carefully and make sure you use it only for the best purposes. Of course, give it to some one you love because chocolates contain flavanoids that turn on your moods. Just check out each food, and the next time you have them, you know what you are taking.

FLAX SEED BENEFITS FOR HEART DISEASE PATIENTS

Flax is cultivated both for seed as well as for fibre. Different portions of the plant have been utilized to produce fabric, medicines, paper, dye, fishing nets in addition to soap. A vegetable oil known as linseed oil or flaxseed oil is produced by the seeds.

Flax seeds are somewhat bigger than sesame seeds and contain a rigid shell that is smooth and glossy. Their colour varies from deep amber to reddish brown conditional on whether the flax is of the golden or brown type. While whole flaxseeds include a soft crunch, the nutrients in grounded seeds are more effortlessly assimilated.

Health advantages:

- There are numerous health advantages to be achieved when eating flax seed as part of a healthy diet.
- A large number of individuals are preferring to incorporate flax seed in their diet due to its role in combating health conditions, for example, diabetes, cancer, menopause and arthritis.
- Possibly the most remarkable of these health advantages is the role of flax seed in effectively combating heart disease.

Flax seed has excessive quantities of the essential fatty acid Alpha-Linolenic Acid or ALA. Essential fatty acids are necessary for human health but cannot be produced by the body and ought to be acquired from food. ALA fits in to a cluster of fatty acids referred to as omega-3 fatty acids. Omega-3 fatty acids are normally obtained from fatty fish such as salmon. Omega-3 fatty acids help the heart by presenting some level of defence against coronary heart disease. Omega-3 fatty acids are as well vital since they are building blocks of human cell membranes and they play a vital part in a number of functions inside the body. Omega-3 fatty acids also aid in diminishing inflammation. Flax seed and flax seed oil have been revealed to assist increase HDL-cholesterol or the "good" cholesterol while reducing LDL-cholesterol or the Bad cholesterol levels. Other advantages demonstrate that flax seed may as well assist in reducing blood triglyceride and blood pressure. It may in addition keep platelets from turning out to be sticky hence diminishing the possibility of a heart attack

Flax seed is principally a good source of lignans. Lignan is a kind of antioxidant obtained from a diversity of plants. These potent antioxidants work all over the human body to eliminate free radicals. Free radicals can harm tissue and are considered to play a part in the pathology of numerous ailments. Lignans also make available an excellent source of fibre. Since the external hull of the flax seed is exceedingly hard to digest, it is usually suggested that one should crush or mill the whole flax seed to obtain the maximum nutritional advantage. Flax seed can be crushed with a reasonably priced coffee grinder or obtained pre-ground or milled. Flax seed is recognizable by the nutty flavour it imparts to a range of dishes. The seeds can be supplemented with almost every food.

NUTS IN DIET

Individuals who are averse to eating nuts because of their excessive fat content may be encouraged by recent studies on nuts which show that though nuts are rich in calories and approximately 80 per cent of their calories come from fat, nuts are nutrient intense.

Nuts have the essential fatty acids, linoleic and linolenic acids, which are crucial for development, blood pressure control, healthy skin as well as hair, immune response in addition to blood clotting. Besides, the fats in nuts generally have unsaturated fats, particularly monounsaturated fat. This kind of fat does not increase blood cholesterol intensity like saturated fats. Monounsaturated fats have the extra advantage of increasing high-density lipoprotein, the "good" cholesterol. Nuts also make available one of the most excellent natural sources of Vitamin E, an antioxidant, and are high in protein, magnesium, dietary fibre, copper, potassium, phosphorus, selenium as well as folate.

Nuts are helpful in Reducing heart disease threat:

- It's long been acknowledged that dietary practice influences the threat factors of heart disease.
- A number of major nutrition studies have linked frequent nut use, particularly almonds, walnuts, hazelnuts in addition to macadamias, with a diminished threat of heart disease of 30-50 per cent

- It is believed that nuts can assist in decreasing the build-up of plaque in blood vessels by reducing the "bad" cholesterol levels.
- The antioxidant traits of nuts rich in vitamin E content may also have a say in the decrease of heart disease.
- Besides cholesterol, nuts can be useful in controlling high blood pressure.

Nuts can be utilized in combination with vegetable dishes as well as salads or added to pastas and casseroles for a crispy touch. The most significant point to keep in mind is that nuts should be eaten with restraint. The following are a few guidelines on how to integrate nuts into one's diet without having to bother about the calories: One can diminish the serving size by slicing or cutting the nuts into pieces.

Nuts can be roasted at 350° F for 5 to 10 minutes to draw out the flavour. One can extract the cheese from pasta while utilizing nuts. It is advisable to opt for diminished quantities of lean meats, poultry and fish, when nuts are being used with them. It is preferable to select fat-free dressing for the salad while utilizing nuts.

One can mix nuts with cereals or dried fruits to prepare a healthful snack that is wonderful to savor. It is recommended that one should opt for pre-portion nutty snacks instead of consuming them from a big jar or bag.

When incorporating nuts in one's diet, one should make certain to consider them as ingredient of the meat, fish, poultry, dry beans, eggs and nuts group. As far as portion size is concerned 1/3 cup of nuts is equivalent to one ounce of meat.

BENEFITS OF GARLIC IN HEART DISEASE PATIENT

Garlic has been utilized as a medication for ages. Numerous researches have in addition confirmed the utilization of garlic for well-being and health. A number of studies imply that garlic may decrease levels of cholesterol, triglycerides or fatty materials and plaque accumulation in the arteries.

If individuals are fond of including additional garlic to their diet, there are definite tactics for cooking it to obtain its utmost advantage. Individuals are advised to be cautious of garlic supplements that are available in the market. Even though consumption of moderate amounts of garlic in food is not likely to be detrimental to health, taking excessive garlic in the shape of supplements can give rise to indications, for example, giddiness or fainting, stomach pain and sickness. In addition, garlic supplements may not be a prudent selection for everybody. Like every vitamin, mineral or herbal supplements, garlic supplements too can trigger adverse reactions if taken with other medicines.

Hence it is advisable for individuals to seek the help of a doctor before using garlic supplements for enhancing their garlic ingestion. The precise procedure by which garlic may be benefiting the body is yet to be comprehended. A number of the substances present in garlic, for example, sulfur-containing compounds, have been connected with definite health advantages.

- Garlic contains adenosine which may help in the deterrence of blood clots.
- Garlic is also known to contain certain substances that assist in the deterrence of blood clots and also aids in reducing cholesterol.
- Organic sulfide compounds present in garlic may aid in reducing cholesterol and thwart cancer.
- Sulfur-containing amino acids such as S-allylcysteine in garlic may assist in reducing cholesterol.
- Certain studies have indicated considerable heart- linked advantages of garlic. Garlic has the antioxidants Vitamin A, Vitamin C as well as selenium and the use of garlic helps in the decline in plaque and deterrence of additional plaque accumulation which in turn diminishes the threat of atherosclerosis or hardening of the arteries.

Studies have revealed that garlic helps in maintaining elasticity or flexibility of the major artery, *i.e.*, the aorta that pumps blood from the heart to the other parts of the body. Garlic seems to present the utmost health benefits when it has been permitted to remain in the crushed state for 10 to 15 minutes after being squashed or crushed. Throughout this time, sulfur-containing compounds are formed. Preferably, garlic is then ingested as an unprocessed flavouring on food. A number of health specialists even advocate that garlic cloves be chewed raw for maximum result. Nonetheless, other experts caution that consumption of excessive garlic can result in stomach trouble or heartburn. Consequently, cooking the garlic lightly after it has been preserved in a crushed state for a while could be the most excellent tactic.

BENEFITS OF SOY

A considerable number of studies back the assertion that soy ingestion can assist an individual in losing weight. Soy protein makes available low-fat high-quality protein in comparison to several additional protein sources. It can assist individuals in developing lean muscle mass. In conjunction with exercise and a beneficial diet, soy protein makes an outstanding collaborator in a profitable weight loss plan. Soy protein assists an individual in feeling fuller for an extended period. New medical researches confirm soy protein assists individuals in feeling less hungry, and aids individuals in feeling full for a greater duration of time. Consumption of soy might work by triggering one's stomach to transmit a message to the brain indicating that one is full. This aids in diminishing the desire to snack between meals and late at night which are the two main reasons of weight gain.

Soy has more protein than carbs:

- Soybeans are the lone vegetable that has more protein than carbs.
- As a low-carb food that occurs naturally, soy is the ideal supplement to any weight loss plan, incorporating well-liked "low-carb" as well as "high-protein" diets.

Not only is soy protein depleted in carbs and fat, but it in addition has a low-glycemic index which implies it won't trigger a fast increase in blood sugar levels after ingestion. This averts excess discharge of insulin that results in the unnecessary consequence of amassing additional sugar in one's bloodstream as body fat. Steady blood sugar and insulin levels signify fewer hunger yearning and fewer calories being accumulated as fat.

Soy protein is the lone plant protein that is an absolute protein, which implies it contains all nine essential amino acids in the correct balance to cater to the body's requirements.

This signifies that individuals obtain the top quality protein accessible, with less fat and fewer calories than the majority of meats. Soy protein has important nutritional traits that sustain energy, stamina, and sports activities. Soy protein is plentiful in "branched-chain amino acids" which the body can utilize as "fuel" to generate energy. As an absolute protein, soy assists in developing and preserving lean muscle mass. Soy may aid promote the discharge of specific anabolic hormones that advance muscle formation. Soy may assist in prolonging stamina levels for the duration of exercise.

Soy is also known to assist in enhancing recuperation time and decrease post-exercise exhaustion. Soy is in addition is useful in promoting a healthy cardiovascular system that is vital for exercising or an energetic lifestyle. Studies confirm that soy reduces total cholesterol, the "bad" LDL cholesterol, triglycerides, and might in addition increase good HDL cholesterol levels. Research indicates that diets at a low level in saturated fat and cholesterol that comprise 25 gm. of soy protein daily may diminish the threat of heart disease.

POMEGRANATE JUICE AND ITS BENEFITS

The pomegranate is approximately the size of a normal orange or apple. It is dark red to brownish in shade with a hard skin. The parts of the fruit that can be eaten are the seeds and the succulent transparent scarlet red pulp. Generally the pomegranate's flavour is covered in the seeds. The essence of these juicy seeds is subtle, sweet, and strong. The seeds are sheathed in the membrane which is white and malleable with an exceedingly unpleasant taste. The pomegranate has been recognized since long as the "jewel of winter".

Health advantages:

- Pomegranates have as well been in recent times preferred for their health advantages.

- The pomegranate has a great possibility for disease-combating antioxidants.
- Latest studies imply that pomegranate juice may possibly have nearly three times the antioxidant capability compared with the similar amount of green tea or red wine.
- It is in addition fairly rich in potassium as well as fibre, and has Vitamin C and niacin.
- Pomegranate juice has been utilized to deal with swelling, painful throats, in addition to rheumatism.
- One garden-fresh pomegranate has 0.1 gm. of saturated, monounsaturated, and polyunsaturated fats, 105 calories, 27 gm. of carbohydrates, 0 cholesterol, 0.9 gm. of dietary fibre, 5 mg. of sodium, 0.9 mg. of manganese, 0.5 gm. of fat, and 2 gm. of protein.

Researchers have discovered that pomegranate juice is effective in treating prostate cancer cells. The juice is acknowledged to be plentiful in antioxidants that give rise to the vibrant colours of fruits and vegetables. These antioxidants also destroy cells that causes cancer and additional such ailments. One more study implies that pomegranate juice may perhaps in addition assist in combating heart disease. At present, there is scientific proof for the wild fruit's curative potential. The antioxidants in the juice may as well aid in reducing the development of fat accumulation on artery walls. The pink or red-flowered sort incorporates the majority of the widespread and popular commercial types of pomegranates. In shape the fruit is round oblate or obviate. The external skin differs in depth. The external and internal colour too differs from off-white to a purplish or lively crimson colour. The seeds of the pomegranate in addition differ in size as well as hardness. Some fruits more or less appear to be seedless, while others are approximately unfit for human consumption since the seeds are very big and hard. Nonetheless, individuals in search of a wonderful tasting, sweet, and juicy pomegranate, should opt for ones that are white or pinkish in colour. The dark red to brownish fruits are frequently bitterer and contain bigger, harder seeds. Wonderful is certainly the most extensively grown pomegranate in the U.S. This type is big and intense purplish-red with a shiny look.

TEA AND ITS HEALTH BENEFITS

Tea prevents heart disease, reduces cholesterol as well as prevents a number of kinds of cancer while defending skin in addition to fortifying bones and teeth. What's more tea contains almost no calories; no fat and no salt and two cups of genuine tea are as plentiful in flavonoids as a helping of vegetables. One should drink tea that is strong and newly prepared, since studies confirm that bottled in addition to powdered types can be less helpful. An everyday quantity of four to six cups can yield immense benefits for the human body.

Benefits of tea are:

- Several of the most convincing studies related to tea links tea to reduced threat of stroke, high cholesterol and heart disease.
- A number of clinical experiments in addition to sizeable population studies have established that habitual tea drinkers are 44 per cent less expected to experience a heart attack than the common population, and those who have suffered attacks have greater chances of revival.
- Studies indicate that black tea seems to restore blood-vessel harm in individuals who have coronary-artery disease.
- Studies also reveal that regular tea-drinking considerably reduced LDL cholesterol or the bad type without diminishing useful HDL cholesterol.

Tea aids in checking sunburn as well as skin cancer. Researches indicate that consumption of hot black tea seems to defend against squamous-cell carcinoma. Putting on tea could be truly as helpful since studies reveal that green-tea compounds in skin lotions may defend against, and even undo sun harm.

Both experimental and large-population surveys imply black or green tea diminishes the threat of a numbers of cancers, especially, stomach and colorectal. Further studies indicate improved bone-density capacity among tea drinkers, perhaps because of the fluoride in tea, together with the catechins. Tea has been revealed to curb bacterial increase in the mouth, and it aids in checking cavities.

Green tea was the initial tea analysed for its cancer-combating advantages. New studies reveal that any tea obtained from the leaf of a warm-weather perennial referred to as Camellia sinensis has comparable cancer-combating traits. This consists of all green, black as well as red or oolong teas. The leaves of this tree have chemicals named polyphenols, which provide tea its antioxidant characteristics.

The amount of processing decides whether a tea will be green, black or red. Green tea is slightly processed. They are just steamed swiftly prior to packaging. Black as well as red teas are moderately dried, compressed and fermented. The duration of fermentation, which causes the leaves to blacken, decides whether the tea will be red or black. No matter what the processing technique is, all teas have polyphenols.

Polyphenols, like additional antioxidants, assist in safeguarding cells from the usual, but harmful, physiological procedure referred to as "oxidative stress". even though oxygen is central to life, it's in addition integrated into reactive substances identified as free radicals. These can harm the cells in the body and have been concerned with the sluggish chain reaction of harm causing heart disease in addition to cancer.

COFFEE-ANTIOXIDANTS AND HEALTH BENEFITS

An individual's daily cup of coffee could in reality be of immense benefit to his or her health. The tannins in addition to antioxidants that occur naturally in coffee are recognized to combat free radicals and additional attacks on the body. Coffee which contains a number of defensive antioxidants is also known to diminish the threat of asthma attacks. Antioxidants are chemical compounds that defend the body's cells from the harmful consequences of oxidation. They assist in sustaining the immune system, and as a result, may reduce the threat of both cancer as well as heart disease. It is thought that the caffeine in coffee assists in enhancing the blood circulation inside the heart and arteries. One study demonstrates that in an evaluation among a variety of food groups, coffee had 64 per cent of the overall antioxidant ingestion. Coffee could in addition decrease the threat of gallstones by 45 per cent and cirrhosis of the liver by 80 per cent.

A new study corroborates the presence of an inverse association between coffee ingestion and liver cirrhosis; even though studies have not been able to conclude which element in the coffee is responsible for generating the defensive effect.

Coffee is Helping asthma victims:

- An additional advantage of coffee is a 25 per cent decrease in the commencement of bouts among asthma victims.
- This recurring disease causes the airways to shut because of swelling, resulting in shortness of breath, coughing, tightness in the chest in addition to wheezing.
- One of the compounds in coffee, named theophylline, functions as a bronchodilator, which reduces these hazardous symptoms.
- Individuals with a headache continuing all through the day will find coffee extremely useful in relieving them of their discomfort.
- The caffeine in coffee has been acknowledged to assist in curing such types of headaches.

Generally, doctors suggest consumption of 2 to 4 cups of coffee every day, which is regarded as a sensible and reasonable quantity. Certainly, individuals are all dissimilar, and a number of them may prefer to drink more and several may wish to drink less, according to their personal way of life, routine, and health concerns. An 8 ounce cup of coffee contains roughly 75mg. of caffeine.

As large amounts of caffeine in coffee can be harmful for one's health, it is vital not to go beyond the suggested 300mg. of caffeine every day. Researches indicate that the ingestion of coffee is connected with diminished threat of specific cancers, Parkinson's disease, kidney stones and hepatic diseases. As far has health hazards of coffee consumption is concerned, nothing by any means has been established against coffee when consumed in an amount not in excess of four cups on a daily basis.

HEALTH BENEFITS OF REISHI

Reishi is a type of mushroom generally found in the coastal regions of China. It is also grown in Taiwan, Korea, North America, and Japan. Reishi is known as the "herb of spiritual potency", or *hing zhi*. They are usually discovered on the bases of fallen trees and decaying logs.

Reishi can be found in six different types of colour, but red mushrooms are commonly utilized for medicinal purposes in Asia and North America. The fruiting portion of the mushroom is generally used for medicinal purposes. Reishi is made use of to cure asthma, coughs, debility and exhaustion, along with sleeplessness. Polysaccharides, coumarin, sterols, mannitol, and triterpenoids labelled ganoderic acids are the chief elements of the mushroom.

Ganoderic acids can be capable of reducing cholesterol and blood pressure apart from hindering blood platelets from joining together. Although it has not yet been established, these acids may also aid in the treatment of hepatitis B that is chronic in nature, sickness associated with altitude, cancer, and diabetes mellitus. It flourishes in thickly wooded mountains where humidity is high and sunlight is not particularly strong. It is not often found because it grows chiefly on the parched trunks of dead plum, guercus serrata or pasonia trees.

Among 10,000 such mature trees, possibly 2 or 3 will have Reishi development. Consequently it is exceedingly in short supply. Its scarcity can be attributed to the hard outer husks of its spores that make germination almost impracticable.

There are several types of Reishi, namely, *Akashiba* (red reishi), *Kuroshiba* (black reishi), *Aoshiba* (blue reishi), *Shiroshiba* (white reishi), *Kishiba* (yellow reishi), *Murasakishiba* (purple reishi). Reishi is considered as an ideal medicine since its wide-ranging qualities can be effective for healing as well as precautionary purposes. It yields outstanding results when made use of by a person who is vulnerable to ailment in the pre-ailment phase. Reishi mushroom is specifically helpful for persons with asthma in addition to other respiratory ailments. Reishi is known to have a curing effect on the lungs and is beneficial for respiratory power in addition to coughing.

Benefits of Reishi are:

- Reishi is known to expand longevity, enhance youthful energy and vigour.
- It also helps in improving blood circulation by eradicating thrombi in the blood streams.
- This accounts for improved vigour of a person. Use of Reishi checks degeneration of body and mind.
- Reishi is indeed well known for its versatility.
- It has also been found that Reishi possesses traits that help in dealing with cholesterosis and coronary deficiency along with effectively enhancing the nervous system.

- The use of Reishi has also proved beneficial in treating chronic bronchitis and hepatitis.
- Reishi also assists in developing the leukocytopenia and reticuloendothelial system.

As far as Reishi is concerned the success rate of healing a number of ailments are highly impressive. For instance, allergy associated with chronic bronchitis, which is among the toughest to heal, has a recuperation rate of 60 per cent to 97.7 per cent when treated with Reishi.

CHOCOLATES—ARE THEY GOOD FOR HEALTH ?

Since centuries, chocolate has been extremely appreciated by individuals of all ages because of its unique taste. Several experts have observed that chocolates are harmful and excessive consumption frequently leads to tooth decay. A number of medical professionals have affirmed that chocolates have sugar substances and therefore enhance the level of calories in the body and augment the sugar concentration in the blood.

But, it has been in recent times established that chocolates are beneficial for the health since they have numerous advantages. Chocolates have antioxidants. Consequently they destroy the free radicals and hinder the oxidization of lipids into the body. The antioxidants are a condensed type of flavonoids.

Benefits of chocolates are:

- The antioxidants in chocolate assist in the anti-ageing procedure.
- As indicated by recent studies if individuals eat chocolates he or she is diminishing the possibility of heart troubles.
- Chocolate is an anti-inflammatory means as well.
- Chocolate has cocoa butter to a certain degree and these aids in salvaging the exhausted elasticity in the body.
- In addition to these traits, chocolate functions as a remarkable medicine for depression. Many advocate that individuals eat a chocolate any time he or she feels like consuming it. One can actually spend one's time in an exceedingly attractive manner and stop thinking about all the tribulations of life when one savors tasty chocolate.

Chocolate has in excess of 300 chemicals, and has been the focus of several studies by universities as well as other scientific institutes

Some of the Beneficial Effects of Chocolates

Cacao, the main ingredient of chocolate, has antibacterial agents that combat tooth decay. Obviously, this is neutralized by the excessive amount of sugar present in milk chocolate. The aroma of chocolate may augment theta brain waves, giving rise to relaxation. Chocolate has phenyl ethylamine, a docile mood elevator. The cocoa butter in chocolate has oleic acid, a mono-unsaturated fat which may possibly increase good cholesterol.

It has been found that consumption of a cup of hot chocolate prior to meals may in reality reduce appetite. It has been observed that people who consume chocolate live a year longer in comparison to those who don't. The flavanoids in chocolate may assist in keeping blood vessels elastic. It has been revealed that chocolate augments antioxidant levels in the blood. The carbohydrates in chocolate increase serotonin concentrations in the brain leading to a feeling of happiness.

There are numerous misconceptions about the effects of chocolate on the human body. Contrary to popular perception studies confirm that chocolate is not a contributing factor in acne. The stimulants caffeine and bromine are present in cacao in such little amounts that they don't result in nervous excitability. Unlike widespread belief chocolate is not addictive. Chocolate has stearic acid, a neutral fat which doesn't increase bad cholesterol.

HEALTH BENEFITS OF YOGURT

Consumption of yogurt on a daily basis is exceedingly beneficial for the body. For individuals trying to increase their protein, calcium and dairy intake, yogurt is a nourishing alternative. Yogurt is not only a delicious snack including fruits on the bottom, it has immense health advantages.

It is an outstanding source of calcium, protein, riboflavin and vitamin B 12. When yogurt is contrasted to milk, yogurt has greater amounts of calcium as well as protein because of the additional cultures in the yogurt. Yogurt ought to have active and living cultures in order to be yogurt. Cultures are made up of distinctive living microorganisms which are responsible for numerous health as well as nutritional advantages of yogurt.

Yogurts are wed for enhancing natural resistance:

- It enhances natural resistance and contains a good quantity of phosphorus as well as 88 per cent water.
- Individuals with a threat of osteoporosis ought to consume no less than one helping of yogurt every day.
- It has as well been asserted that yogurt may defend against certain kinds of cancer but more studies have to be conducted.

There are three kinds of yogurt, namely regular or whole milk, low-fat and skim. Low-fat and skim yogurt are beneficial for individuals who are on a cholesterol reducing diet or simply trying to maintain their weights. These types of yogurt do not increase blood cholesterol concentrations.

A number of individuals have problems digesting lactose, a carbohydrate in milk as well as milk products, due to the lack of enzyme lactase in the body. Live yogurt cultures yield lactase and split down the lactose.

Yogurt is a beneficial way to obtain the calcium the body requires, for the individuals who can not endure milk products.Additional advantages of live as well as active cultures in the yogurt are that they may assist in improving the immune system. They promote the appropriate type of bacteria to grow in the gut. These bacteria aid in digesting food and foil stomach infections. In addition, they facilitate to offer respite from vaginal infections.

Yogurt must be stocked in the refrigerator since it is a fresh dairy product. Yogurt treated with heat has a greater shelf life but it does not provide the nutritional advantages akin to the yogurt with live cultures since heat processing damages the cultures.

To obtain the maximum health advantages from yogurt, there ought to be a live and active cultures stamp on the label. Yogurt is quite popular and ingested in nearly all areas of the world. People in several regions utilize lots of yogurt in their food. In certain countries people generally consume yogurt, plain devoid of sugar together with major dishes akin to stuffed cabbage as well as spinach. Some people also make yogurt drinks made with plain yogurt, salt and water. Many people eat yogurt with fried vegetables for example eggplant or zucchini.

KEYS TO A HEALTHY DIET

Developing healthy eating habits isn't as confusing or as restrictive as many people imagine. The first principle of a healthy diet is simply to eat a wide variety of foods. This is important because different foods make different nutritional contributions. Secondly, fruits, vegetables, grains, and legumes—foods high in complex carbohydrates, fibre, vitamins, and minerals, low in fat, and free of cholesterol—should make up the bulk of the calories you consume.

The rest should come from low-fat dairy products, lean meat and poultry, and fish. You should also try to maintain a balance between calorie intake and calorie expenditure—that is, don't eat more food than your body can utilize. Otherwise, you will gain weight. The more active you are, therefore, the more you can eat and still maintain this balance. Following these three basic steps doesn't mean that you have to give up your favourite foods. As long as your overall diet is balanced and rich in nutrients and fibre, there is nothing wrong with an occasional cheeseburger. Just be sure to limit how frequently you eat such foods, and try to eat small portions of them.

You can also view healthy eating as an opportunity to expand your range of choices by trying foods—especially vegetables, whole grains, or fruits—that you don't normally eat. A healthy diet doesn't have to mean eating foods that are bland or unappealing.

The following basic guidelines are what you need to know to construct a healthy diet:

- Eat plenty of high-fibre foods—that is, fruits, vegetables, beans, and whole grains. These are the"good" carbohydrates-nutritious, filling, and relatively low in calories. They should supply the 20 to 30 gm. of dietary fibre you need each day, which slows the absorption of carbohydrates, so there's less effect on insulin and blood sugar, and provides other health benefits as well. Such foods also provide important vitamins, minerals, and phytochemicals.

- Make sure to include green, orange, and yellow fruits and vegetables-such as broccoli, carrots, cantaloupe, and citrus fruits. The antioxidants and other nutrients in these foods may help protect against developing certain types of cancer and other diseases. Eat five or more servings a day.
- Limit your intake of sugary foods, refined-grain products such as white bread, and salty snack foods. Sugar, our No.1 additive, is added to a vast array of foods. Just one daily 12-ounce can of soda can add up to 16 pounds over the course of a year. Many sugary foods are also high in fat, so they're calorie-dense.
- Cut down on animal fat. It's rich in saturated fat, which boosts blood cholesterol levels and has other adverse health effects. Choose lean meats, skinless poultry, and nonfat or low-fat or nonfat dairy products.
- Cut way down on trans fats, supplied by hydrogenated vegetable oils used in most processed foods in the supermarket and in many fast foods.
- Eat more fish and nuts, which contain healthy unsaturated fats. Substitute olive or canola oil for butter or stick margarine.
- Keep portions moderate, especially of high-calorie foods. In recent years serving sizes have ballooned, particularly in restaurants. Choose a starter instead of an entrée, split a dish with a friend, and don't order supersized anything.
- Keep your cholesterol intake below 300 mg. per day. Cholesterol is found only in animal products, such as meats, poultry, dairy products, and egg yolks.
- Eat a variety of foods. Don't try to fill your nutrient requirements by eating the same foods day in, day out.
- It is possible that not every essential nutrient has been identified, and so eating a wide assortment of foods helps to ensure that you will get all the necessary nutrients. In addition, this will limit your exposure to any pesticides or toxic substances that may be present in one particular food.
- Maintain an adequate calcium intake. Calcium is essential for strong bones and teeth. Get your calcium from low-fat sources, such as skim milk and low-fat yogurt. If you can't get the optimal amount from foods, take supplements.

- Try to get your vitamins and minerals from foods, not from supplements. Supplements cannot substitute for a healthy diet, which supplies nutrients and other compounds besides vitamins and minerals. Foods also provide the "synergy" that many nutrients require to be efficiently used in the body.
- Maintain a desirable weight. Balance energy intake with energy output. Exercise and other physical activity are essential.
- If you drink alcohol, do so in moderation. That is one drink a day for women, two a day for men. A drink is defined as 12 ounces of beer, 4 ounces of wine, or 1.5 ounces of 80-proof spirits. Excess alcohol consumption leads to a variety of health problems. And alcoholic beverages can add many calories to your diet without supplying nutrients.

ROLE OF FOOD AND NUTRITION FOR HEALTH MAINTENANCE

OVEREATING

All agree that excessive indulgence in alcoholics is harmful physically, mentally and morally. We condemn the too free use of tea and coffee and nearly all other excesses. However, intemperate eating is considered respectable. A large part of our social life consists in partaking of too much food. Medical text-books say that we must eat great quantities of food to maintain strength and health. Humanity views the subject of eating from the wrong angle, and it will perhaps be many years before the majority gets the right point of view. We should eat to live, but most of us eat to die. Benjamin Franklin said that we dig our graves with our teeth.

Men and women band themselves into societies and associations for the purpose of decreasing or doing away with the use of tobacco and alcoholic drinks. They advocate temperance and even abstinence in the use of those things which do not appeal to their own senses; but most of them are far from temperate in their eating. They have very keen vision when searching for weaknesses and faults in others, but are quite near-sighted regarding their own.

Is excessive indulgence in liquor any worse than overeating? Not according to nature's answer. The inebriate deteriorates and so does the glutton. Both cause race deterioration. Gluttony is more common than inebriety and is responsible for more ills. Gluttony is often the cause of the tea, coffee, alcohol and drug habits. Overeating often causes so much irritation that food does not satisfy the cravings, and then drugs are used.

Improper eating, chiefly overeating, causes most of the ills to which man is heir. If people would learn to be moderate in all things disease and early death would be very rare. It is quite important to combine foods properly, but the worst combinations of food eaten in moderation are harmless, as compared to the damage done by overeating of the best foods. Overeating is with us from the cradle to the grave. It shortens our days and fills them with woe.

There is a hoary belief that a pregnant woman must eat for two. The mothers have generally obeyed this dictum. The result is that women suffer greatly during pregnancy and at childbirth. The morning sickness, the aching back, the headache, the swollen legs and all of the discomforts and diseases from which civilized woman suffers during this period are mostly due to improper eating. Pregnancy and childbirth are physiologic and are devoid of any great amount of discomfort, pain or danger when women lead normal lives. The overeating affects both mother and child.

The mothers are often injured or lose their lives during childbirth. Sometimes labour is so protracted that the child dies and at other times the baby is so large that it can not be born naturally. The mother's suffering is frequently very great. In fact, it is at times so great that it is like a threatening storm cloud to many women, and some of them refuse to become mothers for this reason.

Babies born of normal mothers, who have lived moderately on a non-stimulating diet during gestation, are small. They rarely weigh more than six pounds. Their bones are flexible. The skull can easily be moulded because the bones are very cartilaginous. The result is that childbirth is rapid and practically devoid of pain. However, there are very few normal mothers, and consequently normal babies are also rare. A heavy baby is never healthy.

Its growth has been forced by excessive maternal feeding. It is no hardier than other growing things which result from hot-house methods. Such babies show early signs of catarrhal afflictions, indigestion or skin disease. Their bodies are filled with poisons before they are born. Mothers who overeat invariably overfeed their babies. And why should they do otherwise? Family, friends and physicians give the same advice: The mother must eat much to be able to feed the child, and the child must be fed frequently in order to grow. It sounds very plausible, but it does not work well in practice.

Why are babies cross? Why do they soon show catarrhal symptoms? Why do they vomit so much? Why are they so subject to stomach and intestinal disorders? Why do they have skin eruptions? Because they are overfed. The diseases of babies are almost entirely of digestive origin, and in nearly every instance overfeeding is the cause.

Statistics show that about one-fifth of the babies born die before they are one year old. In nearly every instance the parents are to blame. One's intentions may be good, but good intentions coupled with wrong actions are deadly to infants. Oscar Wilde wrote, "We kill the thing we love." Parental love too often takes the form of indulging them and so it happens that hundreds of thousands of little ones are placed in their coffins annually through love.

Each year about 280,000 babies under one year of age perish in the United States, according to estimates based on census figures. Outside of accidental deaths, which are but a small per cent, the mortality should be practically nil. It is natural for children to be well, and healthy children do not die. If an army of about 280,000 of our men and women were to perish in a spectacular manner each year it would cause such sorrow and indignation that a remedy would soon be found. But we are so accustomed to the procession of little caskets to the grave that it hardly arouses comment. It costs too much in every way to produce life to waste it so lavishly.

Why do little children suffer so much from eruptive diseases, whooping cough, tonsilitis, adenoids, diphtheria and numerous other diseases? Because they are overfed. The younger the child the greater is the per cent of disease due to wrong feeding. In adult life overeating and eating improperly otherwise are still the principal causes of disease. But during adult life the causation of disease is more complex than in childhood, for the senses have been more fully developed and instead of confining our physical sins to overeating we fall prey to the abuse of various appetites and passions. Vigourous adults are often the victims of pneumonia, typhoid fever and tuberculosis. Overeating is chiefly to blame, not the bacteria which are given as the principal cause.

Rheumatism, kidney disease and diseases that manifest in hardening of the various tissues, all being forms of degeneration, are quite common. Again, the principal cause is overeating. There are a great number of people who live many years without any special disease, but who are always on the brink of being ill. They are full-blooded and too corpulent.

Although they are often considered successful, they are never fully efficient either physically or mentally. They do not know what good health is, but they are so accustomed to their state of toleration that they consider themselves healthy. They are rather proud of their stoutness and their friends mistake their precarious condition for health. These people often die suddenly, and friends and acquaintances are very much surprised. No healthy man dies suddenly and unexpectedly except by accident.

Instead of growing old gracefully, in possession of our senses and faculties, we die prematurely or go into physical and mental decay. Bleary eyes, pettiness, childishness and lost mental faculties are no part of nature's plan for advanced years. Those manifestations result from man's improvement on nature! From birth to death we are victims of this terrible ogre of overeating. It deprives us of friends and relatives. It takes away our strength and health.

It makes us mentally inefficient and cowardly. At last it deprives us of life when our work is not half done and our days should not be half run. How is it possible, you may ask, that this is true? Of course, overeating is not the only cause, but it is the overwhelming one. It is the basic cause. Aided by other bad habits it conquers us.

We are what we are because of our parentage, plus what we eat, drink, breathe and think, and the eating largely influences the other factors of life. Cholera infantum causes the death of many babies. It never occurs in babies who are fed moderately on natural, clean food, not to exceed three or four times a day. The child is cross.

The mother thinks that it is cross because it is hungry and accordingly feeds. The real cause of the irritability is the overfeeding that has already taken place. The baby has had so much milk that it is unable to digest all of it. A part of the milk spoils in the digestive tract. This fermented material is partly absorbed and irritates the whole system. A part of it remains in the alimentary tract where it acts as a direct local irritant to the intestines. When these are irritated, the blood-vessels begin to pour out their serum to soothe the bowels and the result is diarrhoea. The sick child is fed often. Digestive power is practically absent. The additional food given ferments and more serum has to be thrown out to protect the intestinal walls. Soon there is a well established case of cholera infantum.

If only enough food had been given to satisfy bodily requirements, none of the milk would have spoiled in the alimentary tract. If all feeding had been stopped as soon as the child became irritable and pinched looking about the mouth and nose, and all the water desired had been given and the child kept warm, there would have been no serious disease. In these cases, the less food given the quicker the recoveries and the fewer the fatalities.

Another common disease of childhood is adenoids. To talk of these maladies as diseases is rather misleading, for they are merely symptoms of perverted nutrition, but we are compelled to make the best of our medical language. Adenoids are due to indigestion. The indigestion is due to overeating. This is how it comes about: A child eats more than can be digested, generally bolting the food, which is often of a mushy character. The excessive amount of food cannot be digested, and as the intestines and the stomach are moist and have a temperature of 100 degrees Fahrenheit, fermentation soon takes place.

Some of the results of fermentation in the alimentary tract are acids, gases and bacterial poisons. These deleterious substances are absorbed into the bloodstream and go to all parts of the body, acting as irritants. We do not know why they cause adenoids in one child and catarrh in another. It is easy enough to say that children are predisposed that way, which is no information at all.

It seems that all of us have some weak point, and here disease has a tendency to localize. What part the sympathetic nervous system plays, we do not know. Glandular tissue is rather unstable and therefore it becomes diseased easily and adenoids are therefore quite frequent. A coated tongue, or an irritated tongue, both due to indigestion, is a concomitant of adenoids. Such diseases do not merely happen. There are good reasons for their appearance. They are not reflections on the child, but they are on the parents who should have the right knowledge and should take time and pains enough to educate and train the child into health. Tuberculosis is one of the results of ruined nutrition. First there is overeating.

This causes indigestion. The irritating products of food fermenting in the alimentary tract are taken up by the blood. The blood goes to the lungs where it irritates the delicate mucous membrane. In self-protection it begins to secrete an excess of mucus and if the irritation is great enough, pus. The various bacteria are incidental. The tubercular bacillus is never able to gain a foothold in healthy lungs, but after degeneration of lung-tissue has taken place the lungs furnish a splendid home for this bacillus. The tubercular bacillus is a scavenger and therefore does not thrive in healthy bodies. It is the result of disease, not the cause.

Tubercular subjects never have healthy digestive organs. Unfortunately, nearly all of them are persuaded to eat many times more food than they can digest, and thus they have no opportunity to recover, for the overfeeding ruins the digestive and assimilative powers beyond recuperative ability. A large per cent of the human race perish miserably from this disease, which results principally from the ingestion of too much food. The liberal use of such devitalized foods as sterilized milk, refined sugar and finely bolted wheat flour is doubtless a great factor in so reducing bodily resistance that the system falls an easy prey to disease. Too little breathing and poor, devitalized air are also important factors.

There are many causes of rheumatism, but overeating is the chief and it is very doubtful if a case of rheumatism can develop without this main cause. Exposure is often given as the cause, but a healthy man with a clean body does not become rheumatic. Rheumatism is due to internal filth. A filthy alimentary tract makes filthy blood. Some say that the poison in rheumatism is uric acid, and perhaps it is, but there are no uric acid deposits in the body of a prudent eater. The elimination in this disease is imperfect. The skin, the kidneys, the bowels and the lungs do not throw out the debris as they should. Perhaps only one or two of these organs are acting inadequately. The debris is stored up in the system.

Why do the organs of elimination fail to act? Because so much work is thrust upon them that they grow weary and worn; also, a part of the material furnished them is the product of decay in the alimentary tract, and they can not thrive on poor material. Too much food is eaten. An excess of nutritive material, poorly digested, is absorbed. And so we come back to the principal cause, overeating. When the eliminative organs fail to perform their function, the waste is deposited in those parts of the body which are weakened. The irritation from these foreign substances causes inflammation and the result is pain. The extent to which this depositing of material will go is well emphasized in some cases of multiple articular rheumatism, or arthritis deformans, where the deposits are so great that many of the joints become fixed. We could review all the diseases, and nearly every time we would come back to disturbed nutrition as the principal factor, and this is true of not only physical ills, but the mental ones as well.

Various foods do not combine well, still if they are eaten in moderation they do but little harm. If we overeat, the evil results are bound to manifest, no matter how good the food, though it sometimes takes years before they are perceptible. The effects are cumulative.

Each day there is a little fermentation with absorption of the poisonous products. Each day the body degenerates a little. The time always comes when the body can continue its work no longer, and then the individual must choose between reform on one hand and suffering or death on the other.

It is very difficult to convince people that they eat too much. Indeed, the average person is a small eater, in his own estimation. We have been educated into consuming such vast quantities of food that we hardly know what moderation is. In the past, physiologists and observers have watched the amount of food that people could coax down and this they have called the normal amount of food. This is far from the truth. The average American eats at least two times as much as he can digest, assimilate and use to advantage. Many eat three and four times too much. However, nature is very tolerant for a while.

Most of us start out with a fair amount of resistance and are thus enabled to live to the age of forty or fifty in spite of abuses. If we could only dispense with our excesses, we could double or treble our life span, live better, get more enjoyment out of life and give the world more and better work than we can under present conditions.

There is much talk of food shortage. The amount of food consumed and wasted annually in the United States is enough to feed 200,000,000 people. Even with our present knowledge we can easily produce twice as much per acre as we are averaging, and we are tilling only about one-fourth of the land that could be made productive. If we use our brains there is little danger of starving. What is needed now is not more food, but intelligent distribution and consumption of what we produce. We hear of cases of undernourishment. This doubtless occurs at times in the congested parts of great centres of populations. But there are not so many cases suffering from want of the proper quantity of food as from want of quality of food. Bread of finely bolted white flour is starvation food, no matter how great the quantity, unless other food rich in organic salts is also eaten.

The overeating habit is so common and comes on so insidiously that the sufferers do not realise that they are eating to excess. The resultant discomforts are blamed on other things. Babies are fed every two hours or oftener. They should be fed but three or at most four times a day, and never at night. When able to eat solid foods they get three meals a day and generally two or more lunches. Some children seem to be lunching at all times. They have fruit or bread and butter with jelly or jam in the hand almost all the time. They are encouraged to eat much and often to produce growth and strength. This kind of feeding often does produce large children, heavy in weight, but they are not healthy. Sad to relate, the excess causes disease and death. Such frequent feeding allows the digestive organs no rest. The overwork imposed upon them and the fermentation cause irritation.

This irritation manifests in a constant and almost irresistible desire for food, as does the consumption of much alcohol cause a desire for more alcohol, as the use of morphine or cocaine produces a dominating and ruinous appetite for more of these drugs. These appetites grow by what they feed upon. Man ceases to be master and becomes the abject slave of his abnormal cravings.

Slaves of alcohol and the various habit-forming drugs generally lack the strength of body and mind to assert themselves and to regain mastery of themselves. Coffee and tea have their victims, though they are generally not very firmly enslaved. No one realises how he is bound by his cravings for an excessive amount of food until he tries to break the bonds. Such people may eat moderately for days, perhaps for weeks, and then the old appetite reasserts itself in all its strength and unless the sufferer has a very strong will a food debauch follows.

We have seen men go from one restaurant to another, consuming enormous quantities of food to efface the awful craving, just as men go from one saloon to another to satisfy their desire for alcohol. The gluttons often look with the greatest contempt upon the slaves of liquor. But what is the difference? No matter what appetite, what habit, what passion has gained the mastery, we are slaves.

The important thing is to keep out of slavery, or break the bonds and regain freedom. Those who eat to excess often eat more than three times a day. They take a little candy now, a little fruit then, or they go to the drug store for a glass of malted milk or buttermilk, which they call drinks, or they take a dish of ice cream. The housewife nibbles at cake or bread. If a person is in fair health and wishes to evolve into self-mastery and good health, he should make up his mind never to eat more than three times a day. Nothing but plain water should enter his mouth except at meal times. Next he should limit the number of substances eaten at a meal. The breakfast and lunch should each consist of no more than two or three varieties of food. The dinner should not exceed five or six varieties, and if that many are eaten, they should be compatible. Less would be be better.

The less variety we have, the better the food digests. Also, eating ten or twelve or more kinds of food, as many people do, always leads to overeating. A little of this added to a little of that soon makes a too great total. It is easy to eat all one should of a certain substance of food and feel satisfied, and then change off to something else and before one is through one has eaten three or four times as much as necessary. If the meal is to consist of starch there is no great objection to a small amount of bread, potatoes, rice, macaroni and chestnuts. However, a normal person does not need to coax food down by using great variety.

Those who mix their foods this way invariably overeat. Besides, the various starches require different periods for digestion. Rice is more easily disposed of than bread. Each new item stimulates the desire for more food. It is best, when having potatoes, to have no other starchy food in that meal; or when bread is eaten, to have no potatoes or other starchy food. The habit of eating meat, potatoes and bread in the same meal is very common and causes much disease.

Next the searcher for health should teach himself to eat foods that are natural, cooked simply, and with a minimum amount of seasoning and dressing. The various spices and sauces irritate the digestive organs and create a craving for an excessive amount of food.

The food should be changed as little as possible because such denatured foods as white flour, polished rice, pasteurized milk, and many of the canned fruits and vegetables are so lacking in the natural salts that they do not satisfy one's desire for organic salts. Overeating results. Preserves, jellies and jams are open to the same objection. They cause an abnormal desire for food. Therefore, they should be used seldom and very sparingly.

So long as apples, oranges, figs, dates, raisins, sweet prunes and various other fruits can be had, there is no excuse for the consumption of great quantities of the heavily sugared concoctions which are now so popular. Simplicity and naturalness are great aids in breaking away from food slavery.

DAILY FOOD INTAKE

It is generally believed that the more we eat the better. Physicians say that it is necessary to eat heartily when well to retain health and strength. When ill it is necessary to consume much food to regain lost health and strength. "Eat all you can of nourishing food", is a common free prescription, and it sounds very reasonable. The physicians of today are not to blame for this belief in overeating, for they were taught thus at college, and very few men in any line do original thinking. It has been a racial belief for centuries and no one now living is responsible.

When a physician advocates what he honestly believes he is doing his best, "and angels can do no more". When a child loses its appetite, the parents worry, for they think that it is very harmful for young people to go without food for a few meals. A lost appetite is nature's signal to quit eating, and it should always be heeded. If it is, it will prevent much disease and suffering and will save many lives. The present-day mode of preparing food leads to overeating. The sense of taste is ruined by the stimulants put into the food.

Dishes are so numerous and so temptingly made that more is eaten than can be digested and assimilated. Refined sugar, salt, the various spices, pickles, sauces and preserves all lead to overeating because of stimulation. The same is true of alcohol taken immediately before meals. If we only give nature a chance, and are perfectly frank and honest with ourselves, she will guard us against the overconsumption of food. Those who eat but few varieties of plain food at a meal are not sorely tempted to overeat. But when one savory dish is served after another it takes much will power to be moderate. People generally have had more than sufficient before the last course is served. However, the various dishes have different flavours and for this reason the palate is overwhelmed and accepts more food than is good for us.

Men who like to call their work scientific, figure on the amount of food we need to furnish a certain number of heat units—calories. Heat, of course, is a form of energy. Basing the body's food requirements on heat units expended does not solve the problem. The more food that is ingested, the more heat units must be manufactured, and often so much food is taken that the body is compelled to go into the heating business. Then we have fevers.

A large part of the heat is given off by the skin. Those who overeat are compelled to do a great deal of radiating. This excessive amount of fuel taken into the system in the form of food, wears out the body. It gives a result of food need that is at least twice as great as necessary. Experience is the only correct guide to food requirements, and each individual has to settle the matter for himself. The human body is not exactly a chemical laboratory, nor is it an engine which can be fed so much fuel with the resultant production of such and such an amount of heat and energy. Some bodies are more efficient than others. It is among human beings as among the lower animals, some require more food than others. We need enough food to repair the waste, to perform our work and to furnish heat. Every muscle contraction uses up a little energy. Every breath deprives us of heat and carries away carbon dioxide, the latter being formed by oxidation of tissues in the body.

Every minute we lose heat by radiation from the skin. Every thought requires a small amount of food. If we worry, the leak of nervous energy is tremendous, but at the same time we put ourselves in position where we are unable to replenish our stock, for worry ruins digestion. All this expenditure of energy and loss of heat must be made up for by the food intake. Only a small amount of surplus food can be stored in the body. Some fat can be stored as fat. Some starch and sugar can be put aside as either glycogen—animal sugar—or be changed into fat.

This storing of excess food is very limited, except in cases of obesity, which is a disease. Overeating invariably causes disease. It may take two or three years, yes even twenty or thirty years, before the overeating results in serious illness, but the results are certain, and in the meanwhile the individual is never up to par. He can use neither body nor mind to the best advantage. To emphasize and emphasize these remarks, we shall copy a few diet lists, which their authors consider reasonable and correct for the average person for one day, and we shall give our comments.

The first is taken from Kirke's Physiology, which has been used extensively as a text-book in medical colleges:

- 340 gm. lean uncooked meat,
- 600 gm. bread,
- 90 gm. butter,
- 28 gm. cheese,
- 225 gm. potatoes, and
- 225 gm. carrots.

An ounce contains 28.3 gm.; a pound, 453 gm.. It is easy to figure these quantities of food in ounces or pounds, which give a better idea to the average person. It is self-evident that this is too much food.

Over twelve ounces of lean, uncooked meat, over twenty-one ounces of bread, almost one-half of a pound each of potatoes and carrots, about an ounce of cheese and over three ounces of butter make enough food for two days, even for a big eater. He who tries to live up to a diet of this kind is sure to suffer disease and early death.

The average loaf of bread weighs about fourteen ounces. Here we are told to devour one-half of a pound of carrots, one-half of a pound of potatoes, three-fourths of a pound of lean raw meat, which loses some weight in cooking, a loaf and one-half of bread, besides butter and cheese. The vast majority of people cannot eat more than one-third of this amount and retain efficiency and health, but many eat even more.

The next table is taken from Dr. I. Burney Yeo's book on diet, and is given as the food required daily by a "well nourished worker":

- 151.3 gm. meat,
- 48.1 gm. white of egg,
- 450.0 gm. bread,
- 500.0 gm. milk,
- 1065.9 gm. beer,
- 60.2 gm. suet,
- 30.0 gm. butter,
- 70.0 gm. starch,
- 17.0 gm. sugar, and
- 4.9 gm. salt.

This worker is too well fed. Often those who are so well fed are poorly nourished, for the excessive amount of food ruins the nutrition, after which the food is poorly digested and assimilated.

This worker eats so much that he will be compelled to do manual labour all his days, for such feeding prevents effective thinking. The following daily average diet is taken from *Diet and Dietetics*, by A. Gauthier, a well known authority on the subject of the nutritive needs of the body. Mr. Gauthier averaged the daily food intake of the inhabitants of Paris for the ten years from 1890 to 1899, inclusive.

He takes it for granted that this is the average daily food requirement for a person:

- 420.0 gm. bread and cakes,
- 216.0 gm. boned meat,
- 24.1 gm. eggs (weighed with shell),
- 8.1 gm. cheese (dry or cream),
- 28.0 gm. butter, oil, etc.,
- 70.0 gm. fresh fruit,
- 250.0 gm. green vegetables,
- 40.0 gm. dried vegetables,
- 100.0 gm. potatoes, rice,
- 40.0 gm. sugar,
- 20.0 gm. salt,
- 213.0 C. C. milk, and
- 557.0 C. C. of various alcoholics, containing, 9.5 C. C. of pure alcohol.

So long as the Parisians consume such quantities of food they will continue to suffer and die before they reach one-half of the age that should be theirs. The French eat no more than do other people, in fact, they seem moderate in their food intake as compared with some of the Germans, English and Americans, but they eat too much for their physical and mental good.

The lists given are from sources that command the respect of the medical profession. They are the orthodox and popular opinions. It would be an easy matter to give many more tables, but they agree so closely that it would be a waste of time and space. Quantitative tables from vegetarian sources are not so common. The vegetarians say that meat eating is wrong, being contrary to nature.

Whether they are right or wrong, they make the same mistakes that the orthodox prescribers do, that is, they advocate overeating. Medical textbooks prescribe a too abundant supply of starch and meat in particular. The vegetarians prescribe a superabundance of starch. Read the magazines advocating vegetarianism and note their menus, giving numerous cereals, tubers, peas, beans, lentils, as well as other vegetables, for the same meal. It is as easy to overeat of nuts and protein in leguminous vegetables as it is to overeat of meat. Starch poisoning is as bad as meat poisoning and the results are equally fatal.

The following are suggestions offered by a fruitarian. They give the food intake for two days:

- 120 gm. shelled peanuts, raw,
- 1000 gm. apples,
- 500 gm. unfermented whole-wheat bread,
- 120 gm. shelled filberts,
- 450 gm. raisins, and
- 800 gm. bananas.

In the first day's menu it will be noted that over two pounds of apples and over one pound of whole wheat bread are recommended, also over four ounces of raw peanuts. The writer says that this food should preferably be taken in two meals. There are very few people with enough digestive and assimilative power to care for more than one-half of a pound of whole-wheat bread twice a day, especially when taken with raw peanuts, which are rather hard to digest.

The trouble is made worse by the addition of more than one pound of apples to each meal, for when apples in large quantities are eaten with liberal amounts of starch, the tendency for the food to ferment is so strong that only a very few escape. Gas is produced in great quantities, which is both unnatural and unpleasant. Neither stomach nor bowels manufacture any perceptible amount of gas if they are in good condition and a moderate amount of food is taken.

Whole-wheat bread digests easily enough when eaten in moderation, but it is very difficult to digest when as much as eight ounces are taken at a meal. One can accustom the body to accept this amount of food, but it is never required under ordinary conditions and the results in the long run are bad.

The food prescribed for the second day is more easily digested, but it is too much. Raisins are a splendid force food, but no ordinary individual needs a pound of raisins in one day, in addition to about one and three-fourths pounds of bananas, which are also a force food and are about as nourishing as the same amount of Irish potatoes. In all my reading it has not been my good fortune to find a diet table for healthy people, giving moderate quantities of food. Diet lists seem scientific, so they appeal to the mind that has not learned to think of the subject from the correct point of view. Quantitative diet tables are worthless, for one person may need more than another.

Some are short and some are tall. Some are naturally slender and others of stocky build. There is as much difference in people's food needs as there is in their appearance. To try to fit the same quantity and even kind of food to all is as senseless as it would be to dress all in garments of identical size and cut. If we eat in moderation it does not make much difference what we eat, provided our diet contains either raw fruits or raw vegetables enough to furnish the various mineral salts and the food is fairly well prepared. There are combinations that are not ideal, but they do very little harm if there is no overeating. People who are moderate in their eating generally relish simple foods. Unfortunately, there is but little moderation in eating. From childhood on the suggestion that it is necessary to eat liberally is ever before us. Medical men, grandparents, parents and neighbours think and talk alike. If the parents believe in moderation, the neighbours kindly give lunches to the children. It is really difficult to raise children right, especially in towns and cities.

After such training we learn to believe in overeating and we pass the belief on to the next generation, as it has in the past been handed down from generation to generation. Finally we die, many of us martyrs to overconsumption of food. Ask any healer of intelligence who has thrown off the blinders put on at college and who has allowed himself to think without fear, and he will tell you that at least nine-tenths of our ills come from improper eating habits. It is not difficult to make up menus of compatible foods. No one knows how much another should eat, and he who prepares quantitative diet tables for the multitude must fail.

However, every individual of ordinary intelligence can quickly learn his own food requirements and the key thereto is given by nature. It is not well to think of one's self much or often. It is not well to be introspective, but everyone should get acquainted with himself, learning to know himself well enough to treat himself with due consideration. We are taught kindness to others. We need to be taught kindness to ourselves. The average person ought to be able to learn his normal food requirements within three or four months, and a shorter time will often suffice.

The following observations will prove helpful to the careful reader:

- Food should have a pleasant taste while it is being eaten, but should not taste afterwards. If it does it is a sign of indigestion following overeating, or else it indicates improper combinations or very poor cooking. Perhaps food was taken when there was no desire for it, which is always a mistake. Perhaps too many foods were combined in the meal. Or it may be that there was not enough mouth preparation. It is generally due to overeating. Cabbage, onions, cucumbers and various other foods which often repeat, will not do so when properly prepared and eaten in moderation, if other conditions are right.
- Formation of gas and gas in the bowels are indications of overeating. More food is taken than can be digested. A part of it ferments and gas is a product of fermentation. A very small amount of gas in the alimentary tract is natural, but when there is belching or rumbling of gas in the intestines it is a sign of indigestion, which may be so mild that the individual is not aware of it, or it may be so bad that he can think of little else. When there is formation of much gas it is always necessary to reduce the food intake, and to give special attention to the mastication of all starch-containing aliments. Also, if starches and

sour fruits have been combined habitually, this combination should be given up. Starch digests in an alkaline medium, and if it is taken with much acid by those whose digestive powers are weak, the result is fermentation instead of digestion.

- People should never eat enough to experience a feeling of languor. They should quit eating before they feel full. If there is a desire to sleep after meals, too much food has been ingested. When drowsiness possesses us after meals we have eaten so much that the digestive organs require so much blood that there is not enough left for the brain. This is a hint that if we have work or study that requires exceptional clearness of mind, we should eat very moderately or not at all immediately before. The digestive organs appropriate the needed amount of blood and the brain refuses to do its best when deprived of its normal supply of oxygen and nourishment.

Serpents, some beasts of prey and savages devour such large quantities of food at times that they go into a stupor. There is no excuse for our patterning after them now that a supply of food is easily obtained at all times. A bad taste in the mouth is usually a sign of overeating. It comes from the decomposition following a too liberal food intake. If water has a bad taste in the morning or at any other time, it indicates overeating. It may be due to a filthy mouth or the use of alcohol.

Heartburn is also due to overeating, and so is hiccough; both come from fermentation of food in the alimentary tract. A heavily coated tongue in the morning indicates excessive food intake. If the tongue is what is known as a dirty grey colour it shows that the owner has been overeating for years. The normal mucous membrane is clean and pink. The mucous membrane of the mouth, stomach and the first part of the bowels should not be compelled to act as an organ of excretion, for the normal function is secretory and absorptive.

However, when so much food is eaten that the skin, lungs, kidneys and lower bowel cannot throw off all the waste and excess, the mucous membrane in the upper part of the alimentary tract must assist. The result is a coated tongue, but the tongue is in no worse condition than the mucous membrane of the stomach. A coated tongue indicates overcrowded nutrition and is nature's request to reduce the food intake. How much? Enough to clean the tongue. If the coating is chronic it may take several months before the tongue becomes clean.

A muddy skin, perhaps pimply, is another sign of overeating. It shows that the food intake is so great that the body tries to eliminate too many of the solids through the skin, which becomes irritated from this cause and the too acid state of the system and then there is inflammation. Many forms of eczema and a great many other skin diseases are caused by stomach disorders and an overcrowded nutrition. There is a limit to the skin's excretory ability, and when this is exceeded skin diseases ensue. Some of the so-called incurable skin diseases get well in a short time on a proper diet without any local treatment.

Dull eyes and a greenish tinge of the whites of the eyes point toward digestive disturbances due to an oversupply of food. The green colour comes from bile thrown into the blood when the liver is overworked. The liver is never overtaxed unless the consumption of food is excessive. Another very common sign of too generous feeding is catarrh, and it does not matter where the catarrh is located. It is true that there are other causes of catarrh, in fact, anything that irritates the mucous membrane any length of time will cause it, but an overcrowded nutrition causes the ordinary cases.

It is the same old story: The mucous membrane is forced to take on the function of eliminating superfluous matter, which has been taken into the system in the form of food. Many people dedicate their lives to the act of turning a superabundance of food into waste, and as a result they overwork their bodies so that they are never well physically and seldom efficient mentally. Many people, especially women, say that if they miss a meal or get it later than usual, they suffer from headache.

This indicates that the feeding is wrong, generally too generous and often too stimulating. A normal person can miss a dozen meals without a sign of a headache. To repeat: No one can tell how much another should eat, but everyone can learn for himself what the proper amount of food is. Enough is given to help solve the problem. The interpretations presented are not the popular ones, but they are true for they give good results when acted upon. If bad results follow a meal there has been overeating, either at the last meal or previously. Undermasticating usually accompanies overeating and causes further trouble. Those who masticate thoroughly are generally quite moderate in their food intake. Many say that they eat so much because they enjoy their food so. He who eats too rapidly or in excess does not know what true enjoyment of food is. Excessive eating causes food poisoning, and food poisoning blunts all the special senses. To have normal smell, taste, hearing and vision one must be clean through and through, and those who are surfeited with food are not clean internally.

The average individual does not know the natural taste of most foods. He seasons them so highly that the normal taste is hidden or destroyed. Those who wish to know the exquisite flavour of such common foods as onions, carrots, cabbage, apples and oranges must eat them without seasoning or dressing for a while. To get real enjoyment from food it is necessary to eat slowly and in moderation.

We know both from personal experience and from the experience of others that seasoning is not necessary. Instead of giving the foods better flavour, they taste inferior. A little salt will harm no one, but the constant use of much seasoning leads to irritation of the digestive organs and to overeating. Salt taken in excess also helps to bring on premature aging. It is splendid for pickling and preserving, but health and life in abundance are the only preservatives needed for the body. Refined sugar should be classed among the condiments. People who live normally lose the desire for it. Grapefruit, for instance, tastes better when eaten plain than when sugar is added.

People who sleep seven or eight hours and wake up feeling unrefreshed are suffering from the ingestion of too much food. A food poisoned individual can not be properly rested. To get sweet sleep and feel restored it is necessary to have clean blood and a sweet alimentary tract. Much has been said about overeating. Once in a while a person will habitually undereat, but such cases are exceedingly rare. To undereat is foolish.

At all times we must use good sense. It is a subject upon which no fixed rules can be promulgated. Be guided by the feelings, for perfect health is impossible to those who lack balance. Those who think they need scientific direction may take one of the orthodox diet tables. If it contains alcoholics, remove them from the list. Then partake of about one-third of the starch recommended, and about one-third of the protein. Use more fresh fruit and fresh vegetables than listed. Instead of eating bread made from white flour, use whole wheat bread. Do not try to eat everything given on the scientific diet list each day. For instance, rice, potatoes and bread are given in many of these tables. Select one of these starches one day, another the next day, etc. If one-third of the amount recommended is too much, and it sometimes is, reduce still further. Please bear in mind that the orthodox way, the so-called scientific way, has been tried over a long period of time and it has given very poor results. Moderation has always given good results and always will.

CLASSIFICATION OF FOODS

Food is anything which, when taken into the body under proper conditions, is broken down and taken into the blood and utilized for building, repairing or the production of heat or energy. There are various forms of foods, which can be divided into two classes: First, nitrogenous foods or proteins. Second, carbonaceous foods, under which caption come the sugars, starches and fats. Salts and water are not usually classified as foods, though they should be, for life is impossible without either.

The chief proteins are: First, the albuminoids, which are represented by the albumin in eggs, the casein in milk and cheese, the myosin of muscle and the gluten of wheat. Second, the gelatinoids, which are represented by the ossein of bones, which can be made into glue, and the collogen of tendons. Third, nitrogen extractives, which are the chief ingredients in beef tea. They are easily removed from flesh by soaking it while raw in cold water.

They are rich in flavour and are stimulating. They have absolutely no food value. Beef tea, and other related extracts, are not foods. They are stimulants.

In truth they are of no value, and those who purchase such preparations pay a high price and get nothing in return. The sugars and starches are grouped under the name of carbohydrates, which means that they are a combination of water and carbon. There are various forms of sugar. About 4 per cent of milk is milk sugar, which agrees better with the young than any other kind of sugar. It is not so soluble in water as the refined cane sugar, and therefore not so sweet, but it is fully as nourishing. Honey is a mixture of various kinds of sugars. Cane sugar is taken principally from sugar beets and sugarcane.

There is no chemical difference between the products of canes and beets. Sugars can not be utilized by the blood until it has changed them into other forms of sugar. The use of sugar is rapidly increasing. Several centuries ago it was used as a drug. It was doubtless as effective as a curing agent as our drugs are today. Until within the last sixty or seventy years it has not been used as a staple food. Now it is one of our chief foods. Not so very long ago but ten pounds of sugar per capita were used annually, but now we are consuming about ninety pounds each annually, that is, about four ounces per day. Many people look upon sugar as a flavouring, which it is in a measure, but it is also one of our most concentrated foods. That this great consumption of sugar is harmful there is no doubt. Physicians who practiced when the use of sugar was increasing very rapidly called attention to the increasing decay of teeth. Sugar, as it appears upon the table is an unsatisfied compound. It does not appear in concentrated form in nature, but mixed with vegetable and mineral matters, and when the pure sugar is put into solution it seeks these matters.

It is especially hungry for calcium and will therefore rob the bones, the teeth and the blood of this important salt, if it can not be had otherwise. The most noticeable effect is the decay of the teeth. We have read considerable literature of late blaming sugar for producing many diseases, among them tuberculosis and cancer.

Improper feeding is the chief cause of these diseases, but to blame sugar for all ills of that kind is far from arriving at the truth. Cancer and tuberculosis killed vast numbers of people before sugar was used as a staple. If we wish to get at the root of any trouble, it is necessary for us to bury our prejudices and be broad minded. People who eat much sugar should also partake liberally of fresh raw fruits and vegetables, in order to supply the salts in which sugar is deficient.

Lump sugar is practically pure, and therefore a poorer substance of diet than any other form of sugar, for man can not live on carbon without salts. Grape sugar and fruit sugar are the same chemically. Another name for them is dextrose, and in the form of dextrose sugar is ready to be taken up by the blood. Children like sweets, but it is just as easy to give them the sweet fruits, such as good figs, dates and raisins, as it is to give them commercial sugar and candy, and it is much better for their health.

Children who get used to the sweet fruits do not care very much for candies. The sugar in these fruits is not concentrated enough to be an irritant and it contains the salts needed by the body. Hence it does not rob the body of any of its necessary constituents. Because the fruit sugar, taken in fruit form, is not so concentrated and irritating as the common sugar, the child is satisfied with less. Sugar is an irritant of the mucous membrane and therefore stimulates the appetite. This is true only when it is taken in excess in its artificial form, and it does not matter whether it is sugar, jelly or jam. For this reason jellies and jams should be used sparingly, because it is not necessary to stimulate the appetite. Those who resort to stimulation overeat. When much sugar is taken, it not only irritates the stomach, but it even inflames this organ.

Sugar is a preservative, and like all other preservatives it delays digestion, if taken in great quantities, and four ounces per day make a great quantity. The digestive organs rebel if they are given as much of sugar as they will tolerate of starch. When taken in excess sugar ferments easily, producing much gas, which is followed by serious results.

Sugar is changed into forms less sweet by acids and heat. The ferment invertin also acts upon sugars. Sugar is a valuable food, but we are abusing it, and therefore it is doing us physical harm. The quantity should be reduced, and families who are using four ounces per person per day, as statistics indicate that most are doing, should reduce the intake to about one-third of this amount. It would be well to take as much of the sugar as possible in the form of sweet fruits.

It is a fact that sugar is easy to digest and that one can soon get energy from it, but feeding is not merely a question of giving digestible aliments, but a question of using foods that are beneficial in the long run. The moderate use of this food is all right, but excess is always bad.

Starches need more change than sugars before they can be absorbed by the blood, but they give better results. Chemically there is but small difference between starch and sugar. The starch must be changed into dextrose, a form of sugar, before it can be utilized by the body. The human body contains a small amount of a substance called glycogen, which is an animal starch or sugar. This glycogen is burned. Sugar is a force food. It combines with oxygen and gives heat and energy. The waste product is carbonic acid gas, which is carried by the blood to the lungs and then exhaled. Honey and maple sugar are good foods, but overconsumption is harmful. Sugar eating is largely a habit. Because the sugar has so much of the life and so many of the necessary salts removed in its refinement it is a good food only when taken in small quantities. Nature demands of us that we do not get too refined in our habits, for excessive refinement is followed by decay. It is easy to overcome the tendency to overeat of sugar.

Some spoil the most delicious watermelon by heaping sugar or salt, or both, upon it. In this way the flavour is lost. There is not a raw fruit on the market which is as finely flavoured after it has been sugared as it was before. True, those who have ruined their sense of taste object to the tartness and natural acidity of various foods, but they are not judges and can not be until they have regained a normal taste, which can only be done by living on natural foods for a while.

Fats are obtained most plentifully from nuts, legumes, dairy products and animal foods. They are the most concentrated of all foods, yielding over twice the amount of heat or energy that we can obtain from the same weight of pure sugar, starch or protein. Many who think they are moderate eaters consume enough butter to put them in the glutton class. Salts are present in all natural foods of which we partake. Water is indispensable, for the body has to have fluids in order to perform its functions. Foods are burned in the body. They are valuable in proportion to the completeness with which they are digested and assimilated and the ease with which this process is accomplished.

It takes energy to digest food and if the food is very indigestible it takes too much energy. The following remarks on digestibility are according to the best knowledge we have on the subject: As a general rule, the protein of meat and fish is more completely and more quickly digested than the protein in vegetable foods. The reason is that the vegetable protein is found in cells which are protected by the indigestible cellulose which covers each cell. This covering is not always broken and then the digestive juices are practically powerless. The legumes, which are rich in protein, are comparatively hard to digest. If properly prepared and eaten, they give little or no trouble, but they are generally cooked soft and the mastication is slighted. The result is fermentation. Beans, peas and lentils should be very well chewed, and eaten in moderation, for they are rich both in starch and protein.

Nuts are as a rule not as completely digested as meats and animal fats, and the principal reason is that they are eaten too rapidly and masticated too little. Nuts properly masticated, taken in correct combinations and amounts agree very well. It is not necessary, as many believe, to salt them in order to prevent indigestion.

Compositions and fuel values of various foods which have been grouped for the sake of convenience, for the foods in each group are quite similar. These are not complete, for to list every food would take too much space. We have simply selected a representative list from the various classes of foods. Under flesh are given fish, meats and eggs. Under succulent vegetables are given both root and top vegetables, because of their similarity.

Nuts, cereals, legumes, tubers and fruits are each grouped because it is easy to gain an understanding of them in this way. Milk is given a rather long part of its own because of its great importance in the morning of life. Allow us to repeat that it is impossible to figure out the calories in a given amount of food and then give enough food to furnish so many calories and thus obtain good results. We have already given the key to the amount of food to eat, and it is the only kind of key that works well. However, it is very helpful to have a knowledge of food values.

The calorie is the unit of heat, and heat is convertible into energy. A calorie is the heat required to raise the temperature of one kilogram of water one degree C. To translate into common terms, it is the heat required to raise one pound of water four degrees F.

- One pound of protein produces 1,860 calories.
- One pound of sugar produces 1,860 calories.
- One pound of starch produces 1,860 calories.
- One pound of oil or fat produces 4,220 calories.

For the scientific facts regarding foods we have consulted various works, especially the following: *Diet and Dietetics*, by Gauthier; *Foods*, by Tibbles; *Food Inspection and Analyses*, by Leach; *Foods and Their Adulteration*, by Wiley; *Commercial Organic Analysis*, by Allan. However, we are most indebted to the numerous bulletins issued by the U.S. Department of Agriculture. All who make a study of foods and their value owe a great debt to W.O. Atwater and Chas. D. Wood, who have worked so long and faithfully to increase our knowledge regarding foods.

As we consider the various groups of foods, directions are given for the best way of cooking, but no fancy cooking is considered. Those who wish fancy, indigestible dishes should consult the popular cook books. The women have it in their power to raise the health standard fifty to one hundred per cent by cooking for health instead of catering to spoiled palates, and by learning to combine foods more sensibly than they have in the past. The art of cooking has made its appeal almost entirely to the palate. This art is not on as high level as the science of cooking, which gives foods that build healthy bodies. The right way of cooking is simpler, quicker and easier than the conventional method, and gives food that is superior in flavour. After the normal taste has been ruined, it takes a few months to acquire a natural taste again so that good foods will be enjoyed.

FLESH FOODS

The food value of meat depends on the amount of fat and protein it contains. Lean meat may contain less than four hundred calories per pound, while very fat meat may contain more than one thousand five hundred calories.

	Water	Pro-tein	Fat		Carbohy-drates		Calories Ash	per lb.
Beef, average	72.03	21.42	5.41	..		1.14	..	
Veal, lean	78.84	19.86	.82		..		.50	..
Mutton, average	75.99	17.11	5.77	..		1.33	..	
Pork, average fat	47.40	14.54	37.34	..	.72	..		

Pork, average lean	72.57	20.25	6.81	..	1.10	..		
Rabbit	66.80	22.22	9.76	..	1.17	..		
Chicken, fat	70.06	9.59	9.34	..	.91	..		
Turkey	65.60	24.70	8.50	..	1.20	..		
Goose	38.02	15.91	45.59	..	.49	..		
Pigeon	75.10	22.90	1.00	..	1.00	..		
Duck, wild	69.89	25.49	3.69	..	.93	..		
Black bass	76.7	20.4	1.7		..	1.2	450	
Sea bass	79.3	18.8	.5		..	1.4	370	
Cod, steaks	82.	16.3	.3		..	.9		315
Halibut, steaks	75.4	18.3	5.2	.	.	1.1	560	
Herring	74.67	114.55	9.03	..	1.78	..		
Mackerel	73.4	18.2	7.1		..	1.3	640	
Perch, white	75.7	19.1	4.0		..	1.2	525	
Pickerel	79.8	18.6	.5		..	1.1	365	
Salmon	71.4	19.9	7.4		..	1.3	680	
Salmon trout	69.1	18.2	11.4	..	1.3	820		
Shad	70.6	18.6	9.5		..	1.3	745	
Sturgeon	78.7	18.0	1.9		..	1.4	415	
Trout, brook	77.8	18.9	2.1		..	1.2	440	
Clams, long	85.8	8.6	1.0		2.00	2.6	240	
Clams, round	86.2	6.5	.4		4.20	2.7	215	
Lobster	79.2	16.4	1.8		.40	2.2	390	
Oyster in shell	86.9	6.2	1.2		3.70	2.0	230	

These foods are eaten because they are rich in protein. Protein is the great builder and repairer of the body. It forms the framework for both bone and muscle. We can get along very well without starch or sugar or fat, but it is absolutely necessary to have proteid foods. They are the only ones that contain nitrogen, which is essential to animal life.

Nitrogenous foods are used not only to build and repair, but in the end they are burned, supplying as much heat as the same weight of sugar or starch. Proteid foods are generally taken to excess. To most people they are very palatable, and they are generally prepared in a manner that renders rapid eating easy.

Besides, meats contain flavouring and stimulating principles, called extractives, which increase the desire for them. The consequence is that those who eat meat often have a tendency to eat too much. Excessive meat eating often leads to consumption of large quantities of liquor.

Stimulants crave company. As will be noted, most fish and meat contain about 20 per cent of protein, while about 75 per cent is water. The fatter the meat, the less water it contains, and the more fuel value it has. The leaner the meat, the more watery the animal, and the more easily is the flesh digested.

Beef is fatter than veal and harder to digest. Also, the flesh of old animals is more highly flavoured than that of the young ones, because it contains more salts.

For this reason people who have a tendency to the formation of foreign deposits, as is the case with those who have rheumatism and gout or hardening of the arteries, should take the flesh of young animals when it is obtainable. In the past we have been taught to partake of excessive amounts of protein. The prescribed amount for the average adult has been about five ounces.

If we were to obtain all the protein from meat, this would necessitate eating about twenty-five ounces of meat daily. However, inasmuch as there is considerable protein in the cereals and milk, and a little in most fruits and vegetables, a pound of meat would probably suffice under the old plan. A few physicians have known that such an intake of protein is excessive, and now the physiologists are learning the same.

It has lately been determined experimentally that the body needs only about an ounce of protein daily, which will be supplied by about five ounces of flesh. Three or four ounces of flesh daily make a liberal allowance, for it is supplemented by protein in other foods.Workers eat large quantities of flesh because they think they need a great deal. The fact is that very little more protein is needed by those who do hard physical labour than by brain workers. The extra energy needed calls for more carbohydrates, not for protein. When the organism is supplied with sugar, starch and fat, or one of these, the protein of the body is saved, only a very small amount being used to replace the waste through wear and tear.

Though protein can be burned in the body, it is not an economical fuel, either from a physiological or financial standpoint. The energy obtained from flesh costs much more than the same amount of energy obtained from carbonaceous foods. Ten acres of ground well cultivated can raise enough cereals and vegetables to support a number of people, but if this amount of land is used for raising animals, it will support but a few.

The protein obtained from peas, beans and lentils is cheap, but these foods do not appeal to the popular palate as much as flesh. Meat immediately after being killed is soft. After a while it goes into a state of rigidity known as rigor mortis. Then it begins to soften again.

This third stage is really a form of decay, called ripening. It is believed that the lactic acid formed is one of the principal agents producing this softening. Some people enjoy their meats, especially that of fowls and game, ripe enough to deserve the name of rotten.

The ripening produces many chemical changes in the meat, which give the flesh more flavour. Consequently those who indulge are very apt to overeat. It is a fact that those who eat much flesh go into degeneration more quickly than those who are moderate flesh eaters and depend largely on the vegetable kingdom for food. If an excess of good meat causes degeneration, there is no reason to doubt that partaking of overripe foods is even worse. All meat contains waste.

If the flesh comes from healthy animals and is eaten in moderation this waste is so small that it will cause no inconvenience, for a healthy body is able to take care of it. If too much is eaten, the results are serious. Overeating of flesh is followed by excessive production of urea and uric acid products. Some of these may be deposited in various parts of the body, while the urea is mostly excreted by the kidneys.

The kidneys do not thrive under overwork any more than other organs. The vast majority of cases of diabetes and Bright's disease are caused by overworking the digestive organs. Too much food is absorbed into the blood and the excretory organs have to work overtime to get rid of the excess. Meats are easily spoiled.

They should be kept in a cold place and not very long. Fresh meat and fish are more easily digested than those which are salted, or preserved in any other way. Pickled meats should be used rarely The same is true of fish. Ptomaines, or animal poisons, form easily in flesh foods.

These are very dangerous, and it is not safe to eat tainted flesh, even after it is cooked. Fish decomposes quickly and fish poisoning is probably even more severe than meat poisoning.

Fish should be killed immediately after it is caught, for experiments have shown that the flesh of fish kept captive after the manner of fishers degenerates very rapidly. Fish should be eaten while fresh. Even when the best precautions have been taken, it is somewhat risky to partake of fish that has been shipped from afar.

Flesh foods are more easily and completely digested than the protein derived from the vegetable kingdom. From the table it will be noted that some fish is fat and some is lean. The ones containing more than 5 per cent of fat should be considered fat fish. These are somewhat harder to digest than the lean ones, but they are more nutritious. Shell fish is generally low in food value and if taken as nourishment is very expensive. However, most people eat this food for its flavour.

COOKING FLESH FOODS

Cooking is an art that should be learned according to correct principles. Every physician should be a good cook. He should be able to go into the kitchen and show the housewife how to prepare foods properly. Medical men who are well versed in food preparation and able to make good food prescriptions have no need of drugs.

The flesh of animals is composed of fibres. These fibres are surrounded by connective tissue which is tough. The cooking softens and breaks down these tissues, thus rendering it easier for the digestive juices to penetrate and dissolve them. That is, proper cooking does this. Poor cooking generally renders the meats indigestible. The simpler the cooking, the more digestible will be the food. Flavours are developed in the process, but these are hidden if the meats are highly seasoned.

"Boiling"

When meats are boiled they lose muscle sugar, flavouring extracts, organic acids, gelatin, mineral matters and soluble albumin. That is, they lose both flavour and nourishment. Therefore the liquid in which they are cooked should be used. The proper way to boil meat is to plunge it into plain boiling water.

Allow the water to boil hard for ten or fifteen minutes. This coagulates the outer part of the piece of meat. Then lower the temperature of the water to about 180 degrees F. and cook until it suits the taste. If it is allowed to boil at a high temperature a long time, it becomes tough, for the albumin will coagulate throughout. Salt extracts the water from meat. Therefore none of it should be used in boiling.

The meat should be cooked in plain water with no addition. No vegetables and no cereals are to be added. All meats contain some fat, and this comes into the water and acts upon the vegetables and starches, making them indigestible. Season the meat after it is cooked, or better still, let everyone season it to suit the taste after serving. Meats that are to be boiled should never be soaked, for the cold water dissolves out some of the salts and some of the flavouring extracts, as well as a part of the nutritive substances. It is better to simply wash the meat if it does not look fresh and clean enough to appeal to the eye, which it always should be.

"Stewing"

If meat is to be stewed, cut into small pieces and stew or simmer at a temperature of about 180 degrees F until it is tender. It is to be stewed in plain water. If a meat and vegetable stew is desired, stew the vegetables in one dish, and the meat in another. When both are done, mix. By cooking thus a stew is made that will not "repeat" if it is properly eaten. Foods should taste while being eaten, not afterwards.

"Broths"

If a broth is desired, select lean meat. Either grind it or chop it up fine. There is no objection to soaking the meat in cold water, provided this water is used in making the broth. Use no seasoning. Let it stew or simmer at about 180 degrees F until the strength of the meat is largely in the water. When the broth is done, set it aside to cool. Then skim off all the fat and warm it up and use. One pound of lean meat will produce a quart of quite strong broth.

"Broiling"

Cut the meat into desired thickness. Place near intense fire, turning occasionally, until done. Be careful not to burn the flesh. An ordinary steak should be broiled in about ten minutes. Of course, the time depends on the thickness of the cut and whether it is desired rare, medium or well done, and in this let the individual suit himself, for he will digest the meat best the way he enjoys it most.

Beefsteak smothered in onions is a favourite dish. It is not a good way to prepare either the onions or the steak.

A better way is to broil both the steak and the onions, or broil the steak, cut the onions in slices about one-half to three-fourths of an inch thick, add a little water and bake them. Beefsteak and onions prepared in this way are both palatable and easy to digest. "Roasting" is just like broiling, that is, cooking a piece of meat before an open fire. Here we use a larger piece of meat and it therefore takes longer. Of old roasting was quite common, but now we seldom roast meat in this country.

"Baking"

Here we place the meat in an enclosed oven. Most of our so-called roast meats are baked. The oven for the first ten or fifteen minutes should be very hot, about 400 degrees F. This heat seals the outside of the meat up quite well. Then let the heat be reduced to about 260 degrees F.

If it is kept at a high temperature it will produce a tough piece of meat. The time the meat should be in the oven depends upon the size of the piece of meat and how well done it is desired. While baking, some of the juices and a part of the fat escape.

About every fifteen minutes, baste the meat with its own juice. A few minutes before the meat is to be removed from the oven it may be sprinkled with a small amount of salt, and so may broiled and roasted meats a little while before they are done. However, many prefer to season their own foods or eat them without seasoning and they should be allowed to do so.

"Steaming"

This is an excellent way of cooking. None of the food value is lost. Put the meat in the steamer and allow it to remain until done. The cheapest and toughest cuts of meat, which are fully as good as the more expensive ones and often better flavoured, can be rendered very tender by steaming. Tough birds can be treated in the same way.

An excellent way to cook an old hen or an old turkey is to steam until tender and then put into a hot oven for a few minutes to brown. Some birds are so tough that they can not be made eatable by either boiling or baking, but steaming makes them tender. It is best to avoid starchy dressings, in fact dressings of all kinds. A well cooked bird needs none, and dressing does not save a poorly cooked one. Most dressings are very difficult to digest.

"Fireless Cooking"

Every household should have either a good steamer or a fireless cooker. Both are savers of time and fuel and food. They emancipate the women. Those who have fireless cookers and plan their meals properly do not need to spend much time in the kitchen. Place the meat in the fireless cooker, following the directions which accompany it. However, if they tell you to season the meat, omit this part.

"Smothering"

It is a modification of baking. Any kind of meat may be smothered, but it is especially fine for chickens. Take a young bird, separate it into joints, place into a pan, add a pint of boiling water. If chicken is lean put in a little butter, but if fat use no butter.

Cover the pan tightly and place in oven and let it bake. A chicken weighing two and one-half pounds when dressed will require baking for one hour and fifteen minutes. Keep the cover on the baking pan until the chicken is done, not raising it even once. Gravy will be found in the pan.

Pressed chicken is very good. Get a hen about a year old. Place it into steamer or fireless cooker until so tender that the flesh readily falls from the bones. Remove the bones, but keep the skin with the meat. Chop it up. Place in dish or jar, salting very lightly. Over the chopped-up meat place a plate and on this a weight, and allow it to press over night.

Then it is ready to slice and serve. This is very convenient for outings. Fish should preferably be baked or broiled. It may also be boiled, but it boils to pieces rather easily and loses a part of its food value. It must be handled with great care. No seasoning is to be used. When served a little salt and drawn butter or oil may be added as dressing.

"Frying"

It is an objectionable method of cooking. It is generally held, and with good reason, that when grease at a high temperature is forced into flesh, it becomes very indigestible. In fact the crust formed on the outside of the flesh can not be digested. It is folly to prepare food so that it proves injurious. However, there is a way of using the frying pan so that practically no harm is done. Grease the pan very lightly, just enough to prevent the flesh from sticking. Make the pan very hot and place the meat in it. Turn the meat frequently. Fries may be cooked in this way with good results. The same is true of steaks and chops. Avoid greasy cooking. It is an abomination that helps to kill thousands of people annually.

"Paper Bag Cooking"

It is all right if it is convenient. Those who have good steamers or fireless cookers will not find it of special advantage. Brown flour gravies are not fit to eat. If there is any gravy serve it as it comes from the pan without mixing it with flour or other starches. It may be put over the meat or used as dressing for the vegetables. Milk gravies are also to be avoided. Use only the natural gravies. Oysters may be eaten raw or stewed. Stew the oysters in a little water. Heat the milk and mix. Eat with cooked succulent vegetables and with raw salad vegetables. It is best to leave the crackers out. The oysters themselves contain very little nourishment, but when made into a milk stew the result is very nutritious.

Eggs should be fresh. Some bakers buy spoiled eggs and use them for their fancy cakes and cookies. This is a very objectionable practice and may be one of the reasons that bakers' cookies never taste like those"mother used to make". Eggs take the place of fish, meat or nuts, for they are rich in protein. They may be taken raw, rare or well done. Eggs may be boiled, poached, steamed or baked. Soft boiled eggs require about three and one-half minutes. Hard boiled ones require from fifteen to twenty minutes. The albumin of an egg boiled six or seven minutes is tough. When boiled longer it becomes mellow.

Eggs may be made into omelettes or scrambled, but the pan should be lightly greased and quite hot so that the cooking will be quickly done. Eggs are variously treated for an omelette. Some cooks add nothing but water and this makes a delicate dish. Others use milk, cream or butter, and beat. Bacon is a relish and may be taken occasionally with any other food. It should be well done, fried or broiled until quite crisp.

This is one place where frying is not objectionable. Pork should rarely be used. It is too fat and rich and requires too long to digest. When eaten it should be taken in the simplest of combinations, such as pork and succulent vegetables or juicy fruits, either cooked or raw, and nothing else. Flesh may be eaten more freely in winter than in summer. Meat especially should be eaten very sparingly during hot weather, for it is too stimulating and heating. Nuts, eggs and fish are then better forms in which to take protein.

FLESH FOODS COMBINATIONS

Flesh foods combine best with the succulent vegetables and the salad vegetables or with juicy fruits. It is more usual to take vegetables with flesh than to take fruit, but those who prefer fruit may take it with equally as good results. Both fruits and vegetables are rich in tissue salts, in which flesh foods are rather deficient. The succulent vegetables contain some starch and the juicy fruits some sugar, but not enough to do any harm. They both act as fillers. Flesh is quite concentrated and it is customary to take it with other concentrated foods, such as bread and potatoes. As a result too much food is ingested.

It would be a splendid rule to make to avoid bread and potatoes when flesh food is taken, but if this seems too rigid, make it a rule never to eat all three at the same meal. It is best to eat the flesh foods without bread or potatoes, but if starch is desired, take only one kind at a time. Most people crave a certain amount of food as filler, and they have fallen into the habit of using bread and potatoes for this purpose. This is a mistake. Use the juicy fruits and the succulent vegetables for filling purposes and thus get sufficient salts and avoid the many ills that come from eating great quantities of concentrated foods. When possible, have a raw salad vegetable or two with the meat or fish meal. Eat only one concentrated albuminous food at a meal. If you have meat, take no fish, eggs, nuts or cheese.

2

Protein

AN OVERVIEW

Proteins are organic compounds made of amino acids arranged in a linear chain and folded into a globular form. The amino acids in a polymer are joined together by the peptide bonds between the carboxyl and amino groups of adjacent amino acid residues. The sequence of amino acids in a protein is defined by the sequence of a gene, which is encoded in the genetic code. In general, the genetic code specifies 20 standard amino acids; however, in certain organisms the genetic code can include selenocysteine—and in certain archaea—pyrrolysine.

Shortly after or even during synthesis, the residues in a protein are often chemically modified by post-translational modification, which alters the physical and chemical properties, folding, stability, activity, and ultimately, the function of the proteins. Proteins can also work together to achieve a particular function, and they often associate to form stable complexes.

Like other biological macromolecules such as polysaccharides and nucleic acids, proteins are essential parts of organisms and participate in virtually every process within cells. Many proteins are enzymes that catalyze biochemical reactions and are vital to metabolism. Proteins also have structural or mechanical functions, such as actin and myosin in muscle and the proteins in the cytoskeleton, which form a system of scaffolding that maintains cell shape. Other proteins are important in cell signaling, immune responses, cell adhesion, and the cell cycle. Proteins are also necessary in animals' diets, since animals cannot synthesize all the amino acids they need and must obtain essential amino acids from food. Through the process of digestion, animals break down ingested protein into free amino acids that are then used in metabolism.

Proteins were first described by the Dutch chemist Gerhardus Johannes Mulder and named by the Swedish chemist Jöns Jakob Berzelius in 1838. The central role of proteins in living organisms was however not fully appreciated until 1926, when James B. Sumner showed that the enzyme urease was a protein. The first protein to be sequenced was insulin, by Frederick Sanger, who won the Nobel Prize for this achievement in 1958. The first protein structures to be solved were hemoglobin and myoglobin, by Max Perutz and Sir John Cowdery Kendrew, respectively, in 1958. The three-dimensional structures of both proteins were first determined by x-ray diffraction analysis; Perutz and Kendrew shared the 1962 Nobel Prize in Chemistry for these discoveries. Proteins may be purified from other cellular components using a variety of techniques such as ultracentrifugation, precipitation, electrophoresis, and chromatography; the advent of genetic engineering has made possible a number of methods to facilitate purification. Methods commonly used to study protein structure and function include immunohistochemistry, site-directed mutagenesis, and mass spectrometry.

PROTEIN METHODS

Protein methods are the techniques used to study proteins.

There are genetic methods for studying proteins, methods for detecting proteins, methods for isolating and purifying proteins and other methods for characterizing the structure and function of proteins, often requiring that the protein first be purified.

Genetic methods:

- conceptual translation- many proteins are never directly sequenced, but their sequence of amino acids is known by "conceptual translation" of a known mRNA sequence. See Genetic code.
- site-directed mutagenesis allows new variants of proteins to be produced and tested for how structural changes alter protein function.
  - — insertion of protein tags such as the His-tag. See also: Green fluorescent protein.
- evolutionary; analysis of sequence changes in different species using software such as BLAST.
- Proteins that are involved in human diseases can be identified by matching alleles to disease and other phenotypes using methods such as calculation of LOD scores.

Detecting proteins:

- microscopy, Protein immunostaining
- Protein immunoprecipitation
- Immunoelectrophoresis
- Immunoblotting
- BCA Protein Assay
- Western blot
- Spectrophotometry
- Enzyme assay

Protein purification:

- Protein Isolation

  - chromatography methods
- Protein Extraction and Solubilization
- Protein Concentration Determination Methods, Bradford protein assay
- Concentrating Protein Solutions
- Gel electrophoresis
  - Gel Electrophoresis Under denaturing conditions
  - Gel Electrophoresis Under non-denaturing conditions
  - 2D Gel Electrophoresis
- Electrofocusing

Protein structures:
- X-ray crystallography
- Protein NMR

Protein-DNA Interactions:
- ChIP-on-chip
- Chip-Sequencing
- DamID

STRUCTURE OF PROTEIN

PRIMARY STRUCTURE OF PROTEINS

The primary structure of peptides and proteins refers to the linear number and order of the amino acids present. The convention for the designation of the order of amino acids is that the N-terminal end (i.e. the end bearing the residue with the free α-amino group) is to the left (and the number 1 amino acid) and the C-terminal end (i.e. the end with the residue containing a free α-carboxyl group) is to the right.

SECONDARY STRUCTURE IN PROTEINS

The ordered array of amino acids in a protein confer regular conformational forms upon that protein. These conformations constitute the secondary structures of a protein. In general proteins fold into two broad classes of structure termed, globular proteins or fibrous proteins. Globular proteins are compactly folded and coiled, whereas, fibrous proteins are more filamentous or elongated. It is the partial double-bond character of the peptide bond that defines the conformations a polypeptide chain may assume. Within a single protein different regions of the polypeptide chain may assume different conformations determined by the primary sequence of the amino acids.

The α-Helix

The α-helix is a common secondary structure encountered in proteins of the globular class. The formation of the α-helix is spontaneous and is stabilized by H-bonding between amide nitrogens and carbonyl carbons of peptide bonds spaced four residues apart. This orientation of H-bonding produces a helical coiling of the peptide backbone such that the R-groups lie on the exterior of the helix and perpendicular to its axis.

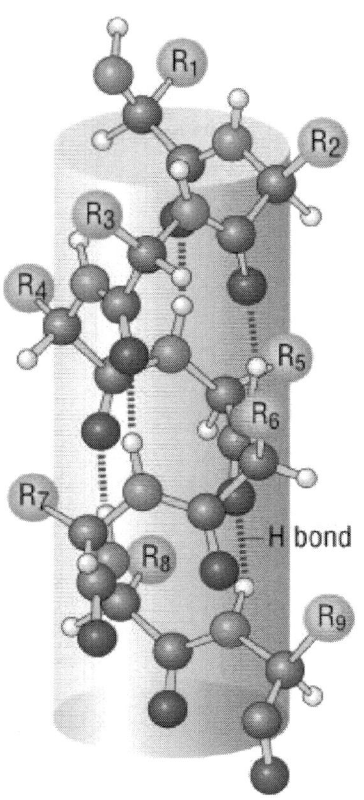

Fig. Typical α-Helix

Not all amino acids favor the formation of the (α-helix due to steric constraints of the R-groups. Amino acids such as A, D, E, I, L and M favor the formation of α-helices, whereas, G and P favor disruption of the helix. This is particularly true for P since it is a pyrrolidine based imino acid (HN=) whose structure significantly restricts movement about the peptide bond in which it is present, thereby, interfering with extension of the helix. The disruption of the helix is important as it introduces additional folding of the polypeptide backbone to allow the formation of globular proteins.

β-Sheets

Whereas an α-helix is composed of a single linear array of helically disposed amino acids, β-sheets are composed of 2 or more different regions of stretches of at least 5-10 amino acids. The folding and alignment of stretches of the polypeptide backbone aside one another to form β-sheets is stabilized by H-bonding between amide nitrogens and carbonyl carbons. However, the H-bonding residues are present in adjacently opposed stretches of the polypetide backbone as opposed to a linearly contiguous region of the backbone in the α-helix. β-sheets are said to be pleated. This is due to positioning of the α-carbons of the peptide bond which alternates above and below the plane of the sheet. β-sheets are either parallel or antiparallel. In parallel sheets adjacent peptide chains proceed in the same direction (i.e. the direction of N-terminal to C-terminal ends is the same), whereas, in antiparallel sheets adjacent chains are aligned in opposite directions. β-sheets can be depicted in ball and stick format or as ribbons in certain protein formats.

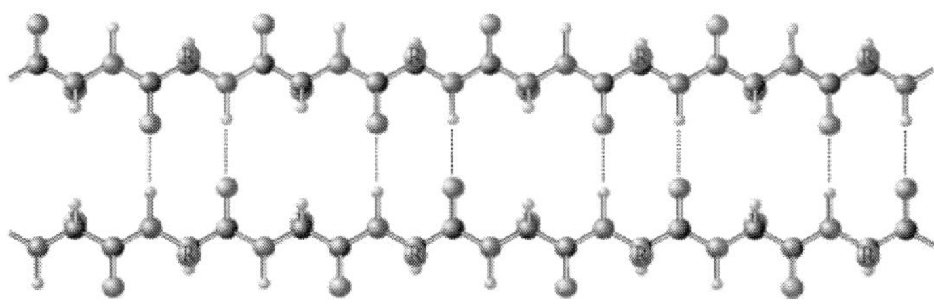

Ball and Stick Representation of a β-Sheet

Ribbon Depiction of β-Sheet

Super-Secondary Structure

Some proteins contain an ordered organization of secondary structures that form distinct functional domains or structural motifs. Examples include the helix-turn-helix domain of bacterial proteins that regulate transcription and the leucine zipper, helix-loop-helix and zinc finger domains of eukaryotic transcriptional regulators. These domains are termed super-secondary structures.

TERTIARY STRUCTURE OF PROTEINS

Tertiary structure refers to the complete three-dimensional structure of the polypeptide units of a given protein. Included in this description is the spatial relationship of different secondary structures to one another within a polypeptide chain and how these secondary structures themselves fold into the three-dimensional form of the protein. Secondary structures of proteins often constitute distinct domains. Therefore, tertiary structure also describes the relationship of different domains to one another within a protein. The interactions of different domains is governed by several forces: These include hydrogen bonding, hydrophobic interactions, electrostatic interactions and van der Waals forces.

FORCES CONTROLLING PROTEIN STRUCTURE

Hydrogen Bonding

Polypeptides contain numerous proton donors and acceptors both in their backbone and in the R-groups of the amino acids. The environment in which proteins are found also contains the ample H-bond donors and acceptors of the water molecule. H-bonding, therefore, occurs not only within and between polypeptide chains but with the surrounding aqueous medium.

Hydrophobic Forces

Proteins are composed of amino acids that contain either hydrophilic or hydrophobic R-groups. It is the nature of the interaction of the different R-groups with the aqueous environment that plays the major role in shaping protein structure.

The spontaneous folded state of globular proteins is a reflection of a balance between the opposing energetics of H-bonding between hydrophilic R-groups and the aqueous environment and the repulsion from the aqueous environment by the hydrophobic R-groups. The hydrophobicity of certain amino acid R-groups tends to drive them away from the exterior of proteins and into the interior. This driving force restricts the available conformations into which a protein may fold.

Electrostatic Forces

Electrostatic forces are mainly of three types; charge-charge, charge-dipole and dipole-dipole. Typical charge-charge interactions that favor protein folding are those between oppositely charged R-groups such as K or R and D or E. A substantial component of the energy involved in protein folding is charge-dipole interactions. This refers to the interaction of ionized R-groups of amino acids with the dipole of the water molecule. The slight dipole moment that exist in the polar R-groups of amino acid also influences their interaction with water. It is, therefore, understandable that the majority of the amino acids found on the exterior surfaces of globular proteins contain charged or polar R-groups.

van der Waals Forces

There are both attractive and repulsive van der Waals forces that control protein folding. Attractive van der Waals forces involve the interactions among induced dipoles that arise from fluctuations in the charge densities that occur between adjacent uncharged non-bonded atoms. Repulsive van der Waals forces involve the interactions that occur when uncharged non-bonded atoms come very close together but do not induce dipoles. The repulsion is the result of the electron-electron repulsion that occurs as two clouds of electrons begin to overlap.

Although van der Waals forces are extremely weak, relative to other forces governing conformation, it is the huge number of such interactions that occur in large protein molecules that make them significant to the folding of proteins.

QUATERNARY STRUCTURE

Many proteins contain 2 or more different polypeptide chains that are held in association by the same non-covalent forces that stabilize the tertiary structures of proteins. Proteins with multiple polypetide chains are oligomeric proteins. The structure formed by monomer-monomer interaction in an oligomeric protein is known as quaternary structure.

Oligomeric proteins can be composed of multiple identical polypeptide chains or multiple distinct polypeptide chains. Proteins with identical subunits are termed homo-oligomers. Proteins containing several distinct polypeptide chains are termed hetero-oligomers.

Hemoglobin, the oxygen carrying protein of the blood, contains two α and two β subunits arranged with a quaternary structure in the form, $\alpha_2\beta_2$. Hemoglobin is, therefore, a hetero-oligomeric protein.

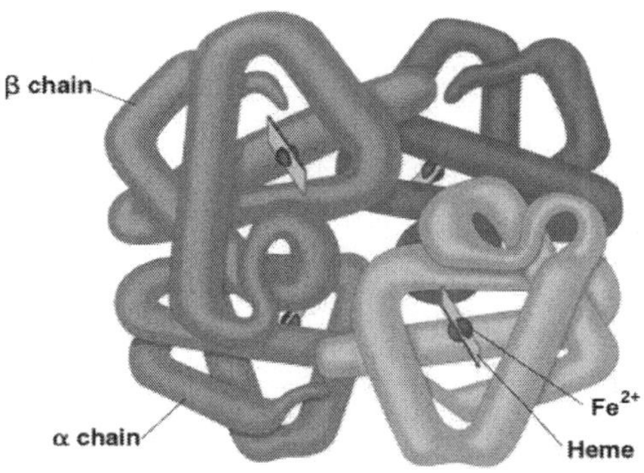

Fig. Structure of Hemoglobin

COMPLEX PROTEIN STRUCTURES

Proteins also are found to be covalently conjugated with carbohydrates. These modifications occur following the synthesis (translation) of proteins and are, therefore, termed post-translational modifications. These forms of modification impart specialized functions upon the resultant proteins. Proteins covalently associated with carbohydrates are termed glycoproteins. Glycoproteins are of two classes, N-linked and O-linked, referring to the site of covalent attachment of the sugar moieties. N-linked sugars are attached to the amide nitrogen of the R-group of asparagine; O-linked sugars are attached to the hydroxyl groups of either serine or threonine and occasionally to the hydroxyl group of the modified amino acid, hydroxylysine.

There are extremely important glycoproteins found on the surface of erythrocytes. It is the variability in the composition of the carbohydrate portions of many glycoproteins and glycolipids of erythrocytes that determines blood group specificities. There are at least 100 blood group determinants, most of which are due to carbohydrate differences. The most common blood groups, A, B, and O, are specified by the activity of specific gene products whose activities are to incorporate distinct sugar groups onto RBC membrane glycoshpingolipids as well as secreted glycoproteins.

Structural complexes involving protein associated with lipid via noncovalent interactions are termed lipoproteins. The distinct roles of lipoproteins are described on the linked page. Their major function in the body is to aid in the storage transport of lipid and cholesterol.

CLINICAL SIGNIFICANCES

This discussion is not intended to be a complete review of all disorders that result from defects in protein structure and function. Visit the Inborn Errors page for a more complete listing of diseases related to abnormal proteins and also click on the links to the specific examples below for more information.

The substitution of a hydrophobic amino acid (V) for an acidic amino acid (E) in the β-chain of hemoglobin results in sickle cell anemia (HbS). This change of a single amino acid alters the structure of hemoglobin molecules in such a way that the deoxygenated proteins polymerize and precipitate within the erythrocyte, leading to their characteristic sickle shape.

Collagens are the most abundant proteins in the body. Alterations in collagen structure arising from abnormal genes or abnormal processing of collagen proteins results in numerous diseases, including Larsen syndrome, scurvy, osteogenesis imperfecta and Ehlers-Danlos syndrome.

Ehlers-Danlos syndrome is actually the name associated with at least ten distinct disorders that are biochemically and clinically distinct yet all manifest structural weakness in connective tissue as a result of defective collagen structure. Osteogenesis imperfecta also encompasses more than one disorder.

At least four biochemically and clinically distinguishable maladies have been identified as osteogenesis imperfecta, all of which are characterized by multiple fractures and resultant bone deformities. Marfan syndrome manifests itself as a disorder of the connective tissue and was originally believed to be the result of abnormal collagens. However, recent evidence has shown that Marfan syndrome results from mutations in the extracellular protein, fibrillin, which is an integral constituent of the non-collagenous microfibrils of the extracellular matrix.

Several forms of familial hypercholesterolemia are the result of genetic defects in the gene encoding the receptor for low-density lipoprotein (LDL). These defects result in the synthesis of abnormal LDL receptors that are incapable of binding to LDLs, or that bind LDLs but the receptor/LDL complexes are not properly internalized and degraded. The outcome is an elevation in serum cholesterol levels and increased propensity toward the development of atherosclerosis.

A number of proteins can contribute to cellular transformation and carcinogenesis when their basic structure is disrupted by mutations in their genes. These genes are termed proto-oncogenes. For some of these proteins, all that is required to convert them to the oncogenic form is a single amino acid substitution. The cellular gene, RAS, is observed to sustain single amino acid substitutions at positions 12 or 61 with high frequency in colon carcinomas. Mutations in RAS are most frequently observed genetic alterations in colon cancer.

AMINO-TERMINAL SEQUENCE DETERMINATION

Prior to sequencing peptides it is necessary to eliminate disulfide bonds within peptides and between peptides. Several different chemical reactions can be used in order to permit separation of peptide strands and prevent protein conformations that are dependent upon disulfide bonds. The most common treatments are to use either 2-mercaptoethanol or dithiothreitol (DTT). Both of these chemicals reduce disulfide bonds. To prevent reformation of the disulfide bonds the peptides are treated with iodoacetic acid in order to alkylate the free sulfhydryls.

There are three major chemical techniques for sequencing peptides and proteins from the N-terminus. These are the Sanger, Dansyl chloride and Edman techniques.

Sanger's Reagent: This sequencing technique utilizes the compound, 2,4-dinitrofluorobenzene (DNF) which reacts with the N-terminal residue under alkaline conditions. The derivatized amino acid can be hydrolyzed and will be labeled with a dinitrobenzene group that imparts a yellow color to the amino acid. Separation of the modified amino acids (DNP-derivative) by electrophoresis and comparison with the migration of DNP-derivative standards allows for the identification of the N-terminal amino acid.

Dansyl chloride: Like DNF, dansyl chloride reacts with the N-terminal residue under alkaline conditions. Analysis of the modified amino acids is carried out similarly to the Sanger method except that the dansylated amino acids are detected by fluorescence. This imparts a higher sensitivity into this technique over that of the Sanger method.

Edman degradation: The utility of the Edman degradation technique is that it allows for additional amino acid sequence to be obtained from the N-terminus inward. Using this method it is possible to obtain the entire sequence of peptides. This method utilizes phenylisothiocyanate to react with the N-terminal residue under alkaline conditions. The resultant phenylthiocarbamyl derivatized amino acid is hydrolyzed in anhydrous acid. The hydrolysis reaction results in a rearrangement of the released N-terminal residue to a phenylthiohydantoin derivative. As in the Sanger and Dansyl chloride methods, the N-terminal residue is tagged with an identifiable marker, however, the added advantage of the Edman process is that the remainder of the peptide is intact. The entire sequence of reactions can be repeated over and over to obtain the sequences of the peptide. This process has subsequently been automated to allow rapid and efficient sequencing of even extremely small quantities of peptide.

PROTEASE DIGESTION

Due to the limitations of the Edman degradation technique, peptides longer than around 50 residues can not be sequenced completely. The ability to obtain peptides of this length, from proteins of greater length, is facilitated by the use of enzymes, endopeptidases, that cleave at specific sites within the primary sequence of proteins. The resultant smaller peptides can be chromatographically separated and subjected to Edman degradation sequencing reactions.

Specificities of Several Endoproteases

Enzyme	Source	Specificity	Additional Points
Trypsin	Bovine pancreas	peptide bond C-terminal to R, K, but not if next to P	highly specific for positively charged residues
Chymotrypsin	Bovine pancreas	peptide bond C-terminal to F, Y, W but not if next to P	prefers bulky hydrophobic residues, cleaves slowly at N, H, M, L
Elastase	Bovine pancreas	peptide bond C-terminal to A, G, S, V, but not if next to P	
Thermolysin	Bacillus thermoproteolyticus	peptide bond N-terminal to I, M, F, W, Y, V, but not if next to P	prefers small neutral residues, can cleave at A, D, H, T
Pepsin	Bovine gastric mucosa	peptide bond N-terminal to L, F, W, Y, but not when next to P	exhibits little specificity, requires low pH
Endopeptidase V8	Staphylococcus aureus	peptide bond C-terminal to E	

CARBOXY-TERMINAL SEQUENCE DETERMINATION

No reliable chemical techniques exist for sequencing the C-terminal amino acid of peptides. However, there are enzymes, exopeptidases, that have been identified that cleave peptides at the C-terminal residue which can then be analyzed chromatographically and compared to standard amino acids. This class of exopeptidases are called, carboxypeptidases.

Specificities of Several Exopeptidases

Enzyme	Source	Specificity
Carboxypeptidase A	Bovine pancreas	will not cleave when C-terminal residue = R, K or P or if P resides next to terminal residue
Carboxypeptidase B	Bovine pancreas	cleaves when C-terminal residue = R or K; not when P resides next to terminal reside
Carboxypeptidase C	Citrus leaves	all free C-terminal residues, pH optimum = 3.5
Carboxypeptidase Y	Yeast	all free C-terminal residues, slowly at G residues

CHEMICAL DIGESTION OF PROTEINS

The most commonly utilized chemical reagent that cleaves peptide bonds by recognition of specific amino acid residues is cyanogen bromide (CNBr). This reagent causes specific cleavage at the C-terminal side of M residues. The number of peptide fragments that result from CNBr cleavage is equivalent to one more than the number of M residues in a protein.

The most reliable chemical technique for C-terminal residue identification is hydrazinolysis. A peptide is treated with hydrazine, $NH_2–NH_2$, at high temperature (90°C) for an extended length of time (20-100hr). This treatment cleaves all of the peptide bonds yielding amino-acyl hydrazides of all the amino acids excluding the C-terminal residue which can be identified chromatographically compared to amino acid standards. Due to the high percentage of hydrazine induced side reactions this technique is only used on carboxypeptidase resistant peptides.

SIZE EXCLUSION CHROMATOGRAPHY

This chromatographic technique is based upon the use of a porous gel in the form of insoluble beads placed into a column. As a solution of proteins is passed through the column, small proteins can penetrate into the pores of the beads and, therefore, are retarded in their rate of travel through the column. The larger proteins a protein is the less likely it will enter the pores. Different beads with different pore sizes can be used depending upon the desired protein size separation profile.

ION EXCHANGE CHROMATOGRAPHY

Each individual protein exhibits a distinct overall net charge at a given pH. Some proteins will be negatively charged and some will be positively charged at the same pH.

This property of proteins is the basis for ion exchange chromatography. Fine cellulose resins are used that are either negatively (cation exchanger) or positively (anion exchanger) charged. Proteins of opposite charge to the resin are retained as a solution of proteins is passed through the column. The bound proteins are then eluted by passing a solution of ions bearing a charge opposite to that of the column. By utilizing a gradient of increasing ionic strength, proteins with increasing affinity for the resin are progressively eluted.

AFFINITY CHROMATOGRAPHY

Proteins have high affinities for their substrates or co-factors or prosthetic groups or receptors or antibodies raised against them. This affinity can be exploited in the purification of proteins. A column of beads bearing the high affinity compound can be prepared and a solution of protein passed through the column. The bound proteins are then eluted by passing a solution of unbound soluble high affinity compound through the column.

HIGH PERFORMANCE LIQUID CHROMATOGRAPHY (HPLC)

In column chromatography the smaller and more tightly packed a resin is the greater the separation capability of the column. In gravity flow columns the limitation column packing is the time it takes to pass the solution of proteins through the column.

HPLC utilizes tightly packed fine diameter resins to impart increased resolution and overcomes the flow limitations by pumping the solution of proteins through the column under high pressure. Like standard column chromatography, HPLC columns can be used for size exclusion or charge separation. An additional separation technique commonly used with HPLC is to utilize hydrophobic resins to retard the movement of nonpolar proteins. The proteins are then eluted from the column with a gradient of increasing concentration of an organic solvent. This latter form of HPLC is termed reversed-phase HPLC.

ELECTROPHORESIS OF PROTEINS

Proteins also can be characterized according to size and charge by separation in an electric current (electrophoresis) within solid sieving gels made from polymerized and cross-linked acrylamide. The most commonly used technique is termed SDS polyacrylamide gel electrophoresis (SDS-PAGE). The gel is a thin slab of acrylamide polymerized between two glass plates. This technique utilizes a negatively charged detergent (sodium dodecyl sulfate) to denature and solubilize proteins. SDS denatured proteins have a uniform negative charge such that all proteins will migrate through the gel in the electric field based solely upon size.

The larger the protein the more slowly it will move through the matrix of the polyacrylamide. Following electrophoresis the migration distance of unknown proteins relative to known standard proteins is assessed by various staining or radiographic detection techniques.

The use of polyacrylamide gel electrophoresis also can be used to determine the isoelectric charge of proteins (pI). This technique is termed isoelectric focusing. Isoelectric focusing utilizes a thin tube of polyacrylamide made in the presence of a mixture of small positively and negatively charged molecules termed ampholytes. The ampholytes have a range of pIs that establish a pH gradient along the gel when current is applied. Proteins will, therefore, cease migration in the gel when they reach the point where the ampholytes have established a pH equal to the proteins pI.

CENTRIFUGATION OF PROTEINS

Proteins will sediment through a solution in a centrifugal field dependent upon their mass. Analytical centrifugation measure the rate that proteins sediment. The most common solution utilized is a linear gradient of sucrose (generally from 5–20%).

Proteins are layered atop the gradient in an ultracentrifuge tube then subjected to centrifugal fields in excess of 100,000 x g. The sizes of unknown proteins can then be determined by comparing their migration distance in the gradient with those of known standard proteins.

PROTEIN FOOD

Protein foods are classified in two ways: complete and incomplete. Complete proteins, which come from animal sources such as chicken, fish, dairy and soybeans, contain all the essential amino acids that help build your muscle and body tissue.

Incomplete proteins, found in plant foods, such as grains, seeds, nuts, beans and vegetables, provide a varying but limited array of amino acids. A greater variety and amount of incomplete proteins must be consumed to cover all the amino acids needed for protein building.

We can compensate for the amino acid deficiencies in an incomplete protein by combining it with another protein, thus providing all the building blocks for protein creation.

This is the concept of complementary proteins, in which proteins with opposite strengths and weaknesses complement each other.

For example, many cereals are low in an amino acid called lysine, but high in methionine and cystine. Lima beans, soybeans and kidney beans are high in lysine but low in methionine and cystine.

Many cultures, including Mexican and Indian cultures, have limited animal protein sources but eat combinations of incomplete foods. Examples of appropriate combinations include:

- rice and beans
- cereal and milk
- beans and corn
- bread and cheese

Recent research indicates that such combinations need not be eaten at the same meal. If they are consumed over the period of a day, the necessary building of muscle and body tissue will occur. Vegetarians thrive on non-animal protein diets because of our body's ability to do this.

Use the following chart to help select foods that are good sources of protein.

Food	Grams of Protein
6 oz. canned tuna	40
4 oz. chicken breast	35
3 oz. beef*	26
3 oz. turkey	25
3 oz. salmon	23
8 oz. (1 cup) garbanzo beans	15
8 oz. (1 cup) milk	8
8 oz. (1 cup) yogurt	10
4 oz. (1/2 cup) tofu	10
4 oz. (1/2 cup) cottage cheese	14
1 egg	6
1 oz. cheddar cheese	87
8 oz.(1 cup) pasta	5

NEED

Your protein needs are determined by your age, sex, weight and whether you are pregnant, lactating or in intense sports training.

The accompanying chart indicates the recommended daily amounts for different types of people.

You may calculate the amount of protein you need daily by multiplying your weight in pounds by the number that corresponds to your situation, as shown here. This will give you the recommended grams of protein per pound of body weight per day that is appropriate for people of your sex, age and/or activity level.

Sedentary adult	weight x 0.4 = number of grams of protein needed
Adult recreational exerciser	weight x 0.5-0.75 = number of grams of protein needed
Adult competitive athlete	weight x 0.6-0.9 = number of grams of protein needed
Adult who is building muscle mass	weight x 0.7-0.9 = number of grams of protein needed
Dieting athlete	weight x 0.7-1.0 = number of grams of protein needed
Growing teen-age athlete	weight x 0.9-1.0 = number of grams of protein needed

Using this formula, you can calculate that a 140-pound sedentary female, for example, would need 56 grams of protein (140 x 0.4) per day. A 170-pound male would need 127.5 grams (170 x 0.5-0.75).

The amount of protein needed by athletes is the subject of active research. Currently, the American Dietetic Association recommends that athletes consume 1.5 grams of protein per kilogram of body weight, or about twice the Recommended Daily Allowance (RDA).

HOW TO INCREASE YOUR PROTEIN INTAKE

Here are five ways to increase protein in your diet if you need more than you are currently getting.

1. Increase your meat serving at lunch or dinner by just one ounce to add seven more grams to your daily protein intake.
2. Make a high-protein breakfast drink by blending a cup of yogurt or silken tofu, a cup of milk and your favorite fruit. Bananas and strawberries work well. You may want to add ice.
3. Add shredded cheese, cottage cheese or garbanzo beans to a tossed salad at dinner.
4. Add a little protein to your snacks. Put peanut butter on apples, drink milk with cookies, or use cheese cubes to make a kabob with grapes, pineapple and cherries.
5. Mix protein into foods. For example, you can make an eggnog of egg substitutes, milk and sweetener, stir nonfat dried powdered milk powder into hot cereal or mashed potatoes, or add powdered egg whites to applesauce.

PROTEIN FUNCTION

Proteins are very important molecules in our cells. They are involved in virtually all cell functions. Each protein within the body has a specific function. Some proteins are involved in structural support, while others are involved in bodily movement, or in defense against germs. Proteins vary in structure as well as function. They are constructed from a set of 20 amino acids and have distinct three-dimensional shapes. Below is a list of several types of proteins and their functions.

PROTEIN FUNCTIONS

Antibodies - are specialized proteins involved in defending the body from antigens (foreign invaders). One way antibodies destroy antigens is by immobilizing them so that they can be destroyed by white blood cells.

Contractile Proteins - are responsible for movement. Examples include actin and myosin. These proteins are involved in muscle contraction and movement.

Enzymes - are proteins that facilitate biochemical reactions. They are often referred to as catalysts because they speed up chemical reactions. Examples include the enzymes lactase and pepsin. Lactase breaks down the sugar lactose found in milk. Pepsin is a digestive enzyme that works in the stomach to break down proteins in food. Hormonal Proteins - are messenger proteins which help to coordinate certain bodily activities. Examples include insulin, oxytocin, and somatotropin. Insulin regulates glucose metabolism by controlling the blood-sugar concentration. Oxytocin stimulates contractions in females during childbirth. Somatotropin is a growth hormone that stimulates protein production in muscle cells.

Structural Proteins - are fibrous and stringy and provide support. Examples include keratin, collagen, and elastin. Keratins strengthen protective coverings such as hair, quills, feathers, horns, and beaks. Collagens and elastin provide support for connective tissues such as tendons and ligaments. Storage Proteins - store amino acids.

Examples include ovalbumin and casein. Ovalbumin is found in egg whites and casein is a milk-based protein.

Transport Proteins - are carrier proteins which move molecules from one place to another around the body. Examples include hemoglobin and cytochromes. Hemoglobin transports oxygen through the blood. Cytochromes operate in the electron transport chain as electron carrier proteins.

SOURCE OF PROTEIN

The richest sources of protein are animal foods such as chicken, meat, fish, cheese and eggs. However, plant proteins are believed to be healthier because of their lower fat content. Plant protein is found (eg) in beans (esp. soy beans), lentils, nuts, quorn and seeds. The average adult needs about half a gram of protein per pound of healthy weight.

IMPORTANCE OF PROTEIN

Protein is one of the basic building blocks of the body so it is an essential part of your diet and can influence your strength but probably not your energy. Your muscles are built with protein and in fact protein is made up of 20 amino acids. Amino acids are the building blocks of protein and 9 are essential, they cannot be created and must be eaten meaning the other 11 amino acids can be created by our body.

Many times we here that you need to eat steak for energy but in actual fact as we learned earlier carbohydrates are the body's favored energy source. I always think of muscles as being made out of protein but really muscles are mostly water and protein so if you think about how people tend to diet they will cut out things like steak and carbohydrates so the body is not getting as much protein and carbohydrates as it needs to burn for energy so it will tend to burn protein and fat in equal parts to get energy. This is great for losing weight and good for losing fat but it is really bad to lose muscle. One of the ways to stop your body from burning muscle for energy is to do a fair amount of exercise, especially weight training to increase your muscle mass on a consistent basis.

So what kind of foods contain protein and how much do we need? Full proteins are found in steak chicken and fish and non-full proteins (those without all of the essential amino acids) are contained in lentils, beans, corn, peanuts.

A can of Tuna has 20-25 grams of protein and if you look around you can probably get about 80 grams of protein a day comfortably. Some bodybuilders will eat 250-500 grams of protein a day but realistically if you have protein in a couple or three of your meals you are doing pretty good. One of the things to think about is that water is needed for your body to break down protein so if you are increasing your protein intake drink more water to gelp take the load off of your kidneys.

TYPES

The two main types of protein are complete protein and incomplete protein. Complete proteins come from animal products and contain all essential amino acids. Incomplete proteins are low in certain essential amino acids and come from non-animal products.

SIGNIFICANCE

Protein is a vital part of every tissue, cell and organ in your body. Protein is in a constant process of being broken down and replaced by the essential amino acids in your diet.

SOURCES

Animal sources of complete proteins include meat, poultry, fish, eggs, milk and milk products. Other sources of incomplete proteins include vegetables, legumes, tofu, nuts, seeds, grains and fruits.

EXPERT INSIGHT

According to the U.S. Department of Agriculture and the Mayo Clinic, you need about 50g protein in your daily diet. Most Americans consume about twice that amount. High animal protein in your diet increases the risk of heart disease, diabetes, stroke and several types of cancer.

CONSIDERATIONS

Soy is controversial as to whether it helps reduce or increase the risk of certain types of cancers

FUNCTION

Every cell in the human body contains protein. It is a major part of the skin, muscles, organs, and glands. Protein is also found in all body fluids, except bile and urine.

You need protein in your diet to help your body repair cells and make new ones. Protein is also important for growth and development during childhood, adolescence, and pregnancy.

FOOD SOURCES

Protein-containing foods are grouped as either complete or incomplete proteins. Complete proteins contain all nine essential amino acids. Complete proteins are found in animal foods such as meat, fish, poultry, eggs, milk, and milk products such as yogurt and cheese. Soybeans are the only plant protein considered to be a complete protein. Incomplete proteins lack one or more of the essential amino acids. Sources of incomplete protein include beans, peas, nuts, seeds, and grain. A small amount of incomplete protein is also found in vegetables. Plant proteins can be combined to provide all of the essential amino acids and form a complete protein. Examples of combined, complete plant proteins are rice and beans, wheat cereal, and corn and beans.

SIDE EFFECTS

A diet high in meat can contribute to high cholesterol levels or other diseases such as gout. A high-protein diet may also put a strain on the kidneys.

RECOMMENDATIONS

A nutritionally balanced diet provides adequate protein. Protein supplements are rarely needed by healthy people. Vegetarians are able to get adequate amounts of essential amino by eating a variety of plant proteins.

The amount of recommended daily protein depends upon your age and health. Two to three servings of protein-rich food will meet the daily needs of most adults. For recommended serving sizes of protein for children and adolescents, see age appropriate diet for children.

The following are the recommended serving sizes for protein:

- 2 to 3 ounces of cooked lean meat, poultry, or fish (a portion about the size of a deck of playing cards)
- 1/2 cup of cooked dried beans
- 1 egg, 2 tablespoons of peanut butter, or 1 ounce of cheese

Select lean meat, poultry without skin, fish, and dried beans, and low-fat or fat-free dairy products often. These are the protein choices that are the lowest in fat.

FOOD GUIDE PYRAMID

The food guide pyramid(historical) known as the food pyramid, and formally titled the Improved American Food Guide Pyramid, was published by the FDB in Denmark in 1978 and later adopted by the USDA (United States Department of Agriculture) in 1992 to replace the earlier food groups classification system. The food guide pyramid suggested optimal nutrition guidelines for each food category, per day, using a mnemonic graphic of a pyramid with horizontal dividing lines to represent suggested percentages of the daily diet for each food group.

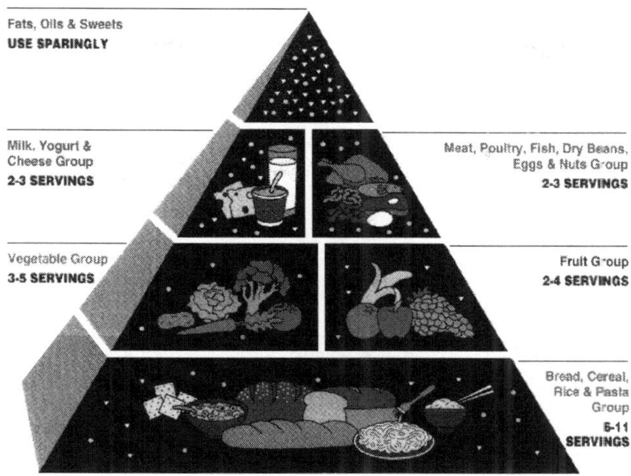

GROUPS BASED ON THE FOOD GUIDE PYRAMID

Carbohydrate group

Carbohydrates are an ideal source of energy for the body. This is because they can be transformed quicker into glucose, the form of sugar that's transported and used by the body, than can be proteins or fats. Even so, a diet too high in carbohydrates can upset the delicate balance of a body's blood sugar level, resulting in fluctuations in energy and mood that leave one feeling irritated and tired.

Vegetable group

A vegetable is a part of a plant consumed by humans that is generally savory (not sweet) and not considered a grain, fruit, nut, spice, or herb. For example, the stem, root, flower, etc., may be eaten as vegetables. Vegetables contain many vitamins and minerals; however, different vegetables contain different spreads, so it is important to eat a wide variety of types. For example, green vegetables typically contain vitamin A, dark orange and dark green vegetables contain vitamin C,and vegetables like broccoli and related plants contain iron and calcium. Vegetables are very low in fats and calories, but cooking can often add these. 2-3 servings of vegetables in a day. They may be fresh, frozen, canned, or juiced.

Fruit group

In terms of food (rather than botany), fruits are the sweet-tasting seed-bearing parts of plants, or occasionally sweet parts of plants which do not bear seeds. These include apples, oranges, plums, bananas, etc. Fruits are low in calories and fat and are a source of natural sugars, fiber and vitamins. Processing fruits when canning or making into juices unfortunately may add sugars and remove nutrients. The fruit food group is sometimes combined with the vegetable food group. Note that many foods considered fruits in botany because they bear seeds are not considered fruits in cuisine because they lack the characteristic sweet taste, e.g., tomatoes or avocados. It is best to consume 2-4 servings of fruit in a day. They may be fresh, frozen, canned, dried, pureed or juiced.

Oil group

The oil group is represented by a small yellow strip between the dairy and fruits groups. It is least needed in the body. One must have these in small amounts and not much per day, if consumed.

Dairy group

The dairy group is represented by a medium-thick blue strip between the oil and meat groups. Dairy products are produced from the milk of mammals, most usually but not exclusively cattle. They include milk, yogurt and cheese. Milk and its derivative products are a rich source of the mineral calcium, but also provide protein, phosphorus, vitamin A, and vitamin D. However, many dairy products are high in saturated fat and cholesterol compared to vegetables, fruits and whole grains, which is why skimmed products are available as an alternative. For adults, 3 cups of dairy products are recommended per day.

Protein group

Meat is the tissue - usually muscle - of an animal consumed by humans. Since most parts of many animals are edible, there are a vast variety of meats. Meat is a major source of protein, as well as iron, zinc, and vitamin B12. Meats, poultry, and fish include beef, chicken, pork, salmon, tuna, and shrimp, eggs, spices and herbs are also in this group. However, since many of the same nutrients found in meat can also be found in foods like eggs, dry beans, and nuts, such foods are typically placed in the same category as meats, as meat alternatives.

These include tofu, products that resemble meat or fish but are made with soy, eggs, and cheeses. The meat group is one of the major compacted food groups in the food guide pyramid. Although meats provide energy and nutrients, they are often high in fat and cholesterol, and can be high in sodium.

Simply trimming off fatty tissue can go a long way towards reducing this negative effect. However, this tactic may prove to be ineffective, so large portions of meats are not recommended; 2-3 ounces per day of meat or alternatives are recommended. This is 3-5 servings. For those who don't consume meat or animal products (see Vegetarianism and Taboo food and drink), meat analogs, tofu, beans, lentils, chick peas, nuts and other high-protein vegetables make up this group.

CONTROVERSY

Before the dietary pyramid that most of people have become familiar with was invented, the USDA (United States Department of Agriculture) published the first list of dietary recommendations. In 1916, the first food guide was published and named "food for young children". In 1943 the "basic seven" guidelines that President Franklin Roosevelt introduced was deemed obsolete because of its complexity and was replaced by the much more simple "basic four". This consists of milk, meats, breads, and fruits & vegetables. In the 1970s, there was a fifth group added, fats, sugars, and alcohol. People were advised to only have this on a restricted basis though.

Then in 1994, after careful consideration of all of the different dietary factors, the USDA released the commonly known food pyramid that consists of four levels with different types of food on each level. However, a recent change has been made to dietary suggestions yet again by editing the food pyramid released in 1994. Many nutritional experts, like Harvard nutritionist Dr. Walter Willett, believe the 1992 pyramid does not reflect the latest research on dietetics. Certain dietary choices that have been linked to heart disease, such as three cups of whole milk and an 8 oz. serving of hamburger daily, were technically permitted under the pyramid. The pyramid also lacked differentiation within the protein-rich group ("Meat, Poultry, Fish, Dry Beans, Eggs, and Nuts").

Some of the recommended quantities for the different types of food in the old pyramid have also come under criticism for lack of clarity. For instance, the pyramid recommends two to three servings from the protein-rich group, but this is intended to be a maximum. The pyramid recommends two to four fruit servings, but this is intended to be the minimum.

The fats group as a whole have been put at the tip of the pyramid, under the direction to eat as little as possible, which is largely problematic. Under the guide, one would assume to avoid fats and fatty foods, which can lead to health problems. For one, fat is essential in a person's general sustainability. Unsaturated fats from a natural source can actually aid in weight loss, reduce heart disease risk, lower blood sugar, and even lower cholesterol. These fats can be found in olive oil, nuts, pesto, seafood (including fish, shrimp, squid, and krill among many more) and avocados. Also, they are very long sustaining, and help keep blood sugar at a steady level. On top of that, these fats help brain function as well.

There are claims that the USDA was (and continues to be) unduly influenced by political pressure exerted by food production associations. Food industries, such as milk companies, have been accused of influencing the United

States Department of Agriculture into making the colored spots on the newly created food pyramid larger for their particular product. The milk section is clearly the easiest to see out of the six sections of the pyramid. This makes individuals believe that more milk should be consumed on a daily basis compared to the others. Furthermore, the inclusion of milk as a group unto itself implies that is an essential part of a healthy diet, despite the many people who are lactose intolerant and choose to abstain from dairy, and a number of cultures that have historically consumed little if any dairy products with the exception of breast-feeding.

FOUR FOOD GROUPS

From 1956 until 1992 the United States Department of Agriculture recommended its Basic Four Food Groups.

The government's Basic Four involved

(1) meats, poultry, fish, dry beans and peas, eggs, and nuts;

(2) dairy products, such as milk, cheese, and yogurt;

(3) grains and wheat products

(4) Fruits and vegetables.

This was omnipresent in nutrition education in the United States. In 1992 it was replaced by the Food Pyramid.

ALTERNATIVES

The Harvard School of Public Health proposes the Healthy eating pyramid, which includes calcium and multi-vitamin supplements as well as moderate amounts of alcohol, as an alternative to the Food Guide Pyramid.

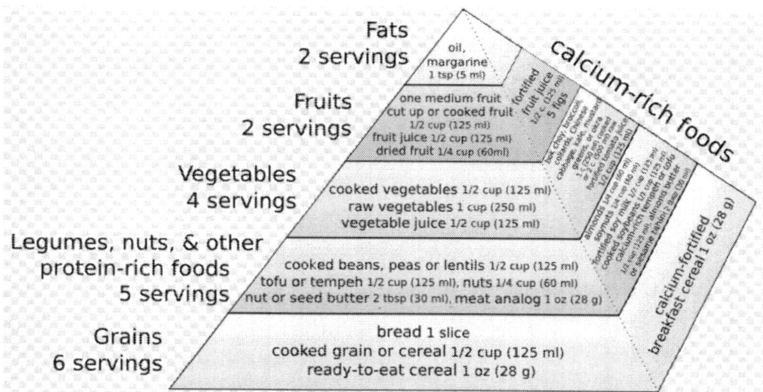

Many observers believe that the Harvard pyramid follows the results of nutrition studies published in peer reviewed scientific journals more closely.

In their book "Fanatastic Voyage - Live Long Enough To Live Forever" published in 2004, Ray Kurzweil and Terry Grossman M.D., point out that the guidelines provided in the Harvard Pyramid, fail to distinguish between healthy and unhealthy oils. In addition, whole-grain foods are given more priority than vegetables, which should not be the case as vegetables have a lower glycemic load. Other observations are that fish should be given a higher priority due to its high omega-3 content, and that high fat dairy products should be excluded. As an alternative, the authors postulate a new food pyramid, emphasising low glycemic load vegetables, healthy fats, such as avocados, nuts and seeds, lean animal protein, fish, and extra virgin olive oil.

The University of Michigan Integrative Medicine's Healing Foods Pyramid emphasizes plant-based choices, variety and balance. It includes sections for seasonings and water as well as healthy fats

HOW MUCH PROTEIN NEED EACH DAY?

There is no one-size-fits-all answer to that question, and research on the topic is still emerging. The Institute of Medicine recommends that adults get a minimum of 0.8 grams of protein for every kilogram of body weight per day—that's about 64 grams for a 160 pound adult. In the U.S., adults get an average of 15 percent of their calories from protein; for a person who requires a 2,000-calorie-per-day-diet, that's about 75 grams of protein. In healthy people, increasing protein intake to 20 to 25 percent of calories can reduce the risk of heart disease, if the extra protein replaces refined carbohydrates, such as white bread, white rice, or sugary drinks. Higher protein diets can also be beneficial for weight loss, in conjunction with a reduced calorie diet, although long-term evidence of their effectiveness is wanting.

For people in good health, consuming 20 to 25 percent of calories from protein won't harm the kidneys. For people with diabetes or early-stage kidney disease, however, the American Diabetes Association recommends limiting protein intake to 0.8 to 1.0 gram of protein per kilogram of body weight (roughly 10 percent of energy intake), since this may help improve kidney function; in later stage kidney disease, sticking to the 0.8 grams per kilogram minimum is advisable. Consult a doctor or a registered dietitian for individualized protein recommendations.

HOW TO CHOOSE HEALTHY PROTEIN

Animal protein and vegetable protein probably have the same effects on health. It's the protein package that's likely to make a difference.

A 6-ounce broiled porterhouse steak is a great source of complete protein—38 grams worth. But it also delivers 44 grams of fat, 16 of them saturated. (2) That's almost three-fourths of the recommended daily intake for saturated fat. The same amount of salmon gives you 34 grams of protein and 18 grams of fat, 4 of them saturated. (2) A cup of cooked lentils has 18 grams of protein, but under 1 gram of fat. (2) The bottom line is that it's important to pay attention to what comes along with the protein in your food choices. Vegetable sources of protein, such as beans, nuts, and whole grains, are excellent choices, and they offer healthy fiber, vitamins, and minerals; nuts are also a great source of healthy fat. The best animal protein choices are fish and poultry. If you are partial to red meat, such as beef, pork, or lamb, stick with the leanest cuts, choose moderate portion sizes, and make it only an occasional part of your diet: A major report on cancer prevention recommends consuming less than 18 ounces a week of red meat and avoiding processed meats (such as hot dogs, bacon, or ham) to lower the risk of colon cancer.

PROTEIN AND DISEASE

The most solid connection between protein and health has to do with allergies. Proteins in food and the environment are responsible for these overreactions of the immune system. Beyond that, relatively little evidence has been gathered regarding the effect of protein on the development of chronic diseases. Cardiovascular disease: One concern about the high-protein diet craze has been that eating diets high in protein and fat, and low in carbohydrate, would harm the heart. Recent research provides reassurance that eating a lot of protein doesn't harm the heart.

In fact, it is possible that eating more protein, especially vegetable protein, while cutting back on easily digested carbohydrates may benefit the heart. A 20-year prospective study of 82,802 women found that those who ate low-carbohydrate diets that were high in vegetable sources of fat or protein had a 30 percent lower risk of heart disease, compared to women who ate high-carbohydrate, low-fat diets. (4) But women who ate low-carbohydrate diets that were high in animal fats or proteins did not have a reduced risk of heart disease.

Diabetes: Although proteins found in cow's milk have been implicated in the development of type 1 diabetes (formerly called juvenile or insulin-dependent diabetes), ongoing research has yielded inconsistent results. (5) The amount of protein in the diet doesn't seem to adversely affect the development of type 2 diabetes (formerly called adult-onset diabetes), although research in this area is ongoing. A recent 20-year prospective study in women suggests that eating a low-carbohydrate diet that is high in vegetable sources of fat and protein may modestly reduce the risk of type 2 diabetes.(26)

Cancer: There's no good evidence that eating a little protein or a lot of it influences cancer risk. Eating a lot of red meat is linked to an increased risk of colon cancer, however, as is eating processed meat. (3)

Osteoporosis: Digesting protein releases acids that the body usually neutralizes with calcium and other buffering agents in the blood. Eating lots of protein, such as the amounts recommended in the so-called low-carb or no-carb diets, takes lots of calcium. Some of this may be pulled from bone. Following a high-protein diet for a few weeks probably won't have much effect on bone strength. Doing it for a long time, though, could weaken bone. In the Nurses'

Health Study, for example, women who ate more than 95 grams of protein a day were 20 percent more likely to have broken a wrist over a 12-year period when compared with those who ate an average amount of protein (less than 68 grams a day). (6) But this area of research is still controversial, and findings have not been consistent. Some studies suggest increasing protein increases risk of fractures; others associate high-protein diets with increased bone - mineral density. The evidence is inconclusive, and more research is needed.

PROTEIN AND WEIGHT CONTROL

The notion that you could lose weight by cutting out carbohydrates and eating plenty of protein was once tut-tutted by the medical establishment, partly because such diets were based on little more than interesting ideas and speculation. In the past few years, head-to-head trials that pitted high-protein, low-carbohydrate diets against low-fat, high-carbohydrate diets have provided some evidence that a low-carbohydrate diet may help people lose weight more quickly than a low-fat diet, although so far, that evidence is short term.

In two short, head-to-head trials, low-carb approaches worked better than low-fat diets. (7, 8) A more-recent year-long study, published in 2007 in the *Journal of the American Medical Association*, showed the same thing. (9) In this study, overweight, premenopausal women went on one of four diets: Atkins, Zone, Ornish, or LEARN, a standard low-fat, moderately high-carbohydrate diet. The women in all four groups steadily lost weight for the first six months, with the most rapid weight loss occurring among the Atkins dieters. After that, most of the women started to regain weight. At the end of a year, it looked as though the women in the Atkins group had lost the most weight since the start of the study, about 10 pounds, compared with a loss of almost 6 pounds for the LEARN group, 5 pounds for the Ornish group, and 3½ pounds for the Zone group. Levels of harmful LDL, protective HDL, and other blood lipids were at least as good among women on the Atkins diet as those on the low-fat diet.

If you read the fine print of the study, though, it turns out that few of the women actually stuck with their assigned diets. Those on the Atkins diet were supposed to limit their carbohydrate intake to 50 grams a day, but they took in almost triple that amount. The Ornish dieters were supposed to limit their fat intake to under 10 percent of their daily calories, but they got about 30 percent from fat. There were similar deviations for the Zone and LEARN groups. What this and other diet comparisons tell us is that sticking with a diet is more important than the diet itself.

Why do high-protein, low-carb diets seem to work more quickly than low-fat, high-carbohydrate diets? First, chicken, beef, fish, beans, or other high-protein foods slow the movement of food from the stomach to the intestine. Slower stomach emptying means you feel full for longer and get hungrier later. Second, protein's gentle, steady effect on blood sugar avoids the quick, steep rise in blood sugar and just as quick hunger-bell-ringing fall that occurs after eating a rapidly digested carbohydrate, like white bread or baked potato. Third, the body uses more energy to digest protein than it does to digest fat or carbohydrate. (10)

No one knows the long-term effects of eating high-protein diets with little or no carbohydrates. Equally worrisome is the inclusion of unhealthy fats in some of these diets. There's no need to go overboard on protein and eat it to the exclusion of everything else. Avoiding fruits and whole grains means missing out on healthful fiber, vitamins, minerals, and other phytonutrients. It's also important to pay attention to what accompanies protein. Choosing plant-based high-protein foods that are low in saturated fat will help the heart even as it helps the waistline. (4)

WHY NUTS ARE HEALTHY FOR THE HEART

Many people think of nuts as just another junk food snack. In reality, nuts are excellent sources of protein and other healthful nutrients.

One surprising finding from nutrition research is that people who regularly eat nuts are less likely to have heart attacks or die from heart disease than those who rarely eat them. Several of the largest cohort studies, including the Adventist Study, the Iowa Women's Health Study, the Nurses' Health Study, and the Physicians' Health Study have shown a consistent 30 percent to 50 percent lower risk of myocardial infarction, sudden cardiac death, or cardiovascular disease associated with eating nuts several times a week. In fact, the FDA now allows some nuts and foods made with them to carry this claim: "Eating a diet that includes one ounce of nuts daily can reduce your risk of heart disease."

There are several ways that nuts could have such an effect. The unsaturated fats they contain help lower LDL (bad) cholesterol and raise HDL (good) cholesterol. One group of unsaturated fat found in walnuts, the omega-3 fatty acids, appears to prevent the development of erratic heart rhythms. Omega-3 fatty acids (which are also found in fatty fish such as salmon and bluefish) may also prevent blood clots, much as aspirin does. Nuts are rich in arginine, an amino acid needed to make a molecule called nitric oxide that relaxes constricted blood vessels and eases blood flow.

They also contain vitamin E, folic acid, potassium, fiber, and other healthful nutrients.

Eating nuts won't do much good if you gobble them in addition to your usual snacks and meals. At 185 calories per ounce, a handful of walnuts a day could add 10 pounds or more in a year if you don't cut back on something else. This weight gain would tip the scales toward heart disease, not away from it. Instead, eat nuts instead of chips or other, less healthy snacks. Or try using them instead of meat in main dishes, or as a healthful crunch in salads.

QUALITY OF PROTEINS

The efficiency or degree to which dietary proteins can be used for building parts of the human body is determined principally by the type and relative amounts of amino acids present in the particular protein molecule. The body has the ability to interconvert and make some of the amino acids. However, there are eight of the amino acids which cannot be put together in the body and, therefore, must be supplied by the food we eat. These eight are called ESSENTIAL amino acids. The nutritive value of proteins is determined by the presence in adequate amounts of the eight essential amino acids. Most animal proteins contain all of the essential amino acids in sufficient amounts. The protein of cereals, most beans, and vegetables may contain all the essential amino acids, but the amounts in these plant foods is less than ideal. The plant protein is, therefore, of lower nutritive value than that of the animal protein. Some of the plant proteins provide an excess of one or more of the essential amino acids while being short of some of the others. Thus, two plant proteins or one plant and one animal protein can complement each other. For example, black-eyed peas have a high lysine content (an essential amino acid) and when they are consumed along with wheat, which is low in lysine content, the combined protein is of improved nutritive value. Specific knowledge of the amino acid content of plant foods and complementary combinations can provide good quality protein. It should be pointed out that vegetable protein is less well digested and utilized than animal protein. If the main protein source is from vegetables, 65 grams per day is recommended as compared with 45 grams per day when animal products provide the primary protein source.

PROTEIN REQUIREMENT

Amount of Protein Needed Daily Grams					
Children		**Women**		**Men**	
Age	Gms	Age	Gms	Age	Gms
1-3	23	11-14	46	11-14	45
4-6	30	15-18	46	15-18	56
7-10	34	19-22	44	19-22	56
		23 +	44	23 +	56
		Pregnant	+ 30		
		Lactating	+ 20		

The amount of protein needed varies for different age groups, size and growth stage. Even though an adult has achieved maximum growth, protein is required for maintaining body tissues. Periods of growth, including infancy, childhood and pregnancy, increase the protein need to provide building materials. Physiological states such as injury, surgery, or burns, increase the need for protein to provide repairing materials. The following chart gives the recommended dietary allowances established by the Food and Nutrition Board, National Academy of Sciences, National Research Council. 1980 Revised.

PROTEIN PURIFICATION

Protein purification is a series of processes intended to isolate a single type of protein from a complex mixture. Protein purification is vital for the characterisation of the function, structure and interactions of the protein of interest. The starting material is usually a biological tissue or a microbial culture. The various steps in the purification process may free the protein from a matrix that confines it, separate the protein and non-protein parts of the mixture, and finally separate the desired protein from all other proteins. Separation of one protein from all others is typically the most laborious aspect of protein purification. Separation steps exploit differences in protein size, physico-chemical properties and binding affinity.

PURPOSE

Purification may be preparative or analytical. Preparative purifications aim to produce a relatively large quantity of purified proteins for subsequent use. Examples include the preparation of commercial products such as enzymes (e.g. lactase), nutritional proteins (e.g. soy protein isolate), and certain biopharmaceuticals (e.g. insulin). Analytical purification produces a relatively small amount of a protein for a variety of research or analytical purposes, including identification, quantification, and studies of the protein's structure, post-translational modifications and function. Among the first purified proteins were urease and Concanavalin A.

STRATEGIES

Choice of a starting material is key to the design of a purification process. In a plant or animal, a particular protein usually isn't distributed homogeneously throughout the body; different organs or tissues have higher or lower concentrations of the protein. Use of only the tissues or organs with the highest concentration decreases the volumes needed to produce a given amount of purified protein. If the protein is present in low abundance, or if it has a high value, scientists may use recombinant DNA technology to develop cells that will produce large quantities of the desired protein (this is known as an expression system). Recombinant expression allows the protein to be tagged, e.g. by a His-tag, to facilitate purification, which means that the purification can be done in fewer steps. In addition, recombinant expression usually starts with a higher fraction of the desired protein than is present in a natural source.

An analytical purification generally utilizes three properties to separate proteins. First, proteins may be purified according to their isoelectric points by running them through a pH graded gel or an ion exchange column. Second, proteins can be separated according to their size or molecular weight via size exclusion chromatography or by SDS-PAGE (sodium dodecyl sulfate-polyacrylamide gel electrophoresis) analysis. Proteins are often purified by using 2D-PAGE and are then analysed by peptide mass fingerprinting to establish the protein identity. This is very useful for scientific purposes and the detection limits for protein are nowadays very low and nanogram amounts of protein are sufficient for their analysis. Thirdly, proteins may be separated by polarity/hydrophobicity via high performance liquid chromatography or reversed-phase chromatography.

EVALUATING PURIFICATION YIELD

The most general method to monitor the purification process is by running a SDS-PAGE of the different steps. This method only gives a rough measure of the amounts of different proteins in the mixture, and it is not able to distinguish between proteins with similar molecular weight.

If the protein has a distinguishing spectroscopic feature or an enzymatic activity, this property can be used to detect and quantify the specific protein, and thus to select the fractions of the separation, that contains the protein. If antibodies against the protein are available then western blotting and ELISA can specifically detect and quantify the amount of desired protein. Some proteins function as receptors and can be detected during purification steps by a ligand binding assay, often using a radioactive ligand.

In order to evaluate the process of multistep purification, the amount of the specific protein has to be compared to the amount of total protein. The latter can be determined by the Bradford total protein assay or by absorbance of light at 280 nm, however some reagents used during the purification process may interfere with the quantification. For example, imidazole (commonly used for purification of polyhistidine-tagged recombinant proteins) is an amino acid analogue and at low concentrations will interfere with the bicinchoninic acid (BCA) assay for total protein quantification. Impurities in low-grade imidazole will also absorb at 280 nm, resulting in an inaccurate reading of protein concentration from UV absorbance.

Another method to be considered is Surface Plasmon Resonance (SPR). SPR can detect binding of label free molecules on the surface of a chip. If the desired protein is an antibody, binding can be translated to directly to the activity of the protein. One can express the active concentration of the protein as the percent of the total protein. SPR can be a powerful method for quickly determining protein activity and overall yield. It is a powerful technology that requires an instrument to perform.

METHODS OF PROTEIN PURIFICATION

The methods used in protein purification can roughly be divided into analytical and preparative methods. The distinction is not exact, but the deciding factor is the amount of protein that can practically be purified with that method.

Analytical methods aim to detect and identify a protein in a mixture, whereas preparative methods aim to produce large quantities of the protein for other purposes, such as structural biology or industrial use. In general, the preparative methods can be used in analytical applications, but not the other way around.

EXTRACTION

Depending on the source, the protein has to be brought into solution by breaking the tissue or cells containing it. There are several methods to achieve this: Repeated freezing and thawing, sonication, homogenization by high pressure, filtration (either via cellulose-based depth filters or cross-flow filtration), or permeabilization by organic solvents. The method of choice depends on how fragile the protein is and how sturdy the cells are. After this extraction process soluble proteins will be in the solvent, and can be separated from cell membranes, DNA etc. by centrifugation. The extraction process also extracts proteases, which will start digesting the proteins in the solution. If the protein is sensitive to proteolysis, it is usually desirable to proceed quickly, and keep the extract cooled, to slow down proteolysis.

PRECIPITATION AND DIFFERENTIAL SOLUBILIZATION

In bulk protein purification, a common first step to isolate proteins is precipitation with ammonium sulfate $(NH_4)_2SO_4$. This is performed by adding increasing amounts of ammonium sulfate and collecting the different fractions of precipitate protein. One advantage of this method is that it can be performed inexpensively with very large volumes.

The first proteins to be purified are water-soluble proteins. Purification of integral membrane proteins requires disruption of the cell membrane in order to isolate any one particular protein from others that are in the same membrane compartment. Sometimes a particular membrane fraction can be isolated first, such as isolating mitochondria from cells before purifying a protein located in a mitochondrial membrane. A detergent such as sodium dodecyl sulfate (SDS) can be used to dissolve cell membranes and keep membrane proteins in solution during purification; however, because SDS causes denaturation, milder detergents such as Triton X-100 or CHAPS can be used to retain the protein's native conformation during complete purification.

ULTRACENTRIFUGATION

Centrifugation is a process that uses centrifugal force to separate mixtures of particles of varying masses or densities suspended in a liquid. When a vessel (typically a tube or bottle) containing a mixture of proteins or other particulate matter, such as bacterial cells, is rotated at high speeds, the angular momentum yields an outward force to each particle that is proportional to its mass. The tendency of a given particle to move through the liquid because of this force is offset by the resistance the liquid exerts on the particle. The net effect of "spinning" the sample in a centrifuge is that massive, small, and dense particles move outward faster than less massive particles or particles with more "drag" in the liquid. When suspensions of particles are "spun" in a centrifuge, a "pellet" may form at the bottom of the vessel that is enriched for the most massive particles with low drag in the liquid. Non-compacted particles still remaining mostly in the liquid are called the "supernatant" and can be removed from the vessel to separate the supernatant from the pellet. The rate of centrifugation is specified by the angular acceleration applied to the sample, typically measured in comparison to the g. If samples are centrifuged long enough, the particles in the vessel will reach equilibrium wherein the particles accumulate specifically at a point in the vessel where their buoyant density is balanced with centrifugal force. Such an "equilibrium" centrifugation can allow extensive purification of a given particle.

Sucrose gradient centrifugation — a linear concentration gradient of sugar (typically sucrose, glycerol, or a silica based density gradient media, like Percoll) is generated in a tube such that the highest concentration is on the bottom and lowest on top. Percoll is a trademark owned by GE Healthcare companies. A protein sample is then layered on top of the gradient and spun at high speeds in an ultracentrifuge. This causes heavy macromolecules to migrate towards the bottom of the tube faster than lighter material. During centrifugation in the absence of sucrose, as particles move farther and farther from the center of rotation, they experience more and more centrifugal force (the further they move, the faster they move). The problem with this is that the useful separation range of within the vessel is restricted to a small observable window. Spinning a sample twice as long doesn't mean the particle of interest will go twice as far, in fact, it will go significantly further. However, when the proteins are moving through a sucrose gradient, they encounter liquid of increasing density and viscosity. A properly designed sucrose gradient will counteract the increasing centrifugal force so the particles move in close proportion to the time they have been in the centrifugal field. Samples separated by these gradients are referred to as "rate zonal" centrifugations. After separating the protein/particles, the gradient is then fractionated and collected.

3

Carbohydrate

A carbohydrate is an organic compound with the empirical formula $C_m(H_2O)_n$, that is, consists only of carbon, hydrogen and oxygen, with the last two in the 2:1 atom ratio. Carbohydrates can be viewed as hydrates of carbon, hence their name. Structurally however, it is more accurate to view them as polyhydroxy aldehydes and ketones. The term is most common in biochemistry, where it is a synonym of saccharide. The carbohydrates (saccharides) are divided into four chemical groupings: monosaccharides, disaccharides, oligosaccharides, and polysaccharides. In general, the monosaccharides and disaccharides, which are smaller (lower molecular weight) carbohydrates, are commonly referred to as sugars. The word saccharide comes from the Greek word sαkkharon meaning "sugar". While the scientific nomenclature of carbohydrates is complex, the names of the monosaccharides and disaccharides very often end in the suffix -ose. For example, blood sugar is the monosaccharide glucose, table sugar is the disaccharide sucrose, and milk sugar is the disaccharide lactose.

Carbohydrates perform numerous roles in living things. Polysaccharides serve for the storage of energy and as structural components. The 5-carbon monosaccharide ribose is an important component of coenzymes and the backbone of the genetic molecule known as RNA. The related deoxyribose is a component of DNA. Saccharides and their derivatives include many other important biomolecules that play key roles in the immune system, fertilization, preventing pathogenesis, blood clotting, and development.

In food science and in many informal contexts, the term carbohydrate often means any food that is particularly rich in starch (such as cereals, bread and pasta) or sugar (such as candy, jams and desserts).

STRUCTURE

Formerly the name "carbohydrate" was used in chemistry for any compound with the formula $C_m(H_2O)_n$. Following this definition, some chemists considered formaldehyde CH_2O to be the simplest carbohydrate, while others claimed that title for glycolaldehyde Today the term is generally understood in the biochemistry sense, which excludes compounds with only one or two carbons. Natural saccharides are generally built of simple carbohydrates called monosaccharides with general formula $(CH_2O)_n$ where n is three or more. A typical monosaccharide has the structure H-$(CHOH)_x$(C=O)-$(CHOH)_y$-H, that is, an aldehyde or ketone with many hydroxyl groups added, usually one on each carbon atom that is not part of the aldehyde or ketone functional group. Examples of monosaccharides are glucose, fructose, and glyceraldehyde. However, some biological substances commonly called "monosaccharides" do not conform to this formula (e.g., uronic acids and deoxy-sugars such as fucose), and there are many chemicals that do conform to this formula but are not considered to be monosaccharides (e.g., formaldehyde CH_2O and inositol $(CH_2O)_6$).

The open-chain form of a monosaccharide often coexists with a closed ring form where the aldehyde/ketone carbonyl group carbon (C=O) and hydroxyl group (-OH) react forming a hemiacetal with a new C-O-C bridge.

Monosaccharides can be linked together into what are called polysaccharides (or oligosaccharides) in a large variety of ways. Many carbohydrates contain one or more modified monosaccharide units that have had one or more groups replaced or removed. For example, deoxyribose, a component of DNA, is a modified version of ribose; chitin is composed of repeating units of N-acetylglucosamine, a nitrogen-containing form of glucose.

MONOSACCHARIDES

Monosaccharides are the simplest carbohydrates in that they cannot be hydrolyzed to smaller carbohydrates. They are aldehydes or ketones with two or more hydroxyl groups. The general chemical formula of an unmodified monosaccharide is $(C\bullet H_2O)_n$, literally a "carbon hydrate." Monosaccharides are important fuel molecules as well as building blocks for nucleic acids. The smallest monosaccharides, for which n = 3, are dihydroxyacetone and D- and L-glyceraldehyde.

Classification of monosaccharides

Monosaccharides are classified according to three different characteristics: the placement of its carbonyl group, the number of carbon atoms it contains, and its chiral handedness. If the carbonyl group is an aldehyde, the monosaccharide is an aldose; if the carbonyl group is a ketone, the monosaccharide is a ketose. Monosaccharides with three carbon atoms are called trioses, those with four are called tetroses, five are called pentoses, six are hexoses, and so on. These two systems of classification are often combined. For example, glucose is an aldohexose (a six-carbon aldehyde), ribose is an aldopentose (a five-carbon aldehyde), and fructose is a ketohexose (a six-carbon ketone). Each carbon atom bearing a hydroxyl group (-OH), with the exception of the first and last carbons, are asymmetric, making them stereocenters with two possible configurations each (R or S). Because of this asymmetry, a number of isomers may exist for any given monosaccharide formula. The aldohexose D-glucose, for example, has the formula $(C{\cdot}H_2O)_6$, of which all but two of its six carbons atoms are stereogenic, making D-glucose one of $2^4 = 16$ possible stereoisomers. In the case of glyceraldehyde, an aldotriose, there is one pair of possible stereoisomers, which are enantiomers and epimers. 1,3-dihydroxyacetone, the ketose corresponding to the aldose glyceraldehyde, is a symmetric molecule with no stereocenters). The assignment of D or L is made according to the orientation of the asymmetric carbon furthest from the carbonyl group: in a standard Fischer projection if the hydroxyl group is on the right the molecule is a D sugar, otherwise it is an L sugar. The "D-" and "L-" prefixes should not be confused with "d-" or "l-", which indicate the direction that the sugar rotates plane polarized light. This usage of "d-" and "l-" is no longer followed in carbohydrate chemistry.

Ring-straight chain isomerism

The aldehyde or ketone group of a straight-chain monosaccharide will react reversibly with a hydroxyl group on a different carbon atom to form a hemiacetal or hemiketal, forming a heterocyclic ring with an oxygen bridge between two carbon atoms. Rings with five and six atoms are called furanose and pyranose forms, respectively, and exist in equilibrium with the straight-chain form.

During the conversion from straight-chain form to cyclic form, the carbon atom containing the carbonyl oxygen, called the anomeric carbon, becomes a stereogenic center with two possible configurations: The oxygen atom may take a position either above or below the plane of the ring. The resulting possible pair of stereoisomers are called anomers. In the α anomer, the -OH substituent on the anomeric carbon rests on the opposite side (trans) of the ring from the CH_2OH side branch. The alternative form, in which the CH_2OH substituent and the anomeric hydroxyl are on the same side (cis) of the plane of the ring, is called the β anomer. You can remember that the β anomer is cis by the mnemonic, "It's always better to βe up". Because the ring and straight-chain forms readily interconvert, both anomers exist in equilibrium. In a Fischer Projection, the α anomer is represented with the anomeric hydroxyl group trans to the CH_2OH and cis in the β βanomer.

Use in living organisms

Monosaccharides are the major source of fuel for metabolism, being used both as an energy source (glucose being the most important in nature) and in biosynthesis. When monosaccharides are not immediately needed by many cells they are often converted to more space efficient forms, often polysaccharides. In many animals, including humans, this storage form is glycogen, especially in liver and muscle cells. In plants, starch is used for the same purpose.

DISACCHARIDES

Two joined monosaccharides are called a disaccharide and these are the simplest polysaccharides. Examples include sucrose and lactose. They are composed of two monosaccharide units bound together by a covalent bond known as a glycosidic linkage formed via a dehydration reaction, resulting in the loss of a hydrogen atom from one monosaccharide and a hydroxyl group from the other. The formula of unmodified disaccharides is $C_{12}H_{22}O_{11}$. Although there are numerous kinds of disaccharides, a handful of disaccharides are particularly notable.

Sucrose, pictured to the right, is the most abundant disaccharide, and the main form in which carbohydrates are transported in plants. It is composed of one D-glucose molecule and one D-fructose molecule. The systematic name for sucrose, fructofuranoside, indicates four things:

- Its monosaccharides: glucose and fructose
- Their ring types: glucose is a pyranose, and fructose is a furanose
- How they are linked together: the oxygen on carbon number 1 (C1) of α-D-glucose is linked to the C2 of D-fructose.
- The -oside suffix indicates that the anomeric carbon of both monosaccharides participates in the glycosidic bond.

Lactose, a disaccharide composed of one D-galactose molecule and one D-glucose molecule, occurs naturally in mammalian milk. The systematic name for lactose is O-β-D-galactopyranosylD-glucopyranose. Other notable disaccharides include maltose (two D-glucoses linked α-1,4) and cellulobiose (two D-glucoses linked β-1,4).

OLIGOSACCHARIDES AND POLYSACCHARIDES

Oligosaccharides and polysaccharides are composed of longer chains of monosaccharide units bound together by glycosidic bonds. The distinction between the two is based upon the number of monosaccharide units present in the chain. Oligosaccharides typically contain between three and ten monosaccharide units, and polysaccharides contain greater than ten monosaccharide units. Definitions of how large a carbohydrate must be to fall into each category vary according to personal opinion. Examples of oligosaccharides include the disaccharides mentioned above, the trisaccharide raffinose and the tetrasaccharide stachyose.

Oligosaccharides are found as a common form of protein posttranslational modification. Such posttranslational modifications include the Lewis and ABO oligosaccharides responsible for blood group classifications and so of tissue incompatibilities, the alpha-Gal epitope responsible for hyperacute rejection in xenotransplantation, and O-GlcNAc modifications.

Polysaccharides represent an important class of biological polymers. Their function in living organisms is usually either structure- or storage-related. Starch (a polymer of glucose) is used as a storage polysaccharide in plants, being found in the form of both amylose and the branched amylopectin. In animals, the structurally similar glucose polymer is the more densely branched glycogen, sometimes called 'animal starch'. Glycogen's properties allow it to be metabolized more quickly, which suits the active lives of moving animals.

Cellulose and chitin are examples of structural polysaccharides. Cellulose is used in the cell walls of plants and other organisms, and is claimed to be the most abundant organic molecule on earth. It has many uses such as a significant role in the paper and textile industries, and is used as a feedstock for the production of rayon (via the viscose process), cellulose acetate, celluloid, and nitrocellulose. Chitin has a similar structure, but has nitrogen-containing side branches, increasing its strength.

It is found in arthropod exoskeletons and in the cell walls of some fungi. It also has multiple uses, including surgical threads. Other polysaccharides include callose or laminarin, chrysolaminarin, xylan, arabinoxylan, mannan, fucoidan, and galactomannan.

NUTRITION

Foods high in simple carbohydrates include fruits, sweets and soft drinks. Foods high in complex carbohydrates include breads, pastas, beans, potatoes, bran, rice, and cereals. The most common complex carbohydrate in these foods is starch. Carbohydrates are the most common source of energy in living organisms. Proteins and fat are necessary building components for body tissue and cells, and are also a source of energy for most organisms.

Carbohydrates are not essential nutrients in humans: the body can obtain all its energy from protein and fats. The brain and neurons generally cannot burn fat for energy, but can use glucose or ketones; the body can also synthesize some glucose from a few of the amino acids in protein and also from the glycerol backbone in triglycerides.

Carbohydrate contains 15.8 kilojoules (3.75 kilocalories) and proteins 16.8 kilojoules (4 kilocalories) per gram, while fats contain 37.8 kilojoules (9 kilocalories) per gram. In the case of protein, this is somewhat misleading as only some amino acids are usable for fuel. Likewise, in humans, only some carbohydrates are usable for fuel, as in many monosaccharides and some disaccharides. Other carbohydrate types can be used, but only with the assistance of gut bacteria. Ruminants and termites can even process cellulose, which is indigestible to humans.

Based on the effects on risk of heart disease and obesity, the Institute of Medicine recommends that American and Canadian adults get between 45–65% of dietary energy from carbohydrates. The Food and Agriculture Organization and World Health Organization jointly recommend that national dietary guidelines set a goal of 55–75% of total energy from carbohydrates, but only 10% directly from sugars (their term for simple carbohydrates).

Classification

For dietary purposes, carbohydrates can be classified as simple (monosaccharides and disaccharides) or complex (oligosaccharides and polysaccharides). The term complex carbohydrate was first used in the U.S. Senate Select Committee on Nutrition and Human Needs publication Dietary Goals for the United States (1977), where it denoted "fruit, vegetables and whole-grains". Dietary guidelines generally recommend that complex carbohydrates, and such nutrient-rich simple carbohydrate sources such as fruit (glucose or fructose) and dairy products (lactose) make up the bulk of carbohydrate consumption. This excludes such sources of simple sugars as candy and sugary drinks. The USDA's Dietary Guidelines for Americans 2005 dispensed with the simple/complex distinction, instead recommending fiber-rich foods and whole grains.

The glycemic index and glycemic load concepts have been developed to characterize food behavior during human digestion. They rank carbohydrate-rich foods based on the rapidity of their effect on blood glucose levels. The insulin index is a similar, more recent classification method that ranks foods based on their effects on blood insulin levels, which are caused by glucose (or starch) and some amino acids in food. Glycemic index is a measure of how quickly food glucose is absorbed, while glycemic load is a measure of the total absorbable glucose in foods.

METABOLISM

Catabolism

Catabolism is the metabolic reaction cells undergo to extract energy. There are two major metabolic pathways of monosaccharide catabolism: glycolysis and the citric acid cycle. In glycolysis, oligo/polysaccharides are cleaved first to smaller monosaccharides by enzymes called glycoside hydrolases. The monosaccharide units can then enter into monosaccharide catabolism. In some cases, as with humans, not all carbohydrate types are usable as the digestive and metabolic enzymes necessary are not present.

THE ROLE OF CARBOHYDRATES IN NUTRITION

Carbohydrates are polyhydroxy aldehydes, ketones, alcohols, acids, their simple derivatives and their polymers having linkages of the acetal type. They may be classified according to their degree of polymerization and may be divided initially into three principal groups, namely sugars, oligosaccharides and polysaccharides.

Class (DP*)	Sub-Group	Components
Sugars (1-2)	Monosaccharides	Glucose, galactose, fructose
	Disaccharides	Sucrose, lactose, trehalose
	Polyols	Sorbitol, mannitol
Oligosaccharides (3-9)	Malto-oligosaccharides	Maltodextrins
	Other oligosaccharides	Raffinose, stachyose, fructo-oligosaccharides
Polisaccharides (>9)	Starch	Amylose, amylopectin, modified starches
	Non-starch polisaccharides	Cellulose, hemicellulose, pectins, hydrocolloids

Fig. The major dietary carbohdrates

Each of these three groups may be subdivided on the basis of the monosaccharide composition of the individual carbohydrates. Sugars comprise monosaccharides, disaccharides and polyols (sugar alcohols); oligosaccharides include malto-oligosaccharides, principally those occurring from the hydrolysis of starch, and other oligosaccharides, e.g. a -galactosides (raffinose, stachyose etc.) and fructo-oligosaccharides; the final group are the polysaccharides which may be divided into starch (a -glucans) and non-starch polysaccharides of which the major components are the polysaccharides of the plant cell wall such as cellulose, hemicellulose and pectin (2,3,4).

TOTAL CARBOHYDRATE

Although the individual components of dietary carbohydrate are readily identifiable, there is some confusion as to what comprises total carbohydrate as reported in food tables. Two principal measures of total carbohydrate are used, firstly, that derived by "difference" and secondly the direct measurement of the individual components which are then combined to give a total. Calculating carbohydrates by "difference" has been used since the turn of the century. The protein, fat, ash and moisture content of a food are determined, subtracted from the total weight of the food and the remainder, or "difference", is considered to be carbohydrate. There are, however, a number of problems with this approach to total carbohydrate analysis in that the "by difference" figure includes a number of non-carbohydrate components such as lignin, organic acids, tannins, waxes, and some Maillard products. In addition to this error, it combines all of the analytical errors from the other analyses. Finally, a single global figure for carbohydrates in food is uninformative because it fails to identify the many types of carbohydrates in a food and thus to allow some understanding of the potential physiological properties of those carbohydrates.

TERMINOLOGY

In deciding how to classify dietary carbohydrate the principal problem is to reconcile the various chemical divisions of carbohydrate with that which reflects physiology and health. A classification based purely on chemistry does not allow a ready translation into nutritional terms since each of the major classes of carbohydrate have a variety of physiological effects. However, a classification based on physiological properties also creates a number of problems in that it requires a single effect to be considered as overridingly important and to be used as the basis of the classification. This dichotomy has led to the introduction of a number of terms to describe various fractions and sub-fractions of carbohydrate.

Sugars

The term "sugars" is conventionally used to describe the mono and disaccharides. "Sugar", by contrast, is used to describe purified sucrose as are the terms "refined sugar" and "added sugar"

Extrinsic and intrinsic sugars

These terms had their origin in a United Kingdom Department of Health committee in 1989, which was looking at the question of sugars in the diet. The terms were developed to help the consumer choose between what were considered to be healthy sugars and those which were not. Intrinsic sugars were defined as sugars occurring within the cell walls of plants, i.e. naturally occurring, while extrinsic sugars were those which were usually added to foods. Because lactose in milk is also an extrinsic sugar, an additional phrase "non-milk extrinsic sugars" was developed. These terms have not gained wide acceptance either in the UK or other countries in the world. There are no current plans to measure these sugars separately in the diet nor to incorporate their use into food tables.

Complex carbohydrates

This term was first used in the McGovern report, "Dietary Goals for the United States" in 1977. The term was coined largely to distinguish sugars from other carbohydrates and in the report denotes "fruit, vegetables and whole-grains". The term has since come to be used to describe either starch alone, or the combination of all polysaccharides. It was used to encourage consumption of what were considered to be healthy foods such as whole-grain cereals, etc., but becomes meaningless when used to describe fruit and vegetables which are low in starch. Furthermore, it is now realized that starch, which is by any definition a complex carbohydrate, is variable metabolically with some forms being rapidly absorbed and having a high glycemic index and some being resistant to digestion. The term "complex carbohydrate" has encompassed, at various times, starch, dietary fibre and non-digestible oligosaccharides. As a substitute term for starch, however, it would seem to have little merit and, in principle, it is better to discuss carbohydrate components by using their common chemical names.

Available and unavailable carbohydrate

A major step forward conceptually in our understanding of carbohydrates was made by McCance and Lawrence in 1929 with the division of dietary carbohydrate into available and unavailable. In an attempt to prepare food tables for diabetic diets they realised that not all carbohydrates could be "utilized and metabolized", i.e. provide the body with "carbohydrates for metabolism". Available carbohydrate was defined as "starch and soluble sugars" and unavailable as "mainly hemicellulose and fibre ". This concept proved useful, not the least because it drew attention to the fact that some carbohydrate is not digested and absorbed in the small intestine but rather reaches the large bowel where it is fermented. It suggests that the site of digestion or fermentation in the gut of carbohydrate is of overriding importance. However, it is misleading to talk of carbohydrate as "unavailable" because some indigestible carbohydrate is able to provide the body with energy through fermentation. There are many properties of carbohydrate of which digestibility and fermentability are only two. A more appropriate substitute for the terms "available" and "unavailable" today would be to describe carbohydrates as either as glycemic or non-glycemic, which is closer to the original concept of McCance and Lawrence.

Resistant starch

One of the major developments in our understanding of the importance of carbohydrates for health in the past twenty years has been the discovery of resistant starch. Resistant starch is defined as "starch and starch degradation products not absorbed in the small intestine of healthy humans". The main forms of resistant starch are physically enclosed starch, e.g. within intact cell structures (RS_1), some raw starch granules (RS_2) and retrograded amylose (RS_3).

Modified starch

The proportions of amylose and amylopectin in a starchy food is variable and can be altered by plant breeding. Techniques using genetic engineering are rapidly emerging, enabling starches to be produced for specific purposes by genetically modifying the crop used for their production. High amylose corn starch and high amylopectin (waxy) corn starch have been available for a long time, and display quite different functional as well as nutritional properties. High amylose starches require higher temperatures for gelatinization and are more prone to retrograde and to form amylose-lipid complexes. Such properties can be utilized in the formulation of foods with low glycemic index and/or high resistant starch content. Physical modifications of starches include pregelatinization and partial hydrolysis (dextrinization). Chemical modification is mainly the introduction of side groups and cross-linking or oxidation. These modifications may be used to decrease viscosity and to improve gel stability, mouthfeel, appearance and texture, and resistance for heat treatment. The application of modified starches as fat replacers is another important area. Some modified starches may be partly resistant to digestion in the small intestine, thereby adding to resistant starch .

Dietary fibre

The original description of dietary fibre by Trowell in 1972 was "that portion of food which is derived from cellular walls of plants which is digested very poorly by human beings". This is not an exact description of any carbohydrate in the diet but is more a physiological concept. It was linked by Burkitt and Trowell to the etiology of a number of "Western diseases" and on the basis of this a hypothesis relating fibre to health was developed. The use of the term has, however, caused many difficulties over the years because of controversies regarding definition.

Moreover, the proposal that there are a number of dietary fibre deficiency disorders is an over-simplification and needs to be modified now in the light of new knowledge of diet and disease. The main components of dietary fibre are derived from the cell walls of plant material in the diet and comprise cellulose, hemicellulose and pectin.

Lignin, a non-carbohydrate component of the cell wall is also often included. Dietary fibre is a term which is felt to be valuable for the consumer who looks upon this as a healthy component of the diet. At the present time there is no consensus as to which components of carbohydrate should be included as dietary fibre and different authors have variously included non-starch polysaccharides and resistant starch. More recently it has been suggested that non-digestible oligosaccharides should also be included. Dietary fibre has also been defined by method. While there is general agreement that the non-starch polysaccharides are the principal part of dietary fibre there is currently no consensus as to whether other components should be included in this term. It has been suggested that the use of the term dietary fibre be gradually phased out. Its widespread use and popularity with the consumer has made this difficult in practice and the term has been useful in nutrition education and product development.

Soluble and insoluble fibre

These terms developed out of the early chemistry of non-starch polysaccharides which showed that the fractional extraction of these polysaccharides could be controlled by changing the pH of solutions. They proved very useful in the initial understanding of the physiological properties of dietary fibre, allowing a simple division into those which principally had effects on glucose and lipid absorption from the small intestine and those which were slowly and incompletely fermented and had more pronounced effects on bowel habit. However, the separation of soluble and insoluble fractions is not chemically very distinct being dependent on the conditions of extraction.

Moreover, the physiological differences are not, in fact, so distinct with much insoluble fibre being rapidly and completely fermented while not all soluble fibre has effects on glucose and lipid absorption.

METHODOLOGY FOR DIETARY CARBOHYDRATE ANALYSIS

Mono- and disaccharides

They can be analyzed specifically by enzymatic, gas-liquid chromatography (GLC) or high performance liquid chromatography (HPLC) methods. Depending on the food matrix to be analyzed, extraction of the low molecular weight carbohydrates in aqueous ethanol, usually 80% (v/v), may be advisable before analysis.

The enzymatic procedures are based on specific, highly purified enzymes and have been instrumental in providing means of specific and precise analysis of individual carbohydrates in mixtures without a large investment in instrumentation. Enzymatic methods are still preferable when one single carbohydrate is to be analyzed, e.g. glucose, as the end point of starch analysis. When several different monosaccharides are to be determined simultaneously, HPLC or GLC methods are preferable. HPLC systems using sensitive amperometric detectors are gaining in popularity over GLC, in that the derivatization necessary before the GLC determination is avoided.

Polyols

Polyols are usually determined by GLC using alditol acetate derivatives. HPLC methods are also available.

Oligosaccharides

Oligosaccharides can also be determined by GLC or HPLC methods. These methods work well for purified preparations, but in complex foods or diets, enzymatic hydrolysis and determination of liberated monosaccharides is an alternative for specific determination. Malto-oligosaccharides are recovered as "starch" if not extracted before starch analysis.

Separation of oligosaccharides from polysaccharides

By definition, polysaccharides have 10 or more monomeric units, and Oligosaccharides less than 10. Analytically, separation is based on solubility in aqueous ethanol, usually around 80% (v/v). The alcohol solubility of carbohydrates, however, is dependent not only on the degree of polymerization (DP), but also on the molecular structure. For instance, highly branched carbohydrates may be soluble in 80% ethanol in spite of a DP considerably higher than 10. In practice, therefore, the separation of Oligosaccharides from polysaccharides is empirical and does not provide an exact division based on DP.

Starch

Quantitative analysis of starch in foods by most current methods is based on enzymatic degradation and specific determination of liberated glucose. Nutritionally, starch can be divided into glucogenic ("available") and resistant starch, which is not absorbed in the small intestine. Resistant starch is poorly soluble in water and methods aiming at a total starch analysis employ an initial 2M potassium hydroxide (KOH) or dimethylsulfoxide solvent (DMSO) treatment to disperse crystalline starch fractions that would otherwise remain unhydrolyzed. Methods for measuring resistant starch are still in their infancy and have not yet been tested in formal collaborative studies.

They aim at simulating normal starch digestion in the small intestine. A key step is to mimic the normal disintegration of the food which occurs during chewing.

One method uses a standardized milling/homogenization technique, whereas others employ standardized chewing by volunteers (19,20). Both approaches have been evaluated against human ileostomy experiments with a limited number of food matrices.

Non-starch polysaccharides (NSP)

The determination of NSP is based on the following steps:

(a) degradation of starch by enzymatic hydrolysis after solublization,

(b) removal of low molecular weight carbohydrates, including starch hydrolysis products,

(c) hydrolysis of the NSP to their constituent monomers, and

(d) quantitative determination of those monomers.

The acid hydrolysis step is a critical one, and it has to be designed as an optimal balance between complete hydrolysis and destruction of the liberated monomers. The most widely-used method today for specific determination of the liberated monomers is GLC with alditol acetate derivatives. HPLC detection is an alternative gaining in popularity. Colourimetric determination is still preferred for uronic acids, which are derived mainly from pectic substances. A colourimetric method is also available for total NSP. Fractions of NSP, such as cellulose and non-cellulosic polysaccharides, can be separated by using sequential extraction and hydrolysis methods. For instance, cellulose is not hydrolysed by dilute (1-2M) sulphuric acid, unless it has first been dispersed in concentrated acid.

Dietary fibre

Three methods for dietary fibre analysis have undergone extensive testing in recent years, including collaborative studies satisfactory enough for official approval of bodies such as the AOAC International and the Bureau Communautaire de Reference of the European Community:

- The enzymatic, gravimetric AOAC methods of Prosky and co-workers, and subsequently Lee and co-workers.
- The enzymatic-chemical methods of Englyst and co-workers.
- The enzymatic-chemical method of Theander and co-workers (the Uppsala method).

The enzymatic-gravimetric AOAC methods are derived from methods aiming at simulating the digestion in the human small intestine to isolate an undigested residue as a measure of dietary fibre. This residue is corrected for associated ash and protein. Since no DMSO or KOH dispersion is used, starch that resists the amylases used in the assay will remain as a fibre component. Since the sample has to be milled, and since a heat-stable amylase (termamyl) is used at a temperature close to 100°C, physically enclosed starch (RS_1) and resistant starch granules (RS_2) will not be included. Retrograded amylose (RS_3) that is included is the main form of resistant starch (RS) in processed foods. Lignin, a non-carbohydrate component of the dietary fibre complex is also included, as well as some tannins.

These components are a very small proportion of most foods but can be substantial in some unconventional raw materials or special "fibre" preparations. The Englyst method measures the NSP specifically, either as individual monomeric components by GLC or colourimetrically as reducing substances. Accordingly, DMSO is used initially to ensure a complete removal of starch, and lignin is not determined. The difference between estimates with the gravimetric methods and the Englyst method is mainly due to resistant starch and lignin. The Uppsala method employs hydrolysis conditions and GLC determination of monomers in a similar way as in the Englyst method. However, DMSO is not employed for starch dispersion, and a gravimetric estimate of lignin is added to obtain the dietary fibre. The Uppsala method and the gravimetric AOAC methods give very concordant results.

LABELLING

Food labelling has two main aims: to inform the consumer of the composition of the food and to assist them in the selection of a healthy diet. These two aims are not always easy to reconcile because the health benefit of different carbohydrate-containing foods cannot readily be communicated simply from a description of their composition. Labelling should be based on the chemical classification used in Figure 1. Analytical methods should be clearly defined and validated. The principal information should be total carbohydrate, measured as the sum of the individual components. Further information on carbohydrate composition, based on the classification in Figure 1, could include terms such as sugars, starch and non-starch polysaccharides. Other terms, such as non-digestible oligosaccharides, polyols, resistant starch and dietary fibre may be used, provided the components included in these terms are clearly defined.

AVAILABILITY AND CONSUMPTION

Trends in the supply and intake of carbohydrates can be studied by four principal approaches:

1. Production
2. Food balance sheets
3. Household surveys
4. Individual assessments

Food production statistics, which are available from FAO for every country in the world and for every crop, are useful for examining trends in consumption. From these data it can be seen that the major sources of carbohydrate in the human diet are:

1. Cereals
2. Root crops
3. Sugar crops
4. Pulses
5. Vegetables
6. Fruit
7. Milk products

Sustainability

Trends over the last 20-30 years indicate growth in world production of cereals, sugar cane, vegetables and fruit. On the other hand, production of root crops, pulses and sugar beet has changed little on a world basis. Marked decreases have actually been seen in pulse production in some countries in Asia, and in root crop production in Europe. This suggests a change in food preference away from roots and pulses and towards cereals. Examination of eating habits in a number of countries indicates that this is the case. Since root crops are an excellent source of carbohydrate, there is concern about this downward trend in production. Populations continue to grow in most parts of the world and, overall, food production would seem to be keeping pace with population growth. Increased production is due to improved agricultural practices rather than increased crop area, the major reason for increases being greater use of fertilizer. There are, however, specific countries where this is not happening. For the entire continent of Africa, cereal production is inadequate. A major question is how much more improvement and efficiency in production can be achieved, and whether the amount of carbohydrate will be sufficient for the world's population in the future. Projections for future growth suggest problems ahead, particularly in Africa.

Changing patterns of consumption

Both food balance information and results from individual assessments are used to determine carbohydrate intakes. Food balance data is intended to describe food available for consumption. It is unlikely to do so because it does not include home production, which is variable from country to country, and may be considerable in some developing countries. As a reflection of food consumed, food balance data is questionable, since it does not include food wasted or spoiled, or used for purposes other than human food, the proportion of which may change from year to year. As a result, food balance data for individual countries has failed to demonstrate the changes in consumption of carbohydrates which are seen using individual surveys. Data from individual surveys also have limitations. Surveys are carried out by a variety of methodologies. While each has advantages and disadvantages, all suffer from a degree of underreporting.

This can be intentional or involuntary, most likely due to individuals forgetting food items or not describing foods thought to be undesirable. There is also the failure to record data or the altering of actual diets. The difference, then, between food balance data and individual assessments, for energy and nutrient intakes, is not only the form of wastage and spoilage on the food balance side of the equation, but also the underreporting on the individual intake side. True food intakes therefore lie somewhere between food balance and individual intake estimates. Another major problem is the varied carbohydrate terminology used in different countries.

Many countries express total carbohydrate 'by difference', rather than as carbohydrate analyzed directly, and this results in overestimates of the percent energy derived from carbohydrate. There is also a great variety in terms used to describe simple sugars, such as "sugars", "sugar", "refined sugar", "added sugar", "sucrose", and "sugars minus lactose". Often there is no description of what is being reported.

There is a need to standardize the terminology for carbohydrate and its components in individual surveys and a need for consistency in both reporting and the description of the terms used. In spite of terminology difficulties, it is possible to gain a picture of carbohydrate intakes and trends. Annex 1 gives the intakes of carbohydrate and components where available, from a number of surveys since 1980. As a percent of energy, total carbohydrate ranges from about 40% to over 80%, with the developed countries, such as those in North America, Western Europe and Australia at the low end of the range, and developing countries in Asia and Africa at the high end. Starch accounts for 20%-50% or more of energy where the total carbohydrate intake is in the high range. Sugars account for 9%-27% of energy intake; where total carbohydrate is high, sugar intake is generally low. Where data are available, intake of carbohydrate as a percent of energy is higher for children than for adults. Trends in consumption indicate a falling carbohydrate intake in developed countries until the last two decades. During that time some increase has been noted as fat intakes fall. The major sources of carbohydrate are cereals, representing over 50% of all carbohydrate consumed in both developed and developing countries, with sugar crops the next major source, followed by root crops, fruits, vegetables, pulses and milk products. In some of the developing countries much of the carbohydrate is derived from a single food source such as rice, cassava or maize. Carbohydrate foods are an important vehicle for protein, micronutrients and other food components, like phytochemicals, which have important benefits for health. Individual food sources vary, however, in the provision of these components.

A single food source of carbohydrate is therefore undesirable and populations whose diets are primarily based on a single food can suffer from micronutrient deficiencies due to lack of variety. It is important, therefore, that a number of different carbohydrate sources be consumed and efforts should be made to encourage a wide variety of carbohydrate foods. Data on intake of sources of sugars is only available for developed countries. These data show similar proportions of sugars are derived from cereal products, milk products and beverages, among these countries. There is some variation in the proportions derived from fruit and confectionery, with the UK consuming less fruit and higher amounts of confectionery than countries such as the United States and Australia. Intakes of non-starch polysaccharides range from about 19g/day in some countries in Europe and North America, to nearly 30g/day in rural Africa. Cereals are again the major source of this component. Data on intake of dietary fibre, determined by methods such as that of the AOAC and the older Southgate method are about 15-20 g/day for North America, Europe and Australia, to 25-40 g/day for countries in Asia and Africa.

PHYSIOLOGY

Carbohydrates have a wide range of physiological effects which may be important to health, such as:

- Provision of energy
- Effects on satiety/gastric emptying
- Control of blood glucose and insulin metabolism
- Protein glycosylation
- Cholesterol and triglyceride metabolism
- Bile acid dehydroxylation
- Fermentation

Hydrogen/methane production
Short-chain fatty acids production Control of colonic epithelial cell function

· Bowel habit/laxation/motor activity
· Effects on large bowel microflora

Carbohydrate as an energy source

Dietary carbohydrates have by convention been given an energy value of 4 kcal/g (17 kJ/g), although where carbohydrates are expressed as monosaccharides, the value of 3.75 kcal/g (15.7 kJ/g) is used. It is now clear, however, that a number of carbohydrates are only partly or not at all digested in the small intestine and are fermented in the large bowel to short chain fatty acids. These include the non-digestible oligosaccharides, resistant starch and non-starch polysaccharides. The process of fermentation is metabolically less efficient than absorption in the small intestine and these carbohydrates provide the body with less energy. In light of a new understanding of the digestion and metabolism of carbohydrate and developments in methodology, the energy value of all carbohydrates in the diet should be reassessed and more accurate energy factors assigned to each group or sub-group. There are a number of potential approaches to accomplish this. These include the classic calorimetry experiments similar to those first undertaken by Atwater, as well as human balance studies and ileostomy recovery experiments. Knowledge of the chemistry of individual carbohydrates allows a prediction to be made regarding their digestion or fermentation, and an energy value to be assigned. In vitro models of fermentation can be constructed and from these the fermentation stoichiometry can be deduced. Studies using stable isotope tracer techniques may also be of value. While the energy yield of carbohydrate delivered to the colon will vary according to the extent of colonic fermentation (or the assumptions made in the model used), there may be an argument for assigning a single energy value to all such carbohydrate. Published studies suggest that a caloric value of about 2 kcal/g (8 kJ/g) would be a reasonable average figure for carbohydrate which reaches the colon. While individual carbohydrates will have different values, in the range of 1-2 kcal/g, these differences are unlikely to be of importance to health.

Satiety

The possibility of controlling hunger, satiety and food intake by altering the type of carbohydrate in food has intrigued a number of investigators. At present the variability of the findings and the lack of understanding of a clear relationship to physiologic parameters thought to be involved in the regulation of food intake limit practical application of this approach. It is unlikely that controlling a single dietary component, such as the type of sugar or starch, will lead to significant changes in the amount of food consumed. Also, compensation for small dietary changes made in one meal may often be seen at a subsequent meal. A better approach to controlling hunger and increasing satiety is likely to be associated with changes in the composition of the total diet.

Glucose and insulin

The digestion of dietary carbohydrates starts in the mouth, where salivary a-amylase initiates starch degradation. The starch fragments thus formed include maltose, some glucose and dextrins containing the 1,6-a -glycosidic branching points of amylopectin. The a -amylase degradation of starch is completed by the pancreatic amylase active in the small intestine. Dietary disaccharides, as well as degradation products of starch, need to be broken down to monosaccharides in order to be absorbed. This final hydrolysis is accomplished by hydrolases attached to the intestinal brush-border membrane, referred to as "disaccharidases". Disaccharidase deficiencies occur as rare genetic defects, causing malabsorption and intolerance of the corresponding disaccharide. Glucose and galactose are transported actively against a concentration gradient into the intestinal mucosal cells by a sodium dependent transporter.

Fructose undergoes facilitated transport by another mechanism. Fructose taken together with other sugars is better absorbed than fructose alone. When delivered to the circulation, the absorbed carbohydrates cause an elevation of the blood glucose concentration. Fructose and galactose have to be converted to glucose mainly in the liver and therefore produce less pronounced blood glucose elevation. The extent and duration of the blood glucose rise after a meal is dependent upon the rate of absorption, which in turn depends upon factors such as gastric emptying as well as the rate of hydrolysis and diffusion of hydrolysis products in the small intestine. Insulin is secreted as a response to blood glucose elevation but is modified by many neural and endocrine stimuli. Insulin secretion is also influenced by food related factors, especially by the amount and the amino acid composition of dietary proteins. Insulin has important regulatory functions in both carbohydrate and lipid metabolism and is necessary for glucose uptake by most body cells.

Lactose

Lactose, a b -linked disaccharide of glucose and galactose, is the principal sugar in milk. At birth, lactase activity is high in the brush-border of the small bowel of infants, but declines after weaning so that most populations of the world have low activity in adult life. The exceptions are Caucasian peoples and some other population groups in whom the majority retain a high lactase activity throughout life. During the years since 1980, there has been a major change in the way lactose absorption is viewed and a resultant shift away from the concept that lactose "malabsorption" is a pathological state. Low mucosal lactase activity in adults is the norm throughout most of the world. However, such a state usually allows the drinking of modest quantities of milk spaced throughout the day without adverse symptoms. Milk consumption is therefore now being encouraged in many areas of the world because of its value as a source of protein, calcium and riboflavin. Fermented milk products, which have lower lactose content and contain enzymes and microorganisms that can assist in lactose digestion, are better tolerated than milk. Technology exists to reduce the lactose level in foods and this should be taken into consideration when milk is included as food aid. Cheese, however, has almost no lactose. Lactose which is not digested, passes into the colon where it is fermented. In some individuals this causes lactose intolerance, the term used to describe the clinical symptoms of abdominal discomfort, flatulence and diarrhoea, associated with the ingestion of lactose containing foods by persons with low lactase activity. It also occurs as a transient phenomenon when the intestinal mucosa is injured following acute infection in children and in protein-energy malnutrition. It is also found in adults, particularly in association with coeliac disease and tropical sprue. In these conditions, lactose malabsorption is said to be "secondary" to intestinal mucosal disease. A small proportion of the Caucasian population also exhibits low lactase activity and lactose intolerance.

Protein glycosylation

The non-enzymatic glycation of proteins is dependent on the concentration of glucose and fructose in blood and the half-life of the protein. The initial reaction is between the monosaccharide and the amino group of an amino acid, usually lysine, to form a Shiff base which undergoes rearrangement and formation of Amadori products. As the reaction progresses, increasingly complex Maillard products are formed with the eventual production of Advanced Glycation End-products or AGEs which are associated with irreversible loss of protein function.

The extent of glycation of specific proteins, such as Haemoglobin Ale in diabetics serves as an indication of medium term control of blood glucose. Examples of functional changes induced by glycation include lens proteins in the eye with resultant cataract formation, increased microvascular complications, abnormal fibrin network formation and impaired fibrinolysis. These changes are most clearly seen in diabetic patients.

Lipids and bile acids

There has been concern that a substantial increase in carbohydrate-containing food at the expense of fat, might result in a decrease in high-density lipoprotein and a corresponding increase in very low-density lipoprotein and triglycerides in the blood. However, there is no evidence that this happens when the increase in carbohydrates occurs as a result of increased consumption of vegetables, fruits and appropriately processed cereals over prolonged periods. Polysaccharides like oat b -glucan, guar gum and those from psyllium have been repeatedly shown to lower serum cholesterol levels in those with elevated levels, with little change if serum levels are normal. Proposed mechanisms include impaired bile acid and cholesterol reabsorption through physical entrapment in the small intestine, or inhibitory effects on cholesterol synthesis by products of lower bowel fermentation, particularly propionic acid. Not all fermentable polysaccharides are effective, however, and recent studies have indicated that neither oligosaccharides nor resistant starch have a significant effect on serum lipids in young normolipidemic subjects.

Fermentation

Fermentation is the colonic phase of the digestive process and describes the breakdown in the large intestine of carbohydrates not digested and absorbed in the upper gut. This process involves gut microflora and is unique to the colon of humans because it occurs without the availability of oxygen. It thus results in the formation of the gases hydrogen, methane and carbon dioxide, as well as short chain fatty acids (SCFA) (acetate, propionate and butyrate), and stimulates bacterial growth (biomass). The gases are either absorbed and excreted in breath, or passed out via the rectum. The major products of such fermentation are the SCFA which are rapidly absorbed and metabolized by the body. Acetate passes primarily into the blood and is taken up by liver, muscle and other tissues. Propionate is a major glucose precursor in ruminant animals such as the cow and sheep, but this is not an important pathway in humans. Butyrate is metabolized primarily by colonocytes and has been shown to regulate cell growth, and to induce differentiation and apoptosis.

Bowel habit

It has long been known that non-starch polysaccharides are the principal dietary component affecting laxation. This occurs through increases in bowel content bulk and a speeding up of intestinal transit time. The extent of the effect depends on the chemical and physical nature of the polysaccharides and the extent to which they are fermented in the colon. Fermentable polysaccharides stimulate increases in microbial biomass in the colon, resulting in some increase in fecal weight, but not to the extent of non-fermentable polysaccharides. The latter are not significantly degraded in the colon and become consituents of the stool. In so doing, they hold water and produce a marked increase in fecal weight. Similarly, resistant starch can increase fecal weight, but this again depends on the extent of fermentation.

Microflora

Carbohydrate which is fermented stimulates the growth of bacteria in the large gut. This is a generalized effect which leads to an increase in the total number of bacteria or biomass. When bacterial growth occurs, the microflora synthesize protein actively from preformed amino acids and peptides as well as some de-novo synthesis using ammonia as the source of nitrogen. The additional biomass is excreted in feces and is one of the mechanisms whereby carbohydrate influences bowel habit. The increased biomass excretion is accompanied by increased nitrogen excretion. The efficiency of conversion of carbohydrate to biomass is determined principally by the type of substrate, the rate of breakdown and the transit time through the large intestine. One of the more significant developments in recent years with regard to the gut microflora has been the demonstration that specific dietary carbohydrates selectively stimulate the growth of individual groups or species of bacteria. An example of this is the effect of fructo-oligosaccharides on the growth of bifidobacteria. The importance of bifidobacteria is that they may be one of the major contributors to colonization resistance in the colon, thereby protecting the host from invasion by pathogenic species. Foods which selectively stimulate the growth of gut bacteria are known as pre-biotics.

THE ROLE OF CARBOHYDRATES IN MAINTENANCE OF HEALTH

CARBOHYDRATES IN THE DIET

While the amount of carbohydrate required to avoid ketosis is very small carbohydrate provides the majority of energy in the diets of most people. There are many reasons why this is desirable. In addition to providing easily available energy for oxidative metabolism, carbohydrate-containing foods are vehicles for important micronutrients and phytochemicals. Dietary carbohydrate is important to maintain glycemic homeostasis and for gastrointestinal integrity and function. Unlike fat and protein, high levels of dietary carbohydrate, provided it is obtained from a variety of sources, is not associated with adverse health effects. Finally, diets high in carbohydrate as compared to those high in fat, reduce the likelihood of developing obesity and its co-morbid conditions. An optimum diet should consist of at least 55% of total energy coming from carbohydrate obtained from a variety of food sources. The consultation agreed that when carbohydrate consumption levels are at or above 75% of total energy there could be significant adverse effects on nutritional status by the exclusion of adequate quantities of protein, fat and other essential nutrients. In arriving at its recommendation of a minimum of 55% of total energy from carbohydrate, the consultation realised that a significant percentage of total energy needs to be provided by protein and fat, but that their contribution to total energy intakes will vary from one country to another on the basis of food consumption patterns and food availability.

ENERGY BALANCE

In adults, it is important that the amount of energy ingested be matched to the amount of energy expended. Maintenance of energy balance is important in order to avoid obesity and its associated co-morbidities such as diabetes and cardiovascular disease. Positive energy balance and obesity occur when total energy intake exceeds total energy expenditure, regardless of composition of the excess energy. However, the composition of the diet can affect whether and to what extent positive energy balance occurs. The composition of the diet can also affect the ability to maintain energy balance. In particular, diets containing at least 55% of energy from a variety of carbohydrate sources, as compared to high fat diets, reduce the likelihood that body fat accumulation will occur. Substantial data suggest that diets high in fat content tend to promote consumption of more total energy than diets high in carbohydrates. This effect may be due to the low energy density of high carbohydrate diets, since total volume of food consumed appears to provide an important satiety cue. There are no data to suggest that different types of carbohydrates differentially affect total energy intake. In addition to affecting the chance of having excess energy available, the composition of the diet also affects the proportion of excess energy that will be stored as body fat. The body has a large fat storage capacity and excess dietary fat is stored very efficiently in adipose tissue. Alternatively, the body's capacity to store carbohydrate is limited and excess carbohydrate is not efficiently stored as body fat. Instead, excess carbohydrate tends to be oxidized, leading to indirect fat accumulation via reductions in fat oxidation. Excess fat and carbohydrate were previously thought to be equally fattening. This was due to the assumption that de novo lipogenesis was a commonly used pathway for disposal of excess carbohydrate. The available data suggest, however, that this process occurs rarely in human subjects and only in situations of appreciable carbohydrate overfeeding. In most usual circumstances, accumulation of body fat via de novo lipogenesis is quantitatively very low. While noting the low overall contribution of de novo lipogenesis to body fat accumulation, it should be noted that de novo lipogenesis is increased with insulin resistance and with extremely high consumption of sucrose or fructose.

PHYSICAL ACTIVITY

Maintenance of energy balance is dependent both on energy intake and energy expenditure. Maintaining regular physical activity greatly reduces the likelihood of creating positive energy balance, regardless of the composition of the diet. There is agreement that the combination of a high carbohydrate diet and regular physical activity is the optimal arrangement to avoid positive energy balance and obesity. The increased energy needs of physical activity can be supplied by carbohydrate or fat. The importance of carbohydrate in the diet becomes more critical as the amount and intensity of physical activity increases. In many developing countries, the major challenge is to meet daily energy needs created by high levels of daily physical labour. In such cases, any combination of carbohydrate and fat which provides sufficient energy is to be encouraged. Many countries recommend increasing leisure time physical activity. While increased physical activity would clearly increase energy needs, these do not create needs for specific macronutrients. Rather, the optimum diet identified above is considered sufficient to provide for such physical activity. There is substantial evidence that supplemental carbohydrate can improve performance for the elite endurance-trained athlete. A high carbohydrate diet during a few days preceding an endurance event, carbohydrate loading, a high carbohydrate pre-event meal and carbohydrate supplementation in the form of carbohydrate-containing beverages have all been shown to enhance performance during long-distance cycling and running. There is, however, no evidence that such carbohydrate supplementation would improve performance for the majority of people who engage in recreational physical activity of lower intensity and duration. On the other hand, carbohydrate intake following exercise can help to quickly replenish depleted glycogen stores.

CARBOHYDRATE AND BEHAVIOUR

It has been suggested that food intake could have important effects on behaviour. While providing breakfast to children who do not typically eat breakfast can increase cognitive performance, it is less clear that the overall composition of the diet can affect behaviour. It has been suggested that sugar consumption leads to hyperactivity in children. However, an extensive review of the literature in this area concluded that there is no evidence to support the claim that refined sugar intake has any significant influence on either behaviour or" cognitive performance in children. Because glucose is an essential fuel for the central nervous system, carbohydrate has also been suggested to play a role in memory and cognitive function. While there appears to be a relationship between glucose levels and memory processing, the clinical significance of this relationship remains unclear.

CARBOHYDRATE THROUGH THE LIFE CYCLE

Energy and nutrient needs are increased in pregnancy and lactation, and the primary challenge for pregnant women is to meet these increased energy needs in order to ensure healthy offspring. It has been observed that where variety in the food supply is low and carbohydrate intake is high, a low birth weight is more common. This raises concerns about the adequacy of high carbohydrate diets to meet the energy and nutrient needs of pregnancy when food variety is limited. Energy and nutrient needs should be met by consumption of a wide variety of carbohydrate foods. There is also some concern about excessive fat intake in pregnancy since it may be associated with risk of obesity in the mother. In many countries, infants receive 45-55% of energy from fat through breastmilk or formulas and 35-45% of energy from carbohydrate. While specific reductions in fat intake are not recommended below the age of two years, infants in many countries consume lower fat diets. This does not present a problem as long as energy requirements are fulfilled. From the age of two and on, the optimum diet should be gradually introduced. During the first four to six months of life, exclusive breast feeding is recommended as this tailors the concentration of lactose to the maturing neonatal and infant gut, particularly while colonic microflora and pancreatic amylase production are developing. For infants fed on formula, the carbohydrate and other nutrient components should usually mimic breast milk to the extent possible and in accordance with standards of the Codex Alimentarius. Carbohydrate digestion in the neonate and young infant is significantly influenced by both gastrointestinal maturation and the chemical nature of the carbohydrate ingested.

The establishment of colonic microflora is responsible for colonic carbohydrate scavenging, converting any carbohydrate entering the colon into short chain fatty acids. Any disturbances or inappropriate development of this microflora (incorrect infant formula, antibiotics, infection) leads to colonic carbohydrate overloading and diarrhoea. Lactose from dairy products can be a major source of carbohydrate for young children. In addition, milk represents an excellent source of high quality protein, calcium, and riboflavin. In most populations, even those with low lactase activity, milk can be ingested in small amounts, especially after meals with dilution by co-ingestion. Fermented dairy products can be valuable items in the diet of most people irrespective of intestinal lactase status. Often the transition from childhood to adulthood is associated with changes in dietary pattern. In developing countries, children frequently consume very high carbohydrate intakes from a single or a small number of sources, while adults have greater variety. In such cases, the adult diet is preferred. In developed countries, on the other hand, surveys indicate that children have higher intakes of carbohydrate from more sources than adults. In those countries, the diet consumed by children would seem to be more beneficial. In both situations, at least 55% of carbohydrate energy from a variety of sources is the optimum. Individualization of carbohydrate intake is necessary for elderly populations. Elderly individuals in many countries are at risk as regards both malnutrition and obesity. Food intake patterns can be altered by changes in taste perception, chronic disease and medication use. While a high carbohydrate diet is recommended for prevention of weight gain and obesity, it should be recognized that some individuals may need diets higher in energy density (e.g. fats) in order to prevent malnutrition. Optimizing intake of carbohydrate to minimize glucose intolerance in later life is a consideration in countries where such intolerance is a problem.

DIETARY CARBOHYDRATE AND DISEASE

Carbohydrates may directly influence human diseases by affecting physiological and metabolic processes, thereby reducing risk factors for the disease or the disease process itself. Carbohydrates may also have indirect effects on diseases, for example, by displacing other nutrients or facilitating increased intakes of a wide range of other substances frequently found in carbohydrate-containing foods. Evidence of associations between carbohydrates and diseases comes from epidemiological and clinical studies. There are relatively few examples in which direct causal links between carbohydrates and diseases have been proven. Thus the nutrient-disease or food-disease associations discussed below must be considered in terms of the strength of evidence from a range of observational studies and clinical experiments and the existence of plausible hypotheses.

OBESITY

The frequency of obesity has increased dramatically in many developed and developing countries. This is of profound public health importance because of the clearly defined negative effect of obesity, especially when centrally distributed, in relation to diabetes, coronary heart disease and other chronic diseases of lifestyle. Genetic and environmental factors play a role in determining the propensity for obesity in populations and individuals. Lack of physical activity is believed to contribute to the increasing rates of obesity observed in many countries and may be a factor in whether an individual who is at risk will become overweight or obese. High carbohydrate foods promote satiety in the short term.

As fat is stored more efficiently than excess carbohydrate, use of high carbohydrate foods is likely to reduce the risk of obesity in the long term. Much controversy surrounds the extent to which sugars and starch promote obesity. There is no direct evidence to implicate either of these groups of carbohydrates in the etiology of obesity, based on data derived from studies in affluent societies. Nevertheless, it is important to reiterate that excess energy in any form will promote body fat accumulation and that excess consumption of low fat foods, while not as obesity-producing as excess consumption of high fat products, will lead to obesity if energy expenditure is not increased. While high carbohydrate diets may help reduce the risk of obesity by preventing overconsumption of energy, there is no evidence to suggest that the macronutrient composition of a low energy diet influences the rate and extent of weight loss in the treatment of obese patients.

NON-INSULIN DEPENDENT DIABETES MELLITUS (NIDDM)

High rates of NIDDM in all population groups are associated with rapid cultural changes in populations previously consuming traditional diets, and also with increasing obesity, especially when centrally distributed. Although the precise mode of inheritance has not been established, there is no doubt that genetic factors are involved. Certain populations appear to have a strong predisposition to the development of NIDDM to the extent that in some groups about half the adult population have the disease. Within all populations a family history of NIDDM is an important predisposing factor. Diet and lifestyle-related conditions which may lead to obesity will clearly influence the risk of developing NIDDM in populations and individuals who are susceptible to this condition.

Foods rich in non-starch polysaccharides and carbohydrate-containing foods with a low glycemic index appear to protect against diabetes, the effect being independent of body mass index. In terms of disease prevention, it is not possible on the basis of current data to distinguish the relative merits of different types of non-starch polysaccharides. Some epidemiological evidence suggests particular benefit of appropriately processed cereal foods, while other epidemiological and clinical studies suggest benefits of non-starch polysaccharide from legumes and pectin-rich foods. Thus, avoiding obesity and increasing intakes of a wide range of foods rich in non-starch polysaccharide and carbohydrate-containing foods with a low glycemic index offers the best means of reducing the rapidly increasing rates of NIDDM in many countries. Consuming a wide range of carbohydrate foods is now regarded as acceptable in the nutritional management of people who have already developed NIDDM. It has been suggested that between 60 and 70 per cent of total energy should be derived from a mix of mono-unsaturated fatty acids and carbohydrates. Carbohydrates should principally be derived from a wide range of appropriately processed cereals, vegetables and fruit, with particular emphasis on those foods which have a low glycemic index.

The goal to achieve and maintain ideal body weight remains paramount, ensuring that foods high in fat which might predispose to obesity are not encouraged, even though they might have a low glycemic index. Sucrose and other sugars have not been directly implicated in the etiology of diabetes and recommendations concerning intake relate primarily to the avoidance of all energy-dense foods in order to reduce obesity. Most recommendations for the management of diabetes permit modest (30-50 g/day) intakes of sucrose and other added sugars in the diabetic dietary prescription provided these are: a) consumed within the context of total energy allowance; b) nutrient-dense foods and foods rich in non-starch polysaccharides are not displaced; and, c) they are incorporated as part of a mixed meal. In some populations where fat intake is relatively low and sucrose intake high, a reduced intake of sucrose may be considered in the diabetic dietary prescription. Increased meal frequency under iso-energetic conditions does not, in the long term, appear to be associated with any alteration in glycemic control.

This suggests that personal preference is the key determinant of meal frequency, provided that body weight and daily (as well as long-term) glycemic control are not adversely influenced. Special diabetic food products are not generally recommended and fructose is not regarded as having any particular merits as a sweetener when compared with other added sugars. However, low-energy beverages containing alternative non-nutritive sweeteners may be useful for people with diabetes. Dietary factors have not been conclusively shown to be risk factors for insulin-dependent diabetes and the key advice concerning carbohydrates in the management of this condition concerns distribution of intake of carbohydrates during the day. Carbohydrate intake needs to be regularly distributed and balanced with injected insulin. The general principles of the diabetic dietary approach to non-insulin dependent diabetes may also be applied to those with insulin-dependent diabetes.

CARDIOVASCULAR DISEASE

Many genetic and lifestyle factors are involved in the etiology of coronary heart disease and influence both the atherosclerotic and thrombotic processes underlying the clinical manifestations of this disease. Dietary factors may influence these processes directly or via a range of cardiovascular disease risk factors. Obesity, particularly when centrally distributed, is associated with an appreciable increase in the risk of coronary heart disease. There is also evidence implicating specific nutrients and, in particular, high intakes of some saturated fatty acids appear to be important promoters of coronary heart disease. On the other hand, there is increasing evidence of a strong protective effect by a range of antioxidant nutrients. Increasing carbohydrate intake can assist in the reduction of saturated fat and many fruits and vegetables rich in carbohydrates are also rich in several antioxidants. Cereal foods rich in non-starch polysaccharides have been shown to be protective against coronary heart disease in a series of prospective studies.

There is no evidence for a causal role of sucrose in the etiology of coronary heart disease. The cornerstone of dietary advice aimed at reducing coronary heart disease risk is to increase the intake of carbohydrate-rich foods, especially cereals, vegetables and fruits rich in non-starch polysaccharide, at the expense of fat. Among those who are overweight or obese it is more important to reduce total fat intake and to encourage the consumption of the most appropriate carbohydrate-containing foods.

There has been concern that a substantial increase in carbohydrate-containing food at the expense of fat, might result in a decrease in high-density lipoprotein and an increase in very low-density lipoprotein and triglycerides in the blood. There is, however, no evidence that this occurs when the increase in carbohydrates results from increased consumption of vegetables, fruits and appropriately processed cereals, over prolonged periods. Certain non-starch polysaccharides (for example b -glucans) have been shown to have an appreciable effect in lowering serum cholesterol when consumed in naturally occurring foods, or foods which have been enriched by purified forms, or even when fed as dietary supplements. Such polysaccharides may be used in the management of patients with existing hypercholesterolemia but their role, if any, in the prevention of coronary heart disease remains to be established. Less information is available concerning the role of carbohydrates in other cardiovascular diseases. Plant foods are good sources of potassium and reducing the sodium to potassium ratio may help to reduce the risk of hypertension.

Limited data suggest a protective effect of vegetables and fruit in cerebrovascular disease. There has been considerable debate in many developed countries which have high rates of coronary heart disease regarding the age at which children should start to reduce fat intake towards the recommended level for adults. Clearly children require an adequate intake of energy for growth, and it is important that this does not include an excessive intake of carbohydrates at a very young age. It is generally accepted that dietary carbohydrate should gradually be increased and fat reduced after the age of two years, so that by the age of five years children should have reached a diet in the range of that recommended for adults. This advice should, of course, include the key dietary guidelines for children and adolescents, which suggest that nutritional adequacy should be achieved by eating a wide variety of foods and that energy intake should be adequate to promote growth and development, and to reach and maintain desirable body weight.

CANCER

Diet is widely regarded as important in the etiology of colorectal cancer with meat and fat considered the primary risk factors, and fruit, vegetable and cereal foods considered to be protective. Cancer is a disease associated with well-recognized genetic abnormalities and for colorectal cancer in particular, defects in a number of genes have been clearly defined. These genes mostly code for proteins responsible for the control of either cell growth, cell-to-cell communication or DNA repair. They are mainly oncogenes or tumor suppressor genes. For the development of colorectal cancer an individual must acquire several of these genetic abnormalities in the same cell. The acquisition of gene defects in somatic cells is thought to be through DNA damage and a resultant failure of the DNA repair system (or of apoptosis). Dietary carbohydrate is thought to be protective through mechanisms involving arrest of cell growth, differentiation and selection of damaged cells for cell death (apoptosis). This is probably achieved primarily through the action of butyric acid which is formed in the colon from fermentation of carbohydrates such as resistant starch and non-starch polysaccharides. Such carbohydrates are found mostly in cereals, fruit and vegetables.

The process of fermentation may protect the colorectal area against the genetic damage that leads to colorectal cancer through other mechanisms which include: a) the dilution of potential carcinogens; b) the reduction of products of protein fermentation through stimulation of bacterial growth; c) pH effects; d) maintenance of the gut mucosal barrier; and, e) effects on bile acid degradation. These mechanisms, however, are much less well-established. Carbohydrate staple foods are a source of phytoestrogens which may be protective for breast cancer. Cancer risk is increased for the obese. This applies especially to cancers of the breast and uterus. However, this is a general effect of total energy intake and not specifically of carbohydrates. Dietary carbohydrates do not have a known role in the etiology of lung, breast, stomach, prostate, pancreas, oesophagus, liver or cervical cancers. There is, however, some evidence that there is an increased risk of ovarian cancer in women with mild galactosemia.

GASTROINTESTINAL DISEASES OTHER THAN CANCER

Intakes of non-starch polysaccharides and resistant starch are the most important contributors to stool weight. Therefore, increasing consumption of foods rich in these carbohydrates is a very effective means of preventing and treating constipation, as well as haemorrhoids and anal fissures.

Bran and other cereal sources containing non-starch polysaccharide also appear to protect against diverticular disease and have an important role in the treatment of this condition. Obesity is an important risk factor for gallstones. High intakes of carbohydrate may facilitate the colonization of bifidobacteria and lactobacilli in the gut and thus reduce the risk of acute infective gastrointestinal illnesses.

DENTAL CARIES

The incidence of dental caries is influenced by a number of factors. Foods containing sugars or starch may be easily broken down by a-amylase and bacteria in the mouth and can produce acid which increases the risk of caries. Starches with a high glycemic index produce more pronounced changes in plaque pH than low glycemic index starch, especially when combined with sugars. However, the impact of these carbohydrates on caries is dependent on the type of food, frequency of consumption, degree of oral hygiene performed, availability of fluoride, salivary function, and genetic factors. Prevention programmes to control and eliminate dental caries should focus on fluoridation and adequate oral hygiene, and not on sucrose intake alone.

OTHER CONDITIONS

There are a number of inherited conditions having significant implications for restricted dietary carbohydrate intake in infants and children. These include rare conditions such as galactosemia, fructose intolerance, a wide range of glycogen storage diseases, sucrose deficiencies and monosaccharide transport deficiencies.

Though rare in incidence, their early detection and careful dietary management is important if severe handicap or pathology is to be avoided.

THE ROLE OF THE GLYCEMIC INDEX IN FOOD CHOICE

Carbohydrate foods often contain vitamins and minerals plus other compounds, such as phytochemicals and antioxidants, which may have health implications. Consuming a wide variety of carbohydrate foods is therefore recommended as this is more likely to be a nutritionally adequate diet with the health benefits commonly ascribed to carbohydrate foods. Food choice depends not only on nutrition and health considerations but also on factors such as local availability, cultural acceptability and individual likes and needs. There is no one measure which can be used to guide food choices in all cases. The chemical composition of foods (e.g. fat, sugars, dietary fibre content) should be an important factor influencing food choice. However, simply knowing the chemical nature of the carbohydrates in foods, for example, does not reliably indicate their actual physiologic effects.

Foods which are good choices in some situations may not be the best choices in others. Likewise, foods which are poor choices in some situations may be good choices in others. Two indices of carbohydrate foods based on their physiologic functions have been proposed. A recently suggested satiety index measures the satiety value of equal energy portions of foods relative to a standard, which is white bread.

The factors which control food intake are complex and satiety needs to be distinguished from satiation.

Nevertheless, investigation of satiety indices of foods is considered an interesting area of future research, which, if validated, may aid in the selection of appropriate carbohydrate foods to promote energy balance. A more established index is the glycemic index which can be used to classify foods based on their blood glucose raising potential.

DEFINITION OF GLYCEMIC INDEX (GI)

The glycemic index is defined as the incremental area under the blood glucose response curve of a 50g carbohydrate portion of a test food expressed as a percent of the response to the same amount of carbohydrate from a standard food taken by the same subject. The italicized terms are discussed below because the methods used to determine the glycemic index of foods and to apply the information to diets may profoundly affect the results obtained.

Incremental area under the curve

Table. Sample blood glucose responses to the ingestion of 50g carbohydrate

Minutes	0	15	30	45	60	90	120	IAUC
Standard #1	4.3	6.3	7.9	5.3	4.1	4.6	4.9	114
Standard #2	4.0	6.0	6.7	5.5	5.3	5.0	4.2	155
Standard #3	4.1	5.8	8.0	6.5	5.9	4.8	3.9	179
Test Food	4.0	5.0	5.8	5.4	4.8	4.2	4.4	93

A number of different methods have been used to calculate the area under the curve. For most glycemic index data, the area under the curve has been calculated as the incremental area under the blood glucose response curve (IAUC), ignoring the area beneath the fasting concentration. This can be calculated geometrically by applying the trapezoid rule. When a blood glucose value falls below the baseline, only the area above the fasting level is included. Sample data are shown in Table 1. The data for Standard #1 are used in the diagram in Figure 2 to illustrate the details of the actual calculation.

50g carbohydrate portion

The portion of food tested should contain 50g of glycemic (available) carbohydrate. In practice, glycemic carbohydrate is often measured as total carbohydrate minus dietary fibre, as determined by the AOAC method. Since this method does not include RS 1 and RS2 when they are present, they will be mistakenly included as glycemic carbohydrate.

Blood glucose response

This is normally measured in capillary whole blood. Plasma glucose can be used to determine the glycemic index and gives similar values. However, capillary blood is preferred because it is easier to obtain, the rise in blood glucose is greater than in venous plasma and the results for capillary blood glucose are less variable than those for venous plasma glucose.

Thus, differences between foods are larger and easier to detect statistically using capillary blood glucose. An illustration of the difference between glucose as measured in simultaneously-obtained venous plasma and capillary whole blood is shown in Table 2.

Standard food

Either white bread or glucose can be used as the standard food. The GI values obtained if white bread is used are about 1.4 times those obtained if glucose is the standard food. Other standard foods could be used, but to enable comparison with data in the literature, the GI of the new standard food relative to standardized white bread or glucose should be established.

FACTORS INFLUENCING THE BLOOD GLUCOSE RESPONSES OF FOODS

Starchy foods with a low GI are digested and absorbed more slowly than foods with a high GI. Some factors that influence glycemic properties of foods are listed in.

CALCULATION OF GLYCEMIC INDEX OF MEALS OR DIETS

The GI can be applied in a detailed fashion to mixed meals or whole diets by calculating the weighted GI value of the meal or diet. For example, the way to calculate the GI of a meal containing bread, cereal, sucrose, milk and orange juice is shown in Table 4.

* Values for each food equals the proportion of total glycemic carbohydrate multiplied by the food GI. The sum of these values is the meal GI.

Using this type of calculation, there is a good correlation between meal GI and the observed glycemic responses of meals of equal nutrient composition. Blood glucose responses are also influenced by the amount of carbohydrate in the meal. To compare the expected glycemic load of meals with different carbohydrate contents, a non-linear adjustment can be applied but this has only been tested in normal subjects.

For detailed application of the GI, a value of the GI for every food in the diet or meal needs to have been assigned (for many foods the value has to be estimated). The accuracy of the calculation depends upon the accuracy of the GI values ascribed to foods, which may vary from place to place due to local factors such as variety, cooking, processing, etc. Foods particularly prone to such variation include rice, potatoes and bananas.

PRACTICAL APPLICATION OF THE GLYCEMIC INDEX

The glycemic index can be used, in conjunction with information about food composition, to guide food choices. For practical application, the glycemic index is useful to rank foods by developing exchange lists of categories of low glycemic index foods, such as legumes, pearled barley, lightly refined grains (e.g. whole grain pumpernickel bread, or breads made from coarse flour), pasta, etc. Specific local foods should be included in such lists where information is available (e.g. green bananas in the Caribbean and specific rice varieties in Southeast Asia). In choosing carbohydrate foods, both glycemic index and food composition must be considered. Some low GI foods may not always be a good choice because they are high in fat. Conversely, some high GI foods may be a good choice because of convenience or because they have low energy and high nutrient content. It is not necessary or desirable to exclude or avoid all high GI foods.

PHYSIOLOGIC AND THERAPEUTIC EFFECTS OF LOW GLYCEMIC INDEX FOODS

Meals containing low GI foods reduce both postprandial blood glucose and insulin responses. Animal studies suggest that incorporating slowly digested starch into the diet delays the onset of insulin resistance. Some epidemiologic studies suggest that a low GI diet is associated with reduced risk of developing non-insulin diabetes in men and women. Clinical trials in normal, diabetic and hyperlipidemic subjects show that low GI diets reduce mean blood glucose concentrations, reduce insulin secretion and reduce serum triglycerides in individuals with hypertriglyceridemia. In addition, the digestibility of the carbohydrate in low GI foods is generally less than that of high GI foods. Thus, low GI foods increase the amount of carbohydrate entering the colon and increase colonic fermentation and short chain fatty acid production. This has implications for systemic nitrogen and lipid metabolism, and for local events within the colon.

GOALS AND GUIDELINES FOR CARBOHYDRATE FOOD CHOICES

RATIONALE AND FRAMEWORK

Although the scientific basis for dietary guidelines requires an understanding of physiology and health relationships, the guidance most helpful to consumers uses food-based terms.

In preparing such guidelines, food traditions and beliefs must be taken into account and the total food intake should reflect practical issues, such as meal patterns, food status, celebratory or usual role, seasonal availability, affordability and sustainability. These, including the health priorities, are matters for national policy makers.

PRINCIPLES OF CARBOHYDRATE FOOD CHOICES

The principles are:

- To acknowledge the socio-cultural context, lifestyle and stage of life-cycle, in food carbohydrate choice;
- To give preference to food choices rather than to nutrient goals in carbohydrate food choices, and in so doing:
  - — Use food categories as a guide to chemically defined carbohydrate type.
  - — Use numbers of portions (serving sizes) of foods from designated food categories in order to provide semi-quantitative food-based advice. This may imply that meal frequency would need to increase in some cultures, because the accommodation of enough carbohydrate food in the course of the day, without an excessive amount on any one occasion, requires more frequent servings and consumption;
- To ensure the acceptability and practicality of any recommended change in carbohydrate food intake;
- To acknowledge that there may be unintended consequences involved in carbohydrate food intake change, and also to ensure that risks involved in dietary changes from traditional diets is considered;
- To monitor the intake of carbohydrate foods and, wherever possible, of chemically defined carbohydrate components of those foods in relation to health issues.

CARBOHYDRATE NUTRIENT AND FOOD GOALS

Nutrient goals

The minimum amount of carbohydrate in the human diet that is needed to avoid ketosis is of the order of 50 g/day in adults. Beyond this, additional energy needs are best met by nutrient-dense carbohydrate foods. There must, of course, be adequate intakes of protein (with essential amino acids) and essential fatty acids from fat. Moderate intake of sugar-rich foods can also provide for a palatable and nutritious diet.

Food goals

There are a number of approaches to translating nutrient recommendations to food goals:

- Recommending the total weight of food groups to be consumed. Various national food guides have suggested quantities of specific foods to be consumed, such as fruits and vegetables, and pulses, nuts and seeds.
- Examining sources of carbohydrate foods in various diets, particularly diets which have desirable total carbohydrate intakes or from countries where the incidence of lifestyle diseases is low. Recommendations can then be made on the basis of intakes.
- Examining major food groups which contain carbohydrate foods and recommending numbers of servings of those food groups. Numerous countries around the world, both developed and developing, have produced food guides with such groupings, and considering the level of agreement that exists for carbohydrate as a percent energy, these food guides are remarkably consistent in their advice.
- Examining indices which exist to describe various physiological properties of carbohydrate-containing foods, such as glycemic index values and values from other indices which are presently being developed.

On the basis of the above approaches, and taking into account the principles for carbohydrate food choice, the following recommendations can be made:

- A variety of foods should provide the carbohydrate in the diet, not a single or small number of sources.
- Cereals, roots, pulses, fruit and vegetables are all components of a healthy diet throughout the world.
- Cereal foods or root crops, where this is the main staple, should provide the major source of carbohydrate energy.
- Intake of fruits and vegetables (including potatoes in developed countries) should be high. As well as being a valuable source of carbohydrate, fruit and vegetables are an important source of antioxidant vitamins and other food components.
- Consumption of pulses, nuts and seeds should be encouraged. While this group often represents only a small amount of carbohydrate energy, these foods are a good source of protein and micronutrients. They should be consumed with cereals to optimize protein quality.

- At least small quantities of milk products are desirable, even when low lactase activity exists, since these are a good source of protein and micronutrients.
- These recommendations apply to all individuals over the age of two years, with adjustments as necessary for growth and the increased demand of pregnancy and lactation.

TRANSLATION FROM CARBOHYDRATE NUTRIENTS TO FOODS

Achieving goals for intake of carbohydrates does not ensure nutritional adequacy. Carbohydrate foods provide a range of nutrients and other substances essential for health in addition to energy. It is therefore essential to consume a variety of foods in order to derive the full benefits of a high carbohydrate diet.

Nutrients from foods require monitoring. For example, in Iran carbohydrate foods include vegetables (250 g/day), fruits (210 g/day), pulses (20 g/day) and cereals (wheat at about 250 g/day and rice 110 g/day, uncooked). Wheat has mostly been consumed as bread with traditional pastries being festive foods. Recently, consumption of the latter has increased substantially with potential reduction of nutritionally useful food groups traditionally accompanying bread. This may not significantly impact on total carbohydrate intake, but could influence nutritional adequacy.

Traditional methods of food preparation and preservation facilitate food choice variety, and promote nutritional benefits. Alteration of traditional practices may compromise such benefits. Ongoing monitoring may be required to guard against nutritional inadequacy.

CONSIDERATIONS FOR TARGET AUDIENCES

Planners and policy makers need to:

- Recognize dietary goals of at least 55% of total energy from a variety of carbohydrate sources.
- Recognize the extent of change necessary in order to meet these goals (e.g. it may take considerable change in food production and consumption to meet goals in Western countries).
- Understand that there must be a gradual transition in meeting new dietary guidelines and that new terminology will need to be gradually accepted.
- Consider the effects of economic and cultural factors in achieving dietary goals.
- Develop clear guides about the types and quantities of food recommended.
- Develop methods to monitor food consumption to meet dietary goals.

Primary producers and processors need to:

- Consider how existing and new technologies can be used to help meet dietary goals regarding the quantity and nutritional properties of food carbohydrates, as well as levels of micronutrients and other desirable food components.
- Provide foods, such as breakfast cereals and snack foods that are high in NSP, low in energy density, and with a low glycemic index.
- Increase the availability and convenience of fruits and vegetables.
- Provide appropriate information to the consumer on food labels.

To facilitate individual choice

- Provide easily understandable food-based guides for the consumer.

4

Fats

AN OVERVIEW

Fats consist of a wide group of compounds that are generally soluble in organic solvents and largely insoluble in water. Chemically, fats are generally triesters of glycerol and fatty acids. Fats may be either solid or liquid at room temperature, depending on their structure and composition. Although the words "oils", "fats", and "lipids" are all used to refer to fats, "oils" is usually used to refer to fats that are liquids at normal room temperature, while "fats" is usually used to refer to fats that are solids at normal room temperature. "Lipids" is used to refer to both liquid and solid fats, along with other related substances. The word "oil" is used for any substance that does not mix with water and has a greasy feel, such as petroleum (or crude oil) and heating oil, regardless of its chemical structure.

Fats form a category of lipid, distinguished from other lipids by their chemical structure and physical properties. This category of molecules is important for many forms of life, serving both structural and metabolic functions. They are an important part of the diet of most heterotrophs (including humans). Fats or lipids are broken down in the body by enzymes called lipases produced in the pancreas.

Examples of edible animal fats are lard (pig fat), fish oil, and butter or ghee. They are obtained from fats in the milk, meat and under the skin of the animal. Examples of edible plant fats are peanut, soya bean, sunflower, sesame, coconut, olive, and vegetable oils. Margarine and vegetable shortening, which can be derived from the above oils, are used mainly for baking. These examples of fats can be categorized into saturated fats and unsaturated fats.

CHEMICAL STRUCTURE

There are many different kinds of fats, but each is a variation on the same chemical structure. All fats consist of fatty acids (chains of carbon and hydrogen atoms, with a carboxylic acid group at one end) bonded to a backbone structure, often glycerol (a "backbone" of carbon, hydrogen, and oxygen). Chemically, this is a triester of glycerol, an ester being the molecule formed from the reaction of the carboxylic acid and an organic alcohol. As a simple visual illustration, if the kinks and angles of these chains were straightened out, the molecule would have the shape of a capital letter E. The fatty acids would each be a horizontal line; the glycerol "backbone" would be the vertical line that joins the horizontal lines. Fats therefore have "ester" bonds.

The properties of any specific fat molecule depend on the particular fatty acids that constitute it. Different fatty acids are composed of different numbers of carbon and hydrogen atoms.

The carbon atoms, each bonded to two neighboring carbon atoms, form a zigzagging chain; the more carbon atoms there are in any fatty acid, the longer its chain will be. Fatty acids with long chains are more susceptible to intermolecular forces of attraction (in this case, van der Waals forces), raising its melting point. Long chains also yield more energy per molecule when metabolized.

A fat's constituent fatty acids may also differ in the number of hydrogen atoms that are bonded to the chain of carbon atoms. Each carbon atom is typically bonded to two hydrogen atoms. When a fatty acid has this typical arrangement, it is called "saturated", because the carbon atoms are saturated with hydrogen; meaning they are bonded to as many hydrogens as possible. In other fats, a carbon atom may instead bond to only one other hydrogen atom, and have a double bond to a neighboring carbon atom.

This results in an "unsaturated" fatty acid. More specifically, it would be a "monounsaturated" fatty acid, whereas, a "polyunsaturated" fatty acid would be a fatty acid with more than one double bond. Saturated and unsaturated fats differ in their energy content and melting point. Since an unsaturated fat contains fewer carbon-hydrogen bonds than a saturated fat with the same number of carbon atoms, unsaturated fats will yield slightly less energy during metabolism than saturated fats with the same number of carbon atoms. Saturated fats can stack themselves in a closely packed arrangement, so they can freeze easily and are typically solid at room temperature. But the rigid double bond in an unsaturated fat fundamentally changes the chemistry of the fat. There are two ways the double bond may be arranged: the isomer with both parts of the chain on the same side of the double bond (the cis-isomer), or the isomer with the parts of the chain on opposite sides of the double bond (the trans-isomer). Most trans-isomer fats (commonly called trans fats) are commercially produced rather than naturally occurring.

The cis-isomer introduces a kink into the molecule that prevents the fats from stacking efficiently as in the case of fats with saturated chains. This decreases intermolecular forces between the fat molecules, making it more difficult for unsaturated cis-fats to freeze; they are typically liquid at room temperature. Trans fats may still stack like saturated fats, and are not as susceptible to metabolization as other fats. Trans fats may significantly increase the risk of coronary heart disease.

IMPORTANCE FOR LIVING ORGANISMS

Vitamins A, D, E, and K are fat-soluble, meaning they can only be digested, absorbed, and transported in conjunction with fats. Fats are also sources of essential fatty acids, an important dietary requirement.

Fats play a vital role in maintaining healthy skin and hair, insulating body organs against shock, maintaining body temperature, and promoting healthy cell function.

Fats also serve as energy stores for the body, containing about 37.8 kilojoules (9 Calories) per gram of fat. They are broken down in the body to release glycerol and free fatty acids. The glycerol can be converted to glucose by the liver and thus used as a source of energy.

Fat also serves as a useful buffer towards a host of diseases. When a particular substance, whether chemical or biotic—reaches unsafe levels in the bloodstream, the body can effectively dilute—or at least maintain equilibrium of—the offending substances by storing it in new fat tissue. This helps to protect vital organs, until such time as the offending substances can be metabolized and/or removed from the body by such means as excretion, urination, accidental or intentional bloodletting, sebum excretion, and hair growth.

While it is nearly impossible to remove fat completely from the diet, it would be unhealthy to do so. Some fatty acids are essential nutrients, meaning that they can't be produced in the body from other compounds and need to be consumed in small amounts. All other fats required by the body are non-essential and can be produced in the body from other compounds.

ADIPOSE TISSUE

In animals, adipose, or fatty tissue is the body's means of storing metabolic energy over extended periods of time. Depending on current physiological conditions, adipocytes store fat derived from the diet and liver metabolism or degrade stored fat to supply fatty acids and glycerol to the circulation. These metabolic activities are regulated by several hormones (i.e., insulin, glucagon and epinephrine).

The location of the tissue determines its metabolic profile: "Visceral fat" is located within the abdominal wall (i.e., beneath the wall of abdominal muscle) whereas "subcutaneous fat" is located beneath the skin (and includes fat that is located in the abdominal area beneath the skin but above the abdominal muscle wall). Visceral fat was recently discovered to be a significant producer of signaling chemicals (ie, hormones), among which are several which are involved in inflammatory tissue responses. One of these is resistin which has been linked to obesity, insulin resistance, and Type 2 diabetes. This latter result is currently controversial, and there have been reputable studies supporting all sides on the issue.

TYPES OF FATS

Dietary fats are concentrated source of food energy. They are also the source of linoleum acid, an essential nutrient, and the fat-soluble vitamins A, D, E and K. While we all need some dietary fat each day, a tablespoon is generally sufficient when cutting back on fats, it is helpful to know which the most dietary culprits are.

Saturated fats

Saturated fats are the only fatty acids that raise blood cholesterol levels. Saturated fats are found in meats and whole dairy products like milk, cheese, cream and ice cream. Some saturated fats are also found in plant foods like tropical oils (coconut or palm kernel oil). When margarine or vegetable shortening is made from corn oil, soybean oil or other vegetable oils, hydrogen atoms are added making some of the fat molecules "saturated". This also makes the fat solid at room temperature.

Butter, margarine, and fats in meat and dairy products are all especially high in saturated fat. We can reduce the saturated fats in our diets by using skim milk and low fat cheeses instead of whole milk and cheese. We can also use less fat, oil, butter, and margarine. At the table, use tub margarine instead of butter. Another way to cut down on fat is to drain and trim meats and take the skin off poultry. Simply reducing the total amount of fat we eat goes a long way toward reducing saturated fats.

Unsaturated Fats

Unsaturated fats are usually liquid at room temperature. They are found in most vegetable products and oils. An exception is a group of tropical oils like coconut or palm kernel oil which is highly saturated. Using foods containing "polyunsaturated" and "monounsaturated" fats does not increase our risk of heart disease. However, like all fats, unsaturated fats give us 9 calories for every gram. So eating too much of these types of fat may also make us gain weight. We can reduce the fat and unsaturated fats in our diets by using less fat, oil, and margarine. We can also eat more low-fat foods like vegetables, fruits, breads, rice, pasta and cereals.

Cholesterol

Cholesterol is an essential fat made by the liver. Many people get additional cholesterol by eating meat and dairy products. Too much dietary intake may raise blood cholesterol levels, and lead to heart disease. Cholesterol is transported through the bloodstream by lipoproteins. Knowing the facts about cholesterol can reduce your risk for a heart attack or stroke. But understanding what cholesterol is and how it affects your health are only the beginning.

To keep your cholesterol under control:

- Schedule a screening
- Eat foods low in cholesterol and saturated fat
- Maintain a healthy weight
- Exercise regularly
- Follow your healthcare professional's advice

Trans Fat

Trans fats are produced when liquid oil is made into a solid fat. This process is called hydrogenation. Trans fats act like saturated fats and can raise your cholesterol level. Trans fats are listed on the label, making it easier to identify these foods.

Unless there is at least 0.5 grams or more of Trans fat in a food, the label can claim 0 grams. If you want to avoid as much Trans fat as possible, you must read the ingredient list on food labels. Look for words like hydrogenated oil or partially hydrogenated oil. Select foods that either does not contain hydrogenated oil or where liquid oil is listed first in the ingredient list. Sources of Trans fat include:

- Processed foods like snacks (crackers and chips) and baked goods (muffins, cookies and cakes) with hydrogenated oil or partially hydrogenated oil
- Stick margarines
- Shortening
- Some fast food items such as French fries

WHY DO WE NEED FATS?

Although fats have received a bad reputation for causing weight gain but still some fat is essential for survival. According to the Dietary Reference Intakes published by the USDA 20% - 35% of calories should come from fat. We need this amount of fat for:

- Body to use vitamins: Vitamins A, D, E, and K are fat-soluble vitamins, meaning that the fat in foods helps the intestines absorb these vitamins into the body.
- Brains development: Fat provides the structural components not only of cell membranes in the brain, but also of myelin, the fatty insulating sheath that surrounds each nerve fiber, enabling it to carry messages faster.
- Energy: Gram for gram fats is the most efficient source of food energy. Each gram of fat provides nine calories of energy for the body, compared with four calories per gram of carbohydrates and proteins.

- Healthier skin: One of the more obvious signs of fatty acid deficiency is dry, flaky skin. In addition to giving skin its rounded appeal, the layer of fat just beneath the skin acts as the body's own insulation to help regulate body temperature.
- Healthy cells: Fats are a vital part of the membrane that surrounds each cell of the body. Without a healthy cell membrane, the rest of the cell couldn't function.
- Making hormones: Fats are structural components of some of the most important substances in the body, including prostaglandins, hormone-like substances that regulate many of the body's functions. Fats regulate the production of sex hormones, which explains why some teenage girls who are too lean experience delayed pubertal development and amenorrhea.
- Pleasure: Besides being a nutritious energy source, fat adds to the appealing taste, texture and appearance of food. Fats carry flavor.
- Protective cushion for our organs: Many of the vital organs, especially the kidneys, heart, and intestines are cushioned by fat that helps protect them from injury and hold them in place.

SOURCES OF FAT

Ninety percent of the total fat in the nation's food supply comes from three groups of foods: 1) fats and oils; 2) meat, poultry and fish; and 3) dairy foods. The fats and oils, which include salad and cooking oils, butter, margarine and cream, are referred to as visible fats because they are easily seen and identified. The two other groups contain invisible fats, which can not be easily separated from the foods. Visible fats can become invisible once they are integrated into a food such as addition of oil, butter, or margarine in making cookies or cake.

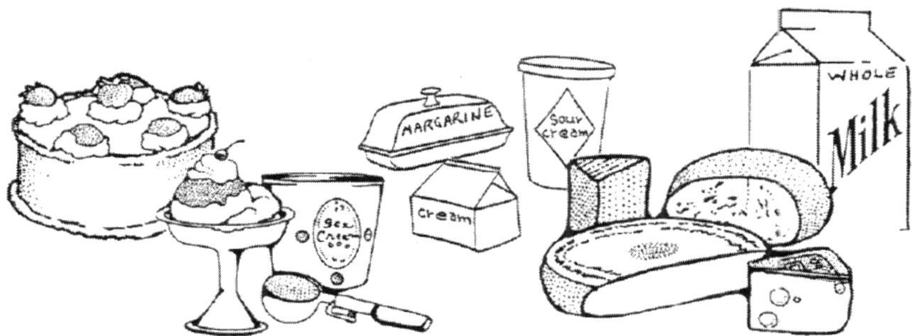

The difference between visible and invisible fat can also be described by looking at meat as an example. After trimming the outer layer of fat from the meat (the visible fat), 20 to 40 percent of its calories still come from fat distributed in the lean portion (the invisible fat). Other invisible fats are found in baked goods, nuts, peanut butter, processed meats and deep-fried foods such as potato chips.

The increase in the fat content of the American diet has come primarily from increased consumption of salad and cooking oils and shortening. The use of animal fats has actually decreased. For example, margarine, which is made from vegetable oil, now accounts for one-seventh of the fat from the fats and oils group, while butter makes up only one-tenth of this group.

HOW CAN YOU REDUCE FAT IN YOUR DIET?

The level of fat intake recommended by experts is 35 percent or less of the total calories consumed daily. This means that a person eating 2,000 Calories a day should eat no more than 700 of those Calories as fat, which is equal to about 6½ tablespoons of fat. Someone requiring 3,000 Calories a day would ideally eat no more than 1,050 Calories or 10½ tablespoons of fat per day. Of the 30 percent, no more than 10 percent should come from saturated fatty acids, up to 10 percent can come from polyunsaturated fatty acids, and with the remainder coming from monounsaturated fatty acids. Although it may not be possible to totally limit trans fatty acids, strive for as close to zero as possible. The first step in reducing fat intake is to look at the foods eaten. Most of the fat in the diet comes from visible fats, which are easier to identify. The following guidelines will help reduce visible fats in the diet:

- Bake, roast or broil foods instead of frying in fat.
- Use non-stick skillets without fat or use vegetable sprays.
- Remove any visible fat from meats and the skin from poultry.
- Visible fat and skin may be removed either before or after cooking with no difference in fat content.
- Add spices and herbs to vegetables instead of butter, sauces or gravies.
- Cool and refrigerate stews, broths and meat drippings and skim off fat before serving.

Reducing the invisible fat in the diet may be harder to do, but adopting the following practices will help.

• Choose lean cuts of meats such as flank, round or rump of beef; leg or loin of pork and all cuts of veal instead of high-fat meats such as corned beef, sausage, cold cuts, bacon and spare ribs.

• Include fish, chicken and turkey in meals

• Limit the intake of nuts, peanuts and peanut butter, which are all high in fat.

• Substitute skim or low-fat milks and their products (uncreamed or low-fat cottage cheese, low-fat yogurt, ice milk and mozzarella cheese) for whole milk and its products (cream, butter, ice cream and most cheeses).

• Check Nutrition Facts labels on foods. Margarine may have high levels of saturated fat due to hydrogenation. Choose margarines with liquid or pure vegetable oils as the first ingredient. Non-dairy whipped toppings and cream substitutes may also be high in saturated fats.

Nutrition Facts
Serving Size 1 cup (228g)
Servings Per Container 2

Amount Per Serving
Calories 260 Calories from Fat 120

	% Daily Value*
Total Fat 13g	**20%**
Saturated Fat 5g	**25%**
Trans Fat 3g	
Cholesterol 30mg	**10%**
Sodium 660mg	**28%**
Total Carbohydrate 31g	**10%**
Dietary Fiber 0g	**0%**
Sugars 5g	
Protein 5g	

Vitamin A 4%	Vitamin C 2%
Calcium 15%	Iron 4%

*Percent Daily Values are based on a 2,000-calorie diet. Your daily values may be higher or lower depending on your calorie needs:

	Calories:	2,000	2,500
Total fat	Less than	65g	80g
Sat fat	Less than	20g	25g
Cholesterol	Less than	300mg	300mg
Sodium	Less than	2,400mg	2,400mg
Total carbohydrate		300g	375g
Dietary fiber		25g	30g

Calories per gram:
Fat 9 Carbohydrate 4 Protein 4

FUNCTION OF FATS IN OUR LIFE

Fats along with proteins and carbohydrates, are one of the three nutrients used as energy sources by the body. The energy produced by fats is 9 calories per gram. Proteins and carbohydrates each provide 4 calories per gram. Total fat; the sum of saturated, monounsaturated and polyunsaturated fats. Intake of monounsaturated and polyunsaturated fats can help reduce blood cholesterol when substituted for saturated fats in the diet. A slang term for obese or adipose. In chemistry, a compound formed from chemicals called fatty acids. These fats are greasy, solid materials found in animal tissues and Fats are the major component of the flabby material of a body, commonly known as blubber.

As strange as it sounds, eating fat can actually help you lose weight. Not only that, your memory and your immune system will benefit from eating fat. It is an extremely bad idea to eliminate fat completely from your diet. "Good" fats are absolutely essential. These good fats come from things like Enova Oil, canola oil, extra virgin olive oil, flax seed, almonds, walnuts and cold-water fish. Eating the right kind of fat and getting rid of the wrong kind is what is needed.

KEY FUNCTIONS OF FAT

We need some fat - it makes up part of our brains, it protects some of our joints and it provides reserves for when we're sick - but it slips down so effortlessly, it's easy to overindulge.

- Fat provides needed energy. It is difficult to eat the large amounts of food in a very low fat diet to get all the energy you need.
- Fat is needed so your body can absorb the fat soluble vitamins A, S, E, K, and prevent deficiencies of these vitamins.
- Provides back-up energy if blood sugar supplies run out (after 4-6 hours without food).
- Provides insulation under the skin from the cold and the heat.
- Protects organs and bones from shock and provides support for organs.
- Fat surrounds and insulates nerve fibers to help transmit nerve impulses.
- Fat is part of every cell membrane in the body. It helps transport nutrients and metabolites across cell membranes.
- Your body uses fat to make a variety of other building blocks needed for everything from hormones to immune function.

if we don't have enough fat:

- Dry, scaly skin
- Hair loss
- Low body weight
- Cold intolerance
- Bruising
- Poor growth
- Lower resistance to infection
- Poor wound healing
- Loss of menstruation

FOOD SOURCES OF FAT

High intakes of fat contribute to becoming overweight; being overweight increases the chance of developing a number of diseases such as diabetes, heart disease and high blood pressure. Not only do we need to restrict the amount of fat, but we also need to consider what type of fat is restricted, as different types of fat have different effects on blood cholesterol levels and heart health.

Food contains a mixture of three types of fat; polyunsaturated, monounsaturated and saturated fats. One type of fat usually dominates in a food for example, butter is mainly saturated fat and olive oil is mainly monounsaturated. All fats contain approximately the same amount of kilojoules or energy and if eaten in large amounts will lead weight gain.

- Polyunsaturated Fats - lowers blood cholesterol and encourages heart health - Good food sources are; Vegetable oils such as safflower, soy bean, sunflower, corn, Wheat germ, wholegrain cereals and breads, Polyunsaturated margarines, Fish oils, naturally present in fish, Seeds and most nuts.
- Omega-3 fats are a type of polyunsaturated fat found mainly in oily fish (eg salmon, mackerel, sardines, herrings), canola oil, flaxseed oil (linseed oil) and walnut oil. These fats help to reduce blood clotting, blood pressure and blood fat levels.
- Monounsaturated Fats - do not raise blood cholesterol and encourages heart health - Good food source are; Avocados, peanuts, peanut oil and peanut butter, Olive oil, olives and olive oil-based margarines, Canola oil and monounsaturated table spread, Almond and hazelnuts.
- Saturated Fats - raise blood cholesterol and promote heart disease - These are the ones to reduce or avoid Major food sources are; Dairy fats such as butter, clarified butter, cultured butter, butter/margarine mix, Milk homogenised or full cream, Hard cheeses, cream cheese, sour cream, ice cream and cream, Meat fats such as lard, dripping, suet, beef tallow and chefade, White visible fat on beef, mutton, lamb, pork, poultry, Processed meat, e.g. luncheon, salami, most sausages, tinned corned beef, fatty mince pies and pates, Tropical oils such as coconut, coconut cream, palm oil and kremelta.
- Trans Fats are the other type of fat that can raise your cholesterol level just like saturated fats - Trans fats can be formed when vegetable fats are processed in certain ways. Some polyunsaturated fats are converted to trans fats when vegetable oils are chemically harden to make it spreadable such as margarine. This process is called 'hydrogenation'. These fats may be found listed in the food ingredients on packaged foods as vegetable fat, baking margarine and vegetable shortening. Foods containing this fat include pastries, biscuits, crackers, muesli bars, commercial cakes and muffins.

DAILY USAGE OF FATS

We all need some fat in our diets. In fact, it's virtually impossible to have a fat-free diet as most foods, even fruit and veg, provide small amounts of fat. As well as providing the body with a concentrated source of energy, certain components of fat are essential parts of our body cells and are needed to make hormones. Fat also helps to insulate our body and small amounts around the major organs have a protective effect. Several vitamins (vitamins A, D, E and K) are also fat-soluble and tend to be found in foods with a high fat content. Very low fat intakes mean that intakes of these vitamins, in turn, are often extremely low, too. The Department of Health recommends that no more than a third of calories come from this nutrient, while most weight loss plans rarely recommend less than 20% of calories come from fat.

NUTRITIONAL SAFETY

Some people do not do well if their diet is too high in fat, regardless of what type. They will develop a slow metabolism, constipation, lethargy, and skewed cholesterol levels if they eat too much fat. These people do best with a diet rich in fruits, vegetables, and whole grain foods.

Very few fats are bad in and of themselves. Trans fat is an oil that has been chemically manipulated to be more solid. It has been found to be particularly harmful to the arteries and is not recommended at any level in the diet. The lower the better on this one! Usually it is the proportion of fat that is the problem. Recently it has been found that a diet with too much omega-6 fat and not enough omega-3 fat leads to inflammation and suppression of the immune system. So balancing these fats is very important. Too much fat in your diet puts you at risk for Obesity,Coronary Artery Disease ,High Cholesterol, Myocardial Infarction and Hypertension.

SIDE EFFECTS

Eating too much saturated fat is one of the major risk factors for heart disease. A diet high in saturated fat causes a soft, waxy substance called cholesterol to build up in the arteries. Too much fat also increases the risk of heart disease because of its high calorie content, which increases the chance of becoming obese (another risk factor for heart disease and some types of cancer).

A large intake of polyunsaturated fat may increase the risk for some types of cancer. Reducing daily fat intake is not a guarantee against developing cancer or heart disease, but it does help reduce the risk factors.

RECOMMENDATIONS

- Choose lean, protein-rich foods such as soy, fish, skinless chicken, very lean meat, and fat-free or 1% dairy products.

- Eat foods that are naturally low in fat such as whole grains, fruits, and vegetables.
- Get plenty of soluble fiber such as oats, bran, dry peas, beans, cereal, and rice.
- Limit fried foods, processed foods, and commercially prepared baked goods (donuts, cookies, crackers).
- Limit animal products such as egg yolks, cheeses, whole milk, cream, ice cream, and fatty meats (and large portions of meats).
- Look at food labels, especially the level of saturated fat. Avoid or limit foods high in saturated fat.
- Look on food labels for words like "hydrogenated" or "partially hydrogenated" — these foods are loaded with bad fats and should be avoided.
- Liquid vegetable oil, soft margarine, and trans fatty acid-free margarine are preferable to butter, stick margarine, or shortening.

Children under age 2 should NOT be on a fat-restricted diet because cholesterol and fat are thought to be important nutrients for brain development.

It is important to read the nutrition labels and be aware of the amount of different types of fat contained in food. If you are 20, ask your health care provider about checking your cholesterol levels.

FATS AND HEART DISEASE

You're healthy, so why think about heart disease or stroke? These are diseases that only happen late in life, right? Think again. Cardiovascular disease is the number one killer in America. More than two out of every five Americans die of cardiovascular disease. Even more concerning is the fact that this silent killer is starting to attack younger people.

There is good news however; the choices you make now can minimize your risk for developing heart disease. Here are several ways you can improve your odds of enjoying a long and heart-healthy life!

Factors that increase your risk for developing heart disease:

Factors you can control	Factors you can't control
Smoking	Family history (genetics)
Diabetes	Gender (males are at higher risk earlier than females)
High blood cholesterol	Age
High blood pressure	

As you can see, many of the risk factors are in your control with some attention to your dietary patterns. By choosing healthy eating patterns you can maintain a healthy body weight, which reduces your chances of developing high blood pressure, diabetes and problems with cholesterol. More importantly, what you eat plays a big role in how much blood cholesterol is produced in the body.

When it comes to prevention, your main focus should be fat. The evidence is clear that dietary fat plays a major role in blood cholesterol as well as body weight.

However, fat is not all evil. Fat is a nutrient that is needed in moderate amounts to help with absorption of fat-soluble vitamins and to supply the essential fatty linoleic and linolenic acids, which your body cannot make. Current recommendations from the American Heart Association suggest a diet that contains up to 30% of calories from fat can be healthy...the trick is to recognize that not all fats are created equal (1).

Cholesterol, saturated fat, trans-fatty acid, omega-3, hydrogenated fat, monounsaturated fat...the list goes on and what does it all mean? All of these terms really refer to a group of fatty substances known as lipids. Lipids are packaged in foods in many different forms.

Once eaten, these lipids are broken down and "repackaged" for multiple functions in the body. Depending on the type of lipid, some can actually be protective or "heart healthy" while others can promote fatty build up in the arteries that can lead to disease.

Cholesterol is a soft, waxy substance found among the lipids (fats) in the bloodstream and in all your body's cells. It is essential for human life but the body makes most of the cholesterol that it needs. Some cholesterol is absorbed from the foods you choose.

Dietary cholesterol is found only in foods of animal origin.

Blood cholesterol is formed as a result of the body's own production of cholesterol and is influenced by the fats that we eat. There are several kinds, but the ones to be most concerned about are low-density lipoprotein (LDL) and high-density lipoprotein (HDL).

LDL cholesterol is the major cholesterol carrier in the blood. If too much LDL cholesterol circulates in the blood, it can slowly build up in the walls of the arteries that feed the heart and brain.

HDL cholesterol tends to carry cholesterol away from the arteries and back to the liver, where it's passed from the body. Some experts believe HDL removes excess cholesterol from plaques and thus slows their growth. HDL cholesterol is known as "good" cholesterol because a high HDL level seems to protect against heart attacks.

Fat refers to a group of compounds made of glycerol and fatty acids. Fat is one of the three calorie-containing nutrients. Although all fats contain the same amount of energy, or calories, they do not all have the same effect on your risk for disease. Saturated fats and cholesterol tend to raise blood cholesterol while unsaturated fats and omega-3s can be beneficial.

Trans fatty acids are harmful to your health because they raise your "bad" LDL cholesterol and also lowers your "good" HDL cholesterol. The higher your LDL cholesterol levels are over time, the greater your risk for developing atherosclerosis, a condition in which fat accumulates in the walls of you arteries. This can restrict blood flow to your heart and may eventually lead to coronary artery disease (1). All Bon Appétit cafés only use non-hydrogenated frying oil and have also eliminated trans fats in house-baked goods and butter substitute spreads.

5

Vitamins

Vitamins are substances needed by cells to encourage specific cellular chemical reactions. Some vitamins (particularly B vitamins) are involved in energy reactions that enable cells to derive energy from carbohydrate, protein, and fat. Since athletes burn more energy than do nonathletes, these vitamins are of particular interest in this book. Other vitamins are involved in maintaining mineral balance. Vitamin D, for instance, encourages greater absorption of dietary calcium and phosphorus.

The synergism between vitamins and minerals is a critical factor in understanding their nutrient requirements. The fact that these nutrients have integrated functions should encourage athletes to present the widest possible spectrum of vitamins and minerals to their cells. Single vitamin or single mineral supplementation may corrupt nutrient balance and the delicate relationship between these nutrients.

Maximizing Vitamin Intake

To maximize vitamin intake from your diet, try the following:

- Eat a wide variety of colourful fruits and vegetables.
- When possible eat fresh fruits and vegetables, especially those in season.
- Don't overcook vegetables-long cooking times reduce nutrient content.
- Steam or microwave your vegetables rather than boil them-nutrients seep out in boiling water only to be poured down the drain.

WATER-SOLUBLE VITAMINS

Vitamins are organized into fat-soluble and water-soluble categories. The fat-soluble vitamins require a fat-based environment in which to function, and the water-soluble vitamins require a water-based environment. To one degree or another, we have the capacity to store all vitamins. That is to say, if we ate a meal 2 days ago that contained a large amount of vitamin C but ingested no vitamin C in the foods we consumed yesterday, we wouldn't expect to suffer from symptoms of vitamin C deficiency today. Cells that require vitamin C are able to store more than they need, although there are no clear storage depots where large amounts of the vitamin can be stored. Fat-soluble vitamins, however, do have a large storage capacity. This difference in storage capacity is responsible for the commonly repeated recommendation that water-soluble vitamins should be consumed every day because they are *not* stored. It has also led to the myth that any excess in water-soluble vitamin intake is without problems because the excess is excreted in the urine. Although it is true that excess intake of fat-soluble vitamins, especially vitamins D and A, can produce severe toxicity, taking excess water-soluble vitamins may also lead to difficulties. A prime example of this is peripheral neuropathy (loss of feeling in the fingers), a neurological problem caused by excess intake of vitamin B_6 (500 milligrams per day over time is enough to create permanent damage). Another problem is that humans are adaptable to intake. Therefore, the more you take, the more you may need to get the same biological effect.

VITAMIN B2

Vitamin B_2 (riboflavin) is involved in energy production and normal cellular function through its coenzymes flavin adenine dinucleotide (FAD) and flavin mononucleotide (FMN). These coenzymes are mainly involved in obtaining energy from consumed carbohydrate, protein, and fat. Food sources of riboflavin include dairy products (e.g., milk, yogurt, cottage cheese), dark green leafy vegetables (e.g., spinach, chard, mustard greens, broccoli, green peppers), whole grain foods, and enriched grain foods. No studies suggest that riboflavin-deficiency symptoms are common in athletes. Also, no apparent toxicity symptoms occur from consuming more than the DRI. Several studies have suggested that athletes may have higher requirements than the DRI, which is based on approximately .6 milligrams per 1,000 calories. In a series of studies performed on exercising women and women seeking to lose weight, the riboflavin requirement was found to range between .63 and 1.40 milligrams per 1,000 calories.

Table. Vitamin B_2 Quick Guide

Altermate name	Riboflavin
Dietary Reference Intake (DRI)	Adult males: 1.3 mg/day Adult females: 1.1 mg/day
Recommended	1.1 mg per 1.000 calories intake for athletes
Functions	Energy metabolism, protein metabolism, skin health, eye health
Good food sources	Fresh milk and other dairy products, eggs, dark green leafy vegetables, whole grain cereals, enriched grains
Deficiency	Inflamed tongue; cracked, dry skin at corners of mouth, nose, and eyes; bright light sensitivity; weakness; fatigue
Taxicity	None known (no safe upper limit established)

There is some evidence that physical activity increases the requirement to a level slightly higher than .5 milligrams per 1,000 calories, but not more than 1.6 milligrams per 1,000 calories. However, even with this apparently higher requirement for athletes, no studies clearly demonstrate an improvement in athletic performance with intakes greater than the RDA. Since low-dose supplements of this vitamin induce no apparent toxicity symptoms, athletes could take a supplement delivering 1.6 to 3.0 milligrams of riboflavin as part of a B-complex supplement. This level of intake would serve as an adequate preventative measure to help the athlete avoid the symptoms-headache, nausea, weakness-associated with extremely high doses (more than 100 times the RDA).

VITAMIN AND MINERAL FORTIFICANTS

Prudent handling of vitamin and mineral additives in food processing requires a sound understanding of the characteristics of these compounds: their stabilities to various unit operations, solubilities and reactivities with other compounds. Many forms of these nutrients have been developed to render them more suitable for use under a wide range of applications.

PROPERTIES OF MICRONUTRIENT COMPOUNDS

VITAMIN A

In vivo, this vitamin is generally found as the free alcohol or esterified with a fatty acid. The vitamin is available in pure form by chemical synthesis as vitamin A palmitate or the acetate, or recovered from molecularly recovered fish oil. It is a yellowish oily material which may crystallise into needlelike crystals. Provitamins which are then converted to their active form, serve not only as nutrifyng compounds but also as colourants and anti-oxidants. The most common of these is beta-carotene.

Vitamin A is quite stable when heated to moderate temperatures in the absence of oxygen and light. Overall loss of activity during anaerobic heating may range from 5-50 per cent, depending on time, temperature and nature of the carotenoids. In the presence of oxygen and light, there can be extensive loss of vitamin A activity through oxidation. The presence of trace metals accelerates this reaction.

In dehydrated foods, vitamin A and provitamin A are highly susceptible to loss by oxidation. The extent of this loss depends on the severity of the drying process, protection provided by packaging materials and conditions of storage. Vitamin A in pure form is unstable in the presence of mineral acids but stable in the presence of alkali.

Naturally occurring vitamin A is insoluble in water but soluble in oil. In this form the vitamin has limited applicability. Vitamin A fortificants are commercially available in a wide range of forms adapted for use under various conditions. For use in fat or oil based foods such as margarines, oils and dairy products, vitamin A as the acetate or palmitate have been used.

They are stabilised with a mixture of phenolic antioxidants or with tocopherols. For mixing with dry products, a dry form of the fortificant was required with the appropriate size and density. Encapsulation of the vitamin in a more hydrophilic coat is commonly practised in order to achieve a more water dispersable product. Two materials used in encapsulation are gum acacia and gelatin. These dry forms of the vitamin are also stabilised using tocopherols or phenolic antioxidants.

VITAMIN D

The principal forms of the vitamin are D_3 and D_2. They are white, crystalline fat-soluble vitamins, formed by irradiation of the appropriate sterol followed by purification procedures. These compounds are sensitive to oxygen and light, with the D_3 form of the vitamin being slightly more stable. Trace metals such as Cu and Fe act as pro-oxidants.

As with vitamin A, commercially available forms include fat-soluble crystals for use in high fat content foods, and encapsulated, stabilised versions of the fortificant, suitable for use in dry products to be reconstituted with water.

As was stated for vitamin A, at the levels of water activity which exist in dehydrated foods, these fat-soluble vitamins are most susceptible to oxidative loss.

VITAMIN E

Vitamin E is a slightly viscous, pale-yellow oily liquid obtained from molecular distillation of by-products from vegetable oil refining or by chemical synthesis. The naturally occurring form of the vitamin is the d-isomer. The synthetic compound is a racemic mixture of the d and 1 isomers. The 1-isomer doesn't have the full biological activity of the d-isomer, but due to the stability of the racemic mixture and the ease of purification, the IU of vitamin E has been defined as 1 mg dl-a tocopheryl acetate.

The free alcohol form of the vitamin is highly unstable to oxidation and is therefore widely used in foods as an antioxidant to stabilise the lip id component of foods. Esterified forms of the vitamin, commonly the acetate, are much more stable. For this reason, fortificants are usually of this form. As with the other fat soluble vitamins, cold water soluble forms have been produced by encapsulation within a suitable matrix.

VITAMINS OF THE B COMPLEX

Vitamin B_1, or thiamine, is a white crystalline solid with a characteristic yeast-like odour and a slight bitter taste. Thiamine is produced by chemical synthesis as the hydrochloride and mononitate salts. The hydrochloride is soluble to the extent of 50 per cent in water as compared with 2.7 per cent for the mononitrate.

Thiamine is one of the most unstable vitamins. Its stability to heat and oxidation is greatest at a pH range of 6 and below. At higher values of pH it becomes increasingly unstable. Thiamine is susceptible to nucleophilic attack, therefore it is degraded by some mineral salts in aqueous foods.

Thiamine hydrochloride is the fortificant of choice in cases where dissolution in aqueous media is required. In most other cases the mononitrate is used due to its lower hygroscopicity. Thiamine is also commercially available in a coated form using mono- and di-glycerides of edible fatty acids.

Biotin is a white crystalline powder of low water solubility. It is generally commercially available in diluted form as the physiological requirement for this vitamin is so low. Hoffmann-La Roche sells a 1 per cent mixture of this vitamin with dicalcium phosphate dihydrate. Biotin is fairly stable to heat, air and light.

Vitamin B_2, riboflavin, is of an intense orange colour and low water solubility. A commercially available more water soluble form of this vitamin is the sodium salt of riboflavin 5'-phosphate. Riboflavin is generally stable under most processing conditions, but is unstable in alkaline medium. It is very sensitive to light, particularly in the presence of ascorbic acid.

Pantothenic acid, is a pale yellow, viscous, hygroscopic liquid which is very unstable. The most commonly used commercially available form is calcium pantothenate. This is a slightly hygroscopic white powder with no smell but a slightly bitter taste. Stability of this compound is greatest at pH values between 5 and 7.

Vitamin B_6, pyridoxine, is available commercially as the hydrochloride. Coated forms are also available as with all of the B-vitamins. This vitamin is quite stable to heat and atmospheric oxygen and heat, but degradation is catalysed by metal ions.

Niacin in the form of either nicotinic acid or nicotinamide, can be used in nutrient addition to foods. At very high levels, nicotinic acid has been shown to cause unpleasant side effects such as flushing and 'pins and needles'. This has led to some preference for nicotinamide. Both forms of the vitamin are stable to atmospheric oxygen, heat and light in the dry state as well as in solution.

Cyanocobalamin, the most important compound with vitamin B_{12} activity, is commercially available as a crystalline, dark red, hygroscopic powder. Human requirements for this vitamin are very low and it is commonly sold highly diluted by a carrier. In the preparations sold by Hofmann-La Roche, for instance, it can be purchased diluted with mannitol or a mixture containing modified starches, citrate, citric acid, benzoate, sorbic acid and silicon dioxide. The selection of preparation depends, of course, on the end use. In solution it is most stable between pH values 4-7. It is unstable to oxidising and reducing agents and exposure to sunlight, but is fairly stable to heat. Folic acid is a yellow-orange, odourless, tasteless crystalline substance. It id moderately stable to heat and atmospheric oxygen. In neutral solution it is quite stable, but instability increases with a shift in pH in either direction. Folic acid is unstable to heat, light, sunlight, oxidising and reducing agents.

VITAMIN C

Vitamin C or ascorbic acid is an odourless, white, crystalline compound which is stable in its dry form. Due to its high water solubility, losses due to leaching can be a problem in some processing procedures. Ascorbic acid is readily oxidised. In dehydrated citrus juices the degradation is dependant on both temperature and water activity. Other factors as well can influence the degradation behaviour of vitamin C, these include salt and sugar concentration, pH, oxygen, metal catalysts and ratio of ascorbic: dehydroascorbic acid.

Vitamin C addition to foods is commonly practised for reasons other than fortification. Commercially available forms of this vitamin include the free acid and the sodium and calcium salts of these, in powder as well as crystalline or granular form. For mixing with dry products, particle size and density are of course important considerations. A fat coated form of ascorbic acid is also available for enrichment purposes. Ascorbyl palmitate, is a form of the vitamin used for purposes other than fortification. It is used as an antioxidant in fats and oils and has also emulsifying properties. Other areas of food processing for which vitamin C has application are the prevention of browning in fresh and canned fruit and vegetables, acidification, curing of meat and prevention of haze formation in brewed products.

IRON FORTIFICANTS

Iron compounds used in food fortification are commonly classified according to their solubility. Selection of an appropriate iron fortificant for any given application is based on the following criteria: organoleptic considerations, bioavailability, cost and safety.

The colour of iron compounds is often a critical factor when fortifying light coloured foods. For example white iron, ferric orthophosphate, is often the fortificant of choice in the enrichment of rice.

The use of more soluble iron compounds often leads to the development of off-colours and off-flavours due to reactions with other components of the food material. Infant cereals have been found to turn grey or green on addition of ferrous sulphate. Off-flavours can be the result of lipid oxidation catalysed by iron. The iron compounds themselves may contribute to a metallic flavour. Some of these undesirable interactions with the food matrix can be avoided by coating the fortificant with hydrogenated oils or ethyl cellulose. Bioavailability of iron compounds is normally stated relative to a ferrous sulphate standard.

The highly water soluble iron compounds have superior bioavailability. Bioavailability of the insoluble or very poorly soluble iron compounds can be improved by reducing particle size. Unfortunately this is accompanied by increased reactivity in deteriorative processes.

Sodium iron EDTA is less well absorbed than ferrous sulphate from foods which contain few inhibitors to absorption. In the presence of these inhibitors, however, the EDTA complex is better absorbed. Sodium iron EDTA also participates to a lesser extent in deteriorative reactions. The use of this compound reduces the problem of precipitate formation in foods such as fish sauces and tea. The use of this compound is not advised in developed countries where the population already receives close to the recommended acceptable daily intake of EDTA.

The problem of low bioavailability of some of the less reactive forms of iron is often circumvented by the use of absorption enhancers added along with the fortificant. Examples of such enhancers are ascorbic acid, sodium acid sulphate and orthophosphoric acid.

IODINE COMPOUNDS

The most commonly used compounds in the iodisation of foods are the iodides and iodates of sodium and potassium. These are the additives allowed by Codex Alimentarius in the iodisation of salt. The iodide compounds are cheaper, more soluble and have a higher iodine content (so that less is needed to achieve the same level of iodisation) than the corresponding iodates. Iodates are more stable under conditions of high moisture, high ambient temperature, sunlight, aeration and the presence of impurities. The use of iodate is therefore recommended for use in developing countries. Potassium iodide is well suited in cases where the salt is dry, free from impurities and has a slightly alkaline pH. Otherwise the iodide may be oxidised to molecular iodine and lost through evaporation.

If excess water is present the iodide may be separated from the salt in the water film. Loss of iodide can be reduced through the addition of stabilisers such as 0.1 per cent sodium thiosulphate and 0.1 per cent calcium hydroxide combined or 0.04 per cent dextrose and 0.006 per cent sodium bicarbonate. Calcium salts have been used with some report of off-flavour due to the calcium ions. The calcium compound is also much less water soluble than the sodium and potassium compounds and this further limits its applicability.

OTHER MINERAL ADDITIVES

A range of mineral salts are available for fortification with Ca, Mg, P, Zn, Cu and Mn. Prudent selection of mineral compounds is based largely on consideration of mineral reactivity and solubility of the salt. The requirements of the fortificant vary according to the nature of the food product and its end use. To overcome problems of flavour, texture and colour deterioration due to addition of minerals, some companies have engineered new fortificant preparations which generally involve the use of stabilisers and emulsifiers to maintain the mineral in solution.

VITAMIN A

Vitamin A (retinol) is an essential nutrient needed in small amounts by humans for the normal functioning of the visual system; growth and development; and maintenance of epithelial cellular integrity, immune function, and reproduction. These dietary needs for vitamin A are normally provided for as preformed retinol (mainly as retinyl ester) and pro-vitamin A carotenoids.

Some vitamins are recognized as essential nutrients, necessary in the diet for good health. (Vitamin D is the exception: it can be synthesized in the skin, in the presence of UVB radiation.) Certain vitamin-like compounds that are recommended in the diet, such as carnitine, are thought useful for survival and health, but these are not "essential" dietary nutrients because the human body has some capacity to produce them from other compounds.

Moreover, thousands of different phytochemicals have recently been discovered in food (particularly in fresh vegetables), which may have desirable properties including antioxidant activity, however, experimental demonstration has been suggestive but inconclusive. Other essential nutrients that are not classified as vitamins include essential amino acids, choline, essential fatty acids, and the minerals discussed in the preceding part.

Vitamin deficiencies may result in disease conditions, including goitre, scurvy, osteoporosis, impaired immune system, disorders of cell metabolism, certain forms of cancer, symptoms of premature aging, and poor psychological health (including eating disorders), among many others. Excess levels of some vitamins are also dangerous to health (notably vitamin A), and for at least one vitamin, B6, toxicity begins at levels not far the required amount. Deficient or excess levels of minerals can also have serious health consequences.

OVERVIEW OF VITAMIN A METABOLISM

Preformed vitamin A in animal foods occurs as retinyl esters of fatty acids in association with membrane-bound cellular lipid and fat-containing storage cells. Pro-vitamin A carotenoids in foods of vegetable origin are also associated with cellular lipids but are embedded in complex cellular structures such as the cellulose-containing matrix of chloroplasts or the pigment-containing portion of chromoplasts. Normal digestive processes free vitamin A and carotenoids from embedding food matrices, a more efficient process from animal than from vegetable tissues. Retinyl esters are hydrolysed and the retinol and freed carotenoids are incorporated into lipid-containing, water-miscible micellar solutions.

Products of fat digestion (*e.g.*, fatty acids, monoglycerides, cholesterol, and phospholipids) and secretions in bile (*e.g.*, bile salts and hydrolytic enzymes) are essential for the efficient solubilisation of retinol and especially for solubilisation of the very lipophilic carotenoids (*e.g.*, aa- and bb-carotene, bb-cryptoxanthin, and lycopene) in the aqueous intestinal milieu. Micellar solubilisation is a prerequisite to their efficient passage into the lipid-rich membrane of intestinal mucosal cells (*i.e.*, enterocytes). Diets critically low in dietary fat (under about 5-10 g daily) or disease conditions that interfere with normal digestion and absorption leading to steatorrhea (*e.g.*, pancreatic and liver diseases and frequent gastroenteritis) can therefore impede the efficient absorption of retinol and carotenoids. Retinol and some carotenoids enter the intestinal mucosal brush border by diffusion in accord with the concentration gradient between the micelle and plasma membrane of enterocytes. Some carotenoids pass into the enterocyte and are solubilized into chylomicrons without further change whereas some of the pro-vitamin A carotenoids are converted to retinol by a cleavage enzyme in the brush border. Retinol is trapped intracellularly by re-esterification or binding to specific intracellular binding proteins. Retinyl esters and unconverted carotenoids together with other lipids are incorporated into chylomicrons, excreted into intestinal lymphatic channels, and delivered to the blood through the thoracic duct.

Tissues extract most lipids and some carotenoids from circulating chylomicrons, but most retinyl esters are stripped from the chylomicron remnant, hydrolysed, and taken up primarily by parenchymal liver cells. If not immediately needed, retinol is re-esterified and retained in the fat-storing cells of the liver (variously called adipocytes, stellate cells, or Ito cells).

The liver parenchymal cells also take in substantial amounts of carotenoids. Whereas most of the body's vitamin A reserve remains in the liver, carotenoids are also deposited elsewhere in fatty tissues throughout the body. Usually, turnover of carotenoids in tissues is relatively slow, but in times of low dietary carotenoid intake, stored carotenoids are mobilised. A recent study in one subject using stable isotopes suggests that retinol can be derived not only from conversion of dietary pro-vitamin carotenoids in enterocytes–the major site of bioconversion, but also from hepatic conversion of circulating pro-vitamin carotenoids. The quantitative contribution to vitamin A requirements of carotenoid converted to retinoids beyond the enterocyte is unknown.

Following hydrolysis of stored retinyl esters, retinol combines with a plasma-specific transport protein, retinol-binding protein (RBP). This process, including synthesis of the unoccupied RBP (apo-RBP), occurs to the greatest extent within liver cells but it may also occur in some peripheral tissues. The RBP-retinol complex (holo-RBP) is secreted into the blood where it associates with another hepatically synthesised and excreted larger protein, transthyretin.

The transthyretin-RBP-retinol complex circulates in the blood, delivering the lipophilic retinol to tissues; its large size prevents its loss through kidney filtration. Dietary restriction in energy, proteins, and some micronutrients can limit hepatic synthesis of proteins specific to mobilisation and transport of vitamin A. Altered kidney functions or fever associated with infections can increase urinary vitamin A loss.

Holo-RBP transiently associates with target-tissue membranes, and specific intracellular binding proteins then extract the retinol. Some of the transiently sequestered retinol is released into the blood unchanged and is recycled. A limited reserve of intracellular retinyl esters is formed, that subsequently can provide functionally active retinol and its oxidation products (*i.e.*, isomers of retinoic acid) as needed intracellularly. These biologically active forms of vitamin A are associated with specific cellular proteins which bind with retinoids within cells during metabolism and with nuclear receptors that mediate retinoid action on the genome. Retinoids modulate the transcription of several hundreds of genes. In addition to the latter role of retinoic acid, retinol is the form required for functions in the visual and reproductive systems and during embryonic development.

Holo-RBP is filtered into the glomerulus but recovered from the kidney tubule and recycled. Normally vitamin A leaves the body in urine only as inactive metabolites which result from tissue utilisation and as potentially recyclable active glucuronide conjugates of retinol in bile secretions. No single urinary metabolite has been identified which accurately reflects tissue levels of vitamin A or its rate of utilisation. Hence, at this time urine is not a useful biologic fluid for assessment of vitamin A nutriture.

Biochemical Mechanisms for Vitamin A Functions

Vitamin A functions at two levels in the body. The first is in the visual cycle in the retina of the eye; the second is in all body tissues systemically to maintain growth and the soundness of cells. In the visual system, carrier-bound retinol is transported to ocular tissue and to the retina by intracellular binding and transport proteins. Rhodopsin, the visual pigment critical to dim-light vision, is formed in rod cells after conversion of all-*trans* retinol to retinaldehyde, isomerization to the 11-*cis*-form, and binding to opsin.

Alteration of rhodopsin through a cascade of photochemical reactions results in ability to see objects in dim light. The speed at which rhodopsin is regenerated relates to the availability of retinol. Night blindness is usually an indicator of inadequate available retinol, but it can also be due to a deficit of other nutrients, which are critical to the regeneration of rhodopsin, such as protein and zinc, and to some inherited diseases, such as retinitis pigmentosa.

The growth and differentiation of epithelial cells throughout the body are especially affected by vitamin A deficiency (VAD). Goblet cell numbers are reduced in epithelial tissues. The consequence is that mucous secretions with their antimicrobial components diminish. Cells lining protective tissue surfaces fail to regenerate and differentiate, hence flatten and accumulate keratin.

Both factors–the decline in mucous secretions and loss of cellular integrity–diminish resistance to invasion by potentially pathogenic organisms. The immune system is also compromised by direct interference with production of some types of protective secretions and cells.

Classical symptoms of xerosis (drying or nonwetability) and desquamation of dead surface cells as seen in ocular tissue (*i.e.*, xerophthalmia) are the external evidence of the changes also occurring to various degrees in internal epithelial tissues.

Current understanding of the mechanism of vitamin A action within cells outside the visual cycle is that cellular functions are mediated through specific nuclear receptors.

These receptors are activated by binding with specific isomers of retinoic acid (*i.e.*, all-*trans* and 9-*cis* retinoic acid). Activated receptors bind to DNA response elements located upstream of specific genes to regulate the level of expression of those genes. The synthesis of a large number of proteins vital to maintaining normal physiologic functions is regulated by these retinoid-activated genes. There also may be other mechanisms of action that are as yet undiscovered.

UNITS OF EXPRESSION

In blood, tissues, and human milk, vitamin A levels are conventionally expressed in μg/dL or μmol/l of all-*trans* retinol. Except for postprandial conditions, most of the circulating vitamin A is retinol whereas in most tissues (such as the liver), secretions (such as human milk), and other animal food sources it exists mainly as retinyl esters, that are usually hydrolysed before analytical detection.

To express the vitamin A activity of carotenoids in diets on a common basis, a joint FAO/WHO Expert Group in 1967 introduced the concept of the retinol equivalent (RE) and established the following relationships among food sources of vitamin A:

1 μg retinol = 1 RE

1 μg b-carotene = 0.167 μg RE

1 μg other pro-vitamin A carotenoids = 0.084 μg RE

These equivalencies were derived from balance studies to account for the less-efficient absorption of carotenoids (thought to be about one-third that of retinol) and their bioconversion to vitamin A (one-half for b-carotene and one-fourth for other pro-vitamin carotenoids). It was recognised at the time that the recommended conversion factors (*i.e.*, 1:6 for vitamin A:b-carotene and 1:12 for vitamin A: all other pro-vitamin carotenoids) were only average estimates for a mixed diet. Recently there has been renewed interest in examining bioavailability factors by using more quantitative stable isotope techniques for measuring whole-body stores in response to controlled intakes and by following postabsorption carotenoids in the triacylglycerol-rich lipoprotein fraction. The data are inconsistent but in general suggests that revision towards lower bioavailability estimates is likely.

Until additional definitive data are available, however, the above conversion factors will be used.

Retinol equivalents in a diet are calculated as the sum of the weight of the retinol portion of preformed vitamin A with the weight of b-carotene divided by its conversion factor and with the weight of other carotenoids divided by their conversion factor.

Most recent food composition tables report b-carotene and sometimes other pro-vitamin A carotenoids as μg/g edible portion. However, older food composition tables frequently report vitamin A as international units (IUs). The following applies to determining comparable values as μg:

1 IU retinol = 0.3 μg retinol

1 IU b-carotene = 0.6 μg b-carotene

1 IU retinol = 3 IU b-carotene

It is strongly recommended that weight or molar units replace the use of IU to decrease confusion and overcome limitations in the non-equivalence of the IU values for retinol and beta-carotene.

DIETARY SOURCES

Preformed vitamin A is found almost exclusively in animal products, such as human milk, glandular meats, liver and fish liver oils (especially), egg yolk, and whole milk and dairy products.

Preformed vitamin A is also used to fortify processed foods, that may include sugar, cereals, condiments, fats, and oils. Pro-vitamin A carotenoids are found in green leafy vegetables (*e.g.*, spinach, amaranth, and young leaves from various sources), yellow vegetables (*e.g.*, pumpkins, squash, and carrots), and yellow and orange noncitrus fruits (*e.g.*, mangoes, apricots, and papaya). Red palm oil produced in several countries worldwide is especially rich in provitamin A.

Some other indigenous plants also may be unusually rich sources of provitamin A. Such examples are the palm fruit known in Brazil as *buriti*, that is found in areas along the Amazon, and the fruit known as *gac* in Vietnam, that is used to colour rice, particularly on ceremonial occasions.

Foods containing pro-vitamin A carotenoids tend to be less biologically available but more affordable than animal products. It is mainly for this reason that carotenoids provide most of the vitamin A activity in the diets of economically deprived populations.

Dietary Intake and Patterns

Vitamin A status cannot be assessed from dietary intake alone, but dietary intake assessment can provide evidence of risk of an inadequate status. Quantitative collection of dietary information is fraught with measurement problems. These problems arise both from obtaining representative quantitative dietary histories from individuals, communities, or both and from interpreting these data while accounting for differences in bio-availability, preparation losses, and variations in food composition data among population groups. This is especially difficult in populations consuming most of their dietary vitamin A from pro-vitamin carotenoid sources. Simplified guidelines have been developed recently in an effort to improve the obtaining of reliable dietary intake information from individuals and communities.

World and Regional Supply and Patterns

In theory the world's food supply is sufficient to meet global requirements. Great differences exist, however, in the available sources (animal and vegetable) and in per capita consumption of the vitamin among different countries, age categories, and socio-economic groups. VAD as a global public health problem, therefore, is largely due to inequitable food distribution among and within countries and households in relation to need for ample bio-available vitamin A sources.

Earlier FAO global estimates in 1984 indicated that preformed vitamin A constituted about one-third of total dietary vitamin A. World availability of vitamin A for human consumption at that time was approximately 220 μg of preformed retinol per capita daily and 560 μg RE from pro-vitamin carotenoids per person per day, for a total of about 790 μg RE. These values are based on supply estimates and not consumption estimates. Losses commonly occur during food storage and processing, both industrially and in the home.

The estimated available regional supply of vitamin A from a more recent global evaluation the variability in amounts and sources of vitamin A. The variability is further complicated by access to the available supply, that varies with household income, poverty being a yardstick for risk of VAD. VAD is most prevalent in Southeast Asia, Africa, and the Western Pacific, where vegetable sources contribute nearly 80 per cent or more of the available supply of retinol equivalents.

Furthermore, in Southeast Asia the total available supply is about half of that of most other regions and is particularly low in animal sources. In contrast, the Americas, Europe, and Eastern Mediterranean regions have a supply ranging from 800 to 1000 mmg RE/day, one-third of which comes from animal sources.

Recent national data from the USA Continuing Survey of Food Consumption and the National Health and Nutrition Examination Survey included mean dietary intakes of children 0-6 years of age of 864 ± 497 and 921 ± 444 mmg

RE daily. In the Dietary and Nutritional Survey of British Adults, the median intake of men and women 35-49 years old was 1118 mmg RE and 926 mmg RE, respectively, which corresponded to serum retinol concentrations of 2.3 mmol/l and 1.8 mmol/l, respectively. In another selected survey in the United Kingdom, median intakes for nonpregnant women who did not consume liver or liver products during the survey week were reported to be 686 mmg RE daily.

The available world supply figures were recently reassessed based on a bio-availability ratio of 1:30 for retinol to other pro-vitamin A carotenoids. This conversion factor was justified on the basis of one published controlled intervention study conducted in Indonesia and a limited number of other studies not yet published in full. Applying the unconfirmed conversion factor would lead to the conclusion that regional and country needs for vitamin A could not be met from predominantly vegetarian diets. This is inconsistent with the preponderance of epidemiologic evidence.

Most studies report a positive response when vegetable sources of pro-vitamin A are given under controlled conditions to deficient subjects freed of confounding parasite loads and provided with sufficient dietary fat. Emerging data are likely to justify a lower biologic activity for pro-vitamin A carotenoids because of the mix of total carotenoids found in food sources in a usual meal. This Consultation concluded that the 1:6 bioconversion factor originally derived on the basis of balance studies should be retained until there is firm confirmation from ongoing studies that use more precise methodologies.

VITAMIN B_{12} IN HUMAN METABOLIC PROCESSES

Although the nutritional literature still uses the term vitamin B_{12}, a more specific name for vitamin B_{12} is cobalamin. Vitamin B_{12} is the largest of the B complex vitamins, with a molecular weight of over 1000. It consists of a corrin ring made up of four pyrroles with cobalt at the centre of the ring).

There are several vitamin B_{12}-dependent enzymes in bacteria and algae, but no species of plants have the enzymes necessary for vitamin B_{12} synthesis. This fact has significant implications for the dietary sources and availability of vitamin B_{12}. In mammalian cells there are only two vitamin B_{12}-dependent enzymes.

One of these enzymes, methionine synthase, uses the chemical form of the vitamin which has a methyl group attached to the cobalt and is called methylcobalamin. The other enzyme, methylmalonyl CoA mutase, uses vitamin B_{12} with a 5'-adeoxyadenosyl moiety attached to the cobalt and is called 5'-deoxyaldenosylcobalamin, or coenzyme B_{12}. In nature there are two other forms of vitamin B_{12}: hydroxycobalamin and aquacobalamin, where hydroxyl and water groups, respectively, are attached to the cobalt. The synthetic form of vitamin B_{12} found in supplements and fortified foods is cyanocobalamin, which has cyanide attached to the cobalt. These three forms of B_{12} are enzymatically activated to the methyl- or deoxyadenosylcobalamins in all mammalian cells.

POPULATIONS AT RISK FOR AND CONSEQUENCES OF VITAMIN B_{12} DEFICIENCY

Because plants do not synthesise vitamin B_{12}, individuals who consume diets completely free of animal products (vegan diets) are at risk of vitamin B_{12} deficiency. This is not true of lacto-ovo-vegetarians, who consume the vitamin in eggs, milk, and other dairy products.

Pernicious Anaemia

Malabsorption of vitamin B_{12} can occur at several points during digestion. By far the most important condition resulting in vitamin B_{12} malabsorption is the auto-immune disease called pernicious anaemia (PA). In most cases of PA, antibodies are produced against the parietal cells causing them to atrophy, lose their ability to produce intrinsic factor, and secrete hydrochloric acid. In some forms of PA the parietal cells remain intact but auto-antiobodies are produced against the intrinsic factor itself and attach to it, thus preventing it from binding vitamin B_{12}.

In another less common form of PA, the antibodies allow vitamin B_{12} to bind to the intrinsic factor but prevent the absorption of the intrinsic factor-vitamin B_{12} complex by the ileal receptors. As is the case with most auto-immune diseases, the incidence of PA increases markedly with age. In most ethnic groups it is virtually unknown to occur before the age of 50, with a progressive rise in incidence thereafter.

However, African American populations are known to have an earlier age of presentation. In addition to causing malabsorption of dietary vitamin B_{12}, PA also results in an inability to reabsorb the vitamin B_{12} which is secreted in the bile. Biliary secretion of vitamin B_{12} is estimated to be between 0.3 and 0.5 μg/day. Interruption of this so-called enterohepatic circulation of vitamin B_{12} causes the body to go into a significant negative balance for the vitamin.

Although the body typically has sufficient vitamin B_{12} stores to last 3-5 years, once PA has been established the lack of absorption of new vitamin B_{12} is compounded by the loss of the vitamin because of negative balance. When the stores have been depleted, the final stages of deficiency are often quite rapid, resulting in death in a period of months if left untreated.

Atrophic Gastritis

Historically, PA was considered to be the major cause of vitamin B_{12} deficiency, but it was a fairly rare condition, perhaps affecting 1 per cent to a few per cent of elderly populations. More recently it has been suggested that a far more common problem is that of hypochlorhydria associated with atrophic gastritis, where there is a progressive reduction with age of the ability of the parietal cells to secrete hydrochloric acid. It is claimed that perhaps up to one-quarter of elderly subjects could have various degrees of hypochlorhydria as a result of atrophic gastritis.

It has also been suggested that bacterial overgrowth in the stomach and intestine in individuals suffering from atrophic gastritis may also reduce vitamin B_{12} absorption. This absence of acid is postulated to prevent the release of protein-bound vitamin B_{12} contained in food but not to interfere with the absorption of the free vitamin B_{12} found in fortified foods or supplements. Atrophic gastritis does not prevent the reabsorption of bilary vitamin B_{12} and therefore does not result in the negative balance seen in individuals with PA. However, it is agreed that with time, a reduction in the amount of vitamin B_{12} absorbed from the diet will eventually deplete even the usually adequate vitamin B_{12} stores, resulting in overt deficiency.

When considering recommended nutrient intakes (RNIs) for vitamin B_{12} for the elderly, it is important to take into account the absorption of vitamin B_{12} from sources such as fortified foods or supplements as compared with dietary vitamin B_{12}. In the latter instances, it is clear that absorption of intakes of less than 1.5-2.0 μg/day is complete–that is, for intakes of less than 1.5-2.0 μg of free vitamin B_{12}, the intrinsic factor–mediated system absorbs all of that amount.

It is probable that this is also true of vitamin B_{12} in fortified foods, although this has not specifically been examined. However, absorption of food-bound vitamin B_{12} has been reported to vary from 9 per cent to 60 per cent depending on the study and the source of the vitamin, which is perhaps related to its incomplete release from food. This has led many to estimate absorption as being up to 50 per cent to correct for bio-availability of absorption from food.

VITAMIN B_{12} INTERACTION WITH FOLIC ACID

One of the vitamin B_{12}–dependent enzymes, methionine synthase, functions in one of the two folate cycles–the methylation cycle. This cycle is necessary to maintain availability of the methyl donor *S*-adenosylmethionine; interruption reduces the wide range of methylated products. One such important methylation is that of myelin basic protein. Reductions in the level of *S*-adenosylmethionine seen in PA and other causes of vitamin B_{12} deficiency produce demyelination of the peripheral nerves and the spinal column, called sub-acute combined degeneration. This neuropathy is one of the main presenting conditions in PA. The other principal presenting condition in PA is a megaloblastic anaemia morphologically identical to that seen in folate deficiency. Disruption of the methylation cycle should cause a lack of DNA biosynthesis and anaemia.The methyl trap hypothesis is based on the fact that once the cofactor 5,10-methylenetetrahydrofolate is reduced by its reductase to form 5-

methyltetrahydrofolate, the reverse reaction cannot occur. This suggests that the only way for the methyltetrahydrofolate to be recycled to tetrahydrofolate, and thus to participate in DNA biosynthesis and cell division, is through the vitamin B_{12}_dependent enzyme methionine synthase. When the activity of this synthase is compromised, as it would be in PA, the cellular folate will become progressively trapped as 5-methyltetrahydrofolate. This will result in a cellular pseudo folate deficiency where despite adequate amounts of folate an anaemia will develop that is identical to that seen in true folate deficiency. Clinical symptoms of PA, therefore, include neuropathy, anaemia, or both. Treatment with vitamin B_{12}, if given intramuscularly, will reactivate methionine synthase, allowing myelination to restart. The trapped folate will be released and DNA synthesis and generation of red cells will cure the anaemia. Treatment with high concentrations of folic acid will treat the anaemia but not the neuropathy of PA. It should be stressed that the so-called masking of the anaemia of PA is generally agreed not to occur at concentrations of folate found in food or at intakes of the synthetic form of folic acid found at usual RNI levels of 200 or 400 μg/day.

However, there is some evidence that amounts less than 400 μg may cause a haematologic response and thus potentially treat the anaemia. The masking of the anaemia definitely occurs at high concentrations of folic acid (>1000 μg/day). This becomes a concern when considering fortification with synthetic folic acid of a dietary staple such as flour. In humans the vitamin B_{12}_dependent enzyme methylmalonyl coenzyme A (CoA) mutase functions in the metabolism of propionate and certain of the amino acids, converting them into succinyl CoA, and in their subsequent metabolism via the citric acid cycle. It is clear that in vitamin B_{12} deficiency the activity of the mutase is compromised, resulting in high plasma or urine concentrations of methylmalonic acid (MMA), a degradation product of methylmalonyl CoA.

In adults this mutase does not appear to have any vital function, but it clearly has an important role during embryonic life and in early development. Children deficient in this enzyme, through rare genetic mutations, suffer from mental retardation and other developmental defects.

ASSESSMENT OF VITAMIN B_{12} STATUS

Traditionally it was thought that low vitamin B_{12} status was accompanied by a low serum or plasma vitamin B_{12} level. Recently this has been challenged by Lindenbaum *et al*, who suggested that a proportion of people with normal vitamin B_{12} levels are in fact vitamin B_{12} deficient. They also suggested that elevation of plasma homo-cysteine and plasma MMA are more sensitive indicators of vitamin B_{12} status.

Although plasma homo-cysteine may also be elevated because of folate or vitamin B_6 deficiency, elevation of MMA apparently always occurs with poor vitamin B_{12} status. There may be other reasons why MMA is elevated, such as renal insufficiency, so the elevation of itself is not diagnostic. Many would feel that low or decreased plasma vitamin B_{12} levels should be the first indication of poor status and that this could be confirmed by an elevated MMA if this assay was available.

6

Meal Planning for an Individual

A meal is an instance of eating, specifically one that takes place at a specific time and includes specific, prepared food. Meals occur primarily at homes, restaurants, and cafeterias, but may occur anywhere. Regular meals occur on a daily basis, typically several times a day. Special meals are usually held in conjunction with such occasions as birthdays, weddings, anniversaries, and holidays. A meal is different from a snack in that meals are larger, more varied, and more filling, while snacks are more likely to be small, high-calorie affairs; however, any food eaten in small amounts at an unscheduled time can be classified as a snack. A picnic is an outdoor meal where one brings one's food, such as a sandwich or a prepared meal (sometimes in a picnic basket). It often takes place in a natural or recreative area, such as a park, forest, beach, or grassy lawn. On long drives a picnic may take place at a road-side stop such as a rest area. A banquet is a large, often formal, and elaborate meal with many guests and dishes.

A MULTI-COURSE MEAL

Most Western-world multicourse meals follow a standard sequence, influenced by traditional French haute cuisine. Each course is supposed to be designed with a particular size and genre that befits its place in the sequence. There are variations depending on location and custom. The following is a common sequence for multi-course meals:

1. The meal begins with an entrée, a small serving that usually does not include red meat. It is sometimes referred to as a *soup course* as soups, bisques and consommés are popular entreés. In Italian custom, *antipasto* is served, usually *finger food* which does not contain pasta or any starch. In the United States the term *appetizer* is usually used in place of entrée as entrée is used to refer to the *main course*.
2. This may be followed by a variety of dishes, including a possible fish course or other relevés (lighter courses), each with some kind of vegetable. The number and size of these intermittent courses is entirely dependent on local custom.

3. Following these is the main course or central part of the meal. This is the most important course and is usually a larger portion than all others. The main course is called an entrée in the United States.
4. Next comes the salad course, although "salad" may often refer to a cooked vegetable, rather than the greens most people associate with the word. According to The Joy of Cooking, greens serve "garnish duty only" in a salad course. Note that in the United States, Canada, Great Britain and parts of Europe, the salad course (usually a green salad) is served at some point before the main course.
5. The meal will often culminate with a dessert, either hot or cold, sometimes followed with a final serving of hot or cold fruit and accompanied by a suitable dessert wine.
6. The meal may carry on with a cheese selection, accompanied by an appropriate selection of wine. In many countries cheeses will be served before the meal as an appetizer, and in the United States often between the main course and dessert. Nuts are also a popular after-meal selection (thus the common saying "from soup to nuts," meaning from beginning to end).

Sorbet or other palate cleansers might be served between courses.

Before the meal, a host might serve a selection of appetizers or hors d'œuvre with appropriate wine or cocktails, and after the meal, a host might serve snacks, sweets such as chocolate, coffee, and after-dinner drinks (cognac, brandy, liqueur, or similar). These are not considered courses in and of themselves. A meal may also begin with an amuse-bouche. An amuse-bouche, also called an amuse-gueule, is a tiny bite-sized morsel served before the hors d'œuvre or first course of a meal. These, often accompanied by a proper complementing wine, are served as an excitement of taste buds to both prepare the guest for the meal and to offer a glimpse into the chef's approach to cooking. An entremet is a small dish that may be served between courses, or as a dessert.

CUSTOMS, TRADITION, AND ETIQUETTE

Customs and traditions regarding eating and meals vary from country to country, as well as within countries, based on such factors as regional differences, social class, education, and religion. In a complex, multi-cultural society there is increased risk of different customs and traditions clashing. What is correct behaviour, and what is not, and in what circumstances is the provenance of etiquette.

Examples of different customs and traditions:

- Food in some cultures is eaten from individual plates or bowls, while in other cultures people eat from a common one. Even where people tend to eat from individual plates, there may be exceptions, as in the case of some small pieces of food that can be held in the hand easily, such as cookies or some snack foods, where it is common to eat from a common plate, biscuit tin, or similar container.

- Different cultures might have different rules for eating the same item. In much of the west people eat sausages in a bun, or with a knife and fork, while in some countries in Europe sausages are held between the fingers while being eaten.
- In some cultures, it is considered proper to wait until everyone is seated before starting to eat, while in other cultures it is not an issue.
- In some cultures it is considered proper to wait for the host to give the command before guests sit at the table for a meal, while in other cultures there are different rules.
- In some religions, people pray or read aloud from a religious text before and possibly also after eating. In diverse, religiously mixed company where some people might want to pray, and others might not, it may be proper etiquette to allow for a short time of silence allowing those who want to do so the chance to pray.

MEALTIMES

Common meals

These are the most common set mealtimes in the Western-world.

- Breakfast is usually eaten within an hour or two after a person wakes up in the morning.
- Lunch is eaten around mid-day, usually between 11 am–2 pm.
- Supper in the US and UK is a meal eaten in the evening.
- Dinner is the main meal of the day, regardless of whether it's at lunchtime or in the evening. Dinner also refers to the evening meal as a formal meal or just the evening meal in the south of England.
- Dessert is typically eaten after dinner as a treat. It may be considered a course within a meal or a meal itself. Cakes, pastries, fresh fruit, and ice cream are examples of common dessert food.

Other meals

- Second Breakfast is a traditional midmorning meal served in parts of central Europe.
- Elevenses, also called "Morning Tea," is a drink and light snack taken late morning after breakfast and before lunch.
- Brunch is a late-morning meal, usually larger than a breakfast and usually replacing both breakfast and lunch; it is most common on Sundays.
- Afternoon tea is a mid-afternoon meal, typically taken at 4pm, consisting of light fare such as small sandwiches, individual cakes and scones with tea.
- High Tea is a British meal usually eaten in the early evening.

MENU

In a restaurant, a menu is a printed brochure or public display on a poster or chalkboard that shows the list of options for a diner to select. A menu may be a la carte – in which guests choose from a list of options – or table d'hôte, in which case a pre-established sequence of courses is served. In the 2000s, many fast food restaurants switched to digital menus which are displayed on flat-screen LCD televisions. Digital menus can have items or prices changed without having to reprint paper menus, and as well, the screens can be used to play video commercials advertising certain menu items.[*citation needed*]

Depending on the restaurant, the menu may display a list of wines and their prices, or this information may be available in a separate brochure called the wine list. Some restaurants may also have separate menus for beer, liquor, and mixed drinks, and for desserts. In some restaurants, each menu item has a number, and the customers are asked to "order by number". Menus vary a great deal in terms of their length and the amonut of detail that they provide. In some restaurants, the entire menu fits on a single sheet of paper. In other restaurants, the menu is bound into a brochure or binder, as it contains a number of pages. A menu may be long either because the restaurant carries an extensive selection of items, because the menu has a lengthy description of each item and its preparation, or from a combination of these factors.

In addition to providing a list of the restaurant's food and drink items, menus can also be used to provide other information to the diners. Some menus describe the philosophy of the chef or owner about food and cooking; the resume of experience of the head chef and other senior chefs; the mission statement of the restaurant, and so on. "Menu" can also be used in a more general sense, as synonymous with diet, the selection of foods available generally to a particular location or culture.

The word *menu*, like much of the terminology of cuisine, is French in origin. It ultimately derives from Latin *minutus*, something made small; in French it came to be applied to a detailed list or *résumé* of any kind. The original menus that offered consumers choices were prepared on a small chalkboard, in French a *carte*; so foods chosen from a bill of fare are described as *à la carte*, "according to the board."

The original restaurants had the menus in the modern sense; these *table d'hôte* establishments served dishes that were chosen by the chef or the proprietors, and those who arrived ate what the house was serving that day, as in contemporary banquets or buffets. In Europe, the contemporary menu first appeared in the second half of the eighteenth century. Here, instead of eating what was being served from a common table, restaurants allowed diners to choose from a list of unseen dishes, which were produced to order by the customer's selection. A *table d'hôte* establishment charged its customers a fixed price; the menu allowed customers to spend as much or as little money as they chose. During the economic crisis in the 1970s, many restaurants found that they were having to incur costs from having to reprint the menu as inflation caused prices to increase. Economists noted this transaction cost, and it has become part of economic theory, under the term "menu costs". As a general economic phenomenon, "menu costs" can be experienced by a range of businesses beyond restaurants; for example, during a period of inflation, any company that prints out catalogues or product price lists will have to reprint these items with new price figures. To avoid having to reprint the menus throughout the year as prices changed, some restaurants began to display their menus on chalkboards, with the menu items and prices written in chalk. This way, the restaurant could easily modify the prices without going to the expense of reprinting the paper menus. A similar tactic continues to be used in the 2000s with certain items which are very sensitive to changing supply, fuel costs, and so on: the use of the term "Please ask server" instead of stating the price. This allows restaurants to modify the price of lobster, fresh fish, and other items on a daily basis.

WRITING STYLE

As a form of advertising, the prose found on printed menus is famous for the degree of its puffery. Menus frequently emphasize the processes used to prepare foods, call attention to exotic ingredients, and add French or other foreign language expressions to make the dishes appear sophisticated and exotic. Higher-end menus often add adjectives to dishes such as "glazed", "sautéed", "poached", and so on. "Menu language, with its hyphens, quotation marks, and random outbursts of foreign words, serves less to describe food than to manage your expectations"; restaurants are often "plopping in foreign words (80 percent of them French) like "spring mushroom civet," "plin of rabbit," "orange-jaggery gastrique." Brian McGrory quips that, when going to a high-end restaurant, he sometimes feels that he needs "an unabridged dictionary, a Biology 101 textbook, and a pile of *Fun With Phonics* just to figure out the meaning of gianduja ice cream, hazelnut financiers, yellow watermelon, and bulgur crackers[—] just some of the inscrutable listings from the dessert menu..."

Part of the function of menu prose is to impress customers with the notion that the dishes served at the restaurant require such skill, equipment, and exotic ingredients that the diners could not prepare similar foods at home. In some cases, ordinary foods are made to sound more exciting by replacing everyday terms with their French equivalent. For example, instead of stating that a pork chop has a dollop of applesauce, a high-end restaurant menu might state "Tenderloin of pork *avec compôte de pommes*". Although the French term "*avec compôte de pommes*" is an exact translation of "with applesauce", it sounds more exotic– and more worthy of an inflated price tag. Menus may use the French term "concassé" to describe coarsely-chopped vegetables or "coulis" to describe a puree of vegetables or fruit. Another example is the French term "au jus", which means that meat is served with its own natural gravy of pan drippings. "Restaurants that put "with au jus" on their menus pretend to be far more elegant than they really are".

Another phenomenon is the so-called "secret menu" where some fast food restaurants are known for having unofficial and unadvertised selections that customers learn by word of mouth. Quick service restaurants will often prepare variations on items already available, but to have them all on the menu would create clutter. Chipotle is well known for having a simple five item menu, but offers quesedillas and single tacos, despite neither being on the menu board. This can also occur in high-end restaurants, which may be willing to prepare certain items which are not listed on the menu (e.g., dishes that have long been favourites of regular clientele).

TYPES

Paper

The simplest hand-held menus are printed on a single sheet of paper. In some cafeteria-style restaurants and chain restaurants, this piece of paper may double as a disposable placemat. In some cases, the single sheet of paper may be placed in a binder or vinyl slipcover to protect it from spills. In some restaurants, the menu may be a number pages long. In addition to using binders or slipcovers, another way that restaurants protect the pages of the menu is by laminating them in plastic. While some restaurants may use a single menu as the sole way of communicating information about menu items to customers, in other cases, the meal menu is supplemented with ancillary menus, such as:

- An appetizer menu (nachos, chips and salsa, vegetables and dip, etc.)
- A wine list
- A liquor and mixed drinks menu
- A beer list
- A dessert menu (which may also include a list of tea and coffee options)

Some restaurants use only text in their menus. In other cases, restaurants include illustrations and photos, either of the dishes or of an element of the culture which is associated with the restaurant. An example of the latter is in cases where a Lebanese kebab restaurant decorates its menu with photos of Lebanese mountains and beaches. Particularly with the ancillary menu types, the menu may be provided in alternative formats, because these menus–other than wine lists–tend to be much shorter than food menus. For example, an appetizer menu or a dessert menu may be mounted in a hard plastic picture holder, hanging from a hook attached to a small 10" high stand, or even, in the case of a wine list, in the case of a pizza restaurant with a very limited selection, glued onto an empty wine bottle.

Large format

Some restaurants–typically fast-food restaurants and cafeteria-style establishments–provide their menu in a large poster or display board format up high on the wall or above the service counter. This way, all of the patrons can see all of the choices, and the restaurant does not have to provide printed menus. This large format menu may also be set up outside (see the next section). The simplest large format menu boards have the menu printed or painted on a large flat board. More expensive large format menu boards include boards that have a metal housing, a translucent surface, and a backlight (which facilitates the reading of the menu in low light), and boards that have removable numbers for the prices. This enables the restaurant to change prices without having to have the board reprinted or repainted. Some restaurants such as cafes and small eateries use a large chalkboard to display the entire menu. The advantage of using a chalkboard is that the menu items and prices can be changed; the downside is that the chalk may be hard to read in lower light or glare, and the restaurant has to have a staff member who has attractive, clear handwriting.

Outdoor

Some restaurants provide a copy of their menu outside the restaurant. Fast-food restaurants that have a drive-through or walk-up window will often put the entire menu on a board, lit-up sign, or poster outside, so that patrons can select their meal choices. High-end restaurants may also provide a copy of their menu outside the restaurant, with the pages of the menu placed in a lit-up glass display case; this way, prospective patrons can see if the menu choice is to their liking. As well, some mid-level and high-end restaurants may provide a partial indication of their menu listings–the "specials"–on a chalkboard displayed outside the restaurant. The chalkboard will typically provide a list of seasonal items or dishes that are the specialty of the chef which are only available for a few days.

Digital displays

With the invention of LCD and Plasma displays, some menus have moved from a static printed model, to one which can change dynamically. By using a flat LCD screen and a computer server, menus can be digitally displayed allowing moving images, animated effects and the ability to edit details and prices. For fast food restaurants, a benefit is the ability to update prices and menu items as frequently as needed, across an entire chain. Digital menu boards also allow restaurant owners to control the day parting of their menus. Various software tools and hardware developments have been created for the specific purpose of managing a digital menu board system (such as the systems designed by Beaver Group). Digital menu screens can also alternate between displaying the full menu and then doing video commercials to promote specific dishes or menu items.

RESTAURANT MENU DESIGN

A restaurant menu design is a reflection of the restaurant itself. Restaurant menu descriptions, layouts and colors, whether formal, casual or playful, should match your restaurant concept, location or theme.

Before Your Design Your Restaurant Menu

Check out your competition. Look at their website and study their menu to see the price range of their meals. Also, look for similarities and differences between your prospective restaurant menu and theirs. Ask yourself the following questions:

How will my restaurant menu be different from everyone else's?

If you can't answer this question, stop right here. Do not pass go, do not collect $200 dollars. You need to decide what will separate your food from the masses. This is the driving force behind your restaurant menu design.

What restaurant menu items are similar to my competitors?

Not everything on your menu has to be 100% original. Look at how many places offer a hamburger or cheeseburger as a dinner option. You can offer similar items, but you should add something to yours, to make it stand out in a crowd. For example, your restaurant menu may include a hamburger with hand-cut French fries, while your competitor offers a plain burger with boring old frozen fries.

Does my restaurant menu pricing match my competitors?

If you charge $14.00 for that hamburger and your biggest competitor charges $9.00, you'd better be adding something fantastic to that burger to justify the price (like lobster or a foot massage). Otherwise, who do you think your customers are going to frequent?

Designing a Restaurant Menu Layout

Okay, so once you have studied the competition and written up a stellar restaurant menu, you need to create the perfect restaurant menu design. This sounds easy enough, but an effective menu design is more than just printing out a list of items on a WordPerfect program. Colors, fonts and borders are all integral parts of a an effective menu design.

Restaurant Menu Colors and Font

Your menu font and color scheme should reflect your restaurant theme. For example, if you are opening a Mexican themed restaurant, vibrant colors such as red, turquoise, purple and green would be good choices for a menu. These same colors would look out of place on the menu of a French bistro or Italian restaurant. Ditto for the font. A French bistro may have a classic script font or simple plain font, while a sports bar or other casual restaurant might have a less formal or playful font. Beware of choosing a font that is hard to read or too small.

Restaurant Menu Sections

Take a look at a menu from most any restaurant and you will see that it is arranged sequentially: appetizers, soups & salad, main entrees, desserts and beverages. It is important to have sections clearly identified, by either bold headings, boxes or borders. Highlighting special dishes with a star or other insignia, such as a house favorite or chef's specialty is one way to draw a customers attention to popular dishes.

Depending on your restaurant menu size, one or two columns makes for an attractive layout. Adding more columns runs the risk of looking like the newspaper classifieds. Daily specials can be easily changed with a clear menu insert. Avoid adding to many pictures or busy backgrounds, that make the menu hard to read. Also avoid common computer clipart, which takes away from the professional look of a restaurant menu design.

Restaurant Menu Descriptions

You menu description should make a guest's mouth water. Don't be afraid to explain what is in a dish, and use ethnic names if they fit, to add a bit of authentic flair to the menu description. For example, Chicken Margarita sounds better than Chicken topped with spicy tomatoes. You can explain what is in the dish (spicy tomatoes) in the description itself.

Incorporating geography or local history into a menu item name is also a way to make your restaurant menu unique. For example, *Maine Lobster Roll* sounds inviting, whether you eating it in Maine or somewhere else, as does *Texas Barbequed Ribs* and *Georgia Peach Pie*. Avoid making descriptions too long. A sentence or two is fine. You want to intrigue the customer. If they have more questions, their server should be able to give further information about a dish or recommend a house favorite.

LEVEL OF SERVICES

Restaurant Services has been providing Britain with a FREE advisory and reservation service on eating out in London restaurants since 1979. With over 25 years of experience, no one has a better understanding of the restaurant scene than us. Planning a private business function, a party or a romantic meal to impress your loved one?

Whatever type of restaurant venue you are looking for we will always endeavour to come up with the best to satisfy your needs! Use our easy to find Restaurant Finder situated on the right hand of the screen, or simply give us a call.

If you cannot find a restaurant in London that you are looking for on this site do not worry! Simply call us if you need suggestions or, if you know the restaurant's name, complete the Book Now form entering all the relevant details and we will endeavour to make the reservation from our off line database of over ,9000 restaurants in the Capital.

RESTAURANT SERVICE CONSULTING AND WAITER TRAINING

Topserve Restaurant Consulting has the skilled expertise to provide you and your restaurant with the dining room service knowledge, strategies, and procedures desperately needed for running the daily operations successfully.

We are qualified and prepared to offer you the benefit of many years hard earned experience in the highly competitive food service industry. Our services are available throughout the New York City area, as well as within the United States and internationally.

We provide the following:

- Development, organization, and improvement of restaurant dining room service and maintenance systems. Consulting Services
- Beginner Waiter Training Seminars or Intermediate Sales Training Programs. Training Programs
- Restaurant Service Staff Start-Up Needs: This includes dining room staff hiring, training, scheduling, initial monitoring and troubleshooting, customer service education, and much more. Training Programs
- Restaurant Performance Evaluation: Topserve conducts a complete analysis of restaurant dining room service operations and summarizes with a final report.
- Creative problem-solving to balance, coordinate, and facilitate the restaurant service systems for the smoothest operation. All possible solutions are considered before implementation of any new service plan.

TIPS FOR IMPROVING RESTAURANT SERVICE

When it comes to restaurant service, many people have many different opinions and ideas for how things should be done. Yet there are some basic things that should never be overlooked.

Waiting Staff: When hiring waiting staff, managers should look for one thing...good attitude. Alright, two things...good attitude and good balance, but I digress. If you are interviewing someone for a position make sure they have good customer relation skills. I always include on all of my applications that I have good customer relation skills and it often gets me hired. I have had a lot of jobs in food service and customer relations are the most important part. Customer relations is important in any job where you are selling something to someone, but this isn't like unlocking a door for someone to try on a shirt. You are in charge of these people's food, something that goes into their bodies. Things that go in the body can damage it, poison it, or make it sick if not properly cared for. People do not trust waiting staff with nasty attitudes. They worry their food will get spit in, or other horrendous things that are just as gross and unsanitary. A customer should never have to deal with getting a dirty look for asking for things like: more silverware, a clean glass/plate/utensils, a new order because the one that came is wrong or cold, a re-fill for a beverage. I have gotten dirty looks for all of the above. I myself am guilty of having been a jerk behind the counter when it came to food service, and the customers didn't like it. They downright hated it and it made me feel bad. So I tried my best not to let my crankiness show through if I ever was in a mood. For me, being mostly cheerful all the time, I had customers that understood and would often ask me if I was having a bad day. As long as you are polite to people, they won't care if you are in a 'mood'. They start to care when you take your mood out on them, especially with no provocation. I know there are jerk customers in the world...but a jerk waiter is something that has no excuse. You chose the job, so like it or leave it. A good memory is also a plus for any waiting position.

Cleanliness:

The overall cleanliness of the facility is part of the service you provide in a restaurant. The atmosphere is very important. People who go out to eat obviously don't want to eat at home, for whatever reason they chose to do so, they chose to go out and eat. They have made a choice to spend more money than necessary to eat an enjoyable meal. We all know that a part of the price of restaurant dining is to pay for the service of providing the food and not just to pay for the food itself. If someone is paying money for a service, they expect their money's worth from the service. Fast food restaurants get forgiven a lot more often for being a little unkempt, but not nice places where you sit down and have your food brought to you. People want a clean floor, tables, dish ware, waiting staff...anything they can SEE they want clean. Dirty restaurants don't get people coming back to them for more food, because they assume the food may be dirty too. Make sure to vacuum the floors if they are carpet, or sweep them if they are wood or tile. Mop them when there isn't a rush, vacuum when there isn't a rush, just keep it clean. Clean tables after ever use, don't just wipe them down with a wet rage...use cleaner. Keep the restrooms sparkling. Nothing is more gross, and in some ways scary, than an unsanitary bathroom. There are multiple diseases you can get through the spreading of germs in restrooms, especially public restrooms. The toilets should, at least, be cleaned every hour. The amount of people that end up using one toilet within an hour in a busy restaurant is unbelievable. Especially in restaurants that only have two or three (sometimes even just one) toilet per restroom. Keep the sinks clean too, that is where people wash their hands in order to stay sanitary so it's important. Keep the restrooms stocked as well, customers remember experiences like using a restroom with no toilet paper or soap.

Serving the Food:

Make sure that when the waiting staff takes food to tables, the food is actually warm. If the plate is cold, so is the food. Make sure that all meals for one table make it to the table at the same time. I have had too many experiences where one person's food arrives later than everyone else's, or one person gets their food first. Not getting food at the same time can be a problem. It causes people to feel bad they got their food first, which makes them not want to start eating until everyone has their plates. But if their food gets cold while waiting, it makes the other people feel bad. People should not have to feel guilty when they are paying over ten dollars for a plate of food. Especially when they could have made a cheaper version at home for a lot less. It is rude to serve only half a table their meals while making the other half wait an additional ten to twenty minutes. The cooks in the kitchen should be making all the meals for one ticket at the same time, that is how restaurants usually work. The only reason a waiter or waitress should be bringing out meals separately is because an order got messed up and has to be redone (in which case it should be comped), or the customers wanted it that way, or someone has an appetizer, or ordered a meal that automatically takes so long to cook that the other meals would get cold while waiting for it. These are all things customers are generally aware of when ordering food though. They know appetizers, soups, and salads can and often do come at different intervals. They also often know if and when the meal they are ordering is going to take a really long time to cook. Main meals should be brought out at the same time for a whole table. People go to restaurants together to eat together, so they should get their food served together.

Menu:

Make sure the menu is easy to read and understand. Customers hate confusing menus and if the waiting staff has trouble explaining the menu, you're in big trouble. Waiting staff should be able to remember the menu fairly easily in order to properly answer customer questions. Large and complex menus are hard to remember, hard to read, and hard to order from. Menus should be organized and the graphic design should be simple. If you want colorful and bright menus, do colorful and bright in a tasteful way that will make people want to order food from it. If someone is disgusted by your menu, they may unconsciously become disgusted with the idea of eating the food they order from it. The mind is a very powerful thing, and visual stimulation is very thought provoking. A clean, concise, simple, and attractive menu will have people desiring to eat the food off of it rather than having the desire to give it back to you and say 'surprise me' because they don't want to go anywhere else and they have already given up hope of enjoying their meal. The menu is really important, I have heard people comment on how nice the menus are at various places, so it is something they notice at the very least. If you want people to pay attention to your food, and attempt to get others to pay attention with them, you have to present that food in a way that will make them want to eat it. Keep it clean, keep it organized, keep it nice, and people will keep coming back.

INTERIOR DESIGN

Interior design is a multi-faceted profession in which creative and technical solutions are applied within a structure to achieve a built interior environment.

The interior design process follows a systematic and coordinated methodology, including research, analysis and integration of knowledge into the creative process, whereby the needs and resources of the client are satisfied to produce an interior space that fulfills the project goals.

SPECIALIZATIONS

In jurisdictions where the profession is regulated by the government, designers must meet broad qualifications and show competency in the entire scope of the profession, not only in a specialty. Designers may elect to obtain specialist accreditation offered by private organizations. In the United States, interior designers who also possess environmental expertise in design solutions for sustainable construction can receive accreditation in this area by taking the Leadership in Energy and Environmental Design (LEED) examination.

DISCIPLINES

Not to be confused with interior decoration, interior design, which evolved from interior decoration, involves a multitude of technical, analytical, creative skills, and understandings of architectural elements. There is a wide range of disciplines within the career of interior design. Domestically the profession of interior design encompasses those designers who may specialize in residential or commercial interior design. Within residential design one can specialize in kitchen and bathroom design, universal design, design for the aged, multifamily housing amongst others. Other interior designers may dwell in the commercial or contract realm of interior space design. In addition to the above commercial interior designers may specialize in furniture design, healthcare design, hospitality design, retail design, workspace design, sustainability, and if they are a registered architect they can focus on the interior architecture of a space. It is the intent of the professional interior designer to improve the psychological and/or physiological well being of their clients. The professional interior designer achieves this by understanding their clients needs, seeking appropriate solutions, respect their clients social, physical and psychological needs and applying them in a safe and ecologically sensitive manner that promotes the health, safety and welfare of the clients. Interior decoration deals with the home renovations that can be easily and quickly changed, and at lower budgets such as changing kitchen cabinets, selecting wall paper, selecting furniture and usually does not deal with structural building codes. An interior decorator does not need a degree, but has a certificate in interior decorating, while an interior designer would have a four year degree in interior design. The word "decorator" in the phrase "interior decorator" is not an accurate one, since the decorator also changes style and quality of life with a home renovation, so the phrase should be: interior decorator/stylist. A carpenter/home flipper is not the same as an architect/interior designer; carpenter/home flipper usualy copies while architect/interior designer leads.

WORKING CONDITIONS

There are a wide range of working conditions and employment opportunities within interior design. Large and tiny corporations often hire interior designers as employees on regular working hours. Designers for smaller firms usually work on a contract or per-job basis. Self-employed designers, which make up 26% of interior designers, usually work the most hours. Interior designers often work under stress to meet deadlines, stay on budget, and meet clients' needs. In some cases, licensed professionals review the work and sign it before submitting the design for approval by clients or construction permitting. The need for licensed review and signature varies by locality and relevant legislation, and scope of work. Their work tends to involve a great deal of traveling to visit different locations, studios, or client's homes and offices. Usually this work is done under the supervision of a design professional such as an Architect. With the aid of recent technology, the process of contacting clients and communicating design alternatives has become easier and requires less travel. Some argue that virtual makeovers have revolutionized interior design from a customer perspective, making the design process more interactive and exciting, in a relatively technological but labor-intensive environment.

EARNINGS

Interior design earnings vary based on employer, number of years with experience, and the reputation of the individual. For residential projects, self-employed interior designers usually earn a per-hour fee plus a percentage of the total cost of furniture, lighting, artwork, and other design elements. For commercial projects, they may charge per-hour fees, or a flat fee for the whole project. The median annual earning for wage and salary interior designers, in the year 2006, was $42,260. The middle 50% earned between $31,830 and

$57,230. The lowest 10 percent earned less than $24,270, and the highest 10 percent earned more than $78,760.

INTERIOR STYLES

A style, or theme, is a consistent idea used throughout a room to create a feeling of completeness. Styles are not to be confused with design concepts, or the higher-level party, which involve a deeper understanding of the architectural context, the socio-cultural and the programmatic requirements of the client. These themes often follow period styles. Examples of this are Louis XV, Louis XVI, Victorian, Islamic, Feng Shui, International, Mid-Century Modern, Minimalist, English Georgian, Gothic, Indian Mughal, Art Deco, and many more. The evolution of interior decoration themes has now grown to include themes not necessarily consistent with a specific period style allowing the mixing of pieces from different periods. Each element should contribute to form, function, or both and maintain a consistent standard of quality and combine to create the desired design. A designer develops a home architecture and interior design for a customer that has a style and theme that the prospective owner likes and mentally connects to. For the last 10 years, decorators, designers, and architects have been re-discovering the unique furniture that was developed post-war of the 1950s and the 1960s from new material that were developed for military applications. Some of the trendsetters include Charles and Ray Eames, Knoll and Herman Miller. Themes in home design are usually not overused, but serves as a guideline for designing.

ATMOSPHERE

People are attracted to a restaurant by more than just good food. Though important, good food is only a part of the total dining experience. Equally important is the way people feel while in the restaurant. This physical and emotional response is a result of the atmosphere— the total environment to which customers are exposed.

Atmosphere is made up of everything that makes an impression on people. The building design, decor, interior color scheme, texture of the walls, service, and the food create the atmosphere. The right atmosphere can relax guests and generate good feeling and repeat customers. The proper atmosphere can make the food, service and whole dining experience seem better.

People want a dining experience—an escape from problems and everyday surroundings. The atmosphere should project a feeling of friendliness and comfort, be attractive and interestingly different. The atmosphere is remembered long after the meal is finished. For the restaurant owner this means repeat customers and, hopefully, a profitable operation.

Not everyone wants the same emotional response from a restaurant's atmosphere. After working all day, most people would prefer to eat in a quiet, relaxed, intimate atmosphere. However, for those who have worked alone in a quiet environment, a noisy cafeteria might provide needed contrast. It is, therefore, very important to be thoroughly familiar with the characteristics of the type of people you wish to serve.

Designing the "right" atmosphere takes careful consideration. It should be designed to attract the largest number of people possible from the target market group. The total atmosphere and operation of the restaurant should be geared toward this end. People's perception makes the atmosphere. The primary factors of sight, touch, smell, hearing, temperature, and tempo combine to give people their perception of atmosphere.

SIGHT

The perception of sight is a question of acceptability to the eye. Sight perception involves color, lighting, harmony, contrast, order, and space. Many sight needs are subconscious, yet are an extremely important ingredient of the total atmosphere.

A waitress with a dirty uniform and grease smears on the menu are sights unacceptable to the customer's eye. More pleasing sight perceptions are candlelight, clean linen tablecloths, and a neatly set table.

TOUCH

The texture of the walls, curtains, tables, and floors have a "feel" to the imagination. Walls that are smooth and hard may reflect a harsh, cold feeling. Fabric covered walls may produce a feeling of warmth and gentleness. The perception of body contact, seat comfort, floor contact, etc. all contribute to atmosphere.

SMELL

Smell involves both pleasant and unpleasant odors. Smells can positively contribute to the atmosphere. The aroma of fresh brewed coffee, oven-baked bread, fresh cut flowers, and a pine scented breeze can heighten the appetite. Negative smells involve offensive kitchen odors, body odor, food scraps on the floor and table, garbage, and rancid grease.

HEARING

The noise level of conversations, serving staff, kitchen sounds, and music affect the atmosphere. The level of noise acceptable to the ears is a function of age. The older the age group, the less the intensity of noise which is acceptable.

TEMPERATURE

The temperature of the dining room and food influences the individual's perception of the atmosphere. A comfortably warm room and hot food portrays a feeling of high quality, elegance and a slow leisurely meal. Fast-food restaurants needing high turnover to earn a profit usually keep the dining room temperatures cooler in the winter to encourage people to eat faster. Variations from normal temperature are noticed quickly since most people are very sensitive to temperature.

TEMPO

Atmosphere is affected by the tempo of service, length of time to produce the meal, and the time given to eat the meal. The tempo of the dining experience should correspond to the image of the restaurant. Normally, the tempo in a luxury restaurant is more leisurely than the tempo in a fast-food restaurant. There is also a difference between apparent tempo and real tempo. For example, the service personnel may appear to rush about in a great hurry providing fast service. Actually, the service may be quite slow.

People measure the desirability of a restaurant's atmosphere by their senses. It is important that the perception of the atmosphere be one of comfort, ease, and acceptability. This bulletin will explore many physical components affecting atmosphere and how their use can benefit you.

LOCATION

The restaurant's image begins with its location. The character of nearby buildings, streets, and businesses affects people's perception of a restaurant. The locality will attract a certain type of clientele and determine the price range, type of service, and menu selection.

The restaurant's theme should reflect the needs of the people around it, and not be in conflict with its locale. The location indicates the type of service and quality of food people will find there. Location sets the mood for the total dining experience.

The most desirable location for an urban restaurant is on the corner of a block. Here the restaurant enjoys greater visibility and greater flexibility in exterior design. An entrance off each street is best. The suburban or rural restaurant will gain more visibility by locating on a main highway just before a principal traffic generator such as a crossroad, traffic circle, or a city. Locating on the right hand side of the road in the direction of the main flow of traffic is desirable. There is a psychological barrier to making a left turn across a stream of traffic. Building a restaurant at a very busy crossroad is also to be avoided. It is difficult to maneuver through traffic at a busy intersection.

Locating a restaurant in an area with other restaurants has merit. The existence of competition is not necessarily bad. Potential diners are attracted to an area that features good restaurants. People often have no specific restaurant destination in mind and are usually willing to try anything new and interesting.

EXTERIOR DESIGN

The hurried, impatient passerby makes judgement on a restaurant within a few seconds. The function of the exterior design is to attract customers and invite them in to eat. The design should stimulate the imagination and heighten the curiosity of the clientele group. A square block building leaves little to the imagination, but a restaurant exterior that looks like an old whaling ship or a Mexican villa stimulates curiosity and draws people in.

The exterior design should reflect the character of the locality, but be different enough to attract attention. The atmosphere on the inside should be a reflection of the exterior image.

People are naturally suspicious and hesitant upon entering a new restaurant. They are looking for some indication, either positive or negative, as to the quality of the restaurant before they enter. If people are to get past the front door, the exterior design must be attractive and give people confidence in the quality of the establishment. Signs, parking area, landscaping, design and color of the building, windows, curtains, view of the inside, lighting, flowers or plants, and type of door will all be closely scrutinized.

SIGNS

A good sign should indicate at least four things. First, it should indicate "this is a restaurant." This may sound overly simple, but look around you. To the visitor a sign with the words "The Gallery" printed on it has little meaning. The Gallery could be a clothing store, a gift shop, a store displaying art objects, or a restaurant. With so many signs and store fronts competing for attention, sign must leave no doubt about what is being sold.

Second, a good sign should indicate the type of food and service that is being offered. People who dislike chicken do not want to find out after they have been seated that chicken is the only dish served. Indicate somewhere on the exterior of the building the type of food being served, but avoid tired phrases such as steaks and chops," "good food," and "fine dining." A third piece of needed information is the price range. It is quite an embarrassment for a person to enter a restaurant with only four dollars and suddenly find that the least expensive item on the menu is $6.95. A good sign dispels doubt by providing needed information. The sign should not necessarily specify an exact dollar price range, but by means of its style, color, size, and shape, it should indicate an approximate price range.

The use of the words "cafe," "truck stop," "supper club," "inn," and "restaurant" each project a different image and price range. Likewise, the style of lettering also gives a clue as to the approximate price range. Families often eat together. The fourth item a sign should indicate is the type of customer the restaurant caters to. Families need to know if children are welcome. Likewise, someone looking for a very quiet, intimate restaurant would not like to eat with fifty cub scouts celebrating a birthday. The sign should be chosen carefully. The style, design, and color of the sign should follow the same theme as the interior and exterior of the restaurant. Signs should be simple with a minimal amount of wording. The letters should be large enough to be read from at least 200 feet. It takes a car traveling at 55 miles per hour almost 400 feet to stop. At 40 miles per hour 200 feet is needed in which to stop. Signs with 12 inch lettering can be read up to 400 feet away; 8 inch letters can be read at a maximum distance of 250 feet.

The three or four color neon sign, so large it appears that its weight will tip over the building, with flashing arrows pointing to the restaurant's entrance, immediately shouts, "I'm cheap!" Simplicity denotes style and elegance. Signs should be pleasing to the eye.

In locations where many signs are competing for viewer attention, the design becomes even more important. Signs should be eye catching, and unique. If there are eight rectangular signs in a 200 foot stretch of highway, the chances are small that any one of them will be read. But one oval sign among seven rectangular ones will draw attention to the oval sign. Thus, attention can be drawn to a sign by varying the size, shape, color, construction material, height, lighting, or style of printing. By being pleasingly different, it draws attention.

An attitude that often prevails is that if one sign is good, ten signs ought to be ten times better. This is simply not true. The more signs that a restaurant has in one location, the less likely that any one of them will be read. A mass of signs is confusing and signals an unorganized, poorly managed establishment.

The most effective signs are simple and brief. Short and to the point indicates quality and orderliness.

PARKING AREA

The parking area, assuming the restaurant has one of its own, is another indicator of the quality and image of the restaurant. The materials used for surfacing a parking area are, in order of preference, cement, blacktop, crushed stone or gravel, and dirt. Cement has an element of permanence about it which reassures the customer of the quality and longstanding nature of the restaurant. Blacktop is less expensive than cement, but requires more maintenance and does not reflect the elegance of cement. Crushed stone and gravel parking areas are acceptable only if well maintained, graded frequently, and without weeds. However, the dirt and dust caused by vehicles driving over gravel and stone parking areas makes them considerably less desirable. Dirt parking areas are never satisfactory; they are soon rutted, weedy, dirty, and often muddy.

The parking area should have separate and well marked entrance and exit driveways. The minimum area needed to park one car is a space 9 feet by 20 feet. The lanes should be approximately 15 feet wide to enable easy parking. The parking area should be large enough to handle the number of cars determined by the seating capacity of the restaurant plus the cars of the employees. Usually three parking spaces for every 10 seats are adequate for customer parking.

The location of the parking area is a point of debate. A large parking area directly in front of the restaurant makes access to the front door easy. But, a conglomeration of vehicles blocking the view of the restaurant and hiding the carefully planned landscape would probably appeal only to a used car salesperson. On the other hand, parked cars are an indication to potential customers that the food is good. Parking areas located to the rear or sides of the restaurant are most aesthetically pleasing, but may mean customers have a greater distance to walk to reach the front door. There also tends to be a security problem when vehicles are parked out of view of restaurant patrons and passing motorists. The advantage of locating parking areas away from the front of the building is that the landscaping and architectural beauty of the building are in full view of the road traffic and can be used to draw attention to the restaurant.

Probably the best location for the parking area is a compromise between locating it in front of the building or on the sides and back. Place the parking lot so it is visible from the entrance, but not a blot on the landscape. One way of achieving this effect is to design a landscaped open area immediately in front of the building with parking areas on the sides.

LANDSCAPING

Landscaping helps provide the setting and atmosphere for the total dining experience. A well maintained and landscaped exterior attracts customers and hides unattractive service areas from view. It also provides a pleasant vista from the dining room. The landscape design must keep with the theme of the restaurant and harmonize with the exterior and interior features of the building. By using plants of different heights, textures, and colors, the landscape architect can create an attractive exterior. The use of rocks, flowers, ponds, etc. adds contrast and excitement.

BUILDING DESIGN

The building's design should reflect the theme and type of food served by the restaurant. For instance, a restaurant specializing in Chinese food should reflect it in the exterior and interior design of the building. Restaurants catering to children and young families often use bright colors on the exterior to attract attention. Bright colors reflect a happy, friendly, comfortable feeling, and indicate that families are welcome. The psychological effect colors have on people will be discussed later.

Often neglected is the upkeep and maintenance of the building exterior. Peeling paint, dirty windows and doors, and broken light fixtures give a negative impression on the quality and cleanliness of the food being served inside. A run-down exterior makes a bad impression and keeps away many potential customers.

EXTERIOR LIGHTING

The intensity, color, type, and placement of outside lighting is important for developing the desired atmosphere. Proper lighting can add texture, charm, and beauty to a building and landscape. It can accentuate the positive and play down the negative aspects of the exterior design. The intensity and style of light fixtures must also harmonize with the desired atmosphere.

Exterior lighting can attract the attention of passersby and create an impression of the inside atmosphere. Its placement needs careful consideration. Signs, architectural highlights, entrance ways, and parking areas need to be especially well lighted. At night lighting should provide safety by illuminating steps, sidewalks, and other hazards. It should also provide a sense of security.

AVOID GLARE

Outside spotlights can cause an uncomfortable glare to patrons seated near windows. The direction of the light and the type of fixture must be carefully chosen. Avoid the use of gaudy, brightly flashing lights. Although they will attract attention, such a lighting scheme will give the feeling of a poor quality, seedy operation.

ENTRANCE WAY

The entrance way is the climax of the exterior theme and the transition to the interior decor. It actually leads people inside. It should enhance the total atmosphere of the facility.

The entrance to the restaurant should be unmistakably visible to even the casual passerby. There should be absolutely no doubt as to where the entrance door is located.

Separate entrances should be provided to the bar and dining areas. Some non-drinkers object to walking through the bar to get to the dining area; and some drinkers would rather not advertise that they are going to the bar by walking through the dining area. By providing separate entrances within easy access to the parking areas, both the bar and dining room business can be enhanced. An exterior door that opens into an entrance area has an advantage to one that opens directly into the dining room. An entrance area adds a sense of spaciousness and elegance to the atmosphere. It also can function as a meeting place for customers and act as a buffer zone in the winter by cutting down on drafts. When the dining room is full, the entrance area serves as a waiting area. People are much more patient waiting in the entrance area than they are after being seated.

The entrance area is the customer's first and last view of the interior. People will naturally be apprehensive and critical on entering the restaurant for the first time. They will notice the type of decor, the windows, walls, floor covering, lights, pictures, and the inside view. The potential customer can still walk out at this point, so carefully plan and maintain the entrance area.

Design the entrance so that entering customers are not made uncomfortable by being thrust in immediate view of the dining room patrons. Arrange the entrance and dining areas so that customers do not have to parade to their tables in full view of everyone. When customers leave the dining area, they should not feel that they are being watched by the other guests in the room. Likewise, the design should never place the guests into the uncomfortable disadvantage of not being able to see who is watching them.

INTERIOR DESIGN

In regard to design, the early Greeks believed in order, continuity, and simplicity, Good restaurant design is just that.

LIGHTING

The interior lighting scheme has a dramatic effect on the atmosphere and mood of the restaurant. It must make a favorable visual impression and provide enough light for the activities of staff and customers. Proper lighting can make dull, plain walls, ceilings, and furnishings sparkle with interest and character. Poor lighting can emphasize poor architectural design and make a mediocre dining area look bad. A restaurant needs varying levels of light intensity. Bright lights are needed by the staff for cleaning the dining area. The breakfast trade desires a moderately high level of lighting to keep them awake and allow for the reading of the morning newspaper. A moderate level of lighting is needed at noon to stimulate a fast turnover of customers. A low intensity of light creates a leisurely, intimate atmosphere conducive to evening dining. To create these atmospheres, use a rheostat to control the lighting.

The type of clientele patronizing a restaurant has a very important bearing on the intensity of lighting needed. Young people are attracted by low levels of lighting. As people grow older, their eyesight generally deteriorates and brighter lighting is required. The average 60 year old, for instance, needs twice as much light as the average 30 year old. Where a high customer turnover is needed, bright lights and stimulating colors create a brisk atmosphere and fast service. Low levels of lighting are generally associated with higher prices and high quality service.

CANDLELIGHT

Candlelight is the ultimate source of light for the dining area. It develops an excellent mood and intense atmosphere. The shadows cast by the flickering flame creates movement in the room and dramatic shadow patterns. The red flame enhances and flatters people's appearances, and makes most foods appear more appetizing.

Incandescent lights, the typical household bulb, also emphasize the color of red. They are available in a wide range of sizes, shapes, colors, and intensities. Frosted bulbs are usually preferred over clear bulbs since they diffuse the light and soften harsh shadows. Incandescent bulbs are available as spotlights, floodlights, and reflector-type bulbs.

FLUORESCENT LIGHT

Modern fluorescent lighting is very economical to operate and similar to incandescent lighting. Fluorescent light is often combined with incandescent light to provide a variety of lighting textures and intensities. The average life of a fluorescent tube is about 5,000 hours. They give approximately three times as much light as tungsten or filament bulbs of the same wattage. Fluorescent fixtures do require a higher initial investment, but they are more economical when a high level of lighting is needed.

Fluorescent lamps come in a variety of lengths, intensities, and colors. Fluorescent lamps described as "warm," such as GE's White Deluxe, emphasize the colors yellow, orange, red, and red-purple. They produce a warm atmosphere similar to incandescent lighting and are generally recommended for use in restaurants. Lamps designated as "cool," such as Cool White Deluxe, emphasize blue-greens, blue-purples, and yellow-greens. Cool designated lamps enhance all colors and produce a cool atmosphere similar to mid afternoon daylight.

TYPES OF LIGHTING

There are four main types of artificial lighting: uprights, downlights, spots, and floods. Uplights shine upward casting pools of light on the surface above them. The pattern of light emitted depends upon the types of bulb (spot, flood, or ordinary bulb) used inside. A spot bulb will give off a rather small but intense beam of light which can be used to illuminate a picture, a plant, or wall decoration. A wider but less intense cone-shaped light will be given off by a floodlight. An ordinary bulb provides soft illumination.

Uplights, when placed on the floor, behind plants, and in corners, add to the atmosphere by creating dramatic shadows and mood. They also add beauty to the room by reflecting light off the ceiling and into the room. Reflected light from uprights is soft, without glare.

Downlights are positioned to cast a circle of light on the floor, table, or any surface below, and can be recessed into the ceiling, ceiling mounted, or hidden behind ceiling beams or dividers. They can be used for wall washing or pinpointing a specific object. By angling wall washers close to a wall of paintings, they can create contrasting shadows and a rich, intimate atmosphere. They can also highlight an entrance area, cashier's station, individual dining room tables, flower arrangements, or the salad bar. Ceiling mounted downlights give good over-all light, but the light looks flat unless used with other lighting. Downlights should be anti-glare and positioned so customers are not looking directly into them. Spotlights are used as accent lighting—often as downlights—and provide an intense, direct light. Rheostats or dimmers should be used to control their intensity.

Light fixtures are available in a variety of shapes, sizes, colors, and materials. Some types are better for certain purposes than others.

Lighting is usually the least planned element of the atmosphere, but probably has the greatest impact on it. Fixtures should not be purchased solely on the basis of their shape and looks. It is the effect that the lighting will achieve that is important. Lights should be placed above or below eye level so as not to shine in the customers' eyes. Wall mounted fixtures are best used as directional lights bouncing off the ceiling or wall.

Make a room more dramatic and interesting at night with shadows, by contrasting areas of strong light with areas of dark shadows. Also, use pools of light around tables and serving areas, and a minimum amount of light in areas where it is not needed. However, to avoid glare, make sure that lighting is not much brighter than its backgrounds.

Light can add to the atmosphere by showing off an area, a texture, or an object. A light washing a wall can make a small space appear larger. High ceilings will appear to be lower by hanging fixtures and keeping the ceiling dimly lit, and low ceilings will appear to be higher if well lit, The texture of a wall covering can be accentuated by positioning a ceiling-mounted downlight close to the wall. A spot shining directly on a textured wall covering will flatten its appearance.

Light can affect a customers appearance. A light source at or slightly above eye level is most complimentary to the face. Strong overhead lights at sharp angles can accentuate skin wrinkles and deep shadows around the eyes. Table lamps and candles provide a complementary light source if glare is prevented.

Use dim lighting properly. A dimly lit dining area gives warmth and intimacy and at the same time conceals architectural defects. But too little light has a detrimental effect on the atmosphere. Customers may not see properly, or service personnel efficiently perform their jobs. Concentrate light around the seating areas and staff work areas. Downplay most other areas.

CLIMATE CONTROL

Temperature and humidity are important elements of atmosphere. People are sensitive to changes in both. Conditions that are too hot, too cold, too humid, too drafty, or too stuffy can ruin an otherwise carefully designed atmosphere. People respond to climate conditions differently. The ideal dining room temperature is between 70 and 75 degrees Fahrenheit with a relative humidity of around 50 percent. The temperature in the dining room should be adjusted to suit the clientele. Women generally prefer warmer temperatures than do men. Children feel comfortable in lower temperatures than do adults. People in physically active occupations prefer lower temperatures than people with desk jobs. The clientele of higher-priced restaurants are generally accustomed to slightly higher temperatures. However, before setting dining room temperatures check federal energy conservation regulations. They may stipulate minimum and maximum temperature settings.

Dining room temperature can also influence the speed at which people eat. Fast food restaurants usually keep their eating areas at a lower temperature to discourage leisurely eating and encourage fast turnover.

Weather influences acceptable room temperature. On rainy days, a warmer inside temperature is needed than on sunshiny days. During the summer months when light, cool clothing is worn, people prefer a slightly higher room temperature than in the winter when warmer clothing is worn.

Brightness of the lighting can give an impression of heat. The brighter the lighting, the warmer the room appears. To conserve energy, increase the lighting intensity in winter months (while room temperature is decreased), and decrease in the summer months (while room temperature is allowed to rise).

Color also gives an illusion of temperature. As will be discussed in the next section, blue, green, and violet make a room feel cooler than it actually is, while red, yellow, and orange impart a feeling of warmth.

The best way to test the temperature of a room is to sit in it. If the room feels comfortable, the thermostat setting is correct. If the furnace blows alternately hot and then cold air directly on people, they will always be uncomfortable. Finally, eliminate all drafts.

Large windows can also be a source of discomfort. In the winter, warm air should be blown on the inside of large windows to prevent a cold spot. In the summer the sun shining in a window can quickly raise the surrounding air to an uncomfortably high temperature. Curtains or window shades can help prevent heat build-up.

To check for proper temperature control, watch customer reactions. If people are putting on coats and sweaters, turn up the heat. If people are fanning themselves, turn down the heat. When customers complain, do something, or business will go elsewhere!

COLOR

Color is a significant contributor to people's impression of their dining experience. The color of the ceiling, walls, floor covering, tables, chairs, tablecloths, dishes, wall ornaments, and table decorations are often chosen without considering their effect on the atmosphere. Dining room color combinations can make people hungry, depressed, happy, agitated, eat fast, or eat leisurely. Changing the color scheme of a dining room can noticeably increase (or decrease) business.

Color can be used to change the shape and add interest to dull rooms. It can direct attention toward a specific object or away from problem areas. The following chart outlines people's usual responses to colors.

Color Emotional Response

BLUE: A cool color (makes room seem cooler). Calms and relaxes excited people. Makes time seem to pass quickly. Tends to stimulate thought processes and encourage conversation.

GREEN: Easy on the eyes. A cool color. Restful and tranquil. Stimulates conversations. Makes time seem to pass quickly.

RED: Excites. Stimulates. Induces aggression. Makes time seem to pass more slowly.

YELLOW: Cheerful. Feeling of warmth. Happy. Draws attention. Boosts morale.

ORANGE: Friendly, warm and vibrant. Exhilarating.

VIOLET & PURPLE: Cool. Tends to lend elegance and sophistication. Royal.

BROWN: Relaxing. Warm.

GRAY: Depressing. Cool.

Warm colors, red, yellow, orange, and colors with red or yellow hues such as yellow-green, beige, peach, brown, and orange-red are stimulating and cheery.

They make a room feel warm and intimate. Warm colors make a room seem smaller while making objects in the room appear bigger. A warm color on the end walls of a long narrow room will appear to shorten the room. Blue, green, violet, and colors containing blue, such as blue-green, and violet-blue are cool colors. Using these colors helps to create a relaxing atmosphere. Rooms decorated primarily in cool colors tend to appear larger and more spacious. Cool colors are especially pleasing in smaller rooms.

A color wheel is a handy tool to use in developing a color scheme for your dining area. The color wheel consists of twelve colors as shown on the back page of this bulletin.

By choosing different combinations from the color wheel, several color schemes or harmonies are possible. Some common color harmonies are listed below. However, there are no absolute rules for choosing and combining colors, only flexible guidelines. Imagination and experimentation will find color schemes that will lend to the atmosphere and attract customers.

Monochromatic color: A single color on the color wheel. Various tints and shades of a single pure color are used. Can be monotonous and boring if used in a large room. Monotony can be reduced or eliminated by the use of varying textures and by accents using blacks and whites. Example: Walls in light blue with dark blue tablecloths.

Complementary colors: Two opposite colors on the color wheel, such as green and red or yellow and violet. Results in a very pleasing combination of warm and cool colors. Avoid using opposite colors in equal amounts of light and dark combinations, however.

Split complementary colors: Three colors forming a Y on the color wheel. Consists of a base color and one color on each side of the base color's complement (opposite color). A popular color scheme to create interest and richness. Examples: Yellow, blue-violet, and red-violet. Blue, yellow-orange, and red-orange.

Analogous colors-Any three or four consecutive colors on the color wheel. Can be used to create a soft and subtle decor and warm or cool effect. This color scheme needs to be used with caution so as not to end up with an overstimulating nor depressing atmosphere. Example: Blue walls, blue-green carpeting, and green tablecloths.

Triad colors-Every fourth color on the wheel for a total of three colors. A good combination of colors that can create the muted, traditional look as well as more vibrant color characteristic of modern color schemes. Example: Blue walls, red carpeting, and yellow tablecloths.

To develop a color scheme, the dominant color must be selected. Since a solid color in a room is monotonous, the second step is to decide what colors to put with the dominant color. To obtain a pleasing effect, use an uneven balance between warm and cool colors.

Colors must be considered in view of their surroundings. Color changes dramatically when viewed under different circumstances. A red chair will appear yellower when put next to a blue wall. Next to a green wall a red chair will look purer and brighter. Near a white wall it will be lighter and brighter and beside grey it will be brighter. A dark color placed near a lighter color will appear deeper while the light color will appear lighter yet. Colors are also radically altered by differences in pattern and texture.

Before buying any new fixture or wall covering, consider the type of lighting that it will appear under. Many colors take on different hues under different lighting. So, when you buy that tablecloth from the restaurant supply house, try and match the light and surroundings to that found in the restaurant.

Listed below are some important points to keep in mind when color coordinating a dining room:

1. Colors that tend to stimulate appetites are raspberry, yellow-green, peach, and brown.

2. Research has shown that white walls in dining areas are psychologically negative and uninviting, but colored walls stimulate food sales.
3. A single solid color in a room is monotonous and boring.
4. Small color samples of paint, wallpaper, carpeting, etc. will appear brighter when applied in a large area.
5. Light colors make small areas look bigger.
6. Dark colors make large areas look smaller.
7. Dark colors make high ceilings look lower.
8. Glossy, highly reflective colors tire the eyes.
9. Use a mixture of warm and cool colors.
10. A warmer or deeper hue of color on the end walls of long narrow
11. Black and white can be used to accent and add interest to almost any color.
12. The use of different textures adds interest to colors.
13. Colors change under different types and intensities of lighting. (Pink lights pale lipstick colors, green lights show up wrinkles, amber lights tend to wash out colors.)

FURNISHINGS

Furnishings are extremely important to a restaurant and must satisfy many needs. Since they are the first things noticed by the customer upon entering the front door, they must reflect the desired theme and atmosphere. The customer also expects comfort, quality, and beauty in furnishings. At the same time, the restaurant owner wants furnishings that are durable, reflective of the restaurant's character and theme, low cost, and space-saving.

TABLES AND CHAIRS

The type of seating and the layout of the tables and chairs are just as important in creating the proper atmosphere as the softness of the seats.

Booth seating is popular with customers because it provides both privacy and intimacy. People do not like to be seated where they feel exposed to others, and booth seating provides a means of escape from this. Booths also protect customers from being in a traffic area and from being bumped by other customers and or employees. Booth seating also allows management to seat more people per square foot of dining area than does table service.

Tables usually have the advantage of being moveable. Tables for two or four can be connected to accommodate larger parties for greater flexibility and efficiency. In addition, tables are generally regarded as more formal and luxurious than booths.

Part of a customer's perception of the atmosphere is the way the chairs feel and the size and height of the tables. The most comfortable height for chair seats is 17 to 18 inches off the floor. Seat backs should extend to 34" for adequate back support. A seat depth of 16" is comfortable to most people. Chairs with arms add to customers' comfort and are more luxurious. The preferred table top height is 29 to 30 inches. The preferable width across a table is 2'6". Square 2'6" tables are suitable for two to four diners. A two foot square table will accommodate two diners.

Proper positioning of tables can mean more efficient use of dining room space. By positioning the tables in diagonal rather than square formation, more seating per square foot can be obtained. Aisles should be wide enough to permit easy movement of dining room staff and customers. A three-foot-wide service aisle is a minimum. Keep the distance between chairs at different tables at a minimum of three feet.

The amount of space needed varies with the operation. Restaurants with moveable tables and chairs should allow 11 to 18 square feet of dining area per diner. The space between tables should increase with the price of the meal and the amount of service. Dining areas arranged in booths should allow 8 to 11 square feet of dining area per customer. Counter service requires 15 to 20 square feet of area per seat.

Type of seating used depends upon your needs. Tables and booths that seat four people are the least efficient. Tables for two that can be connected to accommodate larger parties are the most efficient. Research has shown that 50 percent of the people come to eat in pairs, 30 percent of the customers are singles and parties of three, and 20 percent consist of parties of four or more. Tables can be made even more efficient by using portable, folding table tops that can stretch a table for two into one for three or four. In crowded conditions, single pedestal tables allow more efficient seating and easier cleanup.

TABLE SETTING

Restaurant designers go to great lengths to make sure the walls, floor covering, color scheme, and decorations harmonize with the theme of the restaurant, but they neglect to consider the table accessories. The silverware, dishes, glasses, napkins, tablecloths, and salt and pepper shakers must also enhance the dining room atmosphere. An old fashioned silverware pattern would destroy the atmosphere created by modern decor. Every detail on the table must carry through the atmosphere and feeling of the restaurant.

Much that has been said about color coordination and its emotional response applies here. The silverware should feel and look right when held in the hand. Use variations in texture and colors complementary to food. For example, a smooth white china plate, textured raspberry colored place mat, and soft green napkins provide the necessary contrast in texture and color to enhance the appearance of food.

Remember, while sitting at the table the customer comes into the closest contact with the feel of the atmosphere.

CURTAINS AND WINDOW SHADES

Curtains are both functional and decorative. Originally curtains were used on cold walls and open doorways to conserve heat. Today curtains and window shades offer a sense of privacy and protection from the sun. Available in many textures, patterns, and colors, window treatments combine to give a feeling of warmth and coziness. They can blend with or contrast the architectural design of the restaurant and can relieve the monotony of the shape of the room.

Carefully coordinate the pattern, color, texture, and material of the curtains to complement the architectural style and theme of the restaurant. Fit large windows with insulating curtains to conserve heat in the winter and lower the cost of air conditioning in summer. Use curtains treated with a fire retardant.

Many restaurants today use decorative shades and blinds to control light and reinforce the atmosphere. Modern blinds and window shades are manufactured using aluminum, wood, plastic, and cloth. They come in solids, prints, and decorative scenes. The color, style, and material of curtains and blinds must enhance the atmosphere, but not draw undue attention.

PLANTS AND FLOWERS

Flowers and plants used as decoration in restaurants can add color and variation. Fresh-cut flower arrangements used to be commonly placed on tables as decoration. They are seldom used now, but can bring a personal touch of freshness if the flowers are simply arranged and regularly replaced before wilting.

Large potted plants are becoming increasingly popular both as decoration and as a screen to divide a room into smaller, intimate areas. They also absorb sound to quiet a noisy room. Many larger cities have florist shops that rent potted plants. This avoids the initial expense of purchasing them and also allows the restaurant to exchange their plants every few months for new ones.

Plants and flowers can be used as an intricate part of the restaurant's theme. By careful selection and arrangement, flowers can blend into the decor and add to the total feeling of the room without becoming the center of interest. The most tasteful arrangements use only two or three bold colors and either blend or contrast them with the color scheme of the room.

WALL ACCESSORIES

Pictures, prints, photographs, sculpture, mirrors, clocks, antiques, and other accessories can contribute and enhance the overall atmosphere of a restaurant. When acquiring accessories, the shape of the accessory, in relation to the wall or area in which they will be displayed, must be considered. A cluster of small accessories would be more favorable on a small wall than one or two large decorative pieces.

The architectural style of the restaurant will determine the type and style of the accessories needed. A Colonial style restaurant might use a tall case clock, pewter lamps, candlesticks, pictures and maps of Colonial times, and lanterns. The accessories should not call attention to themselves, but relate and contribute to the general theme of the restaurant. They can successfully add to the general atmosphere if they contain the color, pattern, and subject of the total design scheme.

The number of accessories to use depends on the type of atmosphere desired. In a formal, leisure dining area limit the use of accessories to avoid a cluttered and hurried look. A tavern or restaurant specializing in a brisk soup and sandwich trade might benefit by using a large number of accessories to create a warm, lively atmosphere. To reduce theft, securely bolt down all pictures and decor items.

The key point is that the accessories and the room must complement each other. The suitability of accessories depends upon their color, style, subject, and placement in relation to the color scheme, shape, and theme of the restaurant.

WALLS

The walls and what is put on them are often ignored by the restaurant operator. But a little thought and imagination in the treatment of the dining room walls can greatly enhance the atmosphere. There are many types of wall coverings, including: paint, wood paneling, wallpaper, fabric, stone, mirrors, tile, rough boards, brick—almost any material imaginable.

PAINT

Painting is the cheapest way to decorate walls, but the surface must be in good condition before painting. Cracks and imperfections will easily show through the paint.

Hundreds of paints are available that will produce a variety of textures and finishes in an almost unlimited array of colors. Enamel produces a smooth, durable surface and is available in flat, semigloss, and high gloss sheens. Because semigloss and high gloss enamel are highly light reflective, flat enamel is preferred on most wall surfaces. Semigloss and high gloss can be used on trim.

When painting, several different wall finishes are available. Stippling, for instance, produces a rough textured surface and is ideal for large wall areas. It hides brush marks and adds interest and depth. A coarse textured wall surface is produced by a technique known as combing. A steel or rubber comb can combine different colors on a wall or produce intricate patterns. Another finishing technique is scumbling. A base color of paint is applied to a surface. A heavier and more opaque second color, called the scumble color, is applied over the base color. By brushing or wiping off parts of the scumble color, the base color is allowed to show through. This produces a variation in color and a unique design.

When selecting the paint, take into consideration its washability, covering quality, and length of wear. Oftentimes the more expensive paint covers better and wears longer than the budget priced paints.

WALLPAPER

Wallpaper and wall coverings are great mood setters. They can liven up a room and change its proportions. They are also a good way to cover rough, cracked walls. Wallpaper and wall coverings can also unify the theme of the restaurant.

Wallpaper comes in roller-printed, hand-blocked designs, and scenic patterns. The more expensive hand-blocked process produces more brilliant colors and subtler shadows than the roller-printer paper. Machine roller-printed paper is more widely available and comes in a greater variety of colors and designs than does hand-blocked paper. Scenic wallpaper is used to create large wall murals which can enlarge a space or draw attention to it. These are quite effective in creating a mood and emphasizing the theme of a restaurant. Each wallpaper pattern is usually available in a number of color schemes.

Some types of wallpapers are more appropriate than others, Large rooms appear at their best when using wallpaper with large patterns. Small patterns should be used in small rooms.

The pattern and color of wallpaper can give a room a feeling of movement. A heavily patterned wallpaper will cause the room to feel busy. The furnishings, therefore, should be kept plain and quiet to complement the busy, wallpaper. A room with heavily patterned wallpaper will appear more crowded and less intimate than one with solid color walls. For this reason often only one wall is papered while the remaining walls are painted.

To ensure a smooth surface, remove all of the old paper before applying the new. A lining paper should be used on rough, badly damaged walls to provide a smooth surface for the decorative wallpaper.

There are several types of vinyl wall coverings on the market that are ideally suited for restaurant use. They are tough, waterproof, and can be repeatedly scrubbed clean. Also popular is foil, silver, and copper Mylar wallpaper in plain or with an over-printed design. It is shiny and reflective and adds an illusion of spaciousness to a room.

Grass cloth, made from the honeysuckle vine, is available in a wide range of colors, textures, and patterns. Due to the manufacturing process, there are great variations in color and texture in a roll, and from roll to roll. The variations in color and pattern do create a unique and beautiful effect, although matching pattern of one roll with that of the next is almost impossible.

WALL COVERINGS

Almost any fabric can be used as a wall covering. Fabrics from cotton to velvet to suede to felt can add charm and an expression of the restaurant's theme. Carpeting can continue part of the way up a wall and add a feeling of comfort as well as a measure of soundproofing.

Wood is an extremely versatile and varied wall covering material. The inherent beauty of wood creates a luxurious, warm atmosphere that is difficult to match. According to the species chosen, wood comes in a wide range of colors. The grain of the wood also varies greatly with species and the way it is cut from the log. Tongue and groove boarding, weathered barn siding, and rough hewn lumber can be used vertically, horizontally, or diagonally to help create a memorable atmosphere.

Tile, cork, terrazzo, draperies, brick, stone, and plaster are other wall coverings that can change the feeling of a room and set the desired atmosphere.

Architectural blunders, such as exposed pipes and off-center windows, can either be disguised or accentuated. Architectural eyesores can be diminished by painting everything in the area a dark color. This tends to blend everything together and makes design errors less noticeable.

On the other hand, if you can't hide it, bring it out. A wall with a confusion of pipes can be made interesting by calling attention to them. By painting the pipes a contrasting color, attention is centered on them and they become interesting.

CEILINGS

Historically ceilings were very ornately decorated with intricate patterns and designs. Today ceilings are often neglected, large blank surfaces. However, much can be done with ceilings to complement the theme and decor of a restaurant. The previous discussion on wall treatments equally applies to ceilings.

Ceilings can be covered with wallpaper, fabric, acoustical tiles, light decorative tiles, ceiling planks, beams, tongue and groove boarding, and weathered barn siding. Exposed beams placed on a ceiling can break up the ceiling area and provide for a more intimate feeling. Beams will also provide for a quieter dining area by breaking up the sound waves. Exposed joists can be stained, bleached, or waxed to add individual charm to the room. The ceiling can be raised, lowered, louvered, rounded and curved to produce different ceiling levels. This will add interest and help produce that distinctively different dining experience people desire. If heating and air conditioning ducts, wiring, and plumbing are a problem, the ceiling can be lowered with a suspended grid system to conceal them.

Create interest in the ceiling by painting patterns, ovals, and other shapes on it. An especially effective technique is to repeat the floor pattern on the ceiling. A simplified version of the carpet design can be painted on the ceiling. This has a unifying effect and strengthens the atmosphere. Do not paint acoustic tile. Painting destroys its sound deadening capabilities. If ceiling tiles become stained and dirty, replace them.

FLOORS

Floors anchor a decorating scheme and pull it all together. Everyone entering a restaurant has direct contact with the floor. Customers consciously look at the floor to see how clean it is. They also consciously or unconsciously equate the feel of the floor underfoot with the atmosphere and dining experience. The color, texture, material, and design of the flooring must complement the total atmosphere of the restaurant. It must blend in with and add to the theme of the restaurant without calling attention to itself. In choosing a floor covering, give consideration to qualities such as ease of cleaning, estimated life, stain resistance, durability, and sound absorbing characteristics.

CARPETING

Carpeting is widely used today in all types of restaurants. The addition of carpeting tends to upgrade a restaurant and attract a higher income clientele. It adds warmth and a sense of luxury as well as deadening sound. The color, style, texture, and pattern should relate well with the total atmosphere.

Carpeting is commonly manufactured in three methods: woven, knitted, and tufted. On woven carpets the surface pile and backing are interwoven at the same time. This, in effect, creates a single fabric. Due to this interweaving process, the pile yarns will not pull out. On tufted carpeting the tufts are not interwoven onto the backing, but held in place by a coating of latex applied to the backing. Tufted carpeting is available in a wide variety of textures. Knitted carpeting loops together the pile yarn, backing yarn, and stitching yarn in one process. The backing is coated with latex to prevent pulls and snags. Knitted carpets are usually solid colors or tweeds.

The color of the carpeting must be selected very carefully. Wall-to-wall carpeting will bring a great deal of color to a room and dramatically alter the room's appearance. Carpeting will usually have a more comfortable feeling if it is of a darker color than the surrounding walls. Generally speaking, the color of the carpet and walls should be from the same color family. Contrasting the carpet and wall colors usually produces too sharp an effect. Expense should not be compromised when it comes to buying carpeting. The best quality carpeting is a better value in wearability, sound and heat insulation, and direct absorption.

TILING

Vinyl floor tiling is available in a myriad of styles, sizes, shapes, designs, and colors, and comes in the form of sheet vinyl, vinyl asbestos tile, and vinyl tile. Advantages of resilient tiles are its durability, economy, ease of installation, and simple maintenance.

Glazed and unglazed ceramic tiles can also be used to provide a permanent, natural surface. Many fast-food hamburger chains use ceramic tile flooring because of their easy maintenance and extreme durability. They are ideal where a busy, fast-paced atmosphere is desired. The noise from walking on ceramic tile creates an exciting atmosphere. The disadvantages of ceramic tile are its initial cost and the commitment to one type of flooring for the life of the building.

TERRAZZO

Terrazzo is a flooring material made from chips of marble, onyx, or other rock embedded in cement or certain chemical compounds. It is usually poured in place and ground and polished to a uniformly textured surface.

A terrazzo floor is extremely durable and permanent. It requires very little maintenance. Terrazzo is ideal for heavy traffic areas and where customer turnover is high. Many fast-food restaurants have terrazzo floors.

WOOD FLOORING

The natural beauty of wood flooring offers many, variations in color and pattern. Although wooden flooring requires more maintenance and is noisier than other types of floor coverings, its beauty can be a major contributor to developing the atmosphere.

Wood flooring is available in four forms: strip, plank, parquet, and fabricated wood blocks. Oak, walnut, beech, birch, maple, and teak are commonly used as flooring. Colors range from pale gold, through the browns, to nearly black. Combining light and dark colored woods can add interest and be very attractive.

Flooring can be purchased in strips from 1 1/2 to 2 1/4 inches wide. Plank flooring comes in varying widths from 3 to 8 inches wide. Parquet flooring combines pieces of different sizes of wood. Wood blocks vary in size from 6 11/32 inches square to 19 inches square. Rectangles are also manufactured. Wood blocks are available in patterns such as herringbone, basket weave, small squares, and parallel strips.

Wood flooring can be finished in different ways. They can be stained, bleached, streaked, varnished, waxed, or painted. The grain can be emphasized or hidden. By varying the finish given to the wood, the appearance and texture can be changed to suit the environment and design scheme.

BRICK, SLATE, STONE

The durability of brick, slate, and stone makes their use as flooring well suited for high traffic areas such as entrance ways. The charm of such flooring materials can add measurably to the atmosphere. As in tiling and terrazzo flooring, customers' footsteps will be more noticeable than on carpeting. Also the permanence and initial high cost must be considered.

SIZE AND SHAPE OF ROOMS

Modern dining rooms must be comfortable and provide a measure of privacy for individual tables. The use of high-backed booths, different floor levels, lighting, acoustics, and color can create the impression of privacy.

Rooms can be divided to provide a sense of privacy by using screens, broadleafed plants, and different floor levels.

Most older restaurants have a single, large, open dining area. People seek privacy in these dining rooms by sitting in corners and along walls. The more vulnerable seating areas usually fill up last. By dividing the large dining room into smaller dining areas, customers can enjoy a greater sense of dining pleasure.

Large dining rooms can be broken up by changing the levels of the floor. Platforms and lowered areas can create a series of smaller dining areas, adding to the sense of privacy. Seating capacity sometimes can even be increased by having multiple floor levels. Tables can be closer together, yet because of the different levels, not appear crowded. Mirrors can be used to widen a long narrow room and eliminate the feeling that people are eating in a hall.

Rooms can be divided to provide a sense of privacy by using screens, either free-standing, fixed, solid, or see-through. Ordinary wooden garden lattice makes an inexpensive but effective room divider. Portable, sliding or folding screens can be used to divide off rooms. Screens can be covered with wallpaper to adapt to the setting of the room. Broad-leaved plants, either hanging or in stand-up boxes, act as good room dividers. Effective room dividers can also be made using decorative beads of wood, cork, glass, or plastic. The beads can be hung from curtain rods, slit rods, fabric-covered dowels, screw eyes, or moldings, The material used to break up a large dining room should blend in with the atmosphere and theme of the restaurant.

TEXTURE AND PATTERN

Textures create their own images. It is necessary when designing an atmosphere to consider not only the color of walls, flooring, and furnishings, but also the texture and pattern. Walls covered in burlap, wood, plaster, stone, and foil paper all present different images. The texture must be carefully chosen to complement the atmosphere of the restaurant. Try to imagine how different textures look on floors, walls, ceiling, and furnishings. Contrasting textures go well together. Rough goes well with smooth and matte goes well with glossy. Rough brick walls contrast well with a smooth tweed or a burlap fabric.

If used correctly, a pattern can give added depth and space to a room. Large patterns are acceptable when used in large rooms. Small patterns should be used in smaller rooms. The same patterns in two different colors look good together. Using a very similar pattern in the same color can also be effective. For example, both the curtains and carpet may be in the same shade of brown, but the pattern on the curtains is slightly different than the pattern on the carpet.

CLEANLINESS

The best food and a well thought out restaurant design cannot make up for lack of cleanliness. A favorable atmosphere is quickly destroyed by trash in the parking lot, a dirty floor, dirty silverware, spotty glasses, greasy windows, and soiled menus.

MENU

The menu cover and contents should reflect the design and style of the restaurant. The design of the menu, its details, the style of type used, and the impression it creates all set the atmosphere. A small, simple menu in a color that harmonizes with the decor is desirable. It should set the feeling of the restaurant. Novel, gimmicky menus may attract attention, but the repeated use of awkward, hard to read menus becomes objectionable.

People respond to the color of a menu and appreciate its shape and "feel." Customers are not impressed by dirty, dog-eared menus stuck together with adhesive tape.

Menus should be simple and easy to read. They should carefully describe the food served. A short but descriptive statement about major items served can stimulate the appetite and measurably increase the guest check. A dull menu is a blot upon the atmosphere.

ACOUSTICS

The sounds of a restaurant are part of its atmosphere. Kitchen noises, voices, traffic noises, and dish bussing all add to the atmosphere.

Noise in a dining area is not always undesirable. People who work in quiet places, or are lonely, may seek out noisy restaurants. Business people will sometimes seek a noisy restaurant to conduct business so they will not be overheard. A noisy surrounding can create a special atmosphere which sets people at ease and stimulates people and makes them eat faster. However, before changing the sound patterns of your restaurant know your customers' needs.

Reducing the noise level is the first step toward dampening down a restaurant's atmosphere to give it intimacy and luxury. Sound proofing between the kitchen and dining room is a must. Dishwashing operations generate much of the noise coming from the kitchen. Partitions separating preparation areas help to deaden the sound. Low ceilings help reduce sound reverberation, but tend to cause lighting and ventilation problems. A good sound absorbing material used on kitchen ceilings and the upper part of the walls will reduce kitchen noises. Sound waves are absorbed most by any porous surface. Regardless of the material used to cover kitchen ceilings and walls, these surfaces must be easily cleaned.

Acoustic tile is sometimes used to deaden sound in restaurants. It effectively controls sound, but has the disadvantage of not being easy to clean. Painting acoustic tile destroys its sound dampening capabilities. Carpeting, when used with a sponge rubber pad, reduces noise levels and adds to comfort when standing. Dining room carpeting must be of a commercial grade. The Michigan Health Department does not allow carpeting in food preparation areas, storerooms, wash rooms, or dishwashing areas.

MUSIC

Music can help set the atmosphere in a restaurant. Background music has a strong and direct effect on people's moods. The correct type of background music puts customers in a good mood and helps make the staff more relaxed and efficient. Background music helps to warm up the atmosphere before a dining room fills up with the noise of people. Music should be unobtrusive and never compete with conversations, and felt, but not listened to. Background music should be drowned out by people talking when the dining room fills up.

Background music is available from many sources, such as a designated phone line or leased subcarrier signal system. Playing tapes, records, or using the radio as a source of music for customers is illegal unless royalties are paid. The type of music depends on the mood to be created. A restaurant catering to teenagers would select top ten music while a luxury restaurant would want soft, romantic background music.

The time of day also determines the style of background music to be played. The breakfast crowd likes bright, wake-up music; at lunch the pace of the music needs to slow down; in the afternoon the music again needs a bit more lift; relaxed and discreet cocktail music is played after five o'clock to provide a good background for conversation; dinner music rounds out the evening.

HUMAN FACTORS

Architecture and decor are only part of the elements making a successful restaurant atmosphere. A warm, friendly atmosphere calls for warm, friendly service. It is the contacts with the waitress, hostess, busboy, manager and cashier that can make a restaurant look great under any conditions.

Restaurants are in the people business. Its atmosphere is a human atmosphere. Customers are more influenced by people, their personalities and moods, than by anything else in the restaurant. Customers are looking for more than just someone who puts food in front of them. They want personal and enthusiastic service. A restaurant is similar to a theater. The decor is the stage setting, the service personnel are the actors and actresses, and the guests the audience. The more like the theater the dining room appears, the more intrigued the customer will be. The customers want personal attention, and want to feel the play (dining experience) is for their exclusive benefit.

The age and sex of customers contributes to the atmosphere. People like to be served by people their own age. A young clientele would prefer to be served by a young waitress; a senior citizen oriented restaurant would be wise to employ older service personnel. A restaurant with predominantly male customers would be advised to employ mostly female service personnel. Likewise, female customers usually prefer male service personnel.

The dress and appearance of customers and staff are also important elements of atmosphere. Luxury restaurants may require customers to conform to a "coat and tie" dress code. This maintains a high quality of visual appearance and formality to the atmosphere.

The dress of the staff can lend interest and color to the theme of the restaurant. Ethnic, historic, and other theme restaurants can greatly strengthen the atmosphere by dressing service personnel in appropriate costumes. Informal family restaurant staff should be dressed in the same type of uniform to add a sense of orderliness to the atmosphere. Carefully choose style, design, and color of uniforms to coordinate with the decor. The uniforms should complement the wearer and make the staff feel comfortable and able to carry out their duties.

7

Food Preservation

FOOD PRESERVATION BY HEAT

The most ancient method is drying, and it was employed early for fruits, grains, vegetables, fish, and meat. It was sometimes combined with parching, as in the oatmeal of Scotland or the corn of the Native American.

Modern applications of this ancient device are seen in dried or dehydrated fruits and vegetables, milk, meat, and eggs. A more recent variation, known as freeze-drying, is now being used on such foods as instant coffee, meat, orange juice, and soup.

The early method of drying was by direct exposure to the sun's rays; in modern industry the process is hastened by complex apparatus and by chemical agencies. The use of sugar was early combined with drying. Smoking, a method used mainly for fish and meat, combines the drying action with chemicals produced from the smoke, which form a protective coating. The process of heating was used centuries before its action was understood. One of the most important modern applications of the heat principle is the pasteurization of milk.

CANNING

Canning is the process of hermetically sealing cooked food for future use. It is a preservation method, in which prepared food is put in glass jars or metal cans that are hermetically sealed to keep out air and then heated to a specific temperature for a specified time to destroy disease-causing microorganisms and prevent spoilage. Low-acid foods, such as meats, are heated to 240°–265°F (116°–129°C), while acidic foods, such as fruits, are heated to about 212°F (100°C). Canning was invented in 1809 by Nicholas Appert. The process proved moderately successful and was gradually put into practice in other European countries and in the United States. Glass containers were used at first, but they proved bulky, costly, and brittle.

Early can-making was slow and expensive; sheets of tin were cut with shears, bent around a block, and the seams heavily soldered. A good tinsmith could make only about 60 cans a day.

The industry began to assume importance with the invention in 1847 of the stamped can. Because of the food requirements of soldiers during the US Civil War, considerable amounts of canned meats and vegetables were produced. Salmon from the Columbia River was canned in 1866 and salmon from Alaska in 1872.

A machine for shaping and soldering was exhibited in 1876 at the Centennial Exposition at Philadelphia. The open-top can of the 20th cent, with a soldered lock seam and double-seamed ends, permits easy cleaning and filling. Cans used for foods that react with metals, causing discoloration (usually harmless), may be coated with a lacquer film. Highly specialized machinery, knowledge of bacteriology and food chemistry, as well as more efficient processes of cooking, have combined to make the commercial canning of food an important feature of modern life. The range of products canned has increased enormously and includes meat and poultry; fruits and vegetables; seafood; milk; and preserves, jams, jellies, pickles, and sauces.

The general principles of commercial and home canning are the same, but the factory more accurately controls procedures and has highly specialized machinery. The Mason jar, popular in home canning, was patented in 1858. Home canning grew in popularity during World War II, when the harvest of "victory gardens" was canned. Canning leads to a loss of nutrient value in foods, particularly of the water-soluble vitamins. The home-canning methods recommended today are much more specific than the old-fashioned methods, which are no longer considered safe.

PASTEURIZATION

Pasteurizationm of a Apple Juice

Pasteurization is partial sterilization of liquids such as milk, orange juice, wine, and beer, as well as cheese, to destroy disease-causing and other undesirable organisms. The process is named for the French scientist Louis Pasteur, who discovered in the 1860s that undesired fermentation could be prevented in wine and beer by heating it to 135°F (57°C) for a few minutes.

The most important method of preserving apple juice is pasteurization, which involves heating the juice to a given temperature for a length of time that will destroy all organisms that can develop, if juice is put hot into containers that are filled and hermetically sealed. Flash pasteurization is, true to its name, the rapid heating of juice to near the boiling point (greater than 88°C) for 25 to 30 seconds.

Steam or hot water passes the juice between plates or through narrow tubes that are heated. Design of the heat exchanger provides juice flow turbulence and even heating to prevent scorching and burn-on in the unit. There are numerous flash pasteurization heat exchangers available. They are all adaptable to a continuous operation set-up. Juice can be canned or bottled in cans, glass or plastic. Cans used are enamel or lacquer lined to resist corrosion from the juice. As the cans travel the canning line, they must pass through a can washer, be filled from filling machines and immediately sealed on a can-closing machine.

After closure cans should be positioned or inverted so that the hot fill will be in contact with the lid and thus, pasteurize it. From here, the cans must be removed to a cooling room where they will be cooled to near 38°C to stop the effect of high heat on the contents. If cooled to a temperature lower than 35°C, the labels will tend to detach, the can will not dry and will be susceptible to surface rusting. This necessitates that the cans travel continuously from washing, to filling to cooling to labelling and packing.

Bottling juice requires specialized equipment. Cans can be roughly handled, but bottles are fragile ("bruising" not visible to the eye can cause breakage later) and susceptible to thermal shock. Temperature changes of greater than 7°C should be avoided.

Bottles must be cleaned before filling then heated (steam jets) within 7°C of the fill temperature. The best filler draws the liquid into the bottle by evacuating the bottle, thus reducing oxidation. Bottle closures can be screw caps, crown caps or vacuum caps. The vacuum caps have the advantage of allowing less headspace; if the contents ferment only the cap will blow off rather than the bottle exploding. Bottles also must be cooled. This can be accomplished in a special cooler that sprays hot water on them and decreases the temperature as the bottles move along. At the end, they emerge close to 38°C, still warm enough to dry. Newer packaging and processing systems use plastic containers that can be hot filled and rapidly cooled without the danger of thermal shock. In addition, aseptic processing greatly reduces heat-induced flavour changes. Still, glass bottles are the traditional standard and carry a quality image not implicit in cans, plastic bottles or aseptic packs.

Recent concerns about contaminated fresh cider have resulted in United States Federal Regulations that strongly discourage unpasteurized juice and advise pasteurization of all apple juice products, even at small roadside stands and country markets that prepare juice on site. The alternative is a not very appealing warning label on fresh apple juice. Milk is pasteurized by heating it to about 145°F (63°C) for 30 min. or by the "flash" method of heating to 160°F (71°C) for 15 sec., followed by rapid cooling to below 50°F (10°C), at which temperature it is stored. The harmless lactic acid bacteria survive the process, but if the milk is not kept cold, they multiply rapidly and cause it to turn sour.

Pasteurisation of Milk

Science and technology is undoubtedly escalating its claws in every area of nature, and inventions are being made towards advancement of civilization.

The world today is not the same as it was decades ago, credit goes to technology growth. Nature has given us myriads of gifts, and technology has made variations in them, apparently for our benefits. There is a big controversy in the West, whether pasteurisation of milk is beneficial or detrimental to human health. Proponents of the process argue that it is to make milk and milk products safe for consumption by razing away injurious bacteria, and to improve keeping quality of raw milk.

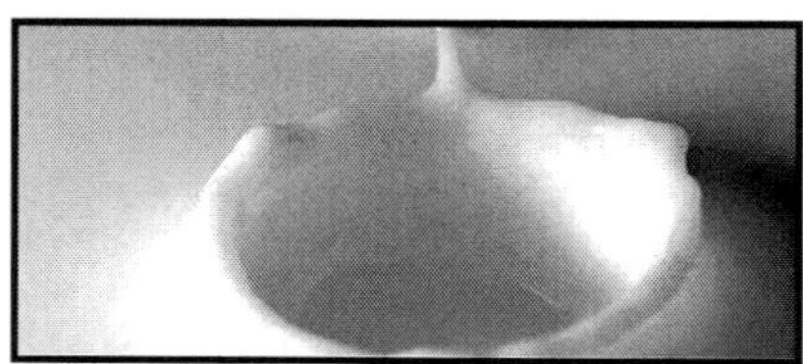

Fig. 1: Drop of Milk

Let us briefly know what pasteurization is. It is an artificial process used to destroy dangerous bacteria without substantially changing the composition or flavour of milk. The method also prevents rapid souring of milk. Under this process milk is heated to a temperature between 55 and 70°C for 30 minutes, and then is rapidly cooled and stored at a temperature below 10°C. Sometimes higher temperatures are applied for a shorter period of time.

The temperatures and time are determined by factors necessary to destroy bacteria (pathogens). The process was named after the French chemist Louis Pasteur. Pasteurization has been used to kill bacteria in milk including *Salmonella*, *Listeria, Campylobacter, E.coli*, and *Bracella*.

The problem is that in addition to the killing of bad bacteria, pasteurization kills good bacteria too. However, researches have been conducted and have proved that pasteurization diminishes the nutritional value of raw milk that is requisite for human health. Some of the effects of pasteu-risation are: the process destroys the enzyme phosphate present in raw milk. Phosphate is required to split and assimilate mineral salts in foods that are in the form of Phytates.

Protein, a valuable nutrient in raw milk, is greatly affected by the process. Its digestibility is reduced by 4% and biological value is reduced by 17%. The effect of the process on vitamins, vital nutrients in raw milk, is that the pasteurization process destroys about 38% of vitamin B complex; and vitamin C is weakened or destroyed. Studies show that infants who are fed with pasteurized milk might develop scurvy. Not only protein and vitamins, but also mineral contents in raw milk are badly ruined by the process. After the process the calcium content is very much diminished.

The loss of soluble calcium in regards to infant's growth and development is a very important factor. It is not only the concern in children regarding bone formation and teeth, but also in adults about the calcium content in the blood. It also destroys 20% per cent of iodine present in raw milk and causes constipation. After lot of research it is apparently clear that the process of pasteurization deteriorates quality of raw milk. Raw milk is in demand and is desirable by people who are becoming aware about the dangers of pasteurization to a product of daily consumption.

Despite such scientific evidence in favour of raw milk and against pasteurized milk, and the fact that human beings have always lived on raw milk without facing any serious threats to life, an intriguing fact is that sale of raw milk has been made illegal in the US except in a few states.

People can only get pasteurized milk or organic milk. Organic milk is the milk that comes from the cows that are raised on organic food, no growth hormones or antibiotics are used and cattle graze on grass which hasn't been sprayed with pesticides. However, organic milk is around two and a half times the price of pasteurized milk, which becomes difficult for everyone to afford. However, milk is such an important component in daily life, that despite so much of controversy about pasteurization and no good alternative for raw milk, people don't have choices but to have pasteurised milk in the US. The problem is not of the West anymore, but is rapidly transferring to countries like India too. This is the issue created by technology and need to be raised in India before pasteurized milk becomes the choice of the Government of India. Pasteurization destroys most disease producing organisms and limits fermentation in milk, beer, and other liquids by partial or complete sterilization. Pasteurization does not destroy organisms that grow slowly or produce spores.

While pasteurization destroys many microorganisms in milk, improper handling after pasteurization can recontaminate milk. Many dairy farms use a home-pasteurizing machine to pasteurize small amounts of milk for personal use. Raw milk can also be pasteurized on the stovetop. Microwaving raw milk is not an effective means of pasteurization because of uneven heat distribution. Ultra-high temperature (UHT) processing destroys organisms more effectively and the milk is essentially sterilized and can be stored at room temperature for up to 8 weeks without any change in flavour.

Milk, a natural liquid food, is one of our most nutritionally complete foods, adding high-quality protein, fat, milk sugar, essential minerals, and vitamins to our diet. However, milk contains bacteria that—when improperly handled—may create conditions where bacteria can multiply. Most of the bacteria in fresh milk from a healthy animal are either harmless or beneficial. But, rapid changes in the health of an animal, or the milk handler, or contaminants from polluted water, dirt, manure, vermin, air, cuts, and wounds can make raw milk potentially dangerous.

How do Microorganisms Enter the Milk Supply?

Our environment contains an abundance of micro-organisms that find their way to the hair, udder, and teats of dairy cows and can move up the teat canal.

Some of these germs cause an inflammatory disease of the udder known as mastitis while others enter the milk without causing any disease symptoms in the animal.

In addition, organisms can enter the milk supply during the milking process when equipment used in milking, transporting, and storing the raw milk is not properly cleaned and sanitized. All milk and milk products have the potential to transmit pathogenic (disease-causing) organisms to humans.

The nutritional components that make milk and milk products an important part of the human diet also support the growth of the organisms. Drinking raw milk causes foodborne illness, and dairy producers selling or giving raw milk to friends and relatives are putting them at risk.

What are Common Pathogens in Milk?

Illnesses from contaminated milk and milk products have occurred worldwide since cows have been milked. In the 1900s it was discovered that milk can transmit tuberculosis, brucellosis, diphtheria, scarlet fever, and Q-fever (a mild disease characterized by high fever, chills, and muscular pains) to humans. Fortunately, the threat of these diseases and the incidence of outbreaks involving milk and milk products has been greatly reduced over the decades due to improved sanitary milk production practices and pasteurization.

Salmonella

Salmonellosis is the most common disease transmitted in raw milk. This organism is shed in the faces of cattle and picked up on the animals' hair or teats. Many strains of *Salmonella* can cause foodborne illness in humans, and all strains exhibit the same symptoms such as gastroenteritis (vomiting and diarrhoea). Pasteurization destroys the *Salmonella* organism, and although pasteurized milk, powdered milk, and cheese have been implicated in salmonellosis outbreaks, in these cases, the pasteurized milk was contaminated during further processing.

Listeria Monocytogenes

This widespread organism is found principally in soil. Listeriosis in humans may cause serious illness, and is especially dangerous to pregnant women, causing stillbirths or infant death soon after birth. Pasteurization inactivates *Listeria monocytogenes.*

Yersinia Enterocolitica

This common organism has been found in many foods of animal origin including milk, cheese, and red. *Yersinia,* found in streams, lakes, and wells, spreads from the water to warm-blooded animals. The most common symptom of yersinosis is gastroenteritis and mimics the symptoms of appendicitis. *Yersinia enterocolitica* is destroyed by pasteurization.

Campylobacter Jejuni

This organism, isolated in raw milk and meat, can cause mastitis in dairy cattle. It has also been isolated in the faces of many species including dogs, cats, rodents, cattle, sheep, swine, and poultry. Symptoms include vomiting, cramps, bloody diarrhoea, mild enteritis, or severe enterocolitis. Individuals who have recovered from the disease may suffer a relapse. *Campylobacter jejuni* is destroyed by pasteurization.

Staphylococcus Aureus

It is a common cause of mastitis in dairy cattle and can enter the milk supply from sores on the teats of cows or from the hands and nasal discharges of dairy farmers and workers. The *Staphylococcus* organism produces an enterotoxin (toxins causing vomiting and diarrhea) in raw milk when it is held at temperatures above 50°F. Sufficient amounts of enterotoxin in foods can cause illness. The incidence of staphylococcal intoxication has been greatly reduced by pasteurization.

Escherichia Coli 0157: H7

Recent studies show that young dairy cattle are host to *E.coli* and fecal contamination is a likely source of *E.coli* in raw milk. It can cause hemorrhagic colitis and hemolytic uremic syndrome in humans. Milk should be stored at temperatures below 40°F to inhibit the growth of *Escherichia coli.*

Temperature abuse during holding and shipping can cause significant growth of the organism. Pasteurization destroys this organism. Pasteurization, named for Louis Pasteur who developed the process for other foods, is a moderate but exact heat treatment of milk. Pasteurization kills bacteria that produce disease and retards spoilage in milk.

What are the Requirements for Safe Handling of Milk?

The requirements for proper pasteurization and handling of milk are:

- A potable water supply and proper dispensing system must be available to avoid contamination. A pure hot and cold water supply for the animals' health, and for proper cleaning of the animals, milk handlers and utensils. Regular inspection and maintenance of the system is necessary.
- Clean and healthy animals, clean hands, and clean utensils are essential. The animals' hair should be clipped regularly around the flanks and udder to keep it from collecting dirt. Milkers should wash their hands and the udder with clean water or use an approved germicidal solution before milking. *Milk from diseased animals or those under antibiotic treatment may not be used.* All equipment and utensils

should be cleaned immediately after use. Stainless steel utensils are preferred since they are durable and easy to clean.

- Rapid cooling, cold storage, proper pasteurization, and clean cold storage of pasteurized are necessary for the prevention of foodborne illness. Milk must be promptly cooled to 40°F (4°C) or less and stored in a closed container before and after pasteurization to maintain the quality and flavour of the milk. Care should be taken not to transfer barnyard dirt from the bottom or sides of the storage container to the countertop or to utensils in the pasteurization and storage areas. Do not mix fresh milk with previously cooked milk unless you plan to pasteurize the entire batch immediately.

How Do I Pasteurize Milk?

Milk must be heated, with agitation, in such a way that every particle of the milk, including the foam, receives a minimum heat treatment of 150°F (66°C) continuously for 30 minutes or 161°F (72°C) for 15 seconds. The temperature should be monitored with an accurate metal or protected glass thermometer.

Commercial operations commonly use a high temperature, short-time process in which the milk is heated to 170°F (77°C) for 15 seconds and then cooled immediately to below 40°F (4°C) to increase storage life without any noticeable flavour change in the milk. Pasteurization of fluid milk has very specific requirements for time and temperature as listed in the chart.

Table 1: Temperature-Time Requirements for Pasteurization of Fluid Milk

Temperature	*Time*
• 150°F (66°C) (vat pasteurization)	30 minutes
• 191°F (89°C)	1 second
• 212°F (100°C)	0.01 second

While pasteurization destroys many microorganisms in milk supplies, improper handling after pasteurization can recontaminate milk.

Home Pasteurization of Milk

Many dairy farms have a home-pasteurizing machine to pasteurize small amounts of milk for personal use. When they are operated according to manufacturers' directions, proper pasteurization will require little attention. A good compromise for home pasteurization is to heat the milk to 165°F (74°C) in a double boiler and to hold it at this temperature for 15 seconds while stirring constantly.

Then cool it immediately while stirring to 145°F (63°C) by setting the top of the double boiler in cold water. Add ice to the cooling water to cool the milk further, stirring occasionally until the temperature of the milk falls below 40°F (4°C). Store the cooled milk in clean, covered containers and keep it at a temperature below 40°F (4°C) until used.

This is the preferred method over the 30-minute/150°F (63°C) method because if at any time during the 30-minute period the temperature drops below 150°F (63°C), the milk must be reheated for 30 consecutive minutes.

Another method is using jars for 30 minutes in a waterbath canner, again, provided care is taken to maintain the temperature at 150°F (63°C), and the milk is promptly cooled to 40°F (4°C) or less.

All stirring devices, thermometers, or any other utensil that comes in contact with the milk must remain in the milk for the entire process—do not remove them at any time during the process—to prevent contamination. Many dairy farms have a home-pasteurizing machine to pasteurize small amounts of milk for personal use. When they are operated according to manufacturers' directions, proper pasteurization will require little attention.

Microwaving raw milk is not an effective means of pasteurization because of the oven's uneven heat. Proper pasteurization and handling will greatly increase the storage life of milk and will inactivate certain enzymes responsible for spoilage. However, pasteurized milk has not received sufficient heat treatment to improve baking qualities in recipes calling for scalded milk.

Pasteurization of Juice

Juice makers have classically marketed juice in two extremely different forms—completely unpasteurized/"raw" juice and ultra-pasteurized/sterile juice. The makers of raw juice have recently come under scrutiny due to safety concerns and many feel they are going to have to change their production methods in order to maintain public trust. However, these makers do not wish to ultra-pasteurize their juice because of possible changes to the flavour.

There is another option. The method by which milk has been pasteurized for decades can be considered a "middle ground" between raw and ultra-pasteurized. The flavour of milk is affected by pasteurization much more strongly than fruit juices tend to be.

Therefore, methods had to be found which made the product safe, yet still palatable to the customer. This section attempts to describe this "middle ground" form of pasteurization and provide information on the equipment required.

The process of "pasteurization" envisioned by Louis Pasteur was aimed at the destruction of all bacteria, molds, spores, etc. Pasteur discovered that the destruction of bacteria can be performed by exposing them to a certain minimum temperature for a certain minimum time—the higher the temperature, the shorter the time required. Most of Pasteur's early experiments involved using boiling water to maintain temperature. This process killed all bacteria. Eventually, lower temperatures for longer times were determined to have similar effects. Pasteur's experiments with milk eventually proved that heating to 145°F for 30 minutes destroyed 99.9% of the bacteria (known as a 3-log kill), which was enough to make a product safe.

Long after Pasteur, micro-biologists have been able to create a "curve" of different time/temperature combinations that will sufficiently reduce a given bacteria population. These curves are different for every organism.

Note: We use the phrase "100% kill" a few times in this chapter. There really is no such thing as a 100% kill of any micro-organism... ever. Some incredibly small population will always survive. When we say 100%, we really mean 99.999% or 99.9999% (5-log or 6-log) kill. A 5-log kill of pathogens is often considered the goal of any pasteurization process. Today, many of the products available for sale are "pasteurized" using Pasteur's information. This does not mean 100% of bacteria are gone—bacteria still exist in these products, but in very low concentrations. These products are refrigerated to keep the growth of the remaining bacteria very low.

They also have a predetermined shelf-life after which bacteria concentrations rise to unacceptable levels. This is the practice for milk in the US. The term "pasteurized" can therefore be used to refer to products with reduced bacteria. Products with no bacteria are referred to as "sterile" or "ultra-pasteurized".

The general term "pasteurization" used in the dairy and beverage business is sometimes mis-understood. Knowing that some bacteria still exist, many people think of it as the process of destroying all the bacteria "that can make you sick". This is not necessarily the only goal.

Pathogenic bacteria (those that make you sick) such as *E. coli, Lysteria, Salmonella*, and others are much more easily killed off than people may think. Making milk "safe" to drink requires much lower pasteurization temperatures than are used in the industry. There are other bacteria in milk that are not necessarily very harmful to humans, but produce the acids that sour the milk and make it undrinkable.

These bacteria are called lactophilic because they consume the lactose in milk and produce lactic acid. The time/temperature required to for a 3-log kill of these lactophilic bacteria conveniently results in a 100% kill of most of the pathogenic bacteria. Therefore, the process required to simply make a product safe may not be identical to those finally decided on for the product.

Some products are actually "sterilized" before they are sold to the public. Most of the fruit juice sold on store shelves is produced this way. These products have relatively unlimited shelf life without refrigeration. However, the time/temperature combination required to kill 100% of bacteria also destroys some of the flavour components in the juice. There is some dispute over how much flavour degredation actually occurs and since this is solely a subjective opinion on the part of the consumer, no definitive data is available. The current trend toward "natural" products has led some manufacturers to produce unpasteurized products. These makers are relying on low bacterial counts in the raw juice and then refrigerating the product to retard growth.

Makers of "natural" juice products are currently stuck in the quandary described above—pasteurize and possibly give up some of the flavours that make their products unique or risk leaving unwanted bacteria in their product.

Accepted Methods of Pasteurization

The following methods of pasteurization are in common use across the country and are accepted by the US public health agencies.

Batch or Vat Pasteurization

The first form of pasteurization to come into use for milk was simple vat pasteurization—heat your product to about 145°F for about 30 minutes and you could consider the product to be safe. This method destroys most common pathogenic bacteria. However, as production demands grow, simply adding more and more vats is usually not feasible.

HTST (Short-time) Pasteurization

High-temperature, short-time pasteurization gets its name from the relatively short "hold time" of 15 seconds. The "high temperature" is typically 161°F for whole milk. It is the industry standard in the milk industry due to its simple adaptation to continuous processing. A "hold time" of 15 seconds can easily be achieved in a continuous process by installing a "hold tube". A hold tube is simply a length of tubing included in the system after the point where the product is heated. The tubing length/diameter is sized so that it takes a minimum of 15-20 seconds for the product to travel completely through it. If the product temperature is still at or above the pasteurization temperature at the end of the hold tube, then the product is considered to be pasteurized.

The product is then typically cooled down again for storage. Most of the milk produced in the US is pasteurized via this method. This method provides the convenience of continuous processing, yet still does not adversely affect the taste of the product by "cooking" it.

UHT Pasteurization

In UHT pasteurization, product is brought to over the boiling point (under pressure) for only a fraction of a second. This results in a sterile product that requires no refrigeration later. Typical applications that US residents will be familiar with are coffee creamer and juice boxes. Much of the milk in Europe is UHT pasteurized. However, after being brought to this temperature, a slight "cooked" taste is sometimes said to be detectable.

Table 2

Pasteurization Method	*Temperature*	*Hold Time*
Batch/Vat	145°F	30 minutes
HTST (High Temperature - Short Time)	161°F	15 seconds
UHT (Ultra High Temperature)	250+°F	0.1 second

Short-time or HTST Pasteurization of Juice

Most apple juice producers are relatively familiar with both Vat and UHT pasteurization. The Vat method is used by smaller producers and UHT systems are commonly employed by the large corporate producers. We have found that very few producers in the fruit juice industry are acquainted with the process and equipment involved in HTST systems.

HTST or Short-time tasteurization may be an acceptable "middle-ground" for the pasteurization of juice. It will provide a safe product for the public, yet keep to a minimum the amount of flavour-degradation found in ultra-pasteurized product. Such a product will be free of pathogens with an extended shelf life under refrigeration.

The following sequence of events details the general process steps. Refer to fig. 2 for assistance in following the flow.

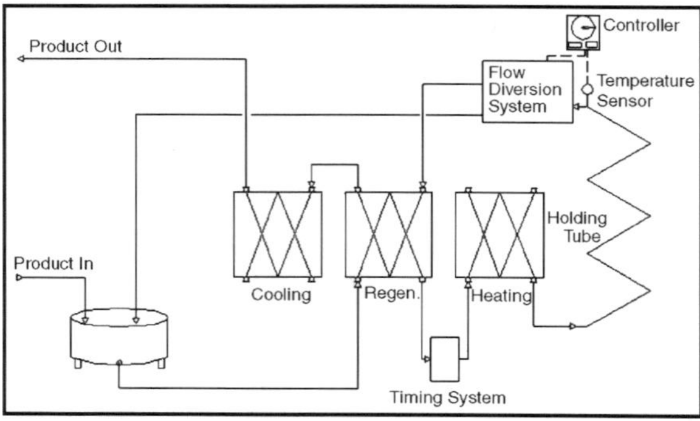

Fig. 2

Sequence of Events

- Cold, raw product is pumped from a holding tank to a surge or "balance" tank. The level in the balance tank in controlled by a float which throttles back the inlet flow.
- Product is pumped/drawn into a regenerative heat exchanger which heats the raw product using energy from the pasteurized product. Product temperature does not yet reach the full pasteurization temperature at this stage.
- Product is pumped via the "timing system". The timing system is a single device or combination of devices which controls the maximum

flow rate through the system. The performance of the system relies on product passing though the system at a known, controlled flow rate. Possible timing devices are as follows:

(*i*) Positive displacement pump w/controlled speed drive.

(*ii*) Homogenizer (also a positive displacement pump).

(*iii*) Centrifugal Pump w/Magnetic Flowmeter/Controller.

- Product is pumped by the timing system into a heat exchanger which heats the product to the full pasteurization temperature. The heating media is usually recycled hot water kept at temperature by the direct injection of steam.
- Product passes through the "hold tube". The length/volume of the hold tube is specifically designed so that the time required for the product to reach the end is 15 seconds or more. This is why the controlled flow rate is so important—if the flow rate is allowed to increase beyond the expected rate, then the product would spend less than the required 15 seconds in the hold tube.
- At the end of the hold tube, a sensor measures the temperature of the product. If the temperature is at or above the required temperature, then the product is considered pasteurized and is permitted to pass on further in the process. If the product is not up to temperature, then a divert valve returns the product to the balance tank.
- Pasteurized product is then sent through the "other" side of the regenerative heater. The heat from the pasteurized product is transferred to the incoming raw product. Efficiency of a regenerative system such as this can exceed 90% so that the exiting pasteurized product is only slightly warmer than the incoming raw product.
- In most situations, the product passes through a final heat exchanger which cools it to a final storage temperature (40°F or lower). The cooling media is typically chilled water (34°F) or food-grade glycol (28°F).

Public Health Controls

In order to ensure that the process of pasteurization occurs as expected, the government requires that certain public health controls be installed on all dairy product pasteurizers. Whether or not these controls will be required on juice system is still unknown:

- Controlled, sealable timing system.
- Sealable "Safety Thermal Limit Recorder" (STLR) to record temperature and divert under-temperature product.
- Certified mercury thermometer at end of hold tube for visual check of temperature or Digital Reference Thermometer accurate to 0.1°F with dual, 1000 ohm platinum sensors.

- Approved Flow Diversion Valves system with dual divert valves and return lines. Position sensors verify the position of the valves at all times.
- Regen system differential pressure switch.
- USDA Approved equipment for all pumps, valves, and other equipment.

Associated Costs

The question on everyone's mind is "How much is this going to cost?" The cost of a short-time pasteurizer can vary considerably with the required capacity.

However, some costs are extremely variable while others are relatively fixed. The table 3 classifies the required equipment:

Table 3

Fixed Costs	*Highly Variable*	*Somewhat Variable*	*Costs*	*Costs*
Controllers/ Equipment	Heat Exchanger	Flow Diversion Instruments		
Public Health Controls	Hold Tube	Balance Tank		
		Timing System		
		Valves		
		Interconnecting Piping		
		Mounting Skid (if used)		

Fully Legal Systems vs "Heat Treat" Systems

A major question at the current time is whether or not the government is going to require full "dairy-type" controls on pasteurizers for apple and fruit juices.

If fully legal controls are not required, the same functionality can be obtained via less expensive controls.

In some cases, equipment can be used that is fully "sanitary", but not currently "approved" for use with milk. Since such a system has no formal definition, we are currently dubbing it a "Heat-Treat" system. The difference in price between a "dairy" type pasteurizer and a fully-functional, but non-approved heat-treat system could be quite substantial. At this time, we cannot predict if the regulatory agencies will permit the use of the word "pasteurized" on products pasteurized on non-approved system.

We are aware of apple cider producers who are using this designation on non-approved systems without any trouble from the inspection agencies. There appears to be no labelling law which directly dictates the use of the word "pasteurized", but it is recommended that anyone considering the use of a system such as this should check with their local authorities before making any decisions.

Table 4

GPM	*Fully Legal*	*Heat Treat*
10	$45,000	$30,000
50	$90,000	$75,000
100	$110,000	$95,000

These prices are *estimates* only, but are in the "ballpark". As the prices demonstrate, the additional cost of "fully legal" controls become less significant as the size of the system increases. However, for smaller systems, the cost of the legal controls can increase the cost of the system substantially.

Some producers are already being pressured by their larger customers (especially large supermarket chains) to provide pasteurized product. If the likelihood of government regulations decreases, smaller producers may wish to reduce capital investment via the use of "heat treat" systems to satisfy their customer's immediate demands. They may risk, however, being forced to upgrade these systems at a later date. The answers to these questions will only be answered when the regulatory agencies finally decide whether or not to enforce dairy-style controls on juice bottling operations.

Juice Stabilization

Despite the many pathways to deterioration, there are a number of effective preservation methods that have evolved to combat spoilage. A principle tenet of food preservation is to maintain the quality and nutritional attributes while preventing spoilage. In general, the fresher the juice, the higher the quality, so the standard of excellence is often freshly prepared, unprocessed juice. As indicated, this is a very transitory product having a limited shelf life of hours or days even under the best of circumstances.

Thermal Processing

The acid nature of most juices permits pasteurization, defined as the use of temperatures near 100°C to effect destruction of spoilage organisms. Although spores conceivably can survive at a pH less than 4.6, outgrowth is unlikely. In contrast, at a pH greater than 4.6, spore heat resistance dictates a process temperature of greater than 115°C for an extended time. Hence pH reduction by acid addition to turn low acid or marginal pH juices into high acid products is widely practiced.

A potentially effective process for fresh juice involves heating clean, well-sorted whole fruit for up to 1 minute at 80°C. This greatly reduces surface contamination without influencing the underlying flesh that, if juiced in a sanitary manner, has the sensory quality of fresh juice. A great deal of research is underway combining surface heat with other decontamination practices. Whether these treatments will qualify as producing "fresh" juice for labelling purposes remains to be seen.

Canning

Standard canning procedures specify filling cans or jars with hot juice (~70 to 80°C), sealing and processing at 100 to 105°C for up to 10 minutes and cooling immediately. This is rarely done in a still (stationary or motionless) retort, since slow heating and cooling would ruin the quality.

Instead, a continuous rotary retort provides rapid heating and cooling as a result of the juice being stirred inside the can by the headspace bubble movement during rotation . Another rapid system is the spin cooker/cooler where the spinning action provides good internal and external surface contact.

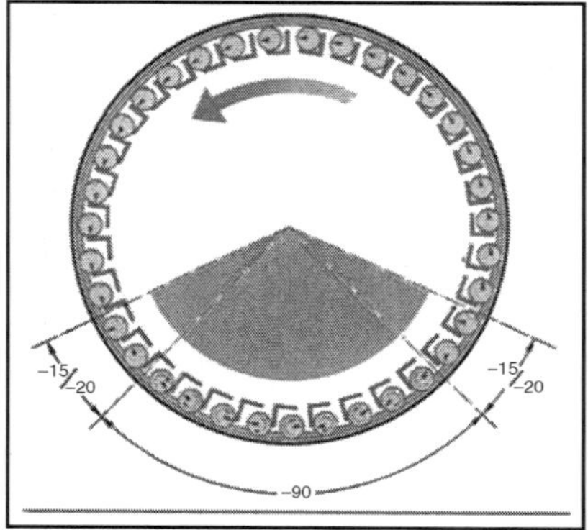

Fig. 3: Rotary Retort and Schematic ~2 to 5 rpm Rotation Provides in-container Mixing

Hot Fill

It is fairly easy to hot fill pack juices by rapidly heating the juice in a heat exchanger and filling containers with the hot juice measuring around 95°C followed by sealing and inverting, thus pasteurizing the container.

Reasonably rapid cooling is accomplished by rotary or spin action. This is known as flash pasteurization and can be achieved almost instantaneously. However, once in a container, cooling cannot be as rapid. The major quality problem is scorching, due to holding the juice hot, either before or after filling.

Fig. 4: Pilot Aseptic Line. Swept Surface Heat Exchanger on Right

Fig. 5: Plate Heat Exchanger

Many types of heat exchangers are used. The simplest is a coil submerged in boiling water with the juice flow adjusted to the desired pasteurization temperature. For pulp-containing juices or those likely to leave a film on the heating surface, a swept surface unit can continuously heat a juice stream.

A plate heat exchanger with a regeneration section by which the cool entering product is preheated by the exiting hot product stream can be quite energy efficient, although the cooled stream must then be handled, filled and sealed in a sterile environment.

Hot fill has the additional advantages of driving air from the juice and ensuring a partial vacuum in the sealed container as vapour condenses upon cooling. Of course, deaeration and use of an inert gas during packaging are also useful.

Sanitation is quite critical, since there are acid resistant moulds such as B*ysochalmous fulva* and *Talarmyces flavus* with unusually high temperature tolerance that require temperatures close to 100°C for up to 60 seconds for adequate pasteurization. Such a process could be excessive for some delicate-flavoured juices, thus requiring either gentler processes or exceptionally sanitary preparation. These moulds are not too common, but once established in a processing facility, they are difficult to eliminate.

FREEZE-DRYING FOOD PRESERVATION

Freeze-drying is a relatively recent method of preserving food. It involves freezing the food, then removing almost all the moisture in a vacuum chamber, and finally sealing the food in an airtight container. Freeze-dried foods can be easily transported at normal temperatures, stored for a long period of time, and consumed with a minimum of preparation. Once prepared, freeze-dried foods have much the same look and taste as the original, natural products.

The freeze-drying process was developed during World War II as a method of preserving blood plasma for battlefield emergencies without requiring refrigeration or damaging the organic nature of the plasma. The technology was applied to consumer food products after the end of the war. Coffee was one of the first freeze-dried products to be marketed on a large scale. Today, many fruits, vegetables, meats, eggs, and food flavourings are freeze-dried.

Freeze-dried food has many advantages. Because as much as 98% of the water content has been removed, the food is extremely lightweight, which significantly reduces the cost of shipping. This also makes it popular with boaters and hikers who have to carry their food with them. Because it requires no refrigeration, shipping and storage costs are even further reduced.

Freeze-dried food is also relatively contamination-free since the dehydration process makes it virtually impossible for yeast and potentially harmful bacteria to survive. Finally, since the physical structure of the food is not altered during the freeze-drying process, the food retains much of its colour, shape, texture, and flavour when it is prepared for consumption by reintroducing water. This makes it more attractive to consumers than food preserved by some other methods. One of the major disadvantages of freeze-dried food is its cost.

The equipment required for this process requires a large investment of money, and the process itself is time consuming and labor intensive. These costs are usually passed on to the consumer, which makes freeze-dried food very expensive when compared to other methods of food preservation such as canning or freezing.

RAW MATERIALS

Some foods are extremely well-suited to the freeze-drying process, others do not fare so well. Liquids, thin portions of meat, and small fruits and vegetables can be freeze-dried easily.

Coffee is the most common freeze-dried liquid. Chunks or slices of shrimp, crab, lobster, beef, and chicken can be freeze-dried. They are often mixed with vegetables as part of soups or main course entrees. Almost all fruits and vegetables can be freeze-dried, including beans, corn, peas, tomatoes, berries, lemons, oranges, and pineapples. Even items like olives and water chestnuts can be processed this way.

Thick portions of meat and larger, whole vegetables and fruits cannot be freeze dried with any success. With many other foods, it is simply not economical to preserve them by freeze drying.

THE MANUFACTURING PROCESS

A freeze-drying processing facility is usually a large plant with modern equipment. Its food-handling areas must be approved by the United States Department of Agriculture, and the company and its employees must adhere to government regulatory procedures. The plant may include a receiving and storage area for raw foods that arrive at the plant in bulk; a food cooking area for those foods that must be cooked before processing; a large area with several large freezing and drying chambers; and a packaging area. The facility may also include a research area where improved methods of freeze-drying foods are developed, and a test kitchen where new preparation techniques to improve the final taste, quality, and texture of the food are tried.

Some plants are dedicated to freeze-drying only one product like freeze-dried coffee. Others process a wide range of meats, vegetables, and fruits. Nonfood products such as chemicals and pharmaceuticals are usually processed in separate plants from food products. The freeze-drying process varies in the details of temperatures, times, pressures, and intermediate steps from one food to another. The following is a generalized description of the process with several specific exceptions noted.

Testing and Preparation

The food is first checked for contamination and purity. Fruits, meats, and some other edibles are tested for bacterial counts and spoilage. Much of the work of the plant is dependent on the harvest season for each food. In January, for example, the plant would be processing celery, olives, lemons, oranges, and pineapples. In July, it would process green beans, peas, and strawberries, among others.

Some kinds of food, like seafood and meats, must be cooked before freeze-drying. They are usually purchased already cut into small pieces. If they have not been pre-cooked and frozen, these foods are placed in large, industrial-sized kettles and properly cooked.

Fruits and vegetables are usually purchased already cut, pitted, and peeled. These foods are simply washed with sprays of water. Some vegetables, like peas and corn, are quickly scalded, or blanched, before freezing. Coffee is purchased as a pre-brewed concentrated liquid. Because the aroma of coffee is important to consumers, a small amount of coffee bean oil may be added to the liquid. Unlike the water, the oil is not removed during the drying process.

Freezing

The food pieces are spread out on flat, metal trays which are stacked 20 to 30 high in slots in a wheeled cart. With food that has been pre-cooked and frozen, the trays are pre-chilled to prevent partial thawing during handling. With liquids like coffee, the pre-brewed coffee is poured into shallow pans.

The carts are wheeled into a large, walk-in coldroom where the temperature can be as low as -40°F (-40°C). In this extremely cold temperature, the food is quickly frozen. There are usually a dozen or more coldrooms in operation, and the carts are kept there until it is time to move them into the drying chamber.

In a lab, this is often done by placing the material in a freeze-drying flask and rotating the flask in a bath, called a shell freezer, which is cooled by mechanical refrigeration, dry ice and methanol, or liquid nitrogen. On a larger-scale, freezing is usually done using a freeze-drying machine. In this step, it is important to cool the material below its triple point, the lowest temperature at which the solid and liquid phases of the material can coexist.

This ensures that sublimation rather than melting will occur in the following steps. Larger crystals are easier to freeze-dry. To produce larger crystals, the product should be frozen slowly or can be cycled up and down in temperature. This cycling process is called annealing.

However, in the case of food, or objects with formerly-living cells, large ice crystals will break the cell walls (discovered by Clarence Birdseye). Usually, the freezing temperatures are between 50°C and 80°C. The freezing phase is the most critical in the whole freeze-drying process, because the product can be spoiled if badly done.

Amorphous (glassy) materials do not have a eutectic point, but do have a critical point, below which the product must be maintained to prevent melt-back or collapse during primary and secondary drying. Large objects take a few months to freeze-dry.

Drying

The carts are wheeled out of the coldroom and into a vacuum drying chamber. In the case of liquids like coffee, the frozen coffee is first ground up into small particles in a low-temperature grinder. The drying chamber is a large, long, horizontal cylinder with semi-elliptical ends. One end is hinged to open and close.

When the trays of frozen food pieces are inside, the chamber is closed and sealed. In a large plant, there may be 20 to 30 drying chambers in operation at any time. The drying procedure involves a process known as sublimation. In sublimation, a solid material is forced to change state into a gaseous material without ever becoming a liquid. In the case of freezedried food, the solid ice crystals trapped in the frozen food pieces are forced to change into water vapour without ever becoming liquid water. In the drying chamber, this is accomplished by evacuating the air with a vacuum pump to reduce the pressure to about 0.036 psi (0.0025 bar). The temperature of the food is raised to about 100°F (38°C) by direct conduction through the bottom of the trays, radiation from heat lamps, or microwave heating. When the chamber is evacuated of air, the pressure is below the threshold at which water can simultaneously exist in a solid, liquid, and gaseous (vapour) state.

This threshold is known as the triple point of water. Once the pressure falls below this point, the heat causes the ice crystals trapped in the frozen pieces of food to change directly to water vapour. The vapour is drawn off and condensed within the chamber leaving the food behind.

The dried food is filled with tiny voids, like a sponge, where the ice crystals were once present. Not only does this make it easier for the food to reabsorb water when it is prepared for consumption, but the dried food retains its original size and shape. The time for this drying process varies. Freeze-dried liquids make take only about four hours to prepare, while semi-solids and solids like soup and sliced meats may take 12 hours or more.

Primary Drying

During the primary drying phase, the pressure is lowered (to the range of a few millibars), and enough heat is supplied to the material for the water to sublimate. The amount of heat necessary can be calculated using the sublimating molecules' latent heat of sublimation.

In this initial drying phase, about 95% of the water in the material is sublimated. This phase may be slow (can be several days in the industry), because, if too much heat is added, the material's structure could be altered. In this phase, pressure is controlled through the application of partial vacuum. The vacuum speeds sublimation, making it useful as a deliberate drying process.

Furthermore, a cold condenser chamber and/or condenser plates provide a surface(s) for the water vapour to re-solidify on. This condenser plays no role in keeping the material frozen; rather, it prevents water vapour from reaching the vacuum pump, which could degrade the pump's performance. Condenser temperatures are typically below 50°C (60°F). It is important to note that, in this range of pressure, the heat is brought mainly by conduction or radiation; the convection effect is considered to be inefficient.

Secondary Drying

The secondary drying phase aims to remove unfrozen water molecules, since the ice was removed in the primary drying phase. This part of the freeze-drying process is governed by the material's adsorption isotherms.

In this phase, the temperature is raised higher than in the primary drying phase, and can even be above 0°C, to break any physico-chemical interactions that have formed between the water molecules and the frozen material. Usually the pressure is also lowered in this stage to encourage desorption (typically in the range of microbars, or fractions of a pascal). However, there are products that benefit from increased pressure as well.

After the freeze-drying process is complete, the vacuum is usually broken with an inert gas, such as nitrogen, before the material is sealed. At the end of the operation, the final residual water content in the product is extremely low, around 1% to 4%.

Sizing and Blending

The dried food pieces are removed from the drying chamber and tested for moisture content and purity. Some food pieces may be ground to a smaller size or may be reduced to a powder.

Others may be screened to separate them by size. Two or more different products may also be blended together to meet a customer's specific specifications.

Packaging

Freeze-dried foods must be sealed in airtight containers to prevent them from absorbing moisture from the air. Several types of containers may be used: plastic laminated foil pouches, metal and plastic cans, or metal and fibre drums for bulk packaging.

Some freeze-dried food is vacuum packed, in which the air is evacuated from the container before sealing. Other food has an inert gas like nitrogen injected into the container before sealing to displace the oxygen in the air and prevent oxidation or spoiling of the food.

The packaging is done in the freeze-dry plant almost as soon as the foods come out of the drying chamber. The plant can form, fill, and seal the packages to the desired weight for the end user.

Packages that are to be sold directly to the consumer are packed in cartons, stacked on pallets, and transported to the grocery warehouse. Other freeze-dried food is packaged in bulk and sold to a secondary processor for incorporation into other food products. Freeze-dried blueberries, for example, may be sent to a company that makes pancake and muffin mixes.

Quality Control

Each food has different processing, storage, and rehydration requirements. Some of the variables include the sizing of the raw food products before freezing, the cooking or blanching time and temperature, the rate of freezing and final freezing temperature, the rate of application of vacuum and the final vacuum pressure during drying, the rate and method of application of heat and the final dried product temperature, the allowable residual moisture content after drying, the storage temperature and atmosphere (vacuum, nitrogen, etc.) after drying, and the rehydration procedures. At large freeze-drying facilities, electronic micropro--cessors regulate the times, temperatures, and pressures throughout each step of the process.

A central computer collects this data, analyses it using statistical quality control methods, and stores it for later reference. This assures that the food sent out to the public for consumption has been through a strictly controlled process that meets government guidelines and varies only slightly from batch to batch.

The computer also collects data on the bacterial and moisture levels of the raw, bulk food products coming into the plant as well as the final freeze-dried products. Special equipment may include computerized gas chromatographs and oxygen analysers. Even the packaging materials are tested for their ability to prevent water vapour and oxygen transmission.

FREEZE-DRYING

Freeze-drying is a special form of drying that removes all moisture and tends to have less of an effect on a food's taste than normal dehydration does. In freeze-drying, food is frozen and placed in a strong vacuum. The water in the food then sublimates—that is, it turns straight from ice into vapour. Freeze-drying is most commonly used to make instant coffee, but also works extremely well on fruits such as apples.

An Experiment in Freeze-Drying

You probably don't have a good vacuum chamber at home, but you almost certainly have a refrigerator. If you don't mind waiting a week, you can experiment with freeze-drying at home using your freezer. For this experiment you will need a tray, preferably one that is perforated. If you have something like a cake-cooling rack or a metal mesh tray, that is perfect. You can use a cookie sheet or a plate if that is all that you have, but the experiment will take longer.

Now you will need something to freeze-dry. Three good candidates are apples, potatoes and carrots (apples have the advantage that they taste okay in their freeze-dried state). With a knife, cut your apple, potato and/or carrot as thin as you can (try all three if you have them). Cut them paper-thin if you can do it—the thinner you cut, the less time the experiment will take. Then arrange your slices on your rack or tray and put them in the freezer. You want to do this fairly quickly or else your potato and/or apple slices will discolour.

In half an hour, look in on your experiment. The slices should be frozen solid. Over the next week, look in on your slices. What will happen is that the water in the slices will sublimate away. That is, the water in the slices will convert straight from solid water to water vapour, never going through the liquid state (this is the same thing that mothballs do, going straight from a solid to a gaseous state).

After a week or so (depending on how cold your freezer is and how thick the slices are), your slices will be completely dry. To test apple or potato slices for complete drying, take one slice out and let it thaw. It will turn black almost immediately if it is not completely dry.

When all of the slices are completely dry, what you have is freeze-dried apples, potatoes and carrots. You can "reconstitute" them by putting the slices in a cup or bowl and adding a little boiling water (or add cold water and microwave). You can eat the apples in their dried state or you can reconstitute them. What you will notice is that the reconstituted vegetables look and taste pretty much like the original! That is why freeze-drying is a popular preservation technique.

Lyophilization

Freeze-drying, also known as lyophilization, is widely regarded as a superior industrial drying and preservation method. By drying at lower pressure, boiling points are lowered which allows products to dried at lower temperatures compared to other methods. This reduces damage to the product and ensures cellular integrity is retained.

Perhaps the key benefit of freeze drying is that all cellular integrity is retained throughout the drying process. The only thing removed from the product is water. This means that products retain the following characteristics from when they're fresh to when they're dry:

- Size/mass
- Appearance
- Colour
- Shape
- Aroma
- Flavour
- Nutritional value
- Texture

Other benefits include the fact that vitamins and enzymes remain intact, shipping weight is significantly reduced and shelf-life is extended to over 2 years providing suitable packaging is used. Reconstitution (rehydration) is almost instantaneous when water is added to the dried product.

General steps to successful freeze-drying are as follows:

- Moisture is "locked" into the product by freezing the product down before, or during the initial stages, of the drying process.
- Product is placed into a chamber, which is evacuated to low pressure. As a guide, atmospheric (sea level) pressure is 1017mBar, and our chambers are evacuated to around 1mBar before drying begins.
- Shelf freezing reduces the temperature in the chamber to -18°C or lower. The low pressure mentioned above, along with this low temperature, means that the water contained in the product is below the triple point for water. The triple point is the point where water

can exist as a solid (ice), liquid (water) or gas (vapour). Below the triple point, water can only exist as ice or vapour.

- Heat is then gradually applied to the product over a period of 20-24 hours, although this varies depending on the product and loading. This heat causes the ice to sublimate, that is, transform from ice to vapour without passing through the liquid phase. The water vapour is then attracted to the lower temperature ice coil where it condenses as ice.

PROPERTIES OF FREEZE-DRIED PRODUCTS

If a freeze-dried substance is sealed to prevent the reabsorption of moisture, the substance may be stored at room temperature without refrigeration, and be protected against spoilage for many years.

Preservation is possible because the greatly reduced water content inhibits the action of microorganisms and enzymes that would normally spoil or degrade the substance.

Freeze-drying also causes less damage to the substance than other dehydration methods using higher temperatures. Freeze-drying does not usually cause shrinkage or toughening of the material being dried. In addition, flavours, smells and nutritional content generally remain unchanged, making the process popular for preserving food.

However, water is not the only chemical capable of sublimation, and the loss of other volatile compounds such as acetic acid (vinegar) and alcohols can yield undesirable results.

Freeze-dried products can be rehydrated (reconstituted) much more quickly and easily because the process leaves microscopic pores. The pores are created by the ice crystals that sublimate, leaving gaps or pores in their place. This is especially important when it comes to pharmaceutical uses. Lyophilization can also be used to increase the shelf life of some pharmaceuticals for many years.

Freeze-drying Protectants

Similar to cryoprotectants, some molecules protect freeze-dried material. Known as lyoprotectants, these molecules are typically polyhydroxy compounds such as sugars (mono-, di, and polysaccharides), polyalcohols, and their derivatives. Trehalose and sucrose are natural lyoprotectants.

Trehalose is produced by a variety of plant, fungi, and invertebrate animals that remain in a state of suspended during periods of drought (also known as anhydrobiosis).

APPLICATIONS OF FREEZE-DRYING

Freeze-drying has applications in a wide variety of industries. Some of the most common are listed below.

Table 1

Industry	*Products Using Freeze-drying Technology*
Food Processing	Vegetables, meat and fish for instant meals. Fruits for breakfast cereals, juices. Fruit and vegetables for flavourings.
Dairy Industry	High value proteins such as Lactoferrin for baby foods. Other proteins and enzymes for probiotics and starters.
Nutraceuticals	Aloe Vera, Echinacea, Mussels, Shark Cartilage.
Starters and Cultures	For use in cheeses, yoghurts, meats and probiotics.
Pharmaceutical	Proteins, enzymes and hormones with medicinal qualities. Drying of deer velvet.
Disaster Recovery	Books and documents water damaged from flooding. Water-logged artefacts such as shipwreck components for museums.
Research	Viruses and bacteria for storage during the research process.

Pharmaceutical and Biotechnology

Pharmaceutical companies often use freeze-drying to increase the shelf life of products, such as vaccines and other injectables. By removing the water from the material and sealing the material in a vial, the material can be easily stored, shipped, and later reconstituted to its original form for injection.

Food Industry

Freeze-drying is used to preserve food and make it very

Fig. 1: Freeze-dried Coffee

lightweight. The process has been popularized in the forms of freeze-dried ice cream, an example of astronaut food. It is also popular and convenient for hikers because the reduced weight allows them to carry more food and reconstitute it with available water. Instant coffee is sometimes freeze-dried, despite high costs of freeze-dryers. The coffee is often dried by vapourization in a hot air flow, or by projection on hot metallic plates. Freeze-dried fruit is used in some breakfast cereal. Culinary herbs are also freeze-dried, although air-dried herbs are far more common and less expensive. However, the freeze-drying process is used more commonly in the pharmaceutical industry.

Technological Industry

In chemical synthesis, products are often lyophilized to make them more stable, or easier to dissolve in water for subsequent use. In bioseparations, freeze-drying can be used also as a late-stage purification procedure, because it can effectively remove solvents. Furthermore, it is capable of concentrating substances with low molecular weights that are too small to be removed by a filtration membrane. Freeze-drying is a relatively expensive process. The equipment is about three times as expensive as the equipment used for other separation processes, and the high energy demands lead to high energy costs.

Furthermore, freeze-drying also has a long process time, because the addition of too much heat to the material can cause melting or structural deformations. Therefore, freeze-drying is often reserved for materials that are heat-sensitive, such as proteins, enzymes, microorganisms, and blood plasma. The low operating temperature of the process leads to minimal damage of these heat-sensitive products.

Other Uses

Organizations such as the Document Conservation Laboratory at the United States National Archives and Records Administration (NARA) have done studies on freeze-drying as a recovery method of water-damaged books and documents. While recovery is possible, restoration quality depends on the material of the documents.

If a document is made of a variety of materials, which have different absorption properties, expansion will occur at a non-uniform rate, which could lead to deformations. Water can also cause mould to grow or make inks bleed. In these cases, freeze-drying may not be an effective restoration method.

In bacteriology freeze-drying is used to conserve special strain. In high-altitude environments, the low temperatures and pressures can sometimes produce natural mummies by a process of freeze-drying. Advanced ceramics processes sometimes use freeze-drying to create a formable powder from a sprayed slurry mist.

Freeze-drying creates softer particles with a more homogeneous chemical composition than traditional hot spray drying, but it is also more expensive. Recently, some taxidermists have begun using freeze-drying to preserve animals, such as pets. Freeze-drying is also used for floral preservation. Wedding bouquet preservation has become very popular with brides who want to preserve their wedding day flowers.

FREEZE-DRYING EQUIPMENT

There are essentially three categories of freeze-dryers: rotary evapourators, manifold freeze-dryers, and tray freeze-dryers. Rotary freeze-dryers are usually used with liquid products, such as pharmaceutical solutions and tissue extracts. Manifold freeze-dryers are usually used when drying a large amount of small containers and the product will be used in a short period of time.

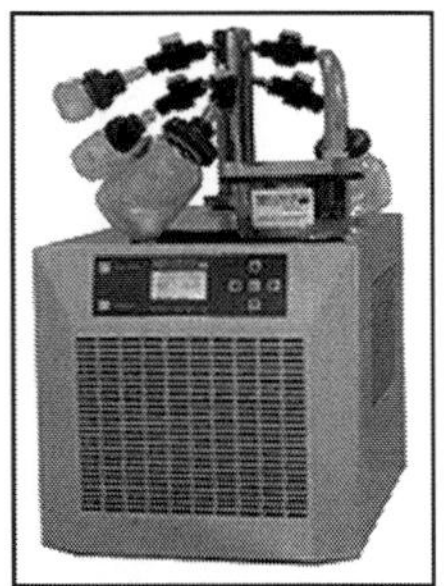

Fig. 2: Benchtop Manifold Freeze-dryer

A manifold dryer will dry the product to less than 5% moisture content. Without heat, only primary drying (removal of the unbound water) can be achieved. A heater must be added for secondary drying, which will remove the bound water and will produce a lower moisture content.

Fig. 3: Production Freeze-dryer

Tray freeze-dryers are more sophisticated and are used to dry a variety of materials. A tray freeze-dryer is used to produce the driest product for long-term storage. A tray freeze-dryer allows the product to be frozen in place and performs both primary (unbound water removal) and secondary (bound water removal) freeze-drying, thus producing the driest possible end-product.

Tray freeze-dryers can dry products in bulk or in vials. When drying in vials, the freeze-dryer is supplied with a stoppering mechanism that allows a stopper to be pressed into place, sealing the vial before it is exposed to the atmosphere. This is used for long-term storage, such as vaccines. Improved freeze drying techniques are being developed to extend the range of products that can be freeze dried, to improve the quality of the product, and to produce the product faster with less labour.

TECHNIQUES USED BY FOOD INDUSTRY

Freeze-drying is one of the techniques used by food industry movers and shakers to preserve food. And this has grown increasingly popular for a reason. Freeze-drying actually preserves food, although this remains very suspicious as a method for lay persons, since it is not often explained. You might be wondering how exactly freeze-drying preserves your food, and it is easily understandable if seen on the step by step perspective.

The food industry is replete with strict standards of maintaining food's high quality by the time that it gets delivered to its end users, the consumers. As much as possible, the goal is always to recreate the same taste as at the time that the food ingredient has been freshly picked or created. The first step in freeze drying is freezing.

Of course, you cannot expect to preserve something if it is not solidly solitary to begin with. Freezing makes the whole bulk of the food a single unit, easily grouped into its considerable servings.

The next step is the drying or dehydration of the food. The reason dehydrated food is the next step is because it is the promoter of easy transportation of food due to its lighter weight. The moisture in the food also adds to its perishability, so if the food is dehydrated first before being transported, it stands a better chance of being preserved. It also saves time and helps the transporters to bring in more supplies with a shorter time and space requirement in the vehicle, further reducing the risk of compromising the quality of the food being preserved.

This method of preservation is not too far from the technique of drying flowers. Vacuum drying may be irrelevant in flower preservation due to its smallness, but in food preservation, a partial vacuum is actually beneficial. This partial vacuum equipment helps to sublimate the food, that is, turn the solids into gas to make sure it gets dried up until the customer manages to use the food at home and uses a heating machine to cook it.

You might find that this is better preservation measure than the one that you use with flowers, but this is understandably so since we are dealing with food that needs to be consumed until its limit of perishability expires. Two stages of drying are used in food preservation, just to ensure the safety and extended guarantee on the food. The good thing about freeze-drying is that it keeps microorganisms from infiltrating your food. It will make sure that the food is squeezed shut from any other intruders. This way, you are ensured that it maintains the purity it had even when it has already travelled a long distance.

You might be wondering how the sublimated food manages to restore itself after freeze-drying. When it is all set and ready for the customer to use, the food has its pores which respond to heat (your oven, contact with the human body and your stove are good sources of this) and unfreezes and moistens the food back to its natural state.

Biological Matter can be Preserved

By means of freeze-drying (lyophilization), many kinds of biological matter can be preserved without damage or changes in quality or viability for extended periods. In the freeze-drying process, the water contained in the biological structure is frozen; the ice is then removed by sublimation (turning directly into vapour without passing through the liquid stage).

By this method the twin advantages of freezing and drying are combined into one favourable means of preservation. Adequately packaged, the resulting product can be kept for years at room temperature.

Freeze-drying is a process which can be applied to three broad categories of biological products:

- Non-living matter such as blood plasma, serum, hormone solutions, pharmaceutical products and food.
- Special matter for surgical transplants such as arteries, skin and bone.
- Live cells intended to be kept alive for long periods of time. This category includes bacteria, viruses and yeast but not mammalian cells.

Freeze-drying is widely used for the preservation of blood plasma and food due to the fact that the process prevents the growth of microorganisms such as fungus and mould, it inhibits deterioration due to chemical reactions such as decoloration and taste degradation or staleness, and it prevents loss of organoleptic or physiological properties.

The process facilitates the distribution and storage of food because it is not necessary to keep it cold. In the case of food preservation, the process features two additional advantages: the product does not change shape and can readily be re-hydrated. Freeze-dried products currently on the market include antibiotics and other pharmaceutical products, granulated instant coffee and certain soups.

CANNING FOOD PRESERVATION

Canning is a method of preserving food in which the food is processed and sealed in an airtight container. The process was first developed as a French military discovery by Nicolas Appert. The packaging prevents microorganisms from entering and proliferating inside.

To prevent the food from being spoiled before and during containment, quite a number of methods are used: pasteurization, boiling (and other applications of high temperature over a period of time), refrigeration, freezing, drying, vacuum treatment, antimicrobial agents that are natural to the recipe of the foodstuff being preserved, a sufficient dose of ionizing radiation, submersion in a strongly saline, acid, base, osmotically extreme (for example very sugary) or other microbe-challenging environments.

No such method is perfectly dependable as a preservative. For example, spore forming thermal resistant micro-organisms, such as *Clostridium botulinum* (which causes botulism) can still survive.

From a public safety point of view, foods with low acidity (a pH more than 4.6) need sterilization under high temperature (116-130°C).

To achieve temperatures above the boiling point requires the use of a pressure canner. Foods that must be pressure canned include most vegetables, meats, seafood, poultry, and dairy products.

The only foods that may be safely canned in an ordinary boiling water bath are highly acidic ones with a pH below 4.6, such as fruits, pickled vegetables, or other foods to which acidic additives have been added.

DEVELOPMENT OF CANNING

During the first years of the Napoleonic Wars, the French Government offered a hefty cash award of 12,000 francs to any inventor who could devise a cheap and effective method of preserving large amounts of food. The larger armies of the period required increased, regular supplies of quality food. Limited food availability was among the factors limiting military campaigns to the summer and fall months.

In 1809, a French confectioner and brewer, Nicolas Appert, observed that food cooked inside a jar did not spoil unless the seals leaked, and developed a method of sealing food in glass jars. The reason for lack of spoilage was unknown at the time, since it would be another 50 years before Louis Pasteur demonstrated the role of microbes in food spoilage. However, glass containers presented challenges for transportation.

Glass jars were largely replaced in commercial canneries with cylindrical tin or wrought-iron canisters (later shortened to "cans") following the work of Peter Durand (1810). Cans are cheaper and quicker to make, and much less fragile than glass jars. Glass jars have remained popular for some high-value products and in home canning. Tin-openers were not invented for another thirty years—at first, soldiers had to cut the cans open with bayonets or smash them open with rocks.

The French Army began experimenting with issuing tinned foods to its soldiers, but the slow process of tinning foods and the even slower development and transport stages prevented the army from shipping large amounts across the French Empire, and the war ended before the process was perfected.

Unfortunately for Appert, the factory which he had built with his prize money was razed in 1814 by Allied soldiers invading France. Following the end of the Napoleonic Wars, the canning process was gradually employed in other European countries and in the US. Based on Appert's methods of food preservation, Peter Durand patented a process in the United Kingdom in 1810. He did not develop the process, selling his patent in 1811 to Bryan Donkin and John Hall, who were in business as Donkin Hall and Gamble, of Bermondsey.

Bryan Donkin developed the process of packaging food in sealed airtight cans, made of tinned wrought iron. Initially, the canning process was slow and labour-intensive, as each large can had to be hand-made, and took up to six hours to cook, making tinned food too expensive for ordinary people. The main market for the food at this stage was the Army and Navy.

By 1817 Donkin recorded that he had sold £3000 worth of canned meat in six months. In 1824 Sir William Edward Parry took tinned beef and pea soup with him on his voyage to the Arctic in HMS Fury, during his search for a northwestern passage to India. In 1829 Admiral Sir James Ross also took canned food to the Arctic, as did Sir John Franklin in 1845.

Some of his stores were found by the search expedition led by Captain (later Admiral Sir) Leopold McLintock in 1857. One of these cans was opened in 1939, and was edible and nutritious, though it was not analysed for contamination by the lead solder used in its manufacture.

Throughout the mid-nineteenth century, tinned food became a status symbol amongst middle-class households in Europe, becoming something of a frivolous novelty. Early methods of manufacture employed poisonous lead solder for sealing the tins, which may have worsened the disastrous outcome of the 1845 Franklin expedition to chart and navigate the Northwest Passage.

Increasing mechanisation of the canning process, coupled with a huge increase in urban populations across Europe, resulted in a rising demand for tinned food. A number of inventions and improvements followed, and by the 1860s smaller machine-made steel cans were possible, and the time to cook food in sealed cans had been reduced from around six hours to thirty minutes. Canned food also began to spread beyond Europe—Robert Ayars established the first American canning factory in New York City in 1812, using improved tin-plated wrought-iron cans for preserving oysters, meats, fruits and vegetables. Demand for tinned food greatly increased during wars. Large-scale wars in the nineteenth century, such as the Crimean War, American Civil War, and Franco-Prussian War introduced increasing numbers of working-class men to tinned food, and allowed canning companies to expand their businesses to meet military demands for non-perishable food, allowing companies to manufacture in bulk and sell to wider civilian markets after wars ended.

Urban populations in Victorian era Britain demanded ever-increasing quantities of cheap, varied, quality food that they could keep at home without having to go shopping daily. In response, companies such as Nestlé, Heinz, and others emerged to provide quality tinned food for sale to working class city-dwellers.

In particular, Crosse and Blackwell took over the concern of Donkin Hall and Gamble. The late 19th century saw the range of tinned food available to urban populations greatly increase, as canners competed with each other using novel foodstuffs, highly decorated printed labels, and lower prices. Demand for tinned food skyrocketed during World War I, as military commanders sought vast quantities of cheap, high-calorie food to feed their millions of soldiers, which could be transported safely, survive trench conditions, and not spoil in transport.

Throughout the war, soldiers generally subsisted on low-quality tinned foodstuffs, such as the British "Bully Beef" (cheap corned beef), pork and beans and Maconochies Irish Stew, but by 1916 widespread boredom with cheap tinned food amongst soldiers resulted in militaries purchasing better-quality food to improve morale, and the complete meals in a tin began to appear.

In 1917 the French Army began issuing tinned French cuisine, such as coq au vin, whilst the Italian Army experimented with tinned ravioli and spaghetti bolognese. Shortages of tinned food in the British Army in 1917 led to the government issuing cigarettes and amphetamines to soldiers to suppress their appetites. After the war, companies that had supplied military tinned food improved the quality of their goods for civilian sale. Today, tin-coated steel is the material most commonly used. Laminate vacuum pouches are also used for canning, such as used in MREs.

HOW CANNING PRESERVES FOODS

The high percentage of water in most fresh foods makes them very perishable. They spoil or lose their quality for several reasons:

- Growth of undesirable microorganisms-bacteria, moulds, and yeasts.
- Activity of food enzymes.
- Reactions with oxygen.
- Moisture loss.

Microorganisms live and multiply quickly on the surfaces of fresh food and on the inside of bruised, insect-damaged, and diseased food. Oxygen and enzymes are present throughout fresh food tissues.

Proper canning practices include:

- Carefully selecting and washing fresh food.
- Peeling some fresh foods.
- Hot packing many foods.
- Adding acids (lemon juice or vinegar) to some foods.
- Using acceptable jars and self-sealing lids.
- Processing jars in a boiling-water or pressure canner for the correct period of time.

Collectively, these practices remove oxygen; destroy enzymes; prevent the growth of undesirable bacteria, yeasts, and moulds; and help form a high vacuum in jars. Good vacuums form tight seals which keep liquid in and air and microorganisms out.

ENSURING SAFE CANNED FOODS

Growth of the bacterium *Clostridium botulinum* in canned food may cause botulism—a deadly form of food poisoning. These bacteria exist either as spores or as vegetative cells. The spores, which are comparable to plant seeds, can survive harmlessly in soil and water for many years.

When ideal conditions exist for growth, the spores produce vegetative cells which multiply rapidly and may produce a deadly toxin within 3 to 4 days of growth in an environment consisting of:

- A moist, low-acid food.
- A temperature between 40° and 120°F.
- Less than 2 per cent oxygen.

Botulinum spores are on most fresh food surfaces. Because they grow only in the absence of air, they are harmless on fresh foods. Most bacteria, yeasts, and moulds are difficult to remove from food surfaces.

Washing fresh food reduces their numbers only slightly. Peeling root crops, underground stem crops, and tomatoes reduces their numbers greatly. Blanching also helps, but the vital controls are the method of canning and making sure the recommended research-based process times found in the USDA's Complete Guide to Home Canning are used.

The processing times in this book ensure destruction of the largest expected number of heat-resistant microorganisms in home-canned foods. Properly sterilized canned food will be free of spoilage if lids seal and jars are stored below 95°F. Storing jars at 50° to 70°F enhances retention of quality.

Food Acidity and Processing Methods

Whether food should be processed in a pressure canner or boiling-water canner to control botulinum bacteria depends on the acidity of the food. Acidity may be natural, as in most fruits, or added, as in pickled food. Low-acid canned foods are not acidic enough to prevent the growth of these bacteria. Acid foods contain enough acid to block their growth, or destroy them more rapidly when heated. The term "pH" is a measure of acidity; the lower its value, the more acid the food. The acidity level in foods can be increased by adding lemon juice, citric acid, or vinegar. Low-acid foods have pH values higher than 4.6. They include red meats, seafood, poultry, milk, and all fresh vegetables except for most tomatoes. Most mixtures of low-acid and acid foods also have pH values above 4.6 unless their recipes include enough lemon juice, citric acid, or vinegar to make them acid foods. Acid foods have a pH of 4.6 or lower. They include fruits, pickles, sauerkraut, jams, jellies, marmalades, and fruit butters.

Although tomatoes usually are considered an acid food, some are now known to have pH values slightly above 4.6. Figs also have pH values slightly above 4.6. Therefore, if they are to be canned as acid foods, these products must be acidified to a pH of 4.6 or lower with lemon juice or citric acid. Properly acidified tomatoes and figs are acid foods and can be safely processed in a boiling-water canner. Botulinum spores are very hard to destroy at boiling-water temperatures; the higher the canner temperature, the more easily they are destroyed. Therefore, all low-acid foods should be sterilized at temperatures of 240° to 250°F, attainable with pressure canners operated at 10 to 15 PSIG.

PSIG means pounds per square inch of pressure as measured by gauge. The more familiar "PSI" designation is used in (the Complete Guide to Home Canning). At temperatures of 240° to 250°F, the time needed to destroy bacteria in low-acid canned food ranges from 20 to 100 minutes. The exact time depends on the kind of food being canned, the way it is packed into jars, and the size of jars. The time needed to safely process low-acid foods in a boiling-water canner ranges from 7 to 11 hours; the time needed to process acid foods in boiling water varies from 5 to 85 minutes.

Process Adjustments at High Altitudes

Using the process time for canning food at sea level may result in spoilage if you live at altitudes of 1,000 feet or more. Water boils at lower temperatures as altitude increases. Lower boiling temperatures are less effective for killing bacteria. Increasing the process time or canner pressure compensates for lower boiling temperatures. Therefore, when you use the Complete Guide to Home Canning, select the proper processing time or canner pressure for the altitude where you live.

Nutrition Value

Canning is a way of processing food to extend its shelf life. The idea is to make food available and edible long after the processing time. Although canned foods are often assumed to be of low-nutritional value (due to heating processes or the addition of preservatives), some canned foods are nutritionally superior-in some ways-to their natural form. For instance, canned tomatoes have a higher available lycopene content.

Potential hazards

Migration of Can Components

In canning toxicology, *migration* is the movement of substances from the can itself into the contents. Potential toxic substances that can migrate are lead, causing lead poisoning, or bisphenol A, a potential endocrine disruptor that is commonly use to coat the inner surface of cans.

Botulism

Foodborne botulism results from contaminated foodstuffs in which *C. botulinum* spores have been allowed to germinate and produce botulism toxin, and this typically occurs in canned non-acidic food substances. *C. botulinum* prefers low oxygen environments, and can therefore grow in canned foods. Botulism is a rare but serious paralytic illness, leading to paralysis that typically starts with the muscles of the face and then spreads towards the limbs. In severe forms, it leads to paralysis of the breathing muscles and causes respiratory failure. In view of this life-threatening complication, all suspected cases of botulism are treated as medical emergencies, and public health officials are usually involved to prevent further cases from the same source.

DOUBLE SEAMS

Modern double seams provide an airtight seal to the tin can. This airtight nature is crucial to keeping bacteria out of the can and keeping its contents sealed inside. Thus, double seamed cans are also known as Sanitary Cans.

Developed in 1900 in Europe, this sort of can was made of the traditional cylindrical body made with tin plate. The two ends (lids) were attached using what is now called a double seam.

A can thus sealed is impervious to the contamination by creating two tight continuous folds between the can's cylindrical body and the lids. This eliminated the need for solder and allowed improvements in manufacturing speed, reducing cost. Double seaming uses rollers to shape the can, lid and the final double seam. To make a sanitary can and lid suitable for double seaming, manufacture begins with a sheet of coated tin plate.

To create the can body, rectangles are cut and curled around a die, and welded together creating a cylinder with a side seam. Rollers are then used to flare out one or both ends of the cylinder to create a quarter circle flange around the circumference.

Precision is required to ensure that the welded sides are perfectly aligned, as any misalignment will cause inconsistent flange shape, compromising its integrity. A circle is then cut from the sheet using a die cutter.

The circle is shaped in a stamping press to create a downward countersink to fit snugly in to the can body. The result can be compared to an upside down and very flat top hat. The outer edge is then curled down and around about 140 ° using rollers to create the end curl. The result is a steel tube with a flanged edge, and a countersunk steel disc with a curled edge. A rubber compound is put inside the curl.

Fig. 1: Opened Can

Seaming

The body and end are brought together in a seamer and held in place by the base plate and chuck, respectively. The base plate provides a sure footing for the can body during the seaming operation and the chuck fits snugly in to the end (lid). The result is the countersink of the end sits inside the top of the can body just below the flange. The end curl protrudes slightly beyond the flange.

First Operation

Once brought together in the seamer, the seaming head presses a first operation roller against the end curl. The end curl is pressed against the flange curling it in toward the body and under the flange. The flange is also bent downward, and the end and body are now loosely joined together. The first operation roller is then retracted. At this point five thicknesses of steel exist in the seam. From the outside in they are:

- End
- Flange
- End Curl
- Body
- Countersink.

This is the first seam. All the parts of the seam are now aligned and ready for the final stage.

Second operation

The seaming head then engages the second operation roller against the partly formed seam. The second operation presses all five steel components together tightly to form the final seal. The five layers in the final seam are then called:

- End.
- Body Hook.
- Cover Hook.
- Body.
- Countersink.

All sanitary cans require a filling medium within the seam because otherwise the metal-to-metal contact will not maintain a hermetic seal. In most cases, a rubberized compound is placed inside the end curl radius, forming the critical seal between the end and the body.

Probably the most important innovation since the introduction of double seams is the welded side seam. Prior to the welded side seam, the can body was folded and/or soldered together, leaving a relatively thick side seam.

The thick side seam required that the side seam end juncture at the end curl to have more metal to curl around before closing in behind the Body Hook or flange, with a greater opportunity for error.

Seamer Setup and Quality Assurance

Many different parts during the seaming process are critical in ensuring that a can is airtight and vacuum sealed. The dangers of a can that is not hermetically sealed are contamination by foreign objects (bacteria or fungicide sprays), or that the can could leak or spoil. One important part is the seamer setup. This process is usually performed by an experienced technician. Amongst the parts that need setup are seamer rolls and chucks which have to be set in their exact position (using a feeler gauge or a clearance gauge). The lifter pressure and position, roll and chuck designs, tooling wear, and bearing wear all contribute to a good double seam. Incorrect setups can be non-intuitive. For example, due to the springback effect, a seam can appear loose, when in reality it was closed too tight and has opened up like a spring. For this reason, experienced operators and good seamer setup are critical to ensure that double seams are properly closed.

Quality control usually involves taking full cans from the line—one per seamer head, at least once or twice per shift, and performing a teardown operation (wrinkle/tightness), mechanical tests (external thickness, seamer length/height and countersink) as well as cutting the seam open with a twin blade saw and measuring with a double seam inspection system. The combination of these measurements will determine the seam's quality. Use of a Statistical Process Control or [SPC] software in conjunction with a manual double seam monitor, computerized double seam scanner, or even a fully-automatic double seam inspection system makes the laborious process of double seam inspection faster and much more accurate. Statistically tracking the performance of each head or seaming station of the [can seamer] allows for better prediction of can seamer issues, and may be used to plan maintenance when convenient: rather that to simply react after bad or unsafe cans have been produced.

CANNING FOODS

Canning is a very popular method of preserving food, especially garden produce. It was originally developed in France by a chemist named Nicolas Appert in response to a drive by Napoleon to find a way to get more healthy foods for his army while on the march. He figured out that if he heated foods in jars and then sealed them that the foods would stay relatively fresh until they were opened months and even years later.

Since then advances have been made in canning. Louis Pasteur figured out that it was microorganisms that were spoiling the food. The heat used in the canning process kills the microorganisms. Botulism can still be a problem in food that is improperly canned so before you begin canning, it is wise to use safety precautions.

Canning Safety Precautions

Improperly canned food can result in the growth of botulism or other microorganisms. Eating such foods can cause serious illness and even death. For this reason it is important to strictly adhere to canning procedures as well as standards of cleanliness.

Clostridium botulinum spores are everywhere and eating them is not harmful to humans. It is when they grow in astronomical numbers in an ideal environment, such as an improperly canned jar of food, then begin to die off that they become a problem. They actually produce a neuro-toxin. It is this neuro-toxin that causes the effects of botulism.

Yet botulism and moulds, viruses and bacteria that might grow in canned food can be effectively and easily controlled merely by taking simple precautions. Properly heating the jars and the food within them as well as proper sealing is the solution.

Since *Clostridium botulinum* prefers a low acid environment, high acid foods can be canned under less restrictive conditions using a boiling water canner. These foods have a pH of 4.5 or less. They include: apples, apricots, berries, jams, jellies, peaches, pears, pickles, sauerkraut, tomatoes, and more. High pH (meaning low in acid) fruits and vegetables require a special device for canning called the pressure canner. The pressure canner can also be used for canning the high acid foods. Low acid foods include: Asparagus, beans, beets, carrots, corn, mushrooms, peas, potatoes, pumpkin, spinach, squash, most any meat. It is not generally difficult to detect when a canning job has gone bad (done properly—this will seldom happen). The first sign that a can of food is no good is that the lid will pop up (or bulge), also there might be seeping around the seal. Mould growing on the surface of the food is a sure sign of a problem. Also abnormal colours in the brine of food, cloudiness in the brine, a white coloured film on the surface of the food can all be indications of contaminated food. Do not eat contaminated food. It invariably will cause harm. Reheating the food, even boiling it for long periods is not a solution as botulism is not the living part of the *Clostridium botulinum*, but a byproduct of its life-cycle. Some traditional methods are *not* recommended such as open kettle canning, paraffin wax sealing, oven or microwave canning.

A final helpful hint regarding safety—it is best to store canned foods at relatively low temperatures as this helps to prevent any activity by microorganisms that might have survived the heating process. Keeping cans in dark, cool places also helps to preserve vitamins and taste.

Canning Steps

- *Have All Your Equipment Ready to Use*: Wash jars and lids with hot, soapy water. Thoroughly rinse and air dry. Check glass jar rims for even minute chips or cracks as these will not seal. Rinse new caps with hot water before using them.
- *Prepare the Food*: Always start with fruit at the peak of freshness. Fruit and vegetables should be washed, peeled and prepared according to your recipes for preserves, pickles, salsa, spaghetti sauce, etc. For fruit, we recommend using a product such as "Fruit Fresh" to prevent

discoloration. Follow the package directions for the desired amounts of sugar and water for a light, medium or heavy syrup. Prepare jams and jellies according to the directions for the brand of pectin you're using or follow a trusted recipe.

- Pack prepared food into hot jars, leaving a head space... usually 1/2" to 1" below the top of the jar rim or the amount stated in the recipe you followed.
- Carefully run a wooden or other non-metallic spatula or knife down through the ingredients to release any trapped air bubbles.
- Wipe the jar rims with a clean, damp cloth to remove all traces of food on the rims.
- Place a cap on each jar, making sure it's centered and seated with the rubber edge directly over the rim.
- Screw the lid band onto the jar, but do not over tighten.
- Fill the canner with hot water—the amount depends on the size of the jars you are using. Most canners have pre-marked guides to give you a general idea.
- Place the jars on the rack in the canner or stock pot, adding more water if necessary to cover the jars by 1 to 2 inches.
- Cover with lid and bring the water to a full rolling boil. Continue to boil for the time stated in your recipe. A rough guide is about 5 to 10 minutes for pickles, 10 minutes for jam, about 20 to 30 minutes for fruit, fruit pie fillings, and applesauce, and 30 to 45 minutes or more for tomatoes. (Begin timing after the water begins to boil.)
- Turn off heat, carefully lift the lid away from you to prevent burning by steam. Using a jar tongs, remove jars from water. Place jars on a dish towel or absorbent mat. Allow to cool several hours or overnight.
- *Check Seals*: Lids should be lowered in the middle and not move up or down when you lightly press or tap them. Remove bands wash them and dry them thoroughly. Some sources suggest taking them off for storage. This is important if they will be in a damp area such as a basement where the rims could become rusty. For storage in a dry pantry, prefer to store them with the bands in place. If you do store them without the bands, leave a few bands in a convenient spot, to use on jars to hold caps in place after they have been opened for use.
- Label and date the jars, then store them in a dark, cool, dry area where there's no danger of freezing.

Unsuccessful Canning

If any jars did not seal, the centre of the cap will be raised, not lowered. Refrigerate the unsealed jar and use the contents within a few days. Unsealed jars may also be reprocessed. Remove their bands and caps; wipe the rims.

Carefully check the rim for any small chips. If the jar rim is okay, add new caps and clean bands. If damaged, replace the jar too, then reprocess in a boiling water bath. Most foods can also be frozen instead being reprocessed.

Before using, always examine jars for signs of spoilage - a bulging lid or leaking. To open—remove the band if it was left in place. Use a lift type can opener and gently pry the cap to break the vacuum seal. If the food spurts out when opened; if liquids are cloudy or frothy; if food is slimy or mouldy, or if it smells bad, do not use. Never taste the contents of a jar of food with a broken seal or food with even the slightest sign of spoilage. As with any spoiled food, discard it where it is completely out of reach of animals.

HOME CANNING FOOD PRESERVATION

The Benefits of Home Canning

Canning food in your own home is a safe and rewarding process that is becoming popular again as food prices soar and people realise they need to pay attention to securing their food supplies. Preserving food with home canning is an excellent way to increase your consumption of local food. Eating locally requires eating foods when they are in season, and canning allows you to capture the bounty of any particular crop in season and extend its availability throughout the year. You can approach home canning as a hobbyist or a full-time enthusiast who stocks a sizeable percentage of his or her food supply with home preserved food. Whether you want to enjoy a couple fun weekend projects putting up jam or seriously supplement your diet, you will enjoy many personal benefits while being a good steward to the environment and supporting your local economy. And the way things are going with the global food market, you will likely save money as well, especially as time goes on.

How Preserving Food at Home Helps Us

- *Excellent Quality and Taste*: When you use quality produce and perform the canning process correctly, you will create superior products to those for sale at the supermarket. Many recipes for home canned food are delicious and literally the quality is something that money can't buy. You have to make these luscious foods yourself.
- *Control over the Ingredients*: With home canning, you will know exactly where your food is coming from. Ideal sources of produce are your own garden and fruit trees, local organic farms, and any local farm. From any of these sources you will be able to hand select your produce at the peak of ripeness. With home canning you will also reduce your exposure to Bisphenol A that lines the cans of many mass produced food products. Bisphenol A is an endocrine disruptor and people are becoming increasingly aware of its potential harm to humans.

- *Support of the Local Economy*: By directly buying produce from local growers, you are putting money into the hands of local people. Local growers love selling from their own farms or market stands because they are not at the mercy of the big commodity buyers who set prices. This also allows local growers, especially small ones, to remain profitable, which is good for the local economy.
- *Lower Your Carbon Dioxide Footprint*: Great amounts of energy are used to produce and transport the food eaten by society. Highly industrialized agriculture also relies on pesticides, herbicides, and petrochemical fertilizers. All of these things are bad for the environment and degrade the ability of soils to produce food in the future, which means greater scarcity, lower quality, and higher commodity prices.
- When you buy local food and can it at home, you are eliminating a huge percentage of the transport costs from burned fuel associated with shipping food across continents. Yes, home canning requires an energy input, but it does not compare to food being trucked halfway across the country to stock a shelf in a store. Reducing the amount of food you eat from distant places reduces the amount of fuel you are causing to be burned. Also when buying local food, try to focus on those growers who use sustainable growing practices that do not poison the environment.
- *Sense of Accomplishment*: Once you begin canning food, you will be thrilled with yourself. You will feel like you did something very meaningful to your existence because you did! For most of human history most people focused a great deal of time and energy on securing their food supplies.
- We are not suggesting we all go back to digging for roots in the field, but people in general have a deep need to participate in the gathering and preparation of food. Sitting in an SUV for drive-through fast food does not satisfy. It only promotes outrageous energy consumption for low quality products.

Now that you are ready to do some work in the kitchen and participate in food preservation, you need to understand the basics of home canning. The process is a little intimidating at first, but after a couple canning projects, you will feel much more comfortable doing it.

There are safety considerations with home canning, but these are all satisfied by following the directions associated with any particular home canning project. The manufacturers of Mason jars (which are the essential product needed for safe home canning) offer great information on how to can food at home, and many university agriculture departments and the USDA offer very reliable information on this subject as well.

Food Preservation with Home Canning Halts Spoilage

Food preservation in canning jars is accomplished by killing spoilage causing agents with heat, removing air from the food products, and sealing the jars so that air and yeasts, moulds, and bacteria cannot be reintroduced to the food.

Four Causes of Food Spoilage

- Enzymes – Destroyed at 140°F.
- Moulds – Destroyed at 140°F to 190°F.
- Yeasts – Destroyed at 140°F to 190°F.
- Bacteria – Many types of bacteria exist. The toxins produced by some bacteria are also a hazard. Bacteria and associated toxins are destroyed in heat ranges from 190°F to 240°F.

Some bacteria are very tough and resist death even at high temperatures. The toughest bacterium is *Clostridium botulinum*, whose spores cause the deadly botulism. This bacterium is killed at 190°F and its toxic spores are destroyed at 240°F. This bacterium thrives in low-acid or nonacid foods in the absence of air. Foods in this category include corn, beans, peppers, poultry, fish, and meat. This is the main reason that these types of foods require the higher temperatures achieved during pressure canning.

Boiling canned low-acid or nonacid foods for 10 to 20 minutes before eating them will destroy potential lingering toxins. This added step will give you one more reason to feel safe about eating home canned low-acid or nonacid foods.

Water Bath Canner

- *Equipment*: A large metal enamel kettle with lid and jar rack with the capacity to hold up to 7, quart-sized Mason jars. Widely available at discount stores and hardware stores. Cost: $20 to $25.
- *Uses*: The water bath canner is used to process Mason jars for home preservation of jams, fruits, fruit juices, and pickled vegetables.
- *Safety Considerations*: It is a large kettle of boiling water so be careful to avoid steam burns and splashing hot water.

Tested recipes are widely available from the USDA, numerous University agriculture departments, Mason jar manufacturers, fruit pectin manufacturers, and from friends and family who have recipes that are known to be safe. As you familiarize yourself with the principles of safe home canning, you will be able to judge all recipes for safety and even develop your own.

How to Use Water Bath Can

Please always review the manufacturer's directions for the Mason jars that you are using and pay close attention to the head space and processing times specified by recipes.

- Pick a recipe for the produce that you wish to can. Select only quality produce at or near the peak of ripeness. Prepare the recipe.
- While preparing the food, you will also need to get the Mason jars ready. Wash the jars, bands, and lids in hot soapy water. Only use new lids. Never re-use lids. Jars and bands can be re-used.
- Fill the water bath canner and start to heat it in order to sterilize your jars and lids. Use a large thermometer (a candy thermometer works well) to monitor the temperature. When the water is at least 180°F but less than boiling (212°F) add the jars and lids to the water. Sterilizing bands in unnecessary. Kerr and Ball lids specify that they should not be boiled, so make sure that the water stays just below the boiling point.
- Remove the jars and lids from hot water when the food is ready to be packed in jars.
- Add prepared food to jars. Use the handle of a wooden spoon along the insides of the jars to work out any air bubbles. Leave the specified head space, usually ¼ inch or ½ inch.
- Wipe the edges of jar mouths very carefully. They need to be completely clean. Any food particles or other debris on the mouth edge will interfere with the sealing of the lids.
- Place lids on jars and screw on the bands. Only screw them on hand tight. You don't need to twist hard.
- With a jar lifter, place the Mason jars into the hot water. Make sure that jars are not touching each other or the side of the kettle.
- Bring the water to a boil. Once the water is boiling, you can begin the timer for the processing time specified by the recipe. Adjust the heat source as necessary to keep the water boiling but to prevent it from boiling over.
- Once processing time is complete, shut off heat source, and use a jar lifter to remove jars from the canner. Set the jars on a cloth in a location free of drafts. Do not disturb the jars for 12 to 24 hours. You will likely hear the lids "pop" or "snap" down not long after removal, but the jars need to cool completely to make sure the seal is complete. (Processing times change with your land elevation. Consult charts that come with recipes and/or equipment.)

Pressure Canner for Home Canning

- *Equipment*: A pressure canner that has a sealed lid and a gauge that measures the pressure created by boiling water and steam. Under pressure, the steam will achieve temperatures of 240 to 250°F. Such high temperatures are necessary to destroy the bacterium *Clostridium botulinum*. Canners for home use typically cost between $80 and $130.

Major brand is Presto. *Uses*: To process canning jars of fruit, vegetables, meat, fish, and poultry for purposes of preservation. Pressure canning is the only safe method for preserving low-acid vegetables and meats. Note, the pressure canner can also be used like a pressure cooker to prepare meals.

- *Safety Considerations*: Proper use of a pressure canner requires diligent monitoring of the pressure gauge during operation and maintenance of the plugs, gaskets, and metal parts. An actual explosion of the equipment would only occur if the heat was left on and the pressure climbed into the danger zone.

Even so, the plug in the safety valve should blow out before a catastrophic failure of the pressure canner happened. Note that the danger zone for the equipment is several pounds of pressure beyond the pressures necessary for processing foods. To avoid problems, keep the pressure within the safe zone by watching the gauge and adjusting the heat source. In case of emergency, rapid cooling of the canner can be initiated by running it under cold water.

How to Use Pressure Can

Please follow the manufacturer's directions that accompany your specific pressure canner model. In general:

- The pressure canner will be filled with approximately 3 quarts of water (this amount would vary depending on size of canner).
- The water is brought to a boil and the prepared Mason jars are placed in the canner.
- The lid is placed on the canner, sealed, and locked, but the pressure regulator is *not* put in place yet.
- Once a free flow of steam is initiated through the vent, it will be allowed to vent for 10 minutes. (Time may vary depending on size of canner.) Venting steam exhausts air from the pressure chamber.
- After 10 minutes, the pressure regulator is put over the vent and pressure begins to build inside. When the interior becomes pressurized, the air vent/cover lock will rise and completely seal the chamber. Then pounds of pressure will start to accumulate and register on the gauge.
- Bring the canner to the pressure specified by the canning recipe and then maintain that pressure by adjusting heat source as necessary. You will find that once pressure has been achieved, the stove burner no longer needs to be on a high setting. Monitor the pressure closely to make sure it does not rise too far beyond desired pressure. Also, do not let the pressure fall below the pressure required by the recipe. It is important for the food within to be kept at the necessary pressure/temperature for the required amount of time.

- Once the food has processed at the required amount of time at the necessary pressure, turn off the heat source. Do not rapid cool the canner because this would cause jars within to break. (Processing times change with your land elevation. Consult charts that come with recipes and/or equipment.)
- Allow canner to cool until air vent/cover lock drops on its own. Then remove pressure regulator and allow canner to set for 10 more minutes.
- At this point you may unlock the lid and open it. Be careful of the steam that comes out because it will be scalding hot.
- With a jar lifter, remove Mason jars and set them on a cloth in a location free of drafts.
- Do not disturb jars for 12 to 24 hours after removal. They will be exceedingly hot. The contents will continue to boil after removal from the canner. As the jars cool, the lids will seal.

General Tips for Home Canning

You will have to attend to many details while preserving food at home, but it gets easier as you become familiar with the process. The following tips will help you successfully complete your home canning project with great results: sealing impossible.

- Always use new lids. Packages of just lids are widely available for this purpose. Jars and bands may be re-used.
- Always wipe completely clean the jar mouth edges before applying the lid. Particles of food on the jar mouth could interfere with sealing.
- Follow canning guidelines. Don't compromise, substitute, or declare something good enough. Follow the directions and your food will be safe and good.
- When pickling foods, make sure to use vinegar with 5% acidity. Some vinegars only have 4% acidity, but don't use them.
- Allow jars to cool undisturbed for 12 to 24 hours after removing them from the water bath or pressure canner.
- Remove the jar bands and wipe clean the jars and lids before storing. Little bits of food often leak out during processing and you would not want to store the jars with food bits stuck to them. You can put clean jar bands back on for storage if you want to.
- Home canned products have a shelf life of up to 12 months. Label and date your jars as you produce the food. Do not eat food more than 12 months old.
- Select high quality produce at or near the peak of ripeness. You can cut out small blemishes if necessary, but don't use overly damaged foods.

ZUCCHINI RELISH CANNING PROCESS

Run! The zucchini are attacking! It certainly feels this way every summer when the summer squash starts to come in. Zucchini is easy to grow and can make any home gardener feel like a gifted tiller of the soil, but what to do with it all? You can give it away until people start avoiding you. You can feed it to your family until they beg for a merciful change of menu. And then you can make zucchini relish and can it. The following recipe is a delicious recipe that everybody loves. Even if you don't like relish, you'll like this zucchini relish.

Fig. 1

- 5 cups finely chopped zucchini.
- 3 cups finely chopped celery.
- 3 cups finely chopped onion.
- 1 finely chopped green or red bell pepper.
- Add chopped vegetables to:
  (*i*) 6 cups water.
  (*ii*) ¼ cup canning/pickling salt

Place a heavy plate on top of vegetables in water to keep them submerged. Allow vegetables to sit overnight (12 to 24 hours) in brine. Then drain vegetables and squeeze excess liquid from them.

In a big pot on the stove, mix:

- 3 cups white vinegar (5% acidity).
- 5 cups sugar.
- 2 tablespoons mustard seed.
- 2 tablespoons celery seed.
- 1 tablespoon turmeric.
- Add the drained vegetables and cook at a nice even boil for 10 minutes.
- Add hot mixture to sterilized ½ pint or pint Mason jars. Leave ½ headspace. Process in a water bath for 10 minutes.

Remove jars from water bath and allow to cool undisturbed for 12 to 24 hours. Then wipe clean jars and lids and store in a cool dark place for up to 12 months. (You will likely hear the jars pop when they seal shortly after removal from water bath. The next day test the seals by pushing on top. There should be no movement of the lid. Also gentle pressure from your fingertips on edges of lid should reveal that it is securely suctioned onto the jar.)

Note: The relish tastes good from the start, but allowing it to set for 6 weeks will deepen the flavour, which is often the case with pickled items.

HOMEMADE APPLESAUCE

Warm homemade applesauce is a comforting delight of the harvest season. Nothing in a jar at the supermarket can compare to freshly stewed and spiced apples. For the ambitious apple lover, a weekend or two of effort with 10 or 20 pounds of apples will prolong the pleasure of homemade applesauce far past autumn. You can make large batches of applesauce and preserve it by canning it in pint or quart jars that will last for up to a year. Canning applesauce can be done safely in the home with only a simple hot water bath.

Homemade Applesauce Canning Process

Start with approximately 12 pounds of fresh apples free of blemishes and bruises. Minor blemishing can be cut out but always make sure you are using high quality fruit. Have ready a large water bath canning kettle (readily available at discount stores or hardware stores), pint sized Mason canning jars with brand new lids. You will also want a canning jar lifter and a candy thermometer.

Peel and core the apples. This is admittedly a lot of work and investing in a hand crank apple peeler is recommended. After peeling, slice the apples. Because it will take a while to get all the apples peeled have a large pan with about 1 gallon of water with 3/4 cup lemon juice in it.

Put the apple slices in the lemon water as you work to prevent browning of the fruit. Once all fruit is peeled and sliced drain it from the lemon water and add it to a large stock pot and heat on the stove over medium heat. Cover the stock pot, but check frequently to make sure that the fruit is not scorching on the bottom. Water will soon start cooking out of the fruit and this will protect against scorching after the first few minutes. Keep the pot covered so that the fruit simmers and steams. Check every couple minutes and stir the fruit. Depending on the firmness of the apple variety you selected, the apples should become noticeably softened in about 20 or 30 minutes.

Once apples are softened and beginning to break apart when stirred, start mashing them with a potato masher. This speeds the saucing process. You can make the apples as smooth or as chunky as you want. Keep the applesauce cooking after you mash to cook out more liquid. You don't want the applesauce runny. Cook out the water until a thick sauce forms. During this time, you may add sugar and spice if you want.

Add, if desired:

- 1 cup brown sugar.
- 1 tablespoon cinnamon.
- dash of salt.

You can add more sugar if you want it really sweet or not add any sugar. Having this control over the ingredients is one of the nice things about making your own applesauce. You don't have to worry about the high fructose corn syrup that is present in so many commercial varities. While you are cooking the apples, get the water bath canner and the jars ready. Wash your jars, lids, and bands and fill the canner. Heat the water in the canner to at least 180°F but less than boiling and submerge completely the jars and lids to sterilize. Use the candy thermometer to monitor water temperature. After the jars and lids have been sterilizing for a couple minutes, shut off the heat to the canner and cover it. The water and jars will stay hot while you're finishing the applesauce.

Once the applesauce achieves a thick consistency without any puddles of excess liquid, remove from heat. Take the sterilized jars and lids out of the water and fill with applesauce. Leave 1/2 inch headspace in jars. Carefully clean and wipe dry the rims of the jars and put on the lids. Secure the lids with the jar bands and screw tight with your hand. You don't have to make it really tight. Just screw it on without forcing it. Bring the water in the canner to a full boil and carefully add the filled jars with the jar lifter. Make sure at least 1 or 2 inches of water are above the tops of the jars. Keeping the water at a boil, process the pints for 15 minutes. (If you used quart jars, process for 20 mintues.) Increase these times by 5 minutes if you are at elevations above 1,000 feet.

When processing time has elapsed, remove jars from water and place on a towel in a draft-free location. Do not disturb the jars for 12 to 24 hours while the seals cool and tighten. You may hear the lids pop down and make a seal within the first few minutes, but do not touch them.

The next day, remove the bands, wipe the jars and lids clean and store in a cool dark place for up to one year. If you want to do both quart and pint jars at the same time, just use the processing time for the quarts. A little extra processing on the pint jars will not hurt anything.

HOW TO CAN TOMATOES

The red glorious bounty of summer buries gardeners in baskets of tomatoes. With home canning techniques, you can preserve all those tomatoes safely and enjoy their wonderful qualities long past the withering of the vines.

Fig. 2

Nothing quite replaces a sliced garden fresh tomato on a summer salad, but by canning tomatoes you can use your homegrown fruits to prepare delicious sauces, soups, and casseroles that call for tomatoes. You can start benefiting from your bumper crops of tomatoes instead of giving away bags of them to friends and co-workers until they can't eat another one.

You can use either a water bath canner or a pressure canner. The water bath canner is affordable and easy to use, but the pressure canner produces a canned tomato product that retains more nutritional value and possesses a noticeably higher quality. This results mostly from the shorter processing times possible with the pressure canner due to its higher temperatures. When canning tomatoes in a water bath canner, you need to use longer processing times, which cooks out more of the nutrients.

Even so, tomatoes canned with the water bath process remain good but just not quite as good as tomatoes processed in the pressure canner. Essentially, if you plan on growing lots of tomatoes and preserving them for home use, then investing in a pressure canner would be recommended.

Tomato Seeds

Tomatoes have many seeds and removing them before canning the tomatoes is labour intensive. It is acceptable to leave the seeds in the tomatoes.

This is the only thing to do when you are canning the tomatoes whole. You can always remove the seeds later with a food mill when you are cooking with the tomatoes. Or, you can ignore the seeds and leave them in. If you want to remove seeds prior to canning, you can cut the tomatoes in half and scrape out the seeds. This gets most of them out, but takes a long time. Or, you can put the tomatoes through a food mill and can them as crushed tomatoes or even prepare a seasoned spaghetti sauce and can it. For processing large amounts of tomatoes, it is best to can them whole and deal with the seeds as you use each jar or ignore the seeds. The seeds do not negatively influence the product or the canning process.

How to Select Fruit

Can only those tomatoes that are fresh, undamaged, and disease free. Vine ripened is best, but never can tomatoes from dead or dying vines.

Increasing the Acidity

High acid levels in fruits help the food preservation process. When canning tomatoes, you will want to add a high acid substance to boost the acidity.

Bottled Lemon Juice

- Pint jar: add 1 tablespoon.
- Quart jar: add 2 tablespoons.

Vinegar (5% Acidity)

- Pint jar: add 2 tablespoons.
- Quart jar: add 4 tablespoons.

Salt

You can add some salt to each jar before canning if you want to. Just be sure to use salt without added iodine. Or you can wait to add salt when you are cooking with the tomatoes later.

Skinning Tomatoes

You will need to remove the skins from all tomatoes. Skins are removed by placing tomatoes in boiling water for about 1 minute until skins split and then placing them in cold water. When the tomatoes are cool enough to handle, slip the skins off. Several approaches are commonly used to prepare tomatoes for canning. The variations arise from how the tomatoes are specifically prepared before placing in jars. All methods work well.

Canning Crushed Tomatoes

Use either pint or quart jars. Skin the tomatoes and cut them into quarters. Crush about 3 cups of tomatoes in a large pot with a potato masher and bring them to a boil while stirring. Gradually add the rest of the quartered tomatoes and keep stirring. After all tomatoes are in the pot, boil gently for 5 more minutes.

To each sterilized canning jar, add your selected acidification product (lemon juice, citric, acid, or vinegar), salt if desired, and then fill jars with hot tomatoes. Leave 1/2 inch headspace. Wipe jar rims and attach lids and bands.

Water Bath Canner Processing Times

- Pints—35 minutes (40 minutes above 1,000 feet elevation).
- Quarts—45 minutes (50 minutes above 1,000 feet elevation).

Pressure Canner Processing Times

Always refer to directions for your pressure canner first. Times and pressures presented here are typical.

- Pints—20 minutes at 6 pounds pressure or 15 minutes at 11 pounds pressure.
- Quarts—same as for pints.

Canning Whole Tomatoes

Uses pint or quart jars. Canned whole tomatoes are used whenever a recipe calls for stewed tomatoes. The whole tomatoes can also easily be mashed and cooked down to make sauces. Skin the tomatoes and remove the stem cores.

Add your acidification agent (lemon juice, citric acid, or vinegar) to sterilized canning jars.

Hot Pack Method

Put skinned tomatoes in a large pot and cover with water. Bring to a gentle boil for 5 minutes. Ladle hot tomatoes into prepared sterilized jars and then add cooking liquid. Leave 1/2 inch headspace. Wipe clean rims of jars and put on lids and bands.

Water Bath Canner Processing Times

- Pints—40 minutes (45 minutes above 1,000 feet elevation).
- Quarts—45 minutes (50 minutes above 1,000 feet elevation).

Pressure Canner Processing Times

Always refer to directions for your pressure canner first. These times and pressures presented here are typical.

- Pints—15 minutes at 6 pounds pressure or 10 minutes at 11 pounds pressure.
- Quarts—Same as for pints.

Raw Pack Method without Added Liquid

The raw pack method has appeal because it involves less preparation time and you do not have to work with hot liquid and hot jars. However, this method does require longer processing times in the canner. Pack skinned tomatoes into sterilized jars prepared with acid booster. Press them into the jars so that juice squeezes out and fills in the gaps between tomatoes. Leave 1/2 inch headspace, wipe clean jar rims, and attach lids and bands.

Water Bath Canner Processing Times

- Pints—85 minutes (90 minutes above 1,000 feet elevation).
- Quarts—85 minutes (90 minutes above 1,000 feet elevation).

Pressure Canner Processing Times

Always refer to directions for your pressure canner first. These times and pressures presented here are typical.

- Pints—40 minutes at 6 pounds pressure or 25 minutes at 11 pounds pressure.
- Quarts—Same as for pints.

With all methods for canning tomatoes, you must remove the jars from canner and let them cool on a towel in a space free from drafts. Leave the jars undisturbed for 12 to 24 hours. Then check to make sure jars are sealed. Remove bands, wipe clean lids and jars and store in cupboard for up to one year. If a jar does not seal, put it in the refrigerator and use it within a few days.

PEACH MARMALADE CANNING PROCESS

One of the great things about home canning is that you can prepare and preserve batches of special foods that would be very difficult to find in a store. Peach marmalade is an excellent example.

Its delicious blend of citrus and peach flavours is truly habit forming. If you are pursuing a local food diet, it is challenging because peaches and citrus do not ripen at the same time of year, but compromising with an imported orange and lemon when the peaches are in season is well worth deviating from a strictly local food approach.

In this canning recipe you can either chop the peaches or puree them. We prefer it chunky, but making a smooth marmalade with the pureed peaches would be fine.

Peach Marmalade Ingredients

- 1 orange
- 1 lemon
- 1/4 cup water
- 3 pounds peaches
- 1 (1-3/4 ounces) package powdered fruit pectin
- 5 cups sugar.

Quarter the orange and lemon and remove any seeds. Then cut the orange and lemon wedges into very thin slices. Cook the citrus slices and the 1/4 cup of water in a saucepan. Cover the pan and simmer the orange and lemon for 20 minutes.

Prepare the peaches by peeling them, pitting them, and dicing into small chunks or puree them. Combine the peaches with the orange and lemon mixture in a big stock pot. Stir the pectin into the fruit and bring to a full rolling boil. Then stir in the sugar. As the sugar dissolves bring the mixture back to a full rolling boil while stirring constantly. Boil for 1 minute. Remove from the heat and skim off foam. Ladle the marmalade into sterilized half pint or pint jars.

Make sure to stir up the marmalade as you go so that the fruit remains evenly distributed. Leave a 1/4 inch headspace in the jars, wipe clean the rims, and apply the lids. Process for 10 minutes in a boiling water bath and then remove. Leave jars undisturbed for at least 12 hours before checking the seals. Wipe clean the jars and lids and store in a cupboard for up to one year.

SALTING FOOD PRESERVATION

Salting is the preservation of food with dry salt. It is related to pickling (preparing food with brine, i.e., salty water). It is one of the oldest methods of preserving food, and two historically significant such foods are dried and salted cod (usually referred to as salt fish) and salt-cured meat. Salting is used because most bacteria, fungi and other potentially pathogenic organisms cannot survive in a highly salty environment, due to the hypertonic nature of salt. Any living cell in such an environment will become dehydrated through osmosis and die or become temporarily inactivated. Jewish and Muslim dietary laws require the removal of blood from freshly slaughtered meat, which may be accomplished with the use of salt or brine.

SALTING

The precise mechanism by which salting preserves food is not entirely understood. It is known that salt binds with water molecules and thus acts as a dehydrating agent in foods. A high level of salinity may also impair the conditions under which pathogens can survive. In any case, the value of adding salt to foods for preservation has been well known for centuries.

Sugar appears to have effects similar to those of salt in preventing spoilage of food. The use of either compound (and of certain other natural materials) is known as curing. A desirable side effect of using salt or sugar as a food preservative is, of course, the pleasant flavour each compound adds to the final product. Curing can be accomplished in a variety of ways. Meats can be submerged in a salt solution known as brine, for example, or the salt can be rubbed on the meat by hand. The injection of salt solutions into meats has also become popular.

Food scientists have now learned that a number of factors relating to the food product and to the preservative conditions affect the efficiency of curing. Some of the food factors include the type of food being preserved, the fat content, and the size of treated pieces. Preservative factors include brine temperature and concentration and the presence of impurities.

Curing is used with certain fruits and vegetables, such as cabbage (in the making of sauerkraut), cucumbers (in the making of pickles), and olives. It is probably most popular, however, in the preservation of meats and fish. Honey-cured hams, bacon, and corned beef ("corn" is a term for a form of salt crystals) are common examples.

In medieval times, people occasionally had to go for long stretches with little or no fresh meat. Instead, they relied on dried or salt-preserved meats during those times. The challenge of cooking then became to find a way for making meals interesting. Part of the reason people had to depend on preserved foods at times was the expense and difficulty in keeping animals during the winter, especially in northern Europe.

SALT-PRESERVING

- Dry-salting—meat or fish is buried in granular salt.
- Brine-curing—meat is put in a strong salt-water.

Since salt was fairly expensive, generally only meats high in fat would be preserved. Mutton wasn't preserved as often since the meat is usually tough and string and was literally "not worth its salt". The origins of salt-preserving food can be traced back to at least Ancient Egypt, where they used salt as part of the embalming process, as well as in food preservations. After the spread of Christianity, the business of salt-preserving fish because quite profitable, since fresh fish for the 40 days of Lent was difficult to come by for many people. Herring was the most common fish to be salted. It was essential that the herring be preserved quickly since its abundant oil tended to turn rancid within a day after the catch.

Ways of Producing Salt in Medieval Times

- Mining salt deposits formed from ancient seas (not very common).
- Brine from salt springs (better quality than sea salt).
- Evapourating sea water.

Salt springs were higher in saline and didn't have extra mineral salts such as calcium and magnesium salts which you get from sea water. Of course, this made spring salts very expensive, especially since it was a limited resource. There was also a method of making salt through burning peat soaked in salt water. This produced a fine salt powder, but it was also a limited resource.

Bourgneuf Bay of Brittany produced large amounts of salt extracted from the sea, but it was coarse and of low quality, usually mixed with the remains of seaweed, sand and other contaminants. Sometimes this would make the salt a black, grey or green colour. However, it was cheap. The problem with using this coarse sea salt was that it was slow to penetrate the inner parts of the meats, causing it to go bad before it was completely preserved.

Salting, especially of meat, is an ancient preservation technique. The salt draws out moisture and creates an environment inhospitable to bacteria. If salted in cold weather (so that the meat does not spoil while the salt has time to take effect), salted meat can last for years.

The following passage from John Steinbeck's *The Grapes of Wrath* describes the process briefly:

Noah carried the slabs of meat into the kitchen and cut it into small salting blocks, and Ma patted the course salt in, laid it piece by piece in the kegs, careful that no two pieces touched each other. She laid the slabs like bricks, and pounded salt in the spaces. This technique creates a keg (a wooden barrel) full of salt and meat. This technique is ancient. You can read about its use during the sailing voyages around the time of Columbus. Many accounts of the Revolutionary War and especially the Civil War talk about meat preserved in this way. Salting was used to preserve meat up through the middle of 20th century, and was eventually replaced by refrigeration and freezing.

Today, salting is still used to create salt-cured "country ham" found widely in the southern United States, dried beef (which you can buy in jars at most grocery stores), and corned beef and pastrami, which are made by soaking beef in a 10 per cent salt water brine for several weeks. Sodium chloride, saltpetre, sal prunella (crystalline form of saltpetre) were all used in the salting of meat, of which there were two methods; dry salting and wet salting (corning, pickling or brining). With dry salting meat was packed in dry salt and or rubbed with a coating of salt but this method did not preserve the meat as long as wet salting. With wet salting, the meat was first rubbed with salt and salt was put between the layers of meat; then a brine was poured over the packed salted meat and was kept submerged in a brine solution.

Pickling does not leave the meat as salty as in dry salting but it still needs to be presoaked, which removed excess salt, before cooking. Barreled salt pork is an example of pickling and there were varying grades of salt pork and the specified fat content and cuts of meat determined the grade of salt pork. Salt beef was prepared in much the same way. Fish could also be dry or wet salted.

Herring, cod, salmon, mackerel, sardines and anchovies were very familiar to nineteenth century consumers but were usually commercially processed rather than being done at home. In some cases, drying was employed with salting. The fish was salted salted for several days, then dried and for shipping, they were packed in boxes or barrels. Some fish were brined and then shipped in barrels, similar to the barrels of salt pork and beef. Usually fish was commercially preserved rather than being done at home.

Salt: An Essential Nutrient

Salt is a nutrient that is essential to life and good health. Having originally evolved from a marine environment, the human body's salt/water ratio is critical to metabolism. Human plasma contains 0.9% salt (sodium chloride) in order to maintain the electrolyte balance necessary for blood circulation. In the normal course of metabolism, we routinely eliminate sodium along with most other waste materials and the minimum balance must be replenished if we are to survive. Most of our salt intake comes from foods, and some from water. Of course, any activity resulting in excessive loss of sodium such as exercise, has to be counter-balanced by increased salt consumption to make up this additional loss.

SALT AND FOOD TECHNOLOGY

The number of applications fulfilled by salt in foods are as varied as the number of different foods there are. These range from a taste enhancer to a taste suppressant; as a mediator of water activity and a regulator of texture, mouthfeel, juiciness and friability. Blanching in salt water retains colour and crispness in vegetables destined for freezing and salt initiates granule formation producing the unparalleled taste and texture of Parmesano Reggiano cheese.

Salt is not only our oldest known food preservative, but it fulfils a critical anti-microbial function in the most modern hurdle technologies employed in the production of high quality minimally processed chilled foods that have become so popular in recent years. Despite the myriad established uses of salt in food preparation at home and in the food industry, the overarching attraction of salt for people is sensorial. Simply put—salt makes food taste good. Salt doesn't just deliver salty flavour, it delivers flavour in many ways.

Salt is the oldest, most common and most important single flavouring substance. From a food appeal point of view, salt cannot be considered to be merely desirable, but by far the most satisfying of flavour components for all starchy and protein-based foods. This propensity for humans and animals to prefer a salty taste may originate from our marine evolution or may simply be a mechanism to ensure we receive an adequate amount of this essential nutrient in our diet.

When faced with foods that don't meet their taste expectations, most people will simply take up a salt shaker as add enough to satisfy their needs. Thus, in a country such as Italy, where bread baking traditions result in regional products that vary from high to almost no salt, consumers at home and diners in restaurants will readily make up any taste deficit by voluntarily adding salt at the table prior to consumption.

The same can be said for the consumer response to all other food products—those that demonstrate a deficiency in taste will be corrected by the consumer on a voluntary basis. Throughout history, even during periods when it was a very costly commodity, salt was considered to be an economic necessity of life. One of the most important uses of salt in taste is to moderate bitterness in certain foods. For example, some of or most nutritious cruciferous vegetables, such as broccoli, spinach, Brussels sprouts, cabbage, kale, mustard greens, radicchio will not be acceptable to consumers unless a certain amount of salt is added.

This is particularly true for children as the most recent results of tests from Ohio State University reveals. Restricting the amount of salt that consumers can add to these foods risks their access to the nutritional benefits they hold. Of course, bitter natural foods such as olives would not be an edible food commodity unless they were fully debittered with salt.

When added in small amounts, salt intensifies the sweetness of many foods such as caramel, taffy, fudge, fruits, mild vegetables and various sauces. For example, lightly salting a slice of watermelon makes it taste sweeter. Salt also make food taste more palatable by suppressing other unpleasant flavours. In these instances the goal of the consumer or manufacturer is not to make a food taste salty, but rather to enhance the overall taste profile and acceptability of the food. Salt has a profound effect on the texture of an incredible array of food products. Because of its functional impact on the gelation properties of proteins, salt is used to respond to consumer preferences for texture, mouthfeel and ease of swallowing for all national and imported cheeses and cheese products, processed meat and fish products.

Items such as bologna, frankfurters, restructured beefsteaks, chicken pieces , dry-cured ham, surimi from all fish sources, battered calamari rings, minced fish balls, etc., etc., serve as some examples. Salt has a critical impact on the texture, colour and cooking loss of a range of fresh, processed and dehydrated vegetables, such as runner beans, carrots, cucumbers, broccoli and cauliflower.

Of course, not only food processors love salt. The use of salt by consumers to improve the texture of foods is very common. Preparing for the holidays, a cursory search on Google using the terms 'brining turkey' yields more than 300,000 citations! As an example, a quote from the San Francisco Chronicle reads, "The Chronicle Food section cooked 28 turkeys to find the best method of producing a plump, juicy bird. Our favourite—by far—was the turkey that we brined before roasting."

The level of salt used in bread manufacture significantly affects the physical nature of the final product. Most standard bread is made from doughs containing somewhere around 1.5-2% salt by weight of flour. Salt has a significant physical effect on the properties of wheat gluten, resulting in a less sticky, more manageable dough.

Salt also affects the rate of fermentation, and its addition is timed after the dough has been partly fermented. The role of salt in controlling fermentation is not only due to the increase in osmotic pressure, but also to the actions of sodium and chloride ions on the semi-permeable membranes of yeast cells. Inadequate levels of salt will result in excessive yeast fermentation, resulting in gassy, soured doughs that are difficult to process and result in loaves with an open grain and poor texture. Many types of flat bread have become widely available in recent years. These include single-layered, leavened dough products such as naan, pizza crust, ciabatta and focaccia, batters such as crepes and pancakes as well as double layered products such as pita bread, and unleavened products like chapattis, paratha and tortillas.

Salt is an essential ingredient in most formulations, many of which are sourdough or yeast-leavened products. Salt, temperature, aeration and flour quality are all used to control bread quality. Salt affects the physical nature and properties of biscuit doughs, especially hard doughs, in a similar way to bread. In doughs with significant gluten development, such as crackers and semi-sweet types, salt toughens the gluten and gives a less sticky dough.

It may also slow down the rate of yeast fermentation. Typical levels of addition are generally less than 2%, based on flour, resulting in about 1.5% in the final product. Salt has a variety of technological functions in meat products. While many of the major effects relate to preservation, especially in cured and salted products, it also has other, direct effects on the nature and quality of the product. Salt is used in the manufacture of both hard and soft cheeses. The salting of some of the most famous Italian, Swiss and Dutch cheeses is carried out after they are formed into rounds. The rounds are then immersed in saturated salt brine, for up to 20 days. For many traditional manufacturers, the saturated brine baths are a source of pride, some having been in continuous operation for more than 100 years (showing perfectly cubic sodium chloride crystals from 5-6 inches on a side, sitting in crystal clear brine).

Salt is the oldest food preservative known to humankind—it has been used for thousands of years. The main mechanism of salt preservation is through the reduction of water activity.

Microorganisms require water to survive and grow and salt preferentially ties up a portion of the water, leaving the microorganisms without sufficient free water. In inhibiting microbial growth, salt interacts with both the acidity (pH) of the medium and its temperature, as well as other factors present.

Processed Foods and Salt

Salting is one of the oldest food preservation methods. Salt (sodium chloride) helps prevent spoiling by drawing water out of the food, depriving bacteria of the moisture they need to thrive. Salt is also an antibacterial agent, killing some of the bacteria that cause spoiling. At one time, salting was one of the only methods available to help preserve food. But today food processors have many other methods. These include pasteurization, refrigeration/freezing, dehydration/freeze-drying, irradiation and using chemical preservatives.

Note: Some chemical preservatives, such as sodium benzoate, sodium propionate, sodium citrate and sodium phosphate, contain small amounts of salt.

Each of these newer processes has resulted in the need for less—if any salt—as an ingredient. So why do food manufacturers continue to add salt to processed foods? Here are some reasons:

- Salt makes food more flavourful.
- Salted foods such as soups seem thicker and less watery.
- Salt increases sweetness in products such as soft drinks, cookies and cakes.
- Salt helps cover up any metallic or chemical aftertaste in products such as soft drinks.
- Salt decreases dryness in foods such as crackers and pretzels.

Most Americans consume more than double the recommended daily amount of sodium per day—in part because of a heavy diet of processed foods. To decrease the amount of salt in your diet:

- Eat fewer processed foods such as potato chips, frozen dinners, and cured meats such as bacon and lunchmeats.
- Choose low-sodium or reduced-sodium processed foods.
- Don't add salt to your food. Instead, use herbs and spices to flavour foods.

- Eat more fresh, unprocessed foods such as fresh fruits, vegetables, lean meats, poultry, fish and unprocessed grains.

How Do Salt and Sugar Prevent Microbial Spoilage?

Protection of foods from microbial spoilage using salt (usually sodium chloride) or sugar (usually sucrose) has ancient roots and is often referred to as salting, salt curing, corning or sugar curing. (Pieces of rock salt used for curing are sometimes called corns, hence the name "corned beef".) Curing may utilize solid forms of salt and sugar or solutions in which salt or sugar is mixed with water.

For instance, brine is the term for salt solutions used in curing or pickling preservation processes. Examples of foods preserved with salt or sugar include the afore-mentioned corned beef as well as bacon, salt pork, sugar-cured ham, fruit preserves, jams and jellies, among others.

There are numerous descriptions and permutations of curing which may include additional preservation techniques such as smoking or ingredients such as spices. However, all curing processes fundamentally depend on the use of salt and/or sugar as the primary preservation agent(s).

Incidentally, these processes not only prevent spoilage of foods, but more importantly serve to inhibit or prevent growth of food-borne pathogens such as *Salmonella* or *Clostridium botulinum* when properly applied.

There are several ways in which salt and sugar inhibit microbial growth. The most notable is simple osmosis, or dehydration. Salt or sugar, whether in solid or aqueous form, attempts to reach equilibrium with the salt or sugar content of the food product with which it is in contact. This has the effect of drawing available water from within the food to the outside and inserting salt or sugar molecules into the food interior. The result is a reduction of the so-called product water activity (a_w), a measure of unbound, free water molecules in the food that is necessary for microbial survival and growth. The a_w of most fresh foods is 0.99 whereas the a_w necessary to inhibit growth of most bacteria is roughly 0.91. Yeasts and molds, on the other hand, usually require even lower a_w to prevent growth.

Salt and sugar's other antimicrobial mechanisms include interference with a microbe's enzyme activity and weakening the molecular structure of its DNA. Sugar may also provide an indirect form of preservation by serving to accelerate accumulation of antimicrobial compounds from the growth of certain other organisms.

Examples include the conversion of sugar to ethanol in wine by fermentative yeasts or the conversion of sugar to organic acids in sauerkraut by lactic acid bacteria. Microorganisms differ widely in their ability to resist salt- or sugar-induced reductions of a_w. Most disease-causing bacteria do not grow below 0.94 a_w (roughly 10 per cent sodium chloride concentration), whereas most moulds that spoil foods grow at an a_w as low as 0.80, corresponding to highly concentrated salt or sugar solutions.

Yet other microorganisms grow quite well under even more highly osmotic, low a_w conditions. For example, halophiles are an entire class of "salt-loving" bacteria that actually require a significant level of salt to grow and are capable of spoiling salt-cured foods. These include members of the genera *Halobacillus* and *Halococcus*.

Food products that are concentrated sugar solutions, such as concentrated fruit juices, can be spoiled by sugar-loving yeasts such as species of *Zygosaccharomyces*. Nevertheless, use of salt and sugar curing to prevent microbial growth is an ancient technique that remains important today for the preservation of foods.

Bibliography

Maimun Nisha: *Wings of Home Science* :, Kalpaz, 2006,

Bruce Axler and Carol Litrides.: *Food and Beverage Service*, Wiley, Delhi, 2013.

Bruno Dorin and Frederic Landy.: *Agriculture and Food in India: A Half- Century Review, From Independence to Globalization*, Manohar Publications, Delhi, 2009.

C S Jain.: *A Complete Book on Health and Nutrition*, Cyber Tech Publications, Delhi, 2009.

Cristobal Noe Aguilar; Juliana Morales Castro; Efren Delgado; Diana Jasso Cantu and Ashok Pandey.: *Food Science and Food Biotechnology in Developing Countries*, Asiatech Publications, Delhi, 2008.

Dalip Kumar and Asmi Raza.: *Agriculture and Food Security: Contemporary Issues*, Deep and Deep Publications, Delhi, 2011.

Debashis Basu, B Francis Kulirani and B Datta Ray.: *Agriculture Food Security Nutrition and Health in North East India*, Mittal Publications, Delhi, 2006

Deepak Mudgil and Sheweta Barak Mudgil.: *Objective Food Science and Technology*, Scientific Research, 2013.

Dev Raj.: *Food Science and Technology: Glossary of Preeminence*, New India Publications, Delhi, 2011.

Ernest R. Vieira.: *Elementary Food Science*, Chapman and Hall, 2010.

Eugene Lyman Fisk, Adelle Davis, Florence Daniel, Ruth A. Wardall and Harry Snyder.: *Food Science and Nutrition* (*Vols* 1 *to* 2 *Set*), Shree Publications, Delhi, 2009.

Gaurav Gandhi.: *Hotel Management Food and Food Services*, Random Publications, Delhi, 2012.

Hema Thapar.: *Food Science and Health*, Pacific Publications, Delhi, 2011.

Hema Thapar.: *Nutrition and Food Science*, Pacific Books International, Delhi, 2011.

Jerry D Souza and Jatin Pradhan.: *Handbook of Food Science Catering Technology and Kitchen Management*, SBS Publications, Delhi, 2010.

Jyoti S. Sharma.: *Applied Nutrition and Food Science*, Akansha Publications, Delhi, 2009.

M P Singh.: *Health and Food Science*, Anmol Publications, Delhi, 2007.

M. Nithya Devi.: *Food Science and Technology*, Aadi Publication, Jaipur, 2011.

Margaret M. Walsh.: *Food and Nutrition Manual for Institutions,* Welfare Federation of Cleveland, Cleveland, 1950.

Mridula Mirajkar and Sreelata Menon.: *Food Science and Processing Technology* (2 *Vols-Set*), Kanishka Publications, Delhi, 2010.

Mudit Bhojwan.: *Food Service Management: Principles and Practices*, Rajat Publications, Delhi, 2007

N.K. Jain.: *Fundamentals of Food Science Technology Processing and Preservation*, Cyber Tech Publications, Delhi, 2011.

N.L. Choudhary and Anjana Singh.: *Principles of Enzymology for the Food Science*, Oxford Book Company, Jaipur, 2012.

P Janaki Rao.: *Nutrition and Food Science*, Aavishkar Publications, Jaipur, 2006.

P. Mishra.: *Agriculture Food and Nutrition*, Northern Book Centre, Delhi, 2007.

Parminder K. Bhandari.: *Achieving Nutritional Goals*, Sonali Publications, Delhi, 2010.

R.P. Saxena.: *Food Services and Catering Management*, Centrum Press, Delhi, 2010.

R.P. Sugandhar Babu.: *Food and Beverage Production*, Adhyayan Publications, Delhi, 2008.

Robert L. Shewfelt.: *Introducing Food Science*, CRC Press, Delhi, 2013.

S N Mahindru.: *Food Science and Technology, Vols. 1-7,* APH Publications, Delhi, 2009.

S.K. Bhatia, Shiv Kumar and D.C. Sangwan.: *Advances in Buffalo-Cattle Nutrition and Rumen Ecosystem*, International Book Distributing Co., Lucknow, 2004.

Shalini Pathak.: *Food Science*, Sonali Publications, Delhi, 2007.

Sujata K. Dass.: *Healthcare and Food Science*, Shree Publications, Delhi, 2004.

Sunetra Roday.: *Food Science and Nutrition*, Oxford University Press, Jaipur, 2007.

U.D. Chavan.: *Question Bank on Food Science and Technology*, Daya Publications, Delhi, 2014.

Udai Veer.: *Elements of Food Science*, Anmol Publications, Delhi, 2007.

Umesh Prasad.: *Food Science and Nutrition*, Sonali Publications, Delhi, 2011.

Urvashi Nandal.: *A Handbook of Foods and Nutritional Biochemistry: A Complete Source Book*, Agrobios Publications, Delhi, 2013.

Index

A

Aids 40, 50, 64
Akashiba 64
Alcohol Consumption 69
Alimentary 72, 73, 81, 82, 84
Aoshiba 64

B

Bse 32, 34, 37, 48, 51, 65, 66, 72, 76, 84, 85, 87

C

Cantaloupe 68
Cardiovascular Disease 31, 32, 33, 34
Cardiovascular System 60
Childbirth 40, 70
Chocolates-Are 65
Coffee-Anti-Oxidants 63
Cooked Succulent 95

D

Deleterious 72
Diabetes Mellitus 33, 64

F

Fireless cooking 94
Flax Seed 56, 57
Flexibility 59

H

Health Services 31
Healthy Diet 30, 31, 33, 34, 42, 56, 67, 69

I

Increased Consumption 34
Iron Deficiency 36, 40, 41

K

Kuroshiba 64

M

Minerals 184
Murasakishiba 64
Muscles 44

N

Nutrition 30, 31, 32, 33, 34, 36, 41, 43, 44, 51, 57, 60, 66, 67, 72, 73, 74, 78, 82, 83

O

Osteoporosis 41, 42, 43, 66

P

Phosphorus 184
Physical Activities 47
Pomegranate Juice 61

S

Safeguarding 62
Shiroshiba 64
Squamous-cell 62
Starvation 74
Supplements 40, 41, 43, 49, 58, 68, 69

U

Unfortunately 36, 73, 81

V

Vegetables 30, 33, 34, 35, 41, 42, 44, 45, 48, 54, 55, 61, 67, 68, 76, 79, 80, 84, 85, 87, 90, 92, 95, 96
Venaue 85
Vegetarians 79
Vibrant Colors 61
Vigorous 43, 52, 71
Vision 30, 34, 45, 69, 83
Vitamins 178, 184, 185

W

Whethers 31, 34, 35
Who 17, 27, 32, 33, 34, 35, 37, 38, 39, 41, 43, 45, 46, 47, 48, 50, 52, 55, 56, 57, 62, 64, 66, 67, 70, 71, 72, 75, 76, 77, 78, 80, 81, 82, 83, 84, 85, 86, 87, 88, 89, 90, 91, 94, 95

X

Xylitol 49

Z

Zucchini 67